CASE CLOSED

VOLUME 8

Gosho Aoyama

Case Briefing:

Subject: Jimmy Kudo, a.k.a. Conan Edogawa
Occupation: High School Student/Detective
Special Skills: Analytical thinking and deductive reasoning, Soccer
Equipment: Bow Tie Voice Transmitter, Super Sneakers, Homing Glasses, Stretchy Suspenders

The subject is hot on the trail of a pair of suspicious men in black when he is attacked from behind and administered a strange substance which physically transforms him into a first grader. When the subject confides in the eccentric inventor Dr. Agasa, they decide to keep the subject's true identity a secret for the safety of everyone around him. Assuming the new identity of first-grader Conan Edogawa, the subject continues to assist the police force on their most baffling cases. The only problem is that most crime-solving professionals won't take a little kid's advice!

Table of Contents

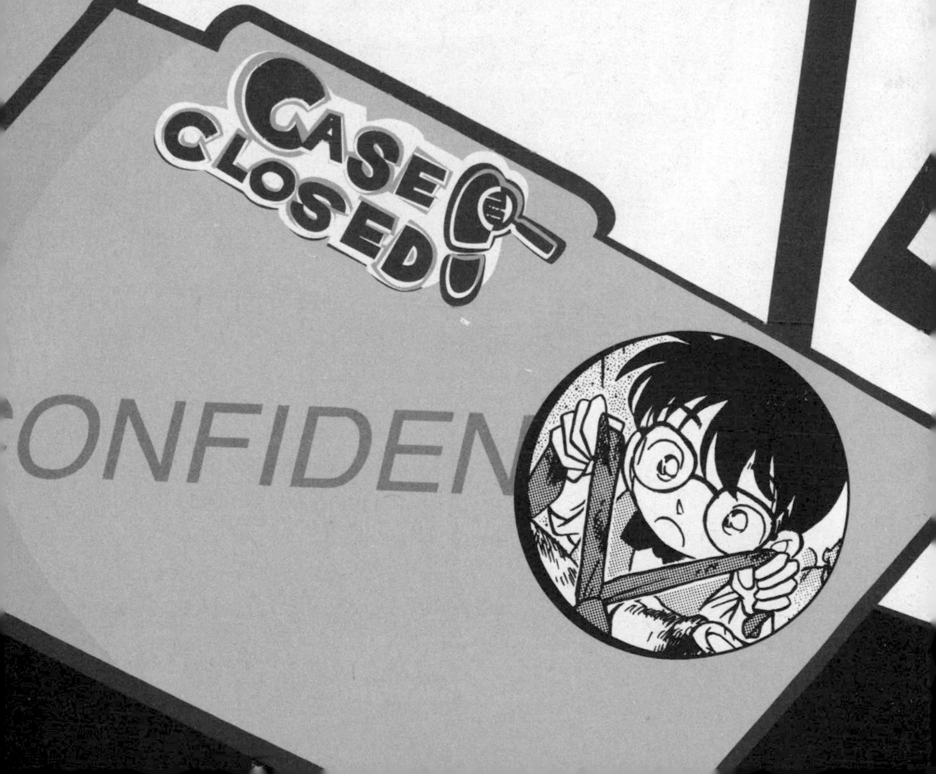

CASE CLOSED
CONFIDEN

CASE CLOSED
Volume 8
Shonen Sunday Edition

Story and Art by GOSHO AOYAMA

MEITANTEI CONAN Vol. 8
by Gosho AOYAMA
© 1994 Gosho AOYAMA
All rights reserved.
Original Japanese edition published by SHOGAKUKAN.
English translation rights in the United States of America, Canada,
the United Kingdom, Ireland, Australia and New Zealand arranged with SHOGAKUKAN.

English Adaptation
Naoko Amemiya

Translation
Joe Yamazaki

Touch-up & Lettering
Walden Wong

Cover & Interior Design
Andrea Rice

Editor
Urian Brown

Printed in the U.S.A.

Published by VIZ Media, LLC
P.O. Box 77010
San Francisco, CA 94107

10 9 8 7 6 5
First printing, October 2005
Fifth printing, March 2020

WWW.SHONENSUNDAY.COM

PARENTAL ADVISORY
CASE CLOSED is rated T+ for Older Teen
and is recommended for ages 16 and up.
This volume contains realistic and graphic
violence.
ratings.viz.com

www.viz.com

FILE 1:
FOUND AT LAST!!

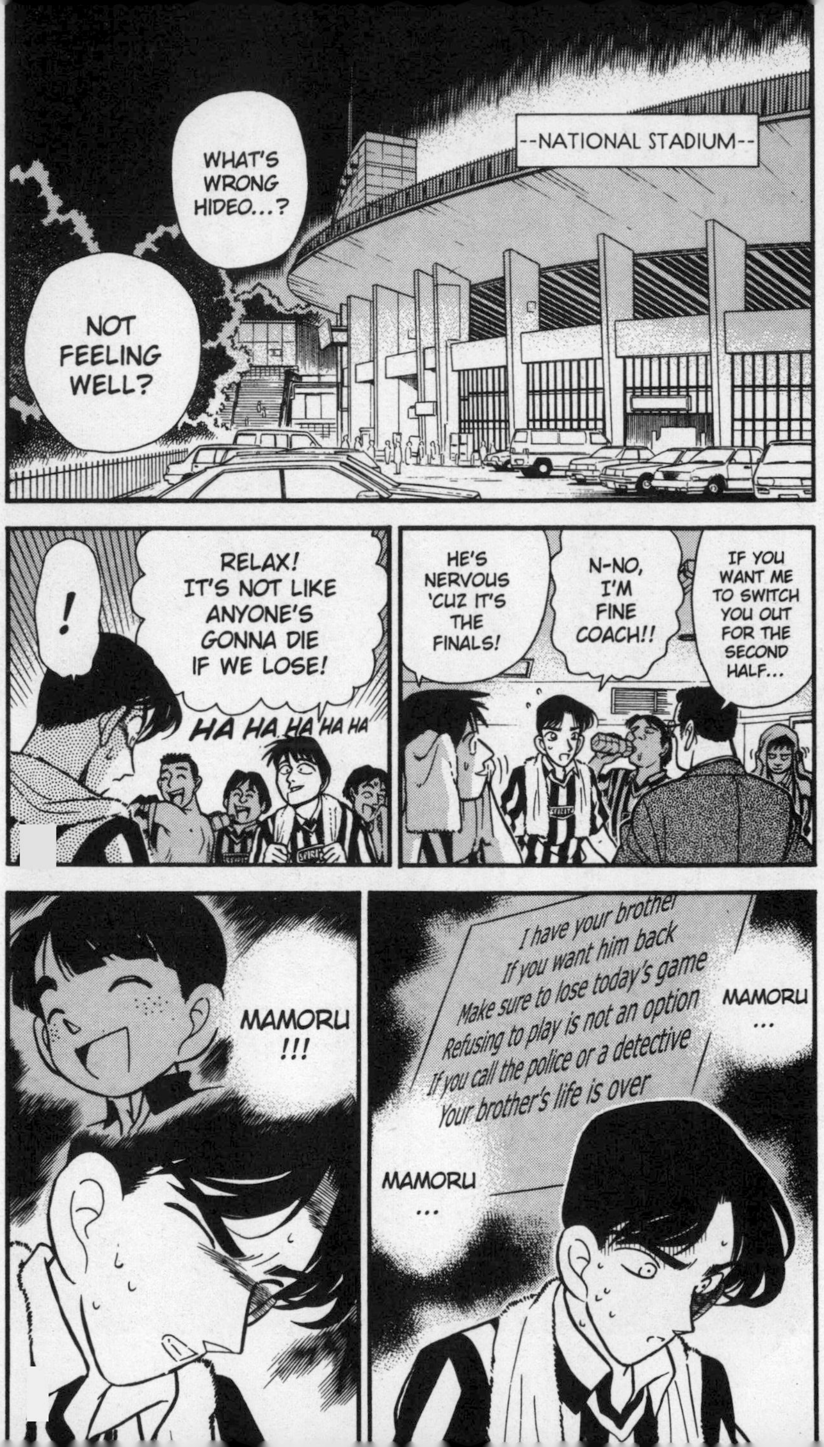
--NATIONAL STADIUM--
WHAT'S WRONG HIDEO...?
NOT FEELING WELL?
IF YOU WANT ME TO SWITCH YOU OUT FOR THE SECOND HALF...
N-NO, I'M FINE COACH!!
HE'S NERVOUS 'CUZ IT'S THE FINALS!
RELAX! IT'S NOT LIKE ANYONE'S GONNA DIE IF WE LOSE!
HA HA HA HA HA
!
I have your brother
If you want him back
Make sure to lose today's game
Refusing to play is not an option
If you call the police or a detective
Your brother's life is over
MAMORU ...
MAMORU ...
MAMORU !!!

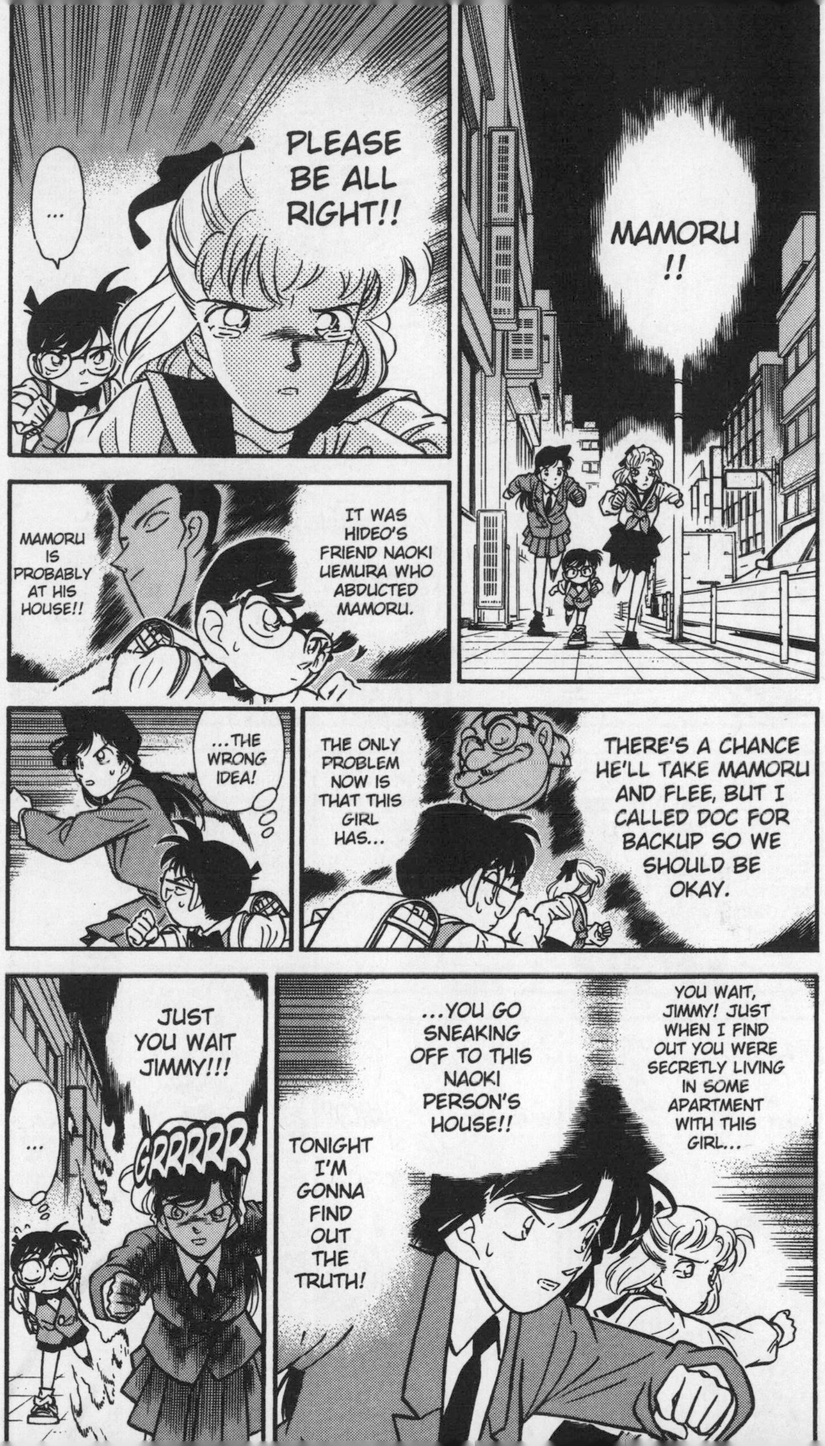
MAMORU !!
PLEASE BE ALL RIGHT!!
...
IT WAS HIDEO'S FRIEND NAOKI UEMURA WHO ABDUCTED MAMORU.
MAMORU IS PROBABLY AT HIS HOUSE!!
THERE'S A CHANCE HE'LL TAKE MAMORU AND FLEE, BUT I CALLED DOC FOR BACKUP SO WE SHOULD BE OKAY.
THE ONLY PROBLEM NOW IS THAT THIS GIRL HAS...
...THE WRONG IDEA!
YOU WAIT, JIMMY! JUST WHEN I FIND OUT YOU WERE SECRETLY LIVING IN SOME APARTMENT WITH THIS GIRL...
...YOU GO SNEAKING OFF TO THIS NAOKI PERSON'S HOUSE!!
TONIGHT I'M GONNA FIND OUT THE TRUTH!
JUST YOU WAIT JIMMY!!!
GRRRRR
...

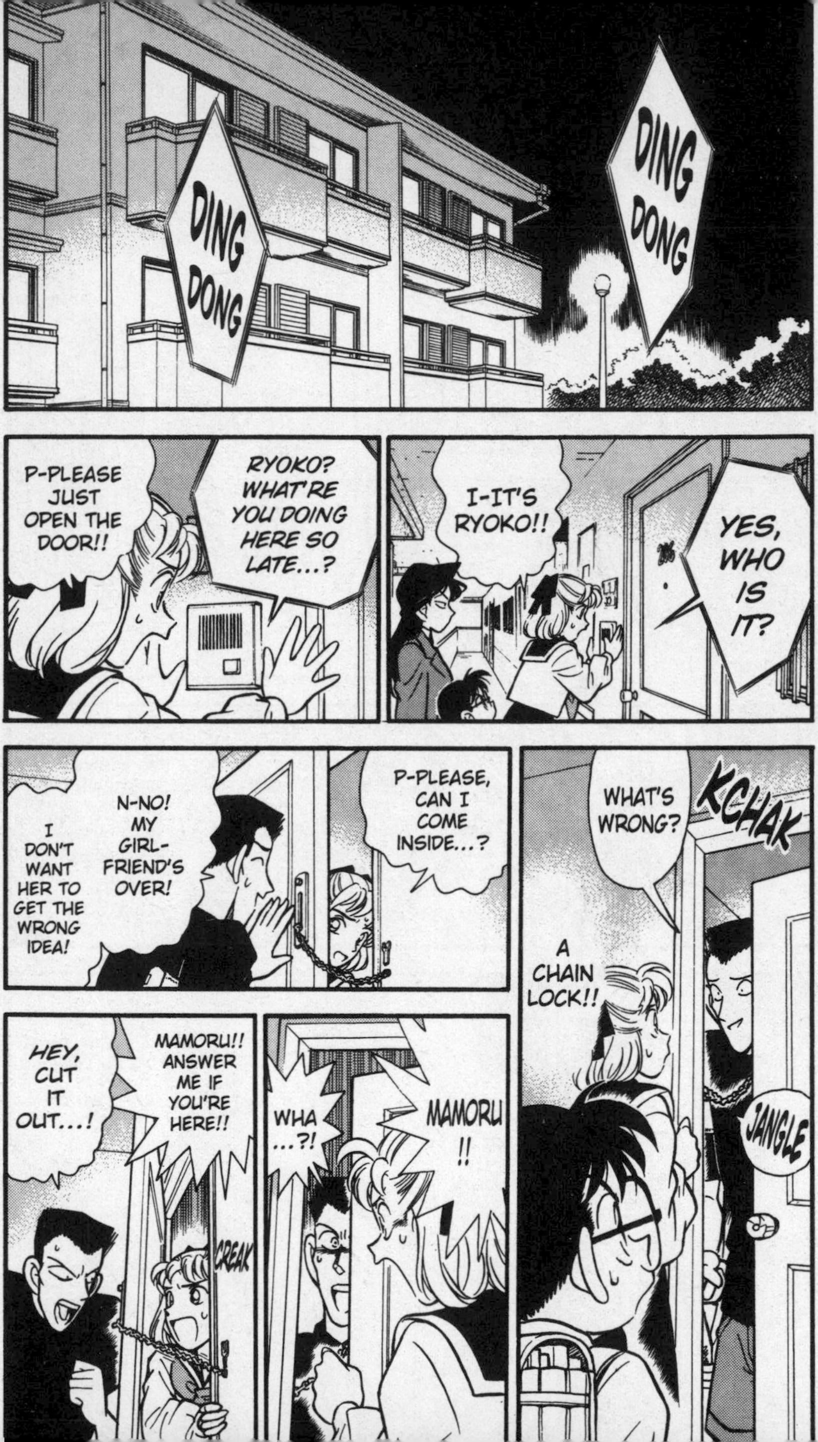
DING DONG
DING DONG
YES, WHO IS IT?
I-IT'S RYOKO!!
RYOKO? WHAT'RE YOU DOING HERE SO LATE...?
P-PLEASE JUST OPEN THE DOOR!!
KCHAK
WHAT'S WRONG?
A CHAIN LOCK!!
JANGLE
P-PLEASE, CAN I COME INSIDE...?
N-NO! MY GIRL-FRIEND'S OVER!
I DON'T WANT HER TO GET THE WRONG IDEA!
MAMORU !!
WHA ...?!
MAMORU!! ANSWER ME IF YOU'RE HERE!!
CREAK
HEY, CUT IT OUT...!

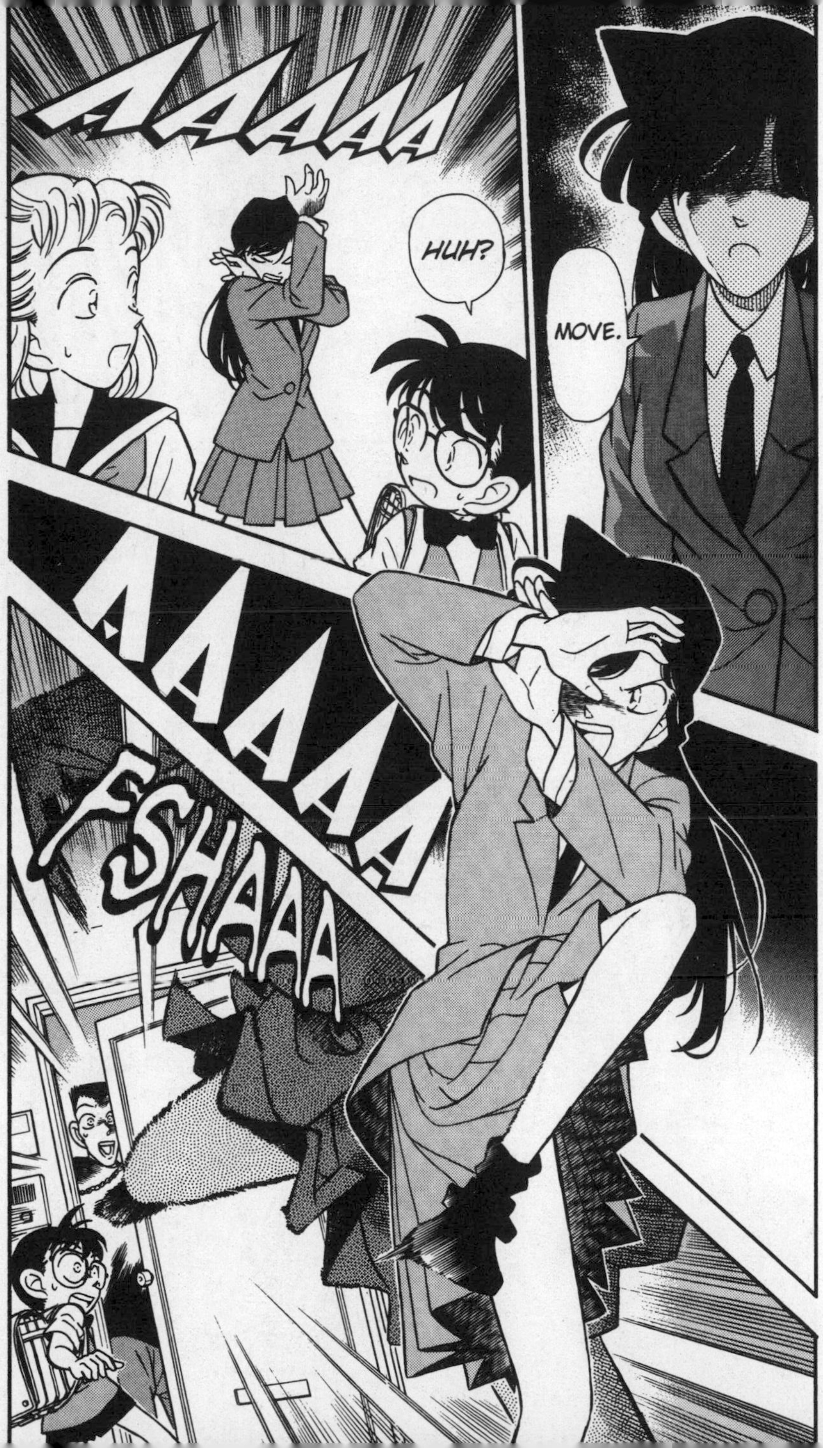
MOVE.
AAAAAA
HUH?
AAAAAA
FSHAAAA

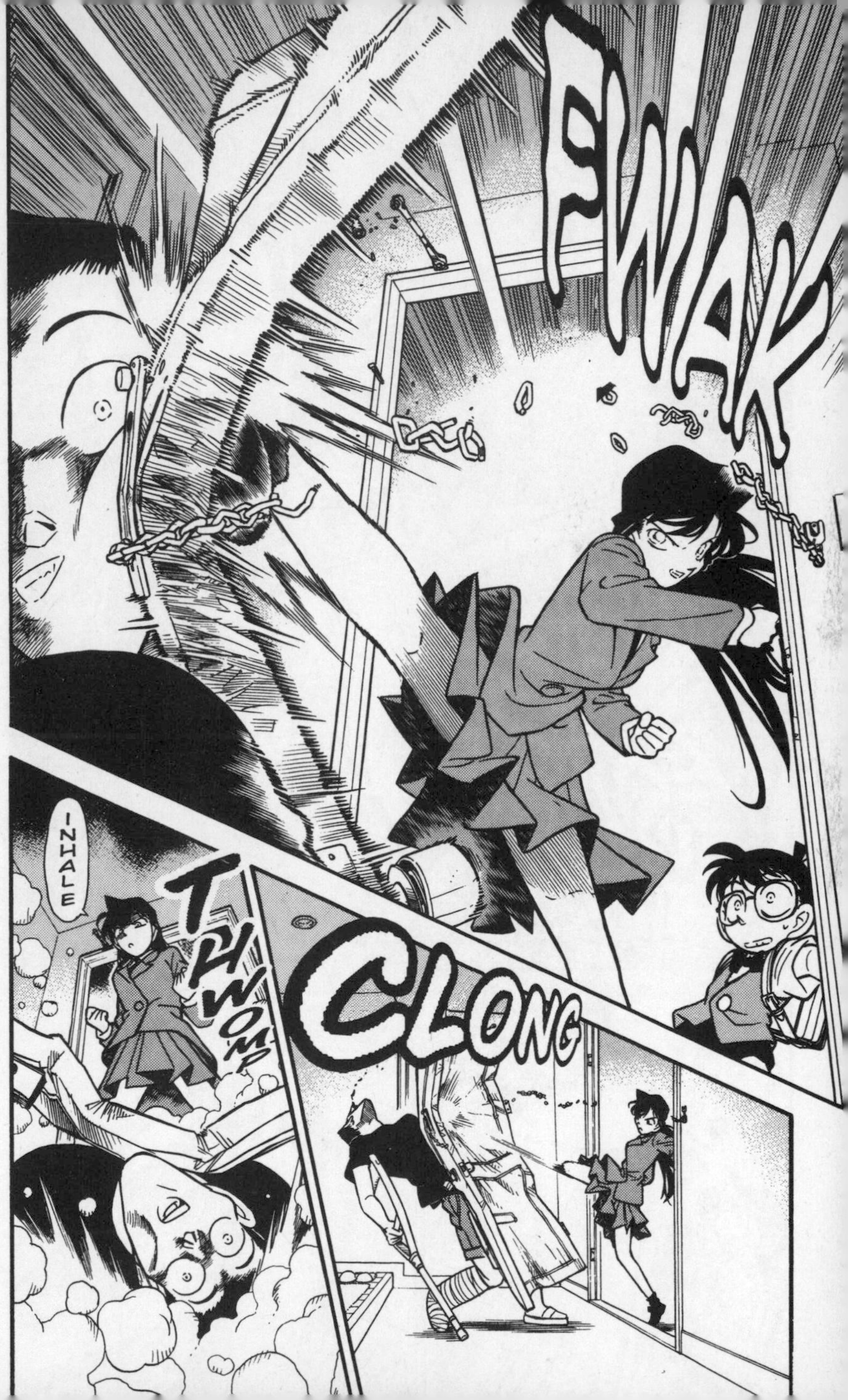
FWAK
CLONG
INHALE
THWOMP

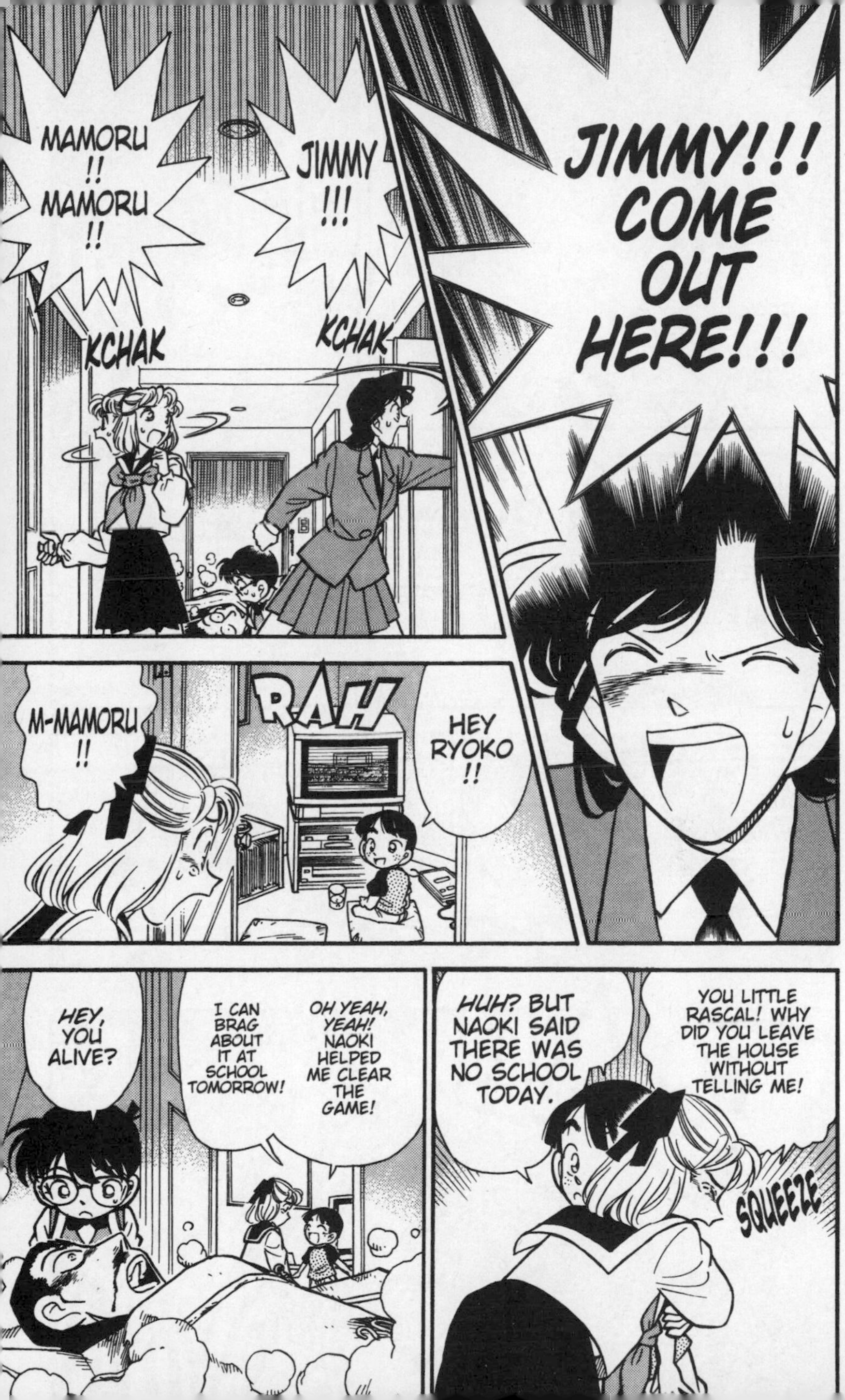
JIMMY!!! COME OUT HERE!!!
JIMMY !!!
KCHAK
MAMORU !! MAMORU !!
KCHAK
HEY RYOKO !!
RAH
M-MAMORU !!
YOU LITTLE RASCAL! WHY DID YOU LEAVE THE HOUSE WITHOUT TELLING ME!
SQUEEZE
HUH? BUT NAOKI SAID THERE WAS NO SCHOOL TODAY.
OH YEAH, YEAH! NAOKI HELPED ME CLEAR THE GAME!
I CAN BRAG ABOUT IT AT SCHOOL TOMORROW!
HEY, YOU ALIVE?

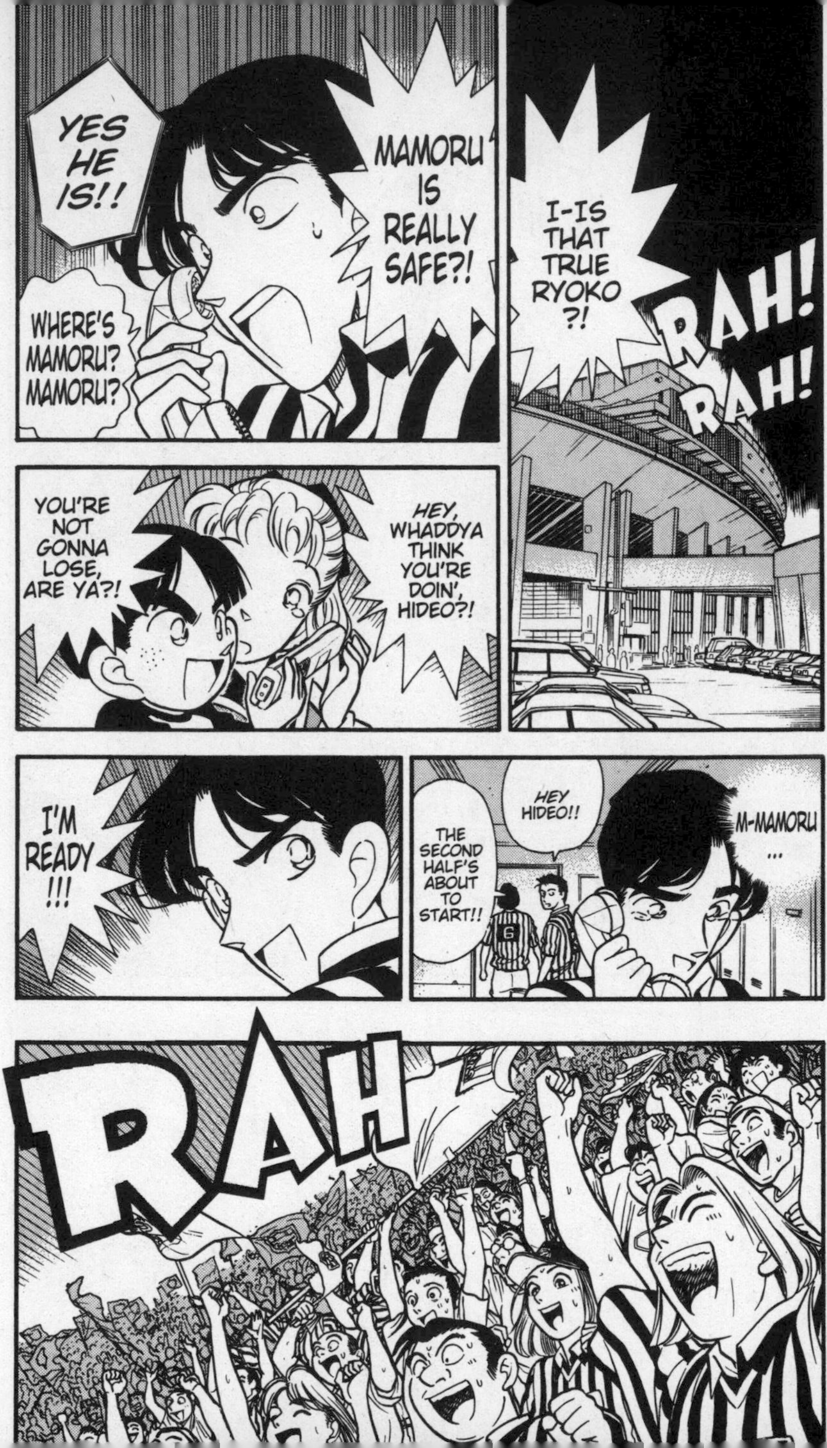
I-IS THAT TRUE RYOKO?!
RAH! RAH!
MAMORU IS REALLY SAFE?!
YES HE IS!!
WHERE'S MAMORU? MAMORU?
HEY, WHADDYA THINK YOU'RE DOIN', HIDEO?!
YOU'RE NOT GONNA LOSE, ARE YA?!
M-MAMORU ...
HEY HIDEO!!
THE SECOND HALF'S ABOUT TO START!!
I'M READY!!!
RAH

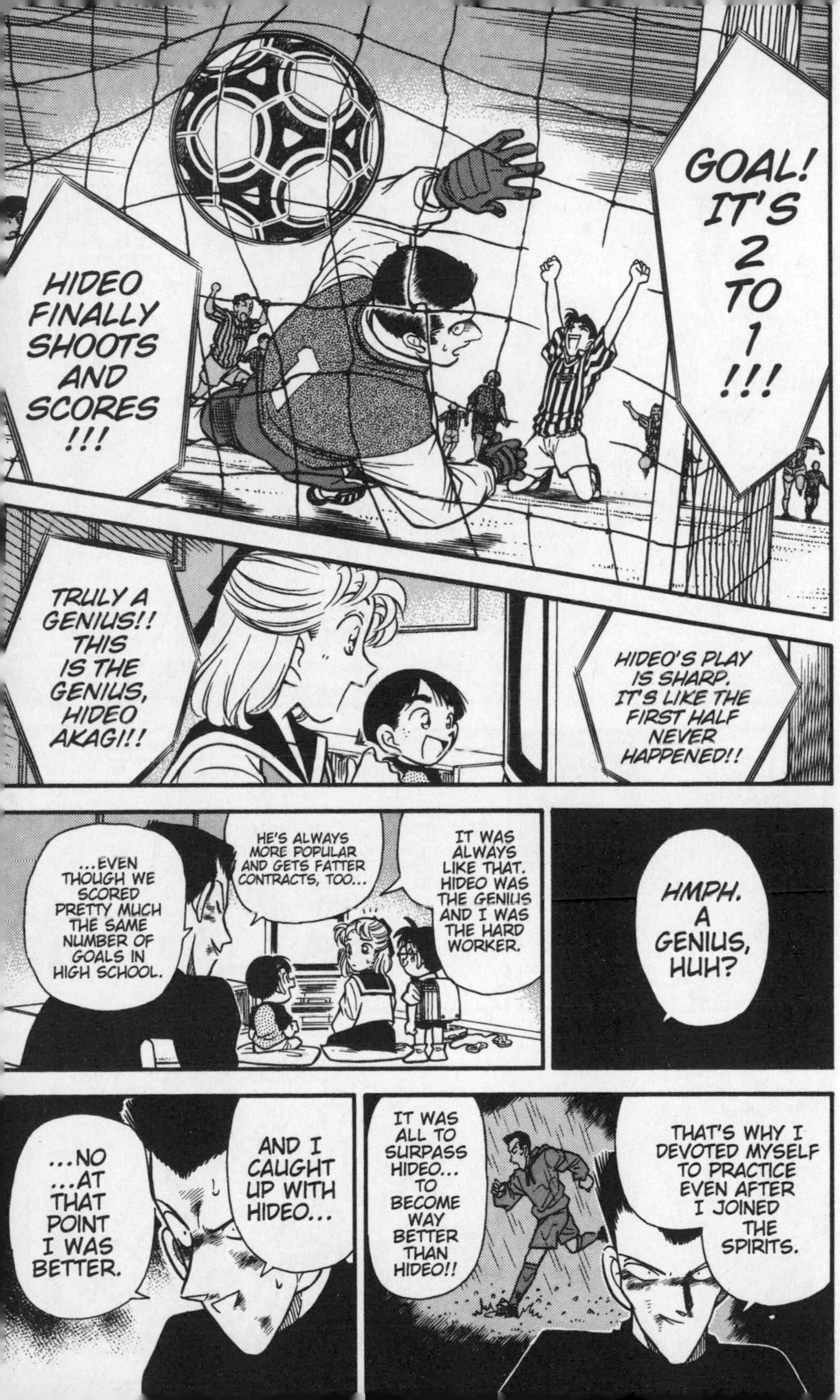
GOAL! IT'S 2 TO 1 !!!
HIDEO FINALLY SHOOTS AND SCORES !!!
HIDEO'S PLAY IS SHARP. IT'S LIKE THE FIRST HALF NEVER HAPPENED!!
TRULY A GENIUS!! THIS IS THE GENIUS, HIDEO AKAGI!!
HMPH. A GENIUS, HUH?
IT WAS ALWAYS LIKE THAT. HIDEO WAS THE GENIUS AND I WAS THE HARD WORKER.
HE'S ALWAYS MORE POPULAR AND GETS FATTER CONTRACTS, TOO...
...EVEN THOUGH WE SCORED PRETTY MUCH THE SAME NUMBER OF GOALS IN HIGH SCHOOL.
THAT'S WHY I DEVOTED MYSELF TO PRACTICE EVEN AFTER I JOINED THE SPIRITS.
IT WAS ALL TO SURPASS HIDEO... TO BECOME WAY BETTER THAN HIDEO!!
AND I CAUGHT UP WITH HIDEO...
...NO ...AT THAT POINT I WAS BETTER.

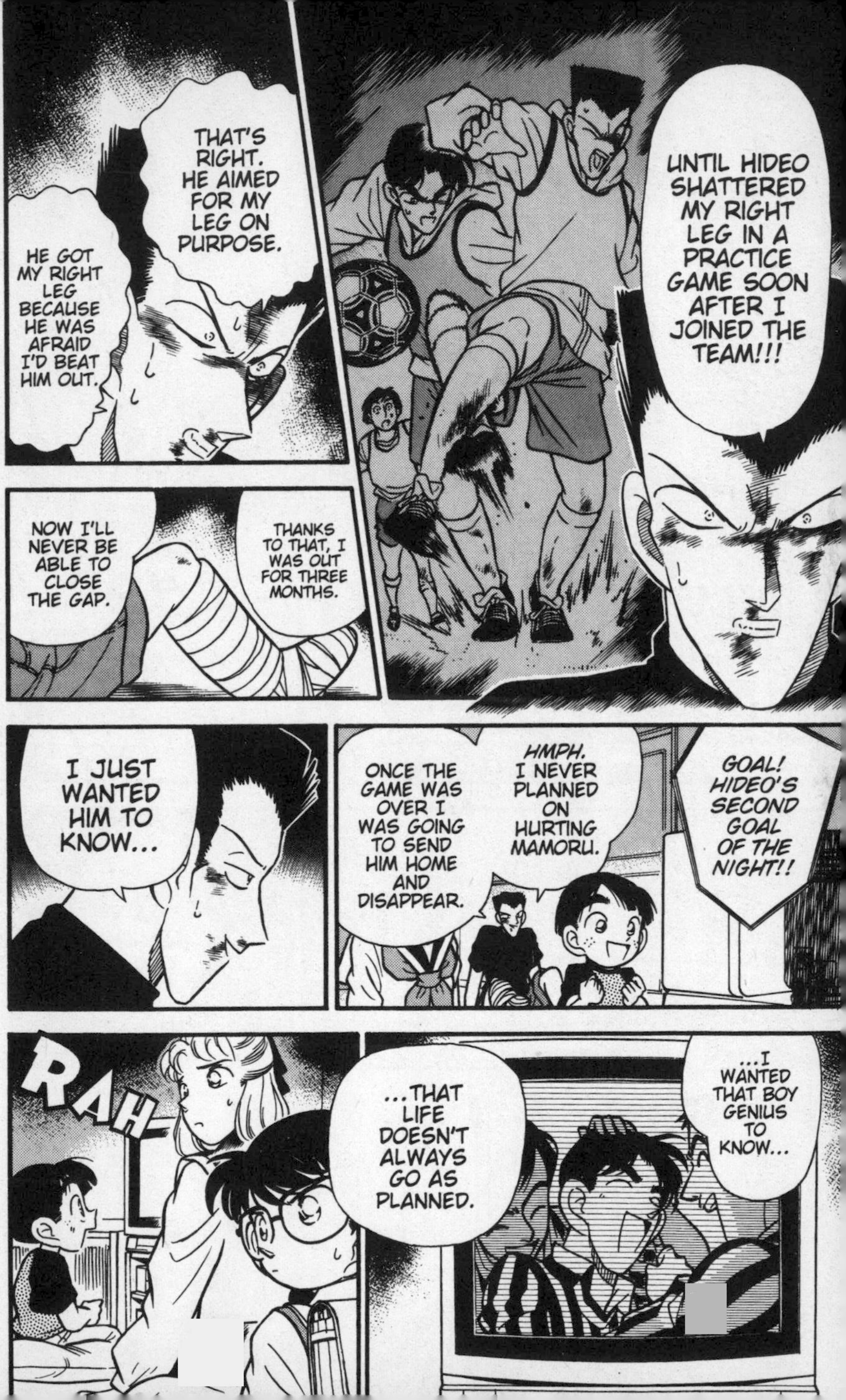
UNTIL HIDEO SHATTERED MY RIGHT LEG IN A PRACTICE GAME SOON AFTER I JOINED THE TEAM!!!
THAT'S RIGHT. HE AIMED FOR MY LEG ON PURPOSE.
HE GOT MY RIGHT LEG BECAUSE HE WAS AFRAID I'D BEAT HIM OUT.
THANKS TO THAT, I WAS OUT FOR THREE MONTHS.
NOW I'LL NEVER BE ABLE TO CLOSE THE GAP.
GOAL! HIDEO'S SECOND GOAL OF THE NIGHT!!
HMPH. I NEVER PLANNED ON HURTING MAMORU.
ONCE THE GAME WAS OVER I WAS GOING TO SEND HIM HOME AND DISAPPEAR.
I JUST WANTED HIM TO KNOW...
...I WANTED THAT BOY GENIUS TO KNOW...
...THAT LIFE DOESN'T ALWAYS GO AS PLANNED.
RAH

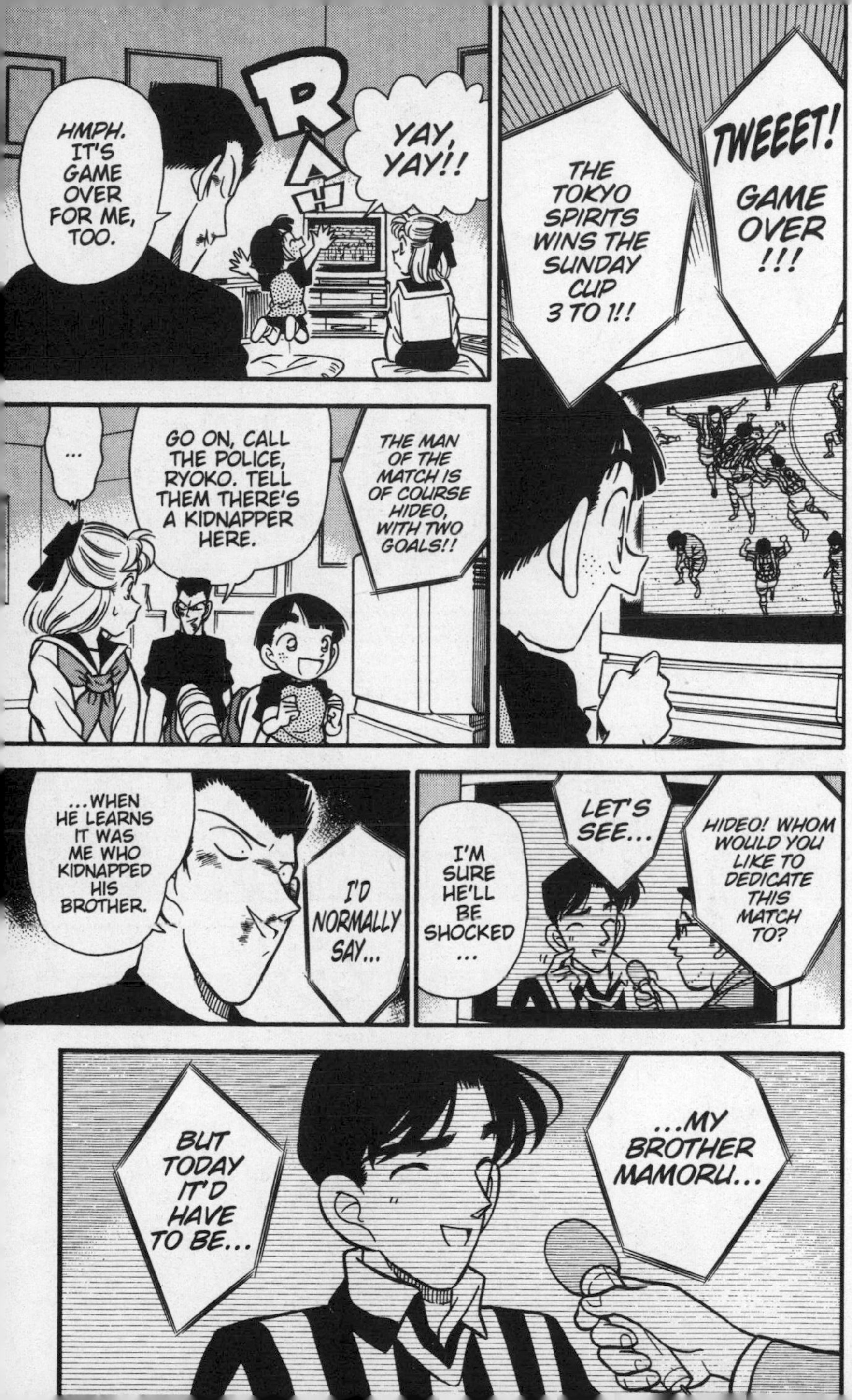

TWEEEET! GAME OVER!!!
THE TOKYO SPIRITS WINS THE SUNDAY CUP 3 TO 1!!
YAY, YAY!!
RAH
HMPH. IT'S GAME OVER FOR ME, TOO.
THE MAN OF THE MATCH IS OF COURSE HIDEO, WITH TWO GOALS!!
GO ON, CALL THE POLICE, RYOKO. TELL THEM THERE'S A KIDNAPPER HERE.
...
HIDEO! WHOM WOULD YOU LIKE TO DEDICATE THIS MATCH TO?
LET'S SEE...
I'M SURE HE'LL BE SHOCKED...
I'D NORMALLY SAY...
...WHEN HE LEARNS IT WAS ME WHO KIDNAPPED HIS BROTHER.
...MY BROTHER MAMORU...
BUT TODAY IT'D HAVE TO BE...

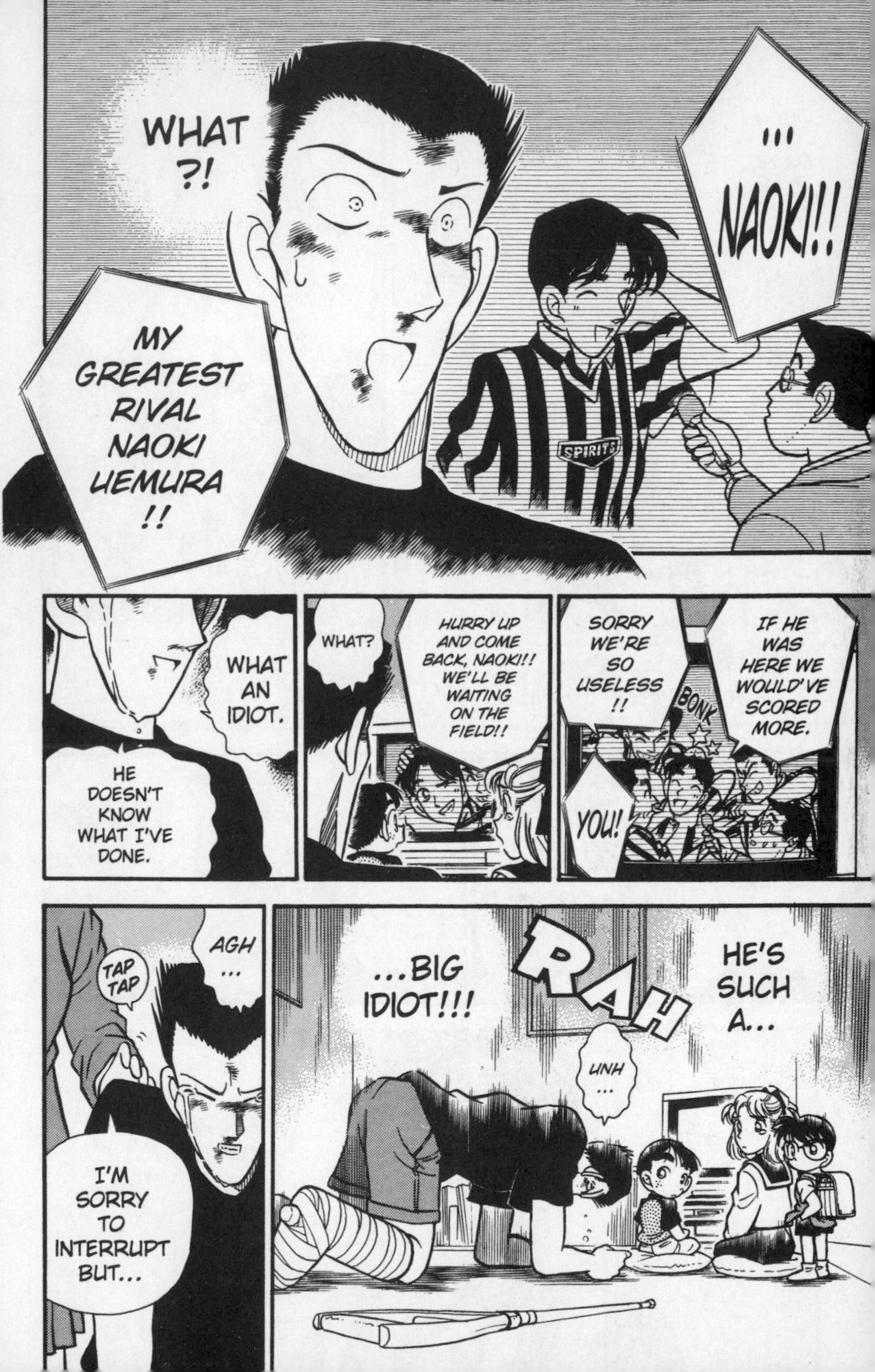
... NAOKI!!
WHAT ?!
MY GREATEST RIVAL NAOKI UEMURA !!
IF HE WAS HERE WE WOULD'VE SCORED MORE.
SORRY WE'RE SO USELESS !!
BONK
YOU!
HURRY UP AND COME BACK, NAOKI!! WE'LL BE WAITING ON THE FIELD!!
WHAT?
WHAT AN IDIOT.
HE DOESN'T KNOW WHAT I'VE DONE.
HE'S SUCH A...
RAH
...BIG IDIOT!!!
UNH ...
AGH ...
TAP TAP
I'M SORRY TO INTERRUPT BUT...

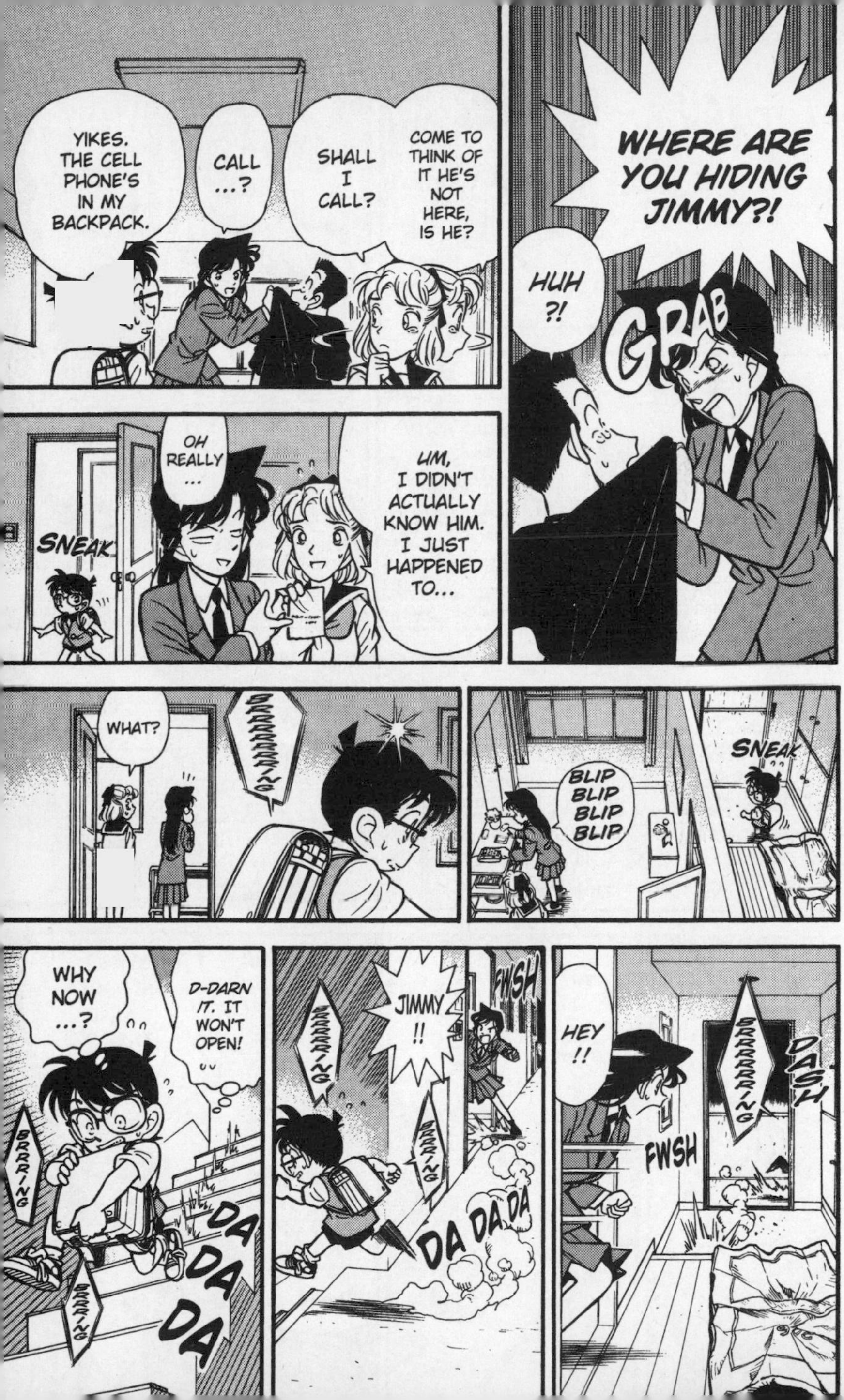
WHERE ARE YOU HIDING JIMMY?!
HUH ?!
GRAB
COME TO THINK OF IT HE'S NOT HERE, IS HE?
SHALL I CALL?
CALL ...?
YIKES. THE CELL PHONE'S IN MY BACKPACK.
UM, I DIDN'T ACTUALLY KNOW HIM. I JUST HAPPENED TO...
OH REALLY ...
SNEAK
SNEAK
BLIP BLIP BLIP BLIP
BRRRRRRRING
WHAT?
DASH
BRRRRRRING
HEY !!
FWSH
FWSH
JIMMY !!
BRRRRRING
BRRRING
DA DA DA
D-DARN IT. IT WON'T OPEN!
WHY NOW ...?
BRRRING
BRRRING
DA DA DA

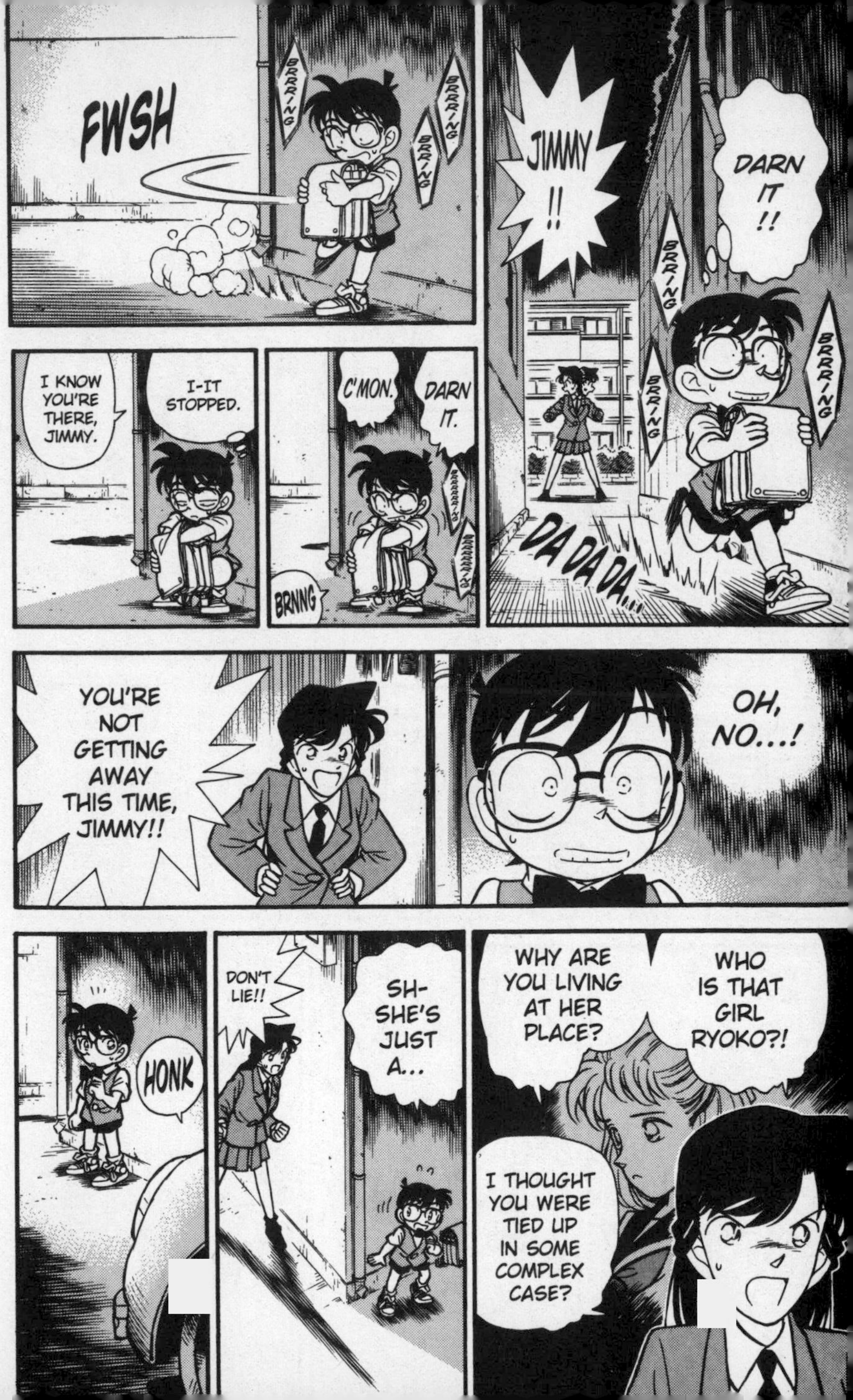
DARN IT!!
BRRRING
BRRRING
BRRRING
JIMMY!!
DA DA DA...
BRRRING
BRRRING
BRRRING
FWSH
DARN IT.
C'MON.
BRRRRING
BRRRRING
BRNNG
I-IT STOPPED.
I KNOW YOU'RE THERE, JIMMY.
OH, NO...!
YOU'RE NOT GETTING AWAY THIS TIME, JIMMY!!
WHO IS THAT GIRL RYOKO?!
WHY ARE YOU LIVING AT HER PLACE?
I THOUGHT YOU WERE TIED UP IN SOME COMPLEX CASE?
SH-SHE'S JUST A...
DON'T LIE!!
HONK

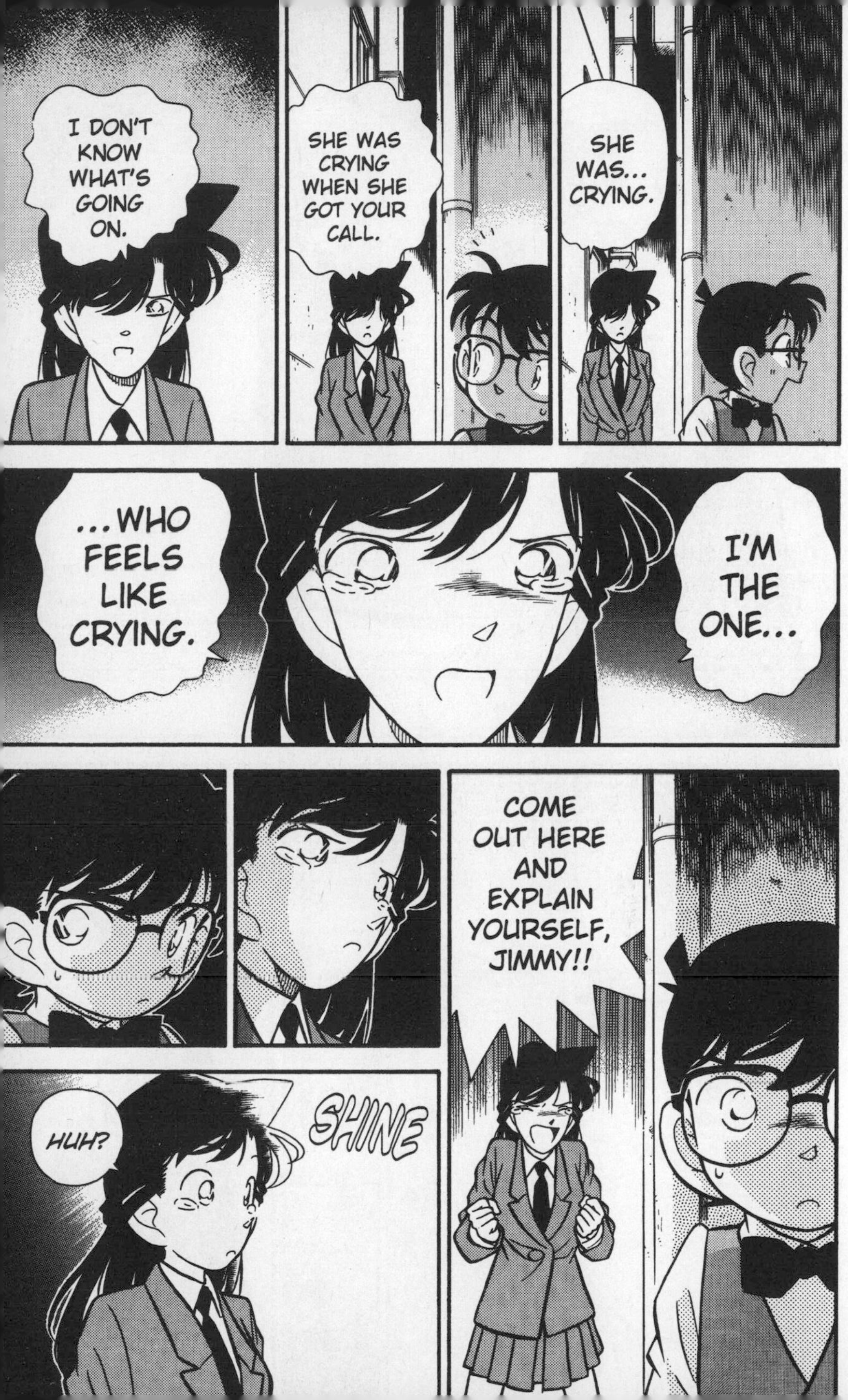
SHE WAS... CRYING.
SHE WAS CRYING WHEN SHE GOT YOUR CALL.
I DON'T KNOW WHAT'S GOING ON.
I'M THE ONE...
...WHO FEELS LIKE CRYING.
COME OUT HERE AND EXPLAIN YOURSELF, JIMMY!!
SHINE
HUH?

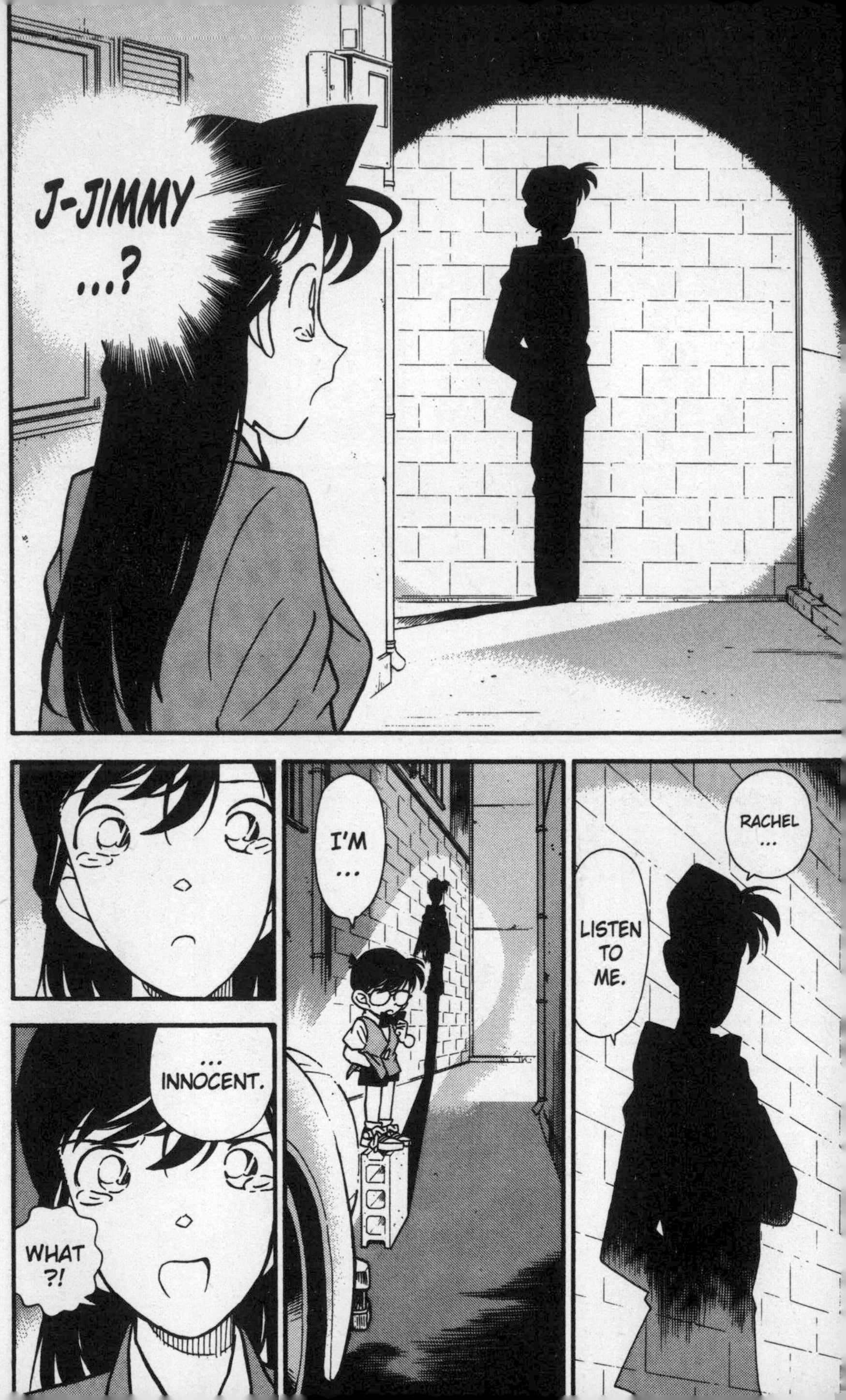

J-JIMMY ...?
RACHEL ...
LISTEN TO ME.
I'M ...
... INNOCENT.
WHAT ?!

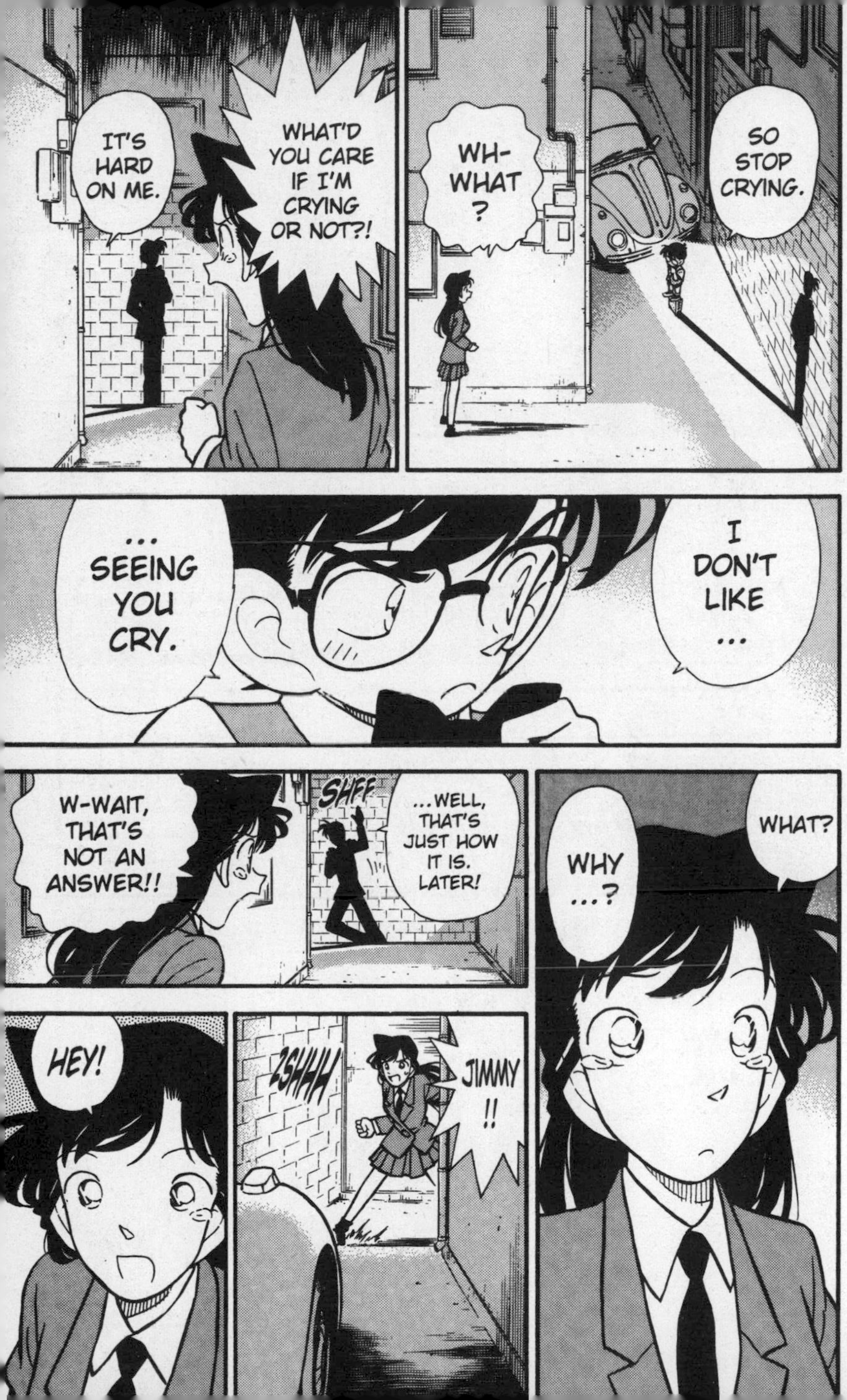
SO STOP CRYING.
WH-WHAT?
WHAT'D YOU CARE IF I'M CRYING OR NOT?!
IT'S HARD ON ME.
I DON'T LIKE ...
... SEEING YOU CRY.
WHAT?
WHY ...?
SHFF
...WELL, THAT'S JUST HOW IT IS. LATER!
W-WAIT, THAT'S NOT AN ANSWER!!
JIMMY !!
ZSHHH
HEY!

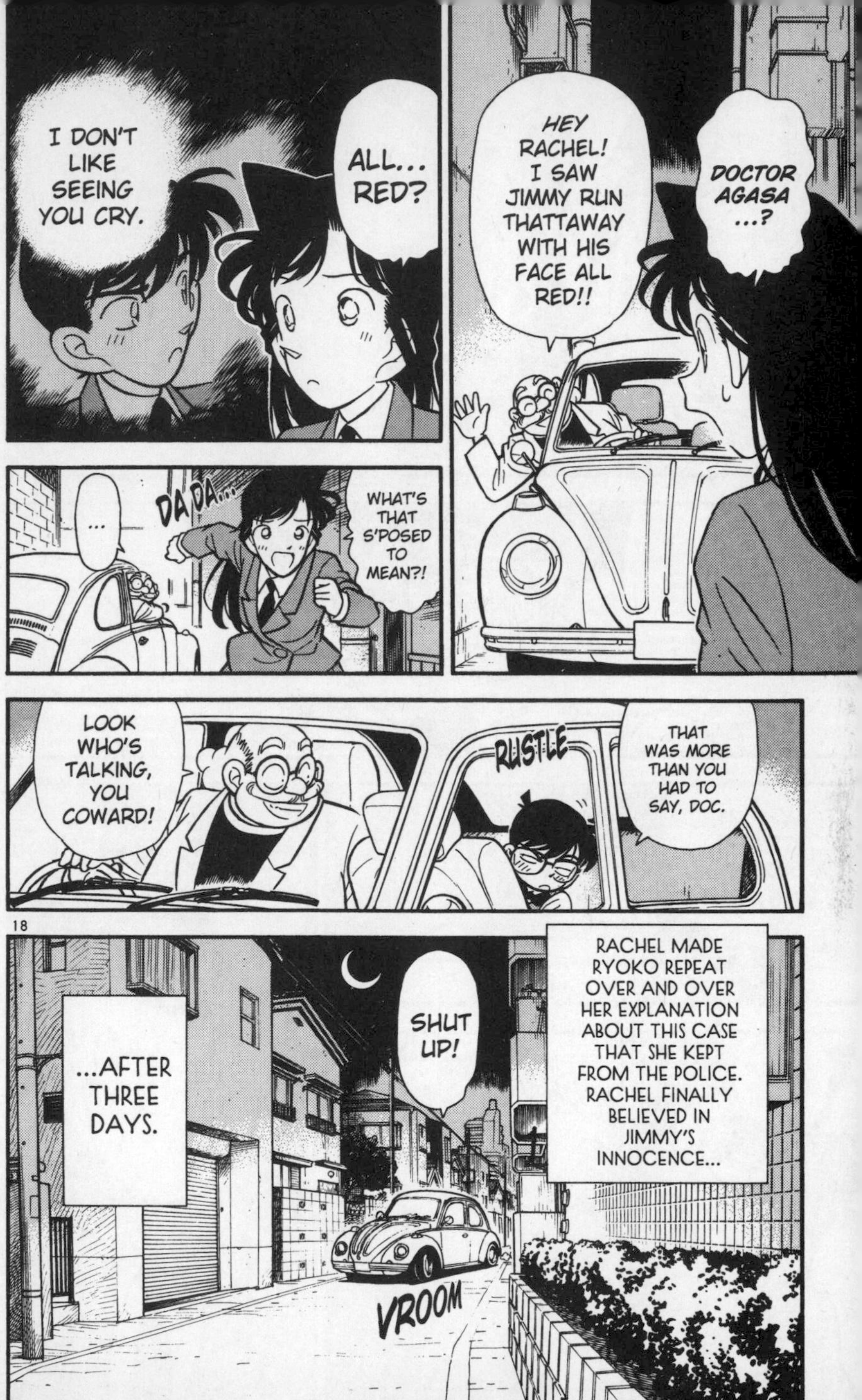
DOCTOR AGASA ...?
HEY RACHEL! I SAW JIMMY RUN THATTAWAY WITH HIS FACE ALL RED!!
ALL... RED?
I DON'T LIKE SEEING YOU CRY.
WHAT'S THAT S'POSED TO MEAN?!
DA DA...
...
THAT WAS MORE THAN YOU HAD TO SAY, DOC.
RUSTLE
LOOK WHO'S TALKING, YOU COWARD!
RACHEL MADE RYOKO REPEAT OVER AND OVER HER EXPLANATION ABOUT THIS CASE THAT SHE KEPT FROM THE POLICE. RACHEL FINALLY BELIEVED IN JIMMY'S INNOCENCE...
SHUT UP!
...AFTER THREE DAYS.
VROOM

FILE 2: THE NIGHT BARON

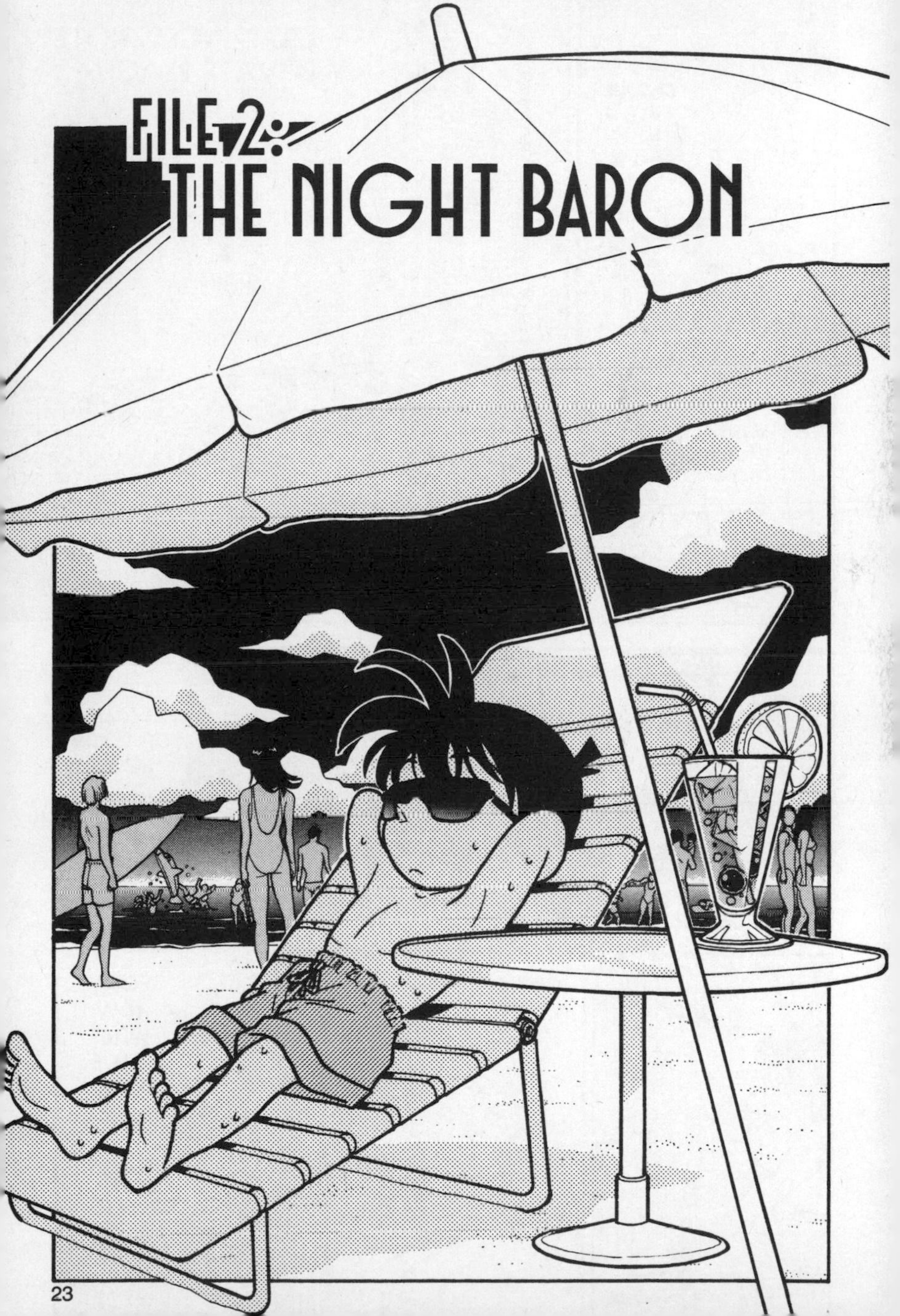

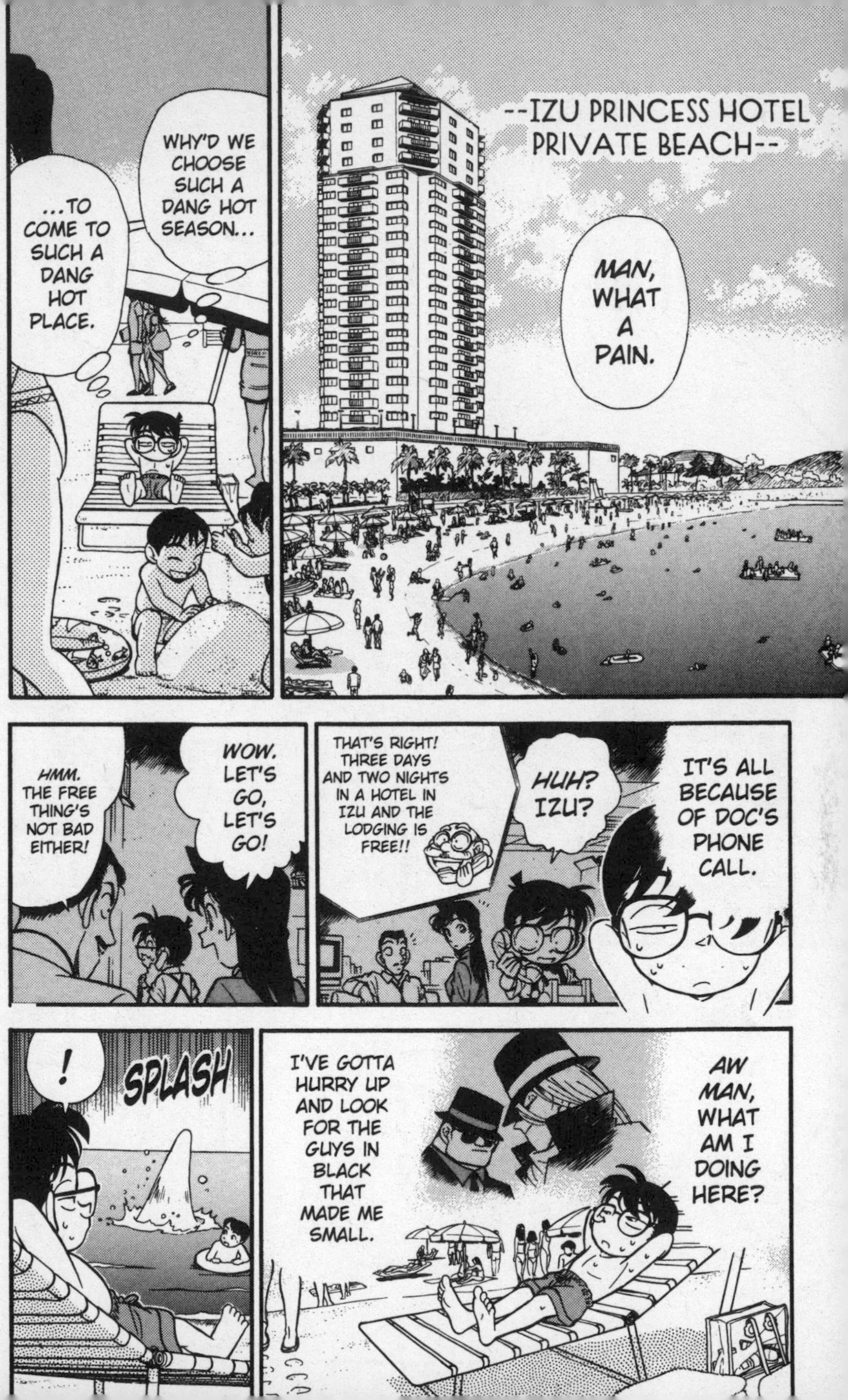
--IZU PRINCESS HOTEL PRIVATE BEACH--
MAN, WHAT A PAIN.
WHY'D WE CHOOSE SUCH A DANG HOT SEASON...
...TO COME TO SUCH A DANG HOT PLACE.
IT'S ALL BECAUSE OF DOC'S PHONE CALL.
HUH? IZU?
THAT'S RIGHT! THREE DAYS AND TWO NIGHTS IN A HOTEL IN IZU AND THE LODGING IS FREE!!
WOW. LET'S GO, LET'S GO!
HMM. THE FREE THING'S NOT BAD EITHER!
AW MAN, WHAT AM I DOING HERE?
I'VE GOTTA HURRY UP AND LOOK FOR THE GUYS IN BLACK THAT MADE ME SMALL.
SPLASH
!

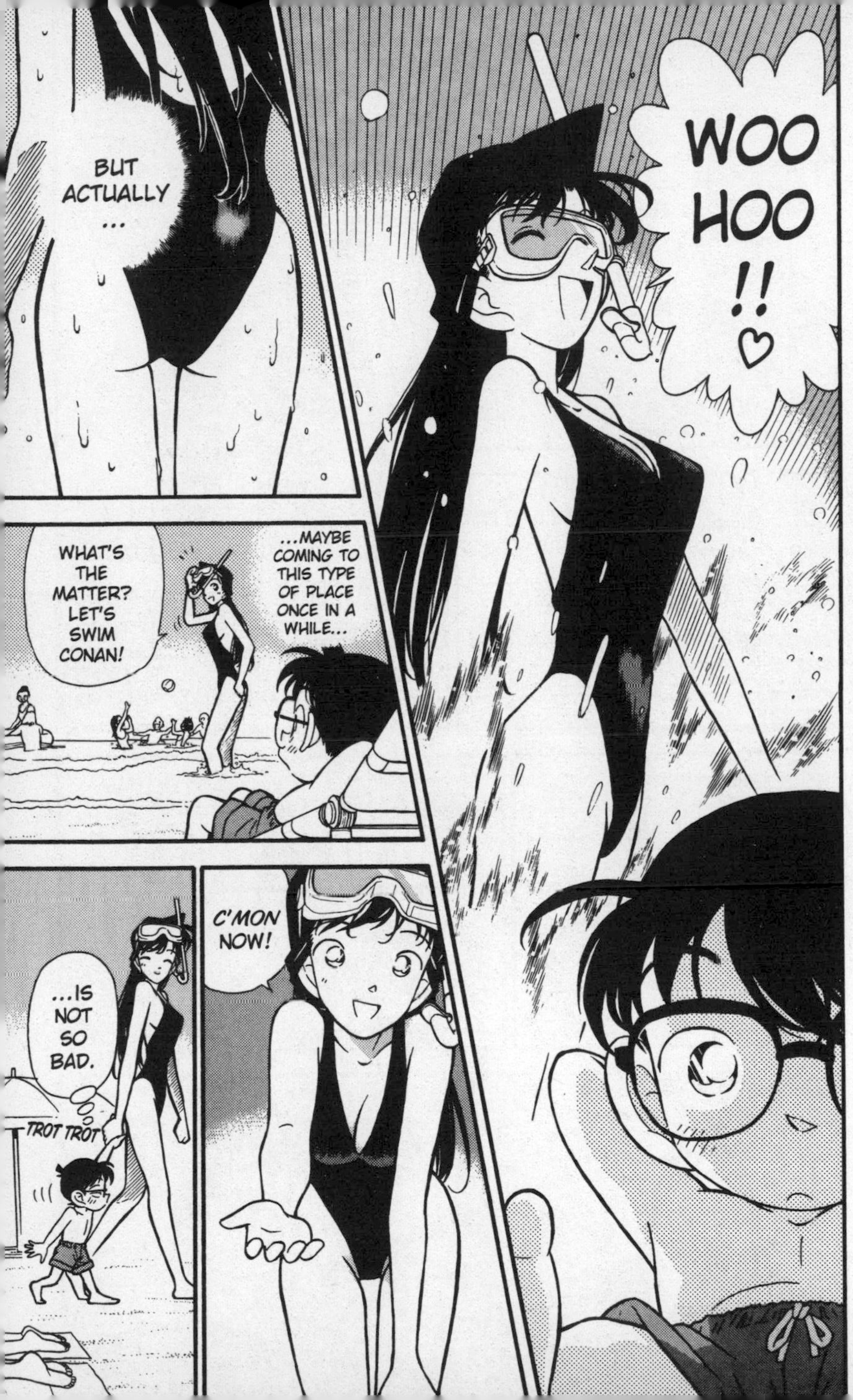
WOO HOO !! ♡
BUT ACTUALLY ...
...MAYBE COMING TO THIS TYPE OF PLACE ONCE IN A WHILE...
WHAT'S THE MATTER? LET'S SWIM CONAN!
C'MON NOW!
...IS NOT SO BAD.
TROT TROT

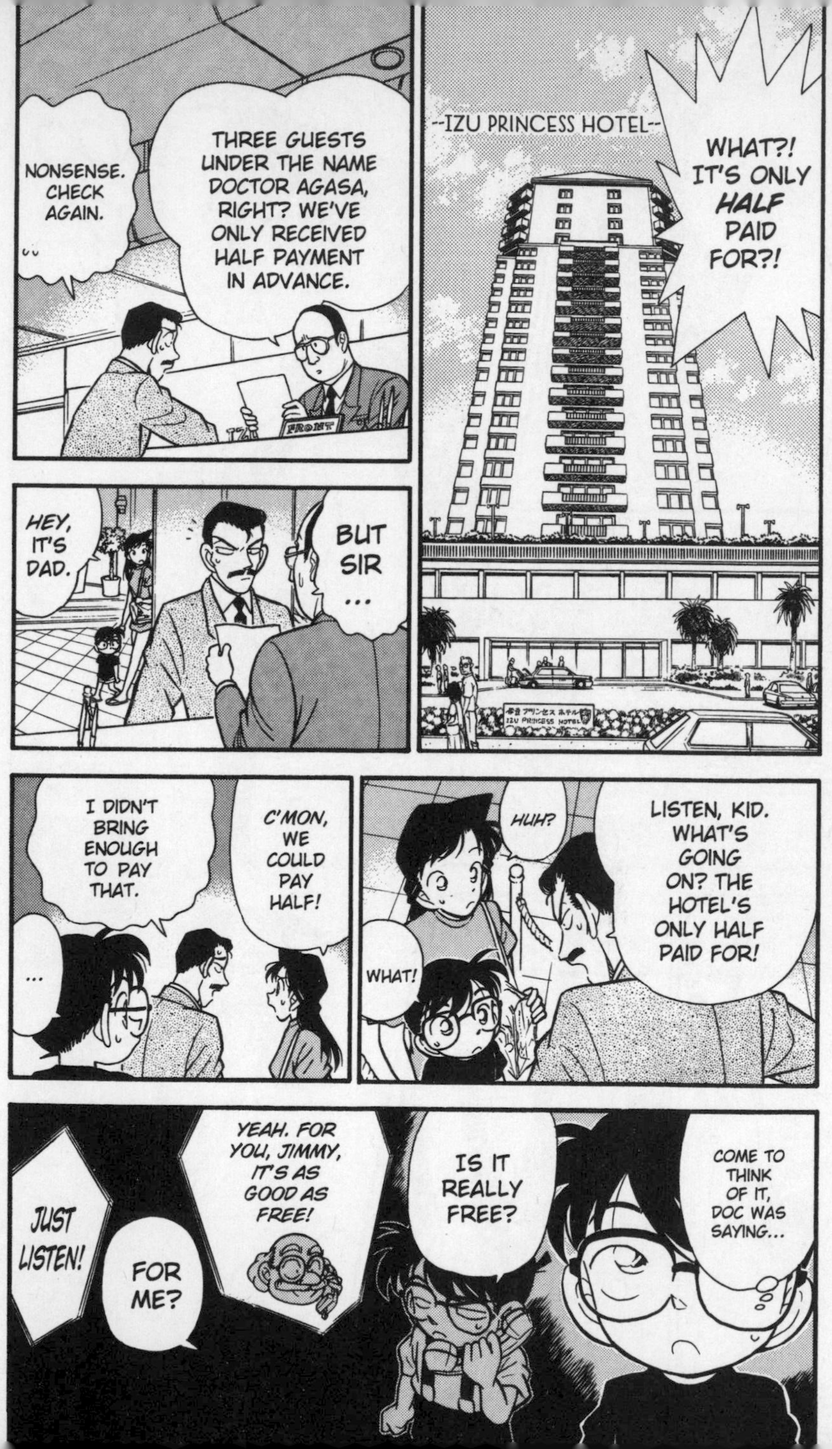
--IZU PRINCESS HOTEL--
WHAT?! IT'S ONLY HALF PAID FOR?!
THREE GUESTS UNDER THE NAME DOCTOR AGASA, RIGHT? WE'VE ONLY RECEIVED HALF PAYMENT IN ADVANCE.
NONSENSE. CHECK AGAIN.
BUT SIR ...
HEY, IT'S DAD.
LISTEN, KID. WHAT'S GOING ON? THE HOTEL'S ONLY HALF PAID FOR!
HUH?
WHAT!
C'MON, WE COULD PAY HALF!
I DIDN'T BRING ENOUGH TO PAY THAT.
...
COME TO THINK OF IT, DOC WAS SAYING...
IS IT REALLY FREE?
YEAH. FOR YOU, JIMMY, IT'S AS GOOD AS FREE!
FOR ME?
JUST LISTEN!

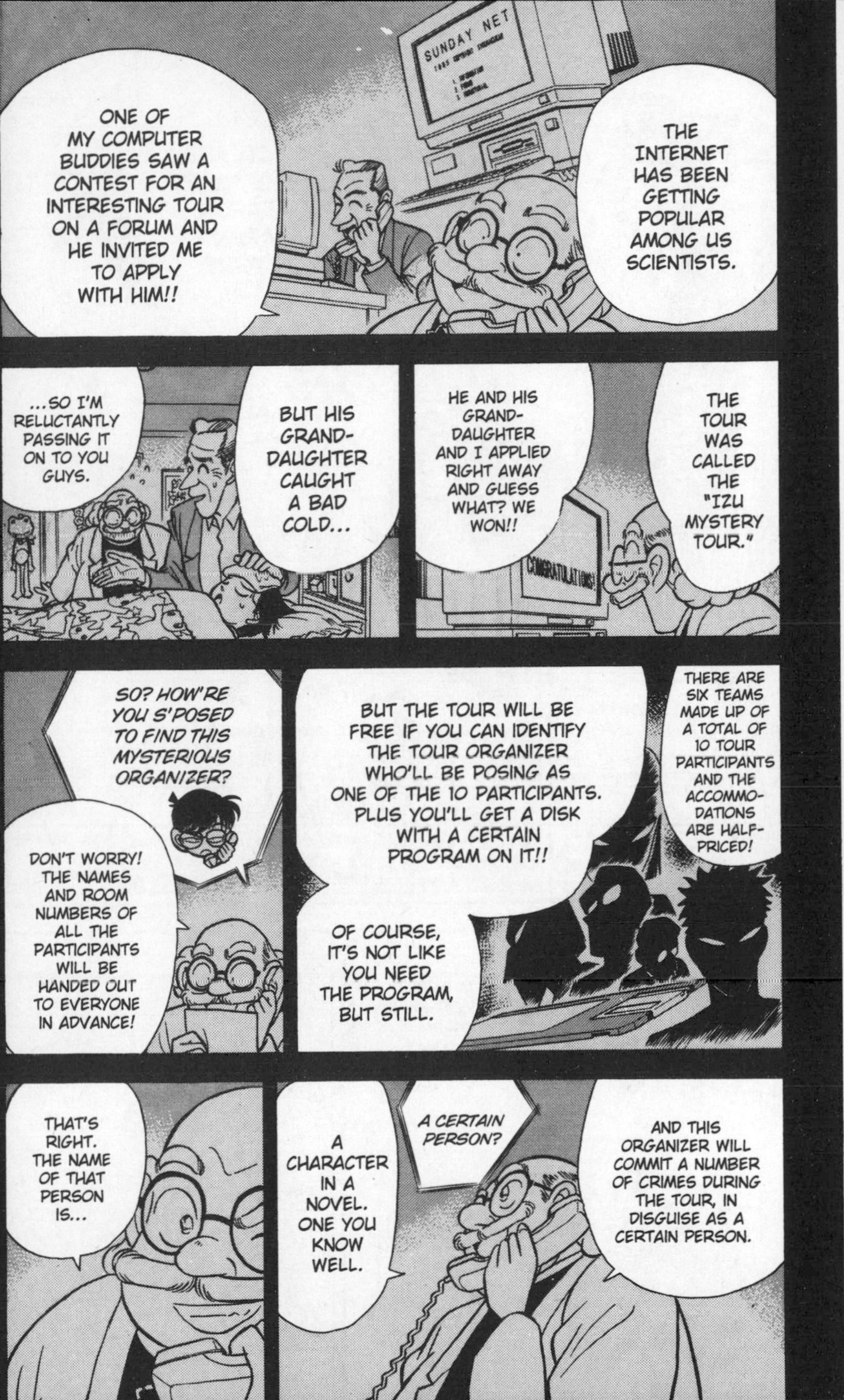
SUNDAY NET
THE INTERNET HAS BEEN GETTING POPULAR AMONG US SCIENTISTS.
ONE OF MY COMPUTER BUDDIES SAW A CONTEST FOR AN INTERESTING TOUR ON A FORUM AND HE INVITED ME TO APPLY WITH HIM!!
THE TOUR WAS CALLED THE "IZU MYSTERY TOUR."
HE AND HIS GRAND-DAUGHTER AND I APPLIED RIGHT AWAY AND GUESS WHAT? WE WON!!
CONGRATULATIONS!
BUT HIS GRAND-DAUGHTER CAUGHT A BAD COLD...
...SO I'M RELUCTANTLY PASSING IT ON TO YOU GUYS.
THERE ARE SIX TEAMS MADE UP OF A TOTAL OF 10 TOUR PARTICIPANTS AND THE ACCOMMO-DATIONS ARE HALF-PRICED!
BUT THE TOUR WILL BE FREE IF YOU CAN IDENTIFY THE TOUR ORGANIZER WHO'LL BE POSING AS ONE OF THE 10 PARTICIPANTS. PLUS YOU'LL GET A DISK WITH A CERTAIN PROGRAM ON IT!!
OF COURSE, IT'S NOT LIKE YOU NEED THE PROGRAM, BUT STILL.
SO? HOW'RE YOU S'POSED TO FIND THIS MYSTERIOUS ORGANIZER?
DON'T WORRY! THE NAMES AND ROOM NUMBERS OF ALL THE PARTICIPANTS WILL BE HANDED OUT TO EVERYONE IN ADVANCE!
AND THIS ORGANIZER WILL COMMIT A NUMBER OF CRIMES DURING THE TOUR, IN DISGUISE AS A CERTAIN PERSON.
A CERTAIN PERSON?
A CHARACTER IN A NOVEL. ONE YOU KNOW WELL.
THAT'S RIGHT. THE NAME OF THAT PERSON IS...

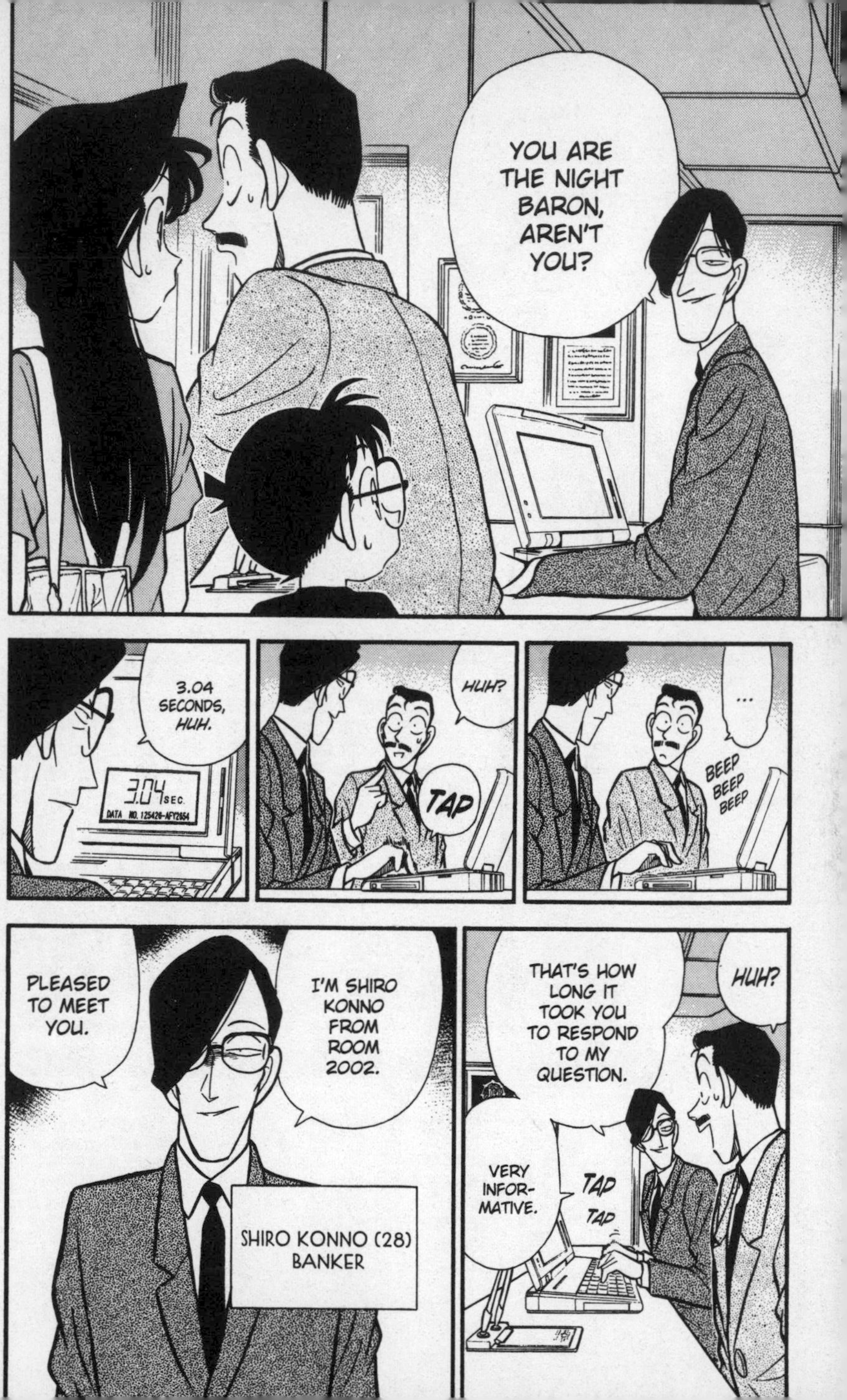
YOU ARE THE NIGHT BARON, AREN'T YOU?
...
BEEP BEEP BEEP
HUH?
TAP
3.04 SECONDS, HUH.
3.04 SEC.
DATA NO. 125426-AFY2654
HUH?
THAT'S HOW LONG IT TOOK YOU TO RESPOND TO MY QUESTION.
VERY INFORMATIVE.
TAP
TAP
I'M SHIRO KONNO FROM ROOM 2002.
PLEASED TO MEET YOU.
SHIRO KONNO (28) BANKER

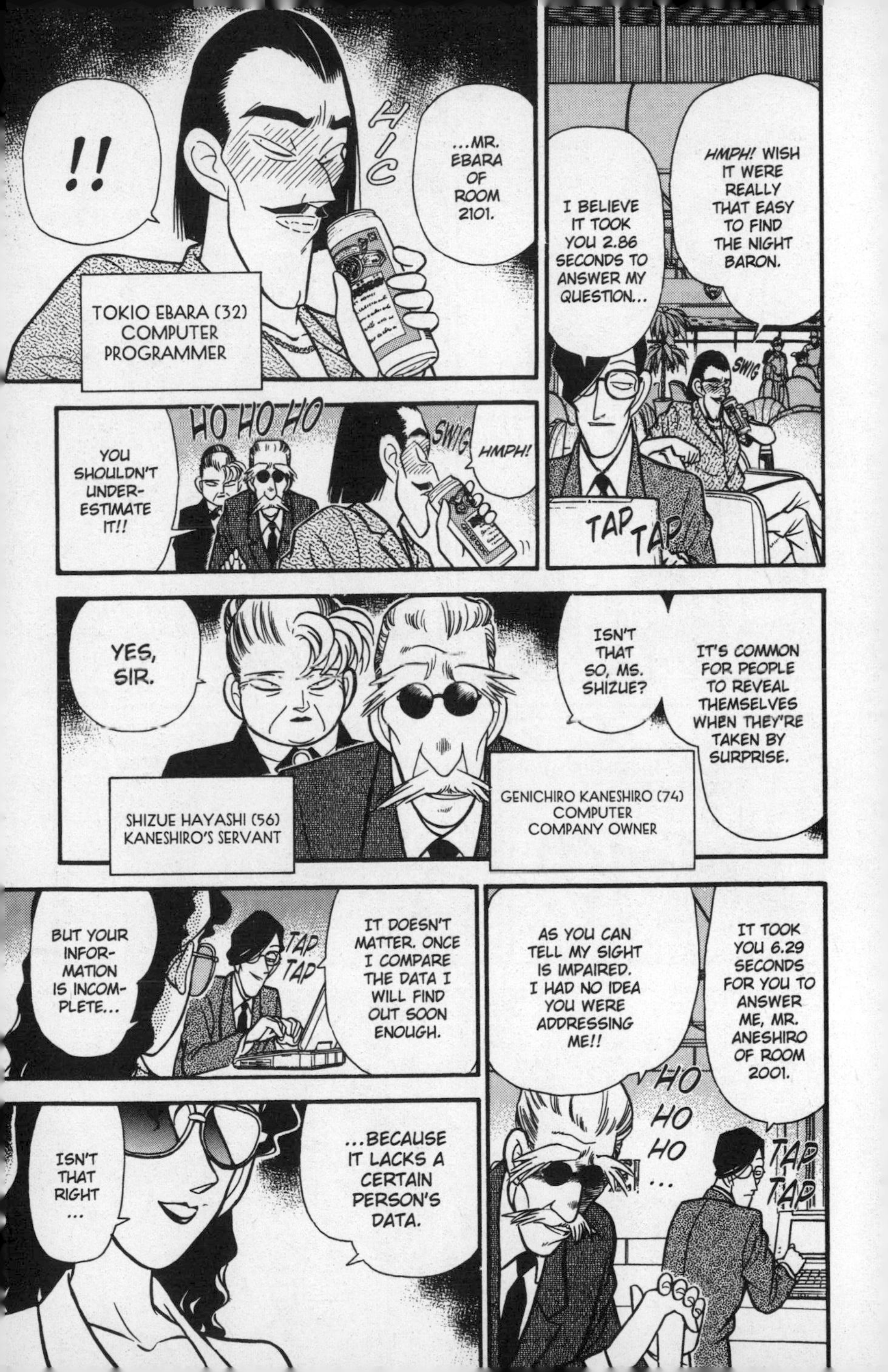
HMPH! WISH IT WERE REALLY THAT EASY TO FIND THE NIGHT BARON.
I BELIEVE IT TOOK YOU 2.86 SECONDS TO ANSWER MY QUESTION...
SWIG
TAP TAP
...MR. EBARA OF ROOM 2101.
HIC
!!
TOKIO EBARA (32) COMPUTER PROGRAMMER
HMPH!
SWIG
HO HO HO
YOU SHOULDN'T UNDER-ESTIMATE IT!!
IT'S COMMON FOR PEOPLE TO REVEAL THEMSELVES WHEN THEY"RE TAKEN BY SURPRISE.
ISN'T THAT SO, MS. SHIZUE?
GENICHIRO KANESHIRO (74) COMPUTER COMPANY OWNER
YES, SIR.
SHIZUE HAYASHI (56) KANESHIRO'S SERVANT
IT TOOK YOU 6.29 SECONDS FOR YOU TO ANSWER ME, MR. ANESHIRO OF ROOM 2001.
AS YOU CAN TELL MY SIGHT IS IMPAIRED. I HAD NO IDEA YOU WERE ADDRESSING ME!!
HO HO HO...
TAP TAP
IT DOESN'T MATTER. ONCE I COMPARE THE DATA I WILL FIND OUT SOON ENOUGH.
TAP TAP
BUT YOUR INFOR-MATION IS INCOM-PLETE...
...BECAUSE IT LACKS A CERTAIN PERSON'S DATA.
ISN'T THAT RIGHT...

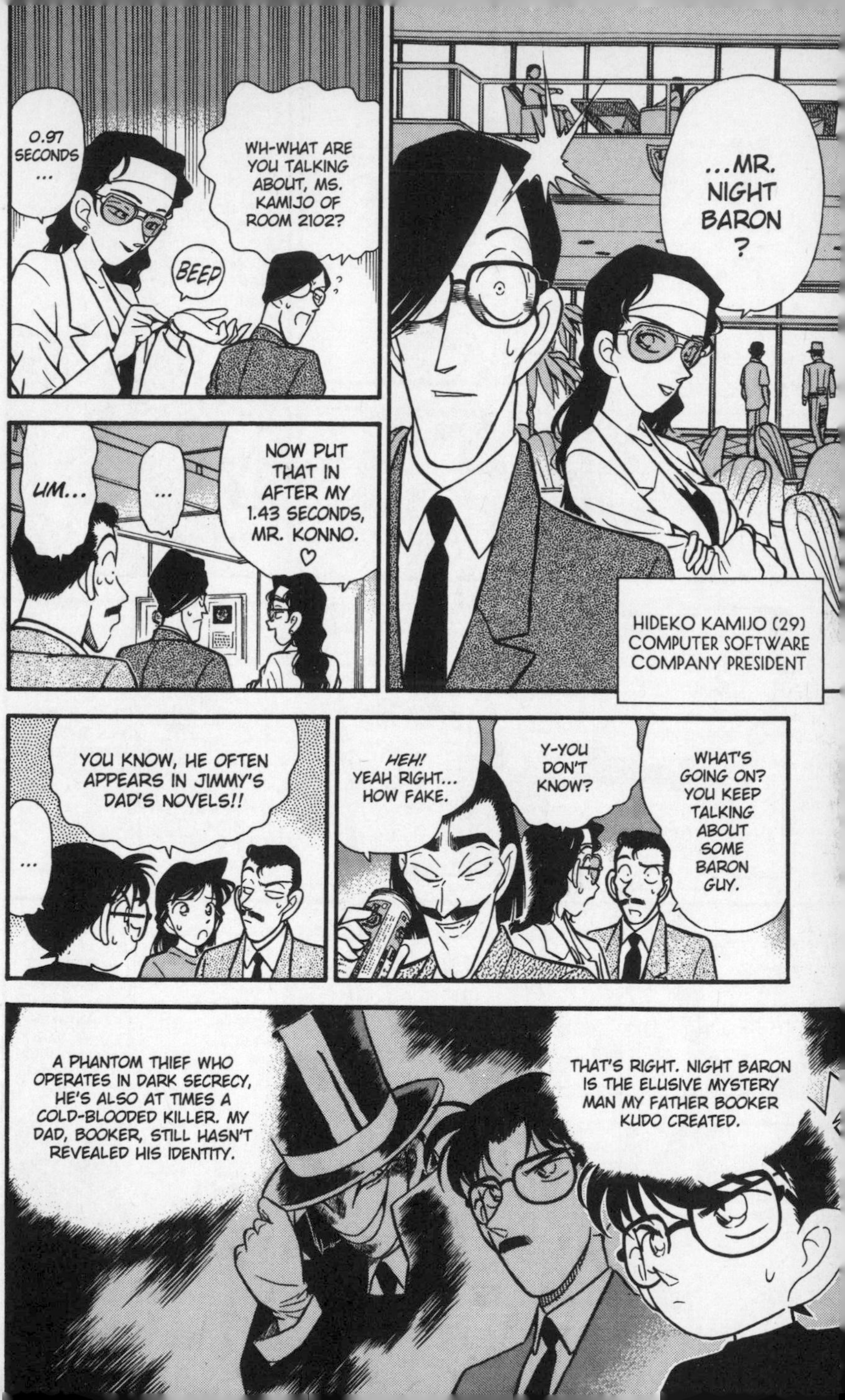
...MR. NIGHT BARON ?
HIDEKO KAMIJO (29) COMPUTER SOFTWARE COMPANY PRESIDENT
WH-WHAT ARE YOU TALKING ABOUT, MS. KAMIJO OF ROOM 2102?
0.97 SECONDS ...
BEEP
NOW PUT THAT IN AFTER MY 1.43 SECONDS, MR. KONNO. ♡
...
UM...
WHAT'S GOING ON? YOU KEEP TALKING ABOUT SOME BARON GUY.
Y-YOU DON'T KNOW?
HEH! YEAH RIGHT... HOW FAKE.
YOU KNOW, HE OFTEN APPEARS IN JIMMY'S DAD'S NOVELS!!
...
THAT'S RIGHT. NIGHT BARON IS THE ELUSIVE MYSTERY MAN MY FATHER BOOKER KUDO CREATED.
A PHANTOM THIEF WHO OPERATES IN DARK SECRECY, HE'S ALSO AT TIMES A COLD-BLOODED KILLER. MY DAD, BOOKER, STILL HASN'T REVEALED HIS IDENTITY.

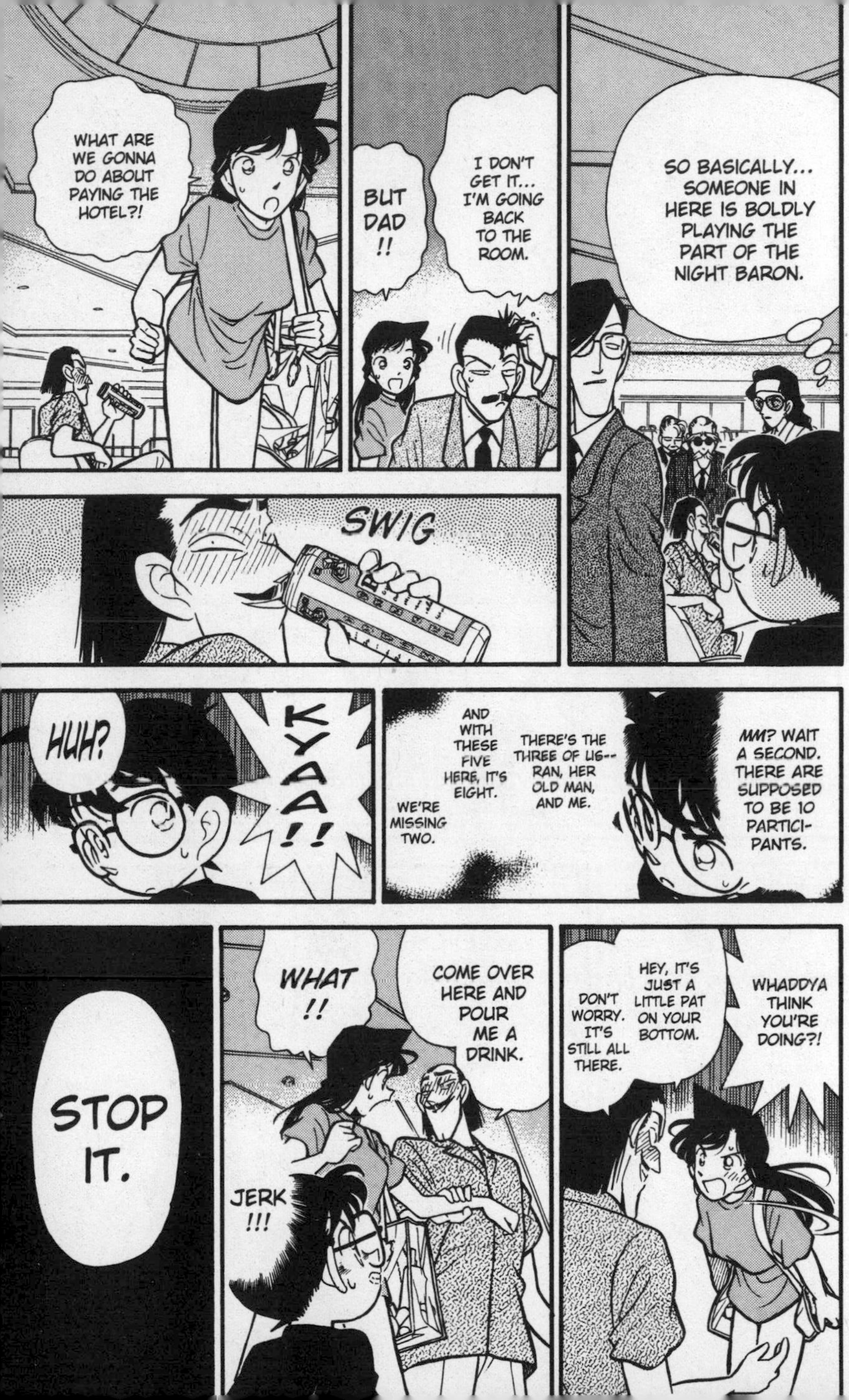
SO BASICALLY... SOMEONE IN HERE IS BOLDLY PLAYING THE PART OF THE NIGHT BARON.
I DON'T GET IT... I'M GOING BACK TO THE ROOM.
BUT DAD !!
WHAT ARE WE GONNA DO ABOUT PAYING THE HOTEL?!
SWIG
MM? WAIT A SECOND. THERE ARE SUPPOSED TO BE 10 PARTICI-PANTS.
THERE'S THE THREE OF US-- RAN, HER OLD MAN, AND ME.
AND WITH THESE FIVE HERE, IT'S EIGHT.
WE'RE MISSING TWO.
KYAAA!!
HUH?
WHADDYA THINK YOU'RE DOING?!
HEY, IT'S JUST A LITTLE PAT ON YOUR BOTTOM.
DON'T WORRY. IT'S STILL ALL THERE.
COME OVER HERE AND POUR ME A DRINK.
WHAT !!
JERK !!!
STOP IT.

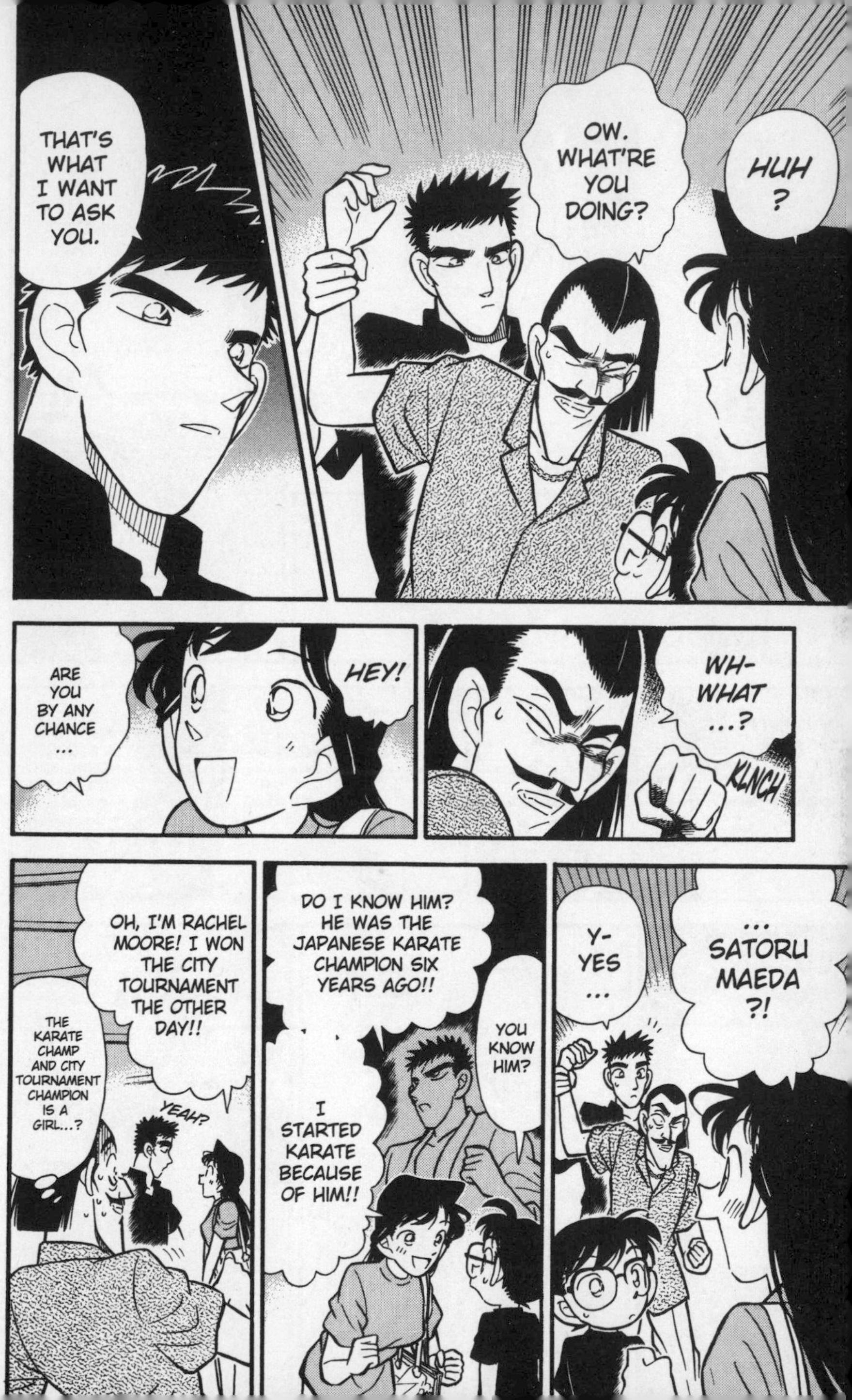
HUH?
OW. WHAT'RE YOU DOING?
THAT'S WHAT I WANT TO ASK YOU.
WH-WHAT...?
KLNCH
HEY!
ARE YOU BY ANY CHANCE...
...SATORU MAEDA?!
Y-YES...
DO I KNOW HIM? HE WAS THE JAPANESE KARATE CHAMPION SIX YEARS AGO!!
YOU KNOW HIM?
I STARTED KARATE BECAUSE OF HIM!!
OH, I'M RACHEL MOORE! I WON THE CITY TOURNAMENT THE OTHER DAY!!
YEAH?
THE KARATE CHAMP AND CITY TOURNAMENT CHAMPION IS A GIRL...?

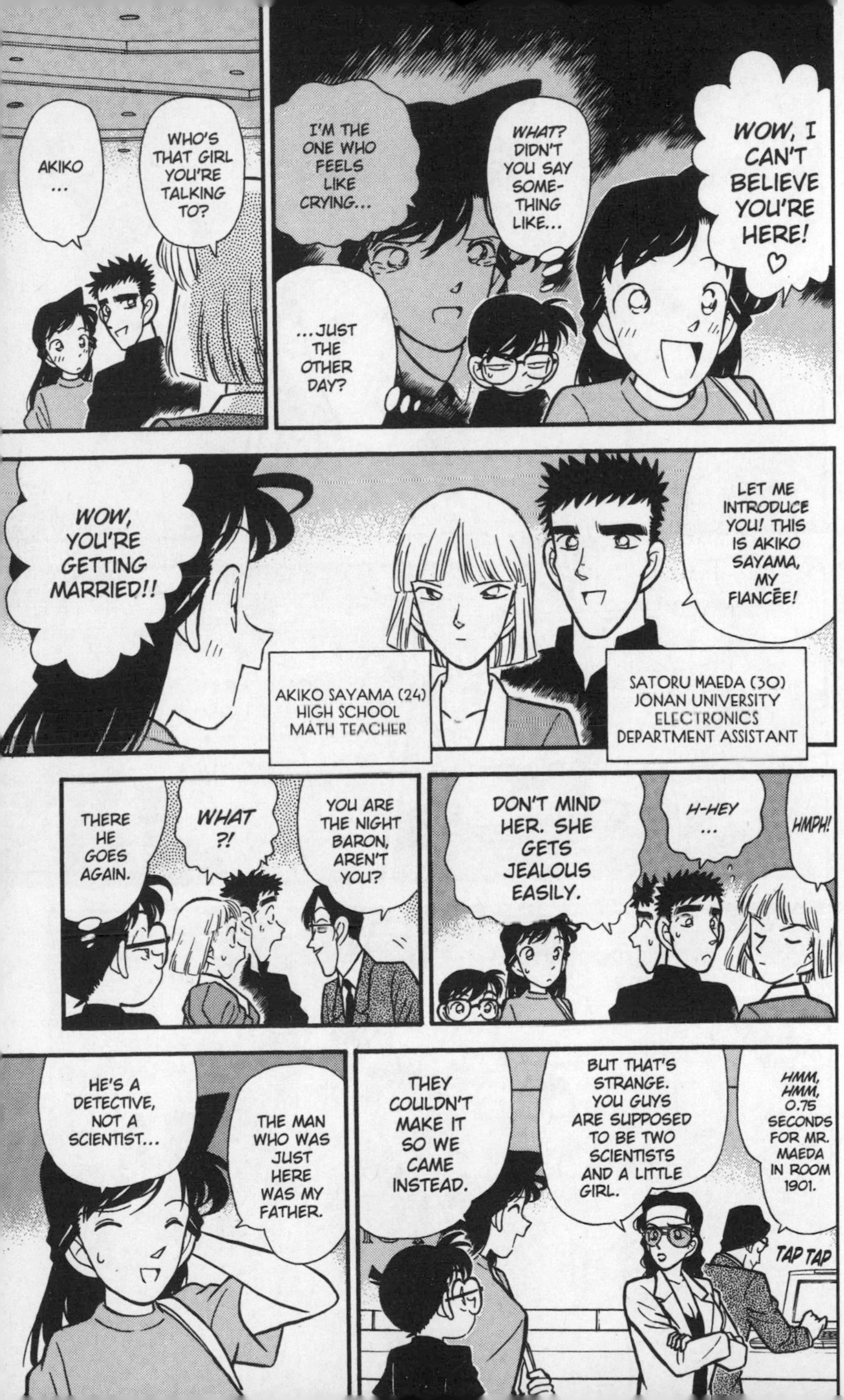
WOW, I CAN'T BELIEVE YOU'RE HERE! ♡
WHAT? DIDN'T YOU SAY SOMETHING LIKE...
I'M THE ONE WHO FEELS LIKE CRYING...
...JUST THE OTHER DAY?
WHO'S THAT GIRL YOU'RE TALKING TO?
AKIKO ...
LET ME INTRODUCE YOU! THIS IS AKIKO SAYAMA, MY FIANCÉE!
WOW, YOU'RE GETTING MARRIED!!
SATORU MAEDA (30) JONAN UNIVERSITY ELECTRONICS DEPARTMENT ASSISTANT
AKIKO SAYAMA (24) HIGH SCHOOL MATH TEACHER
HMPH!
H-HEY ...
DON'T MIND HER. SHE GETS JEALOUS EASILY.
YOU ARE THE NIGHT BARON, AREN'T YOU?
WHAT ?!
THERE HE GOES AGAIN.
HMM, HMM, 0.75 SECONDS FOR MR. MAEDA IN ROOM 1901.
TAP TAP
BUT THAT'S STRANGE. YOU GUYS ARE SUPPOSED TO BE TWO SCIENTISTS AND A LITTLE GIRL.
THEY COULDN'T MAKE IT SO WE CAME INSTEAD.
THE MAN WHO WAS JUST HERE WAS MY FATHER.
HE'S A DETECTIVE, NOT A SCIENTIST...

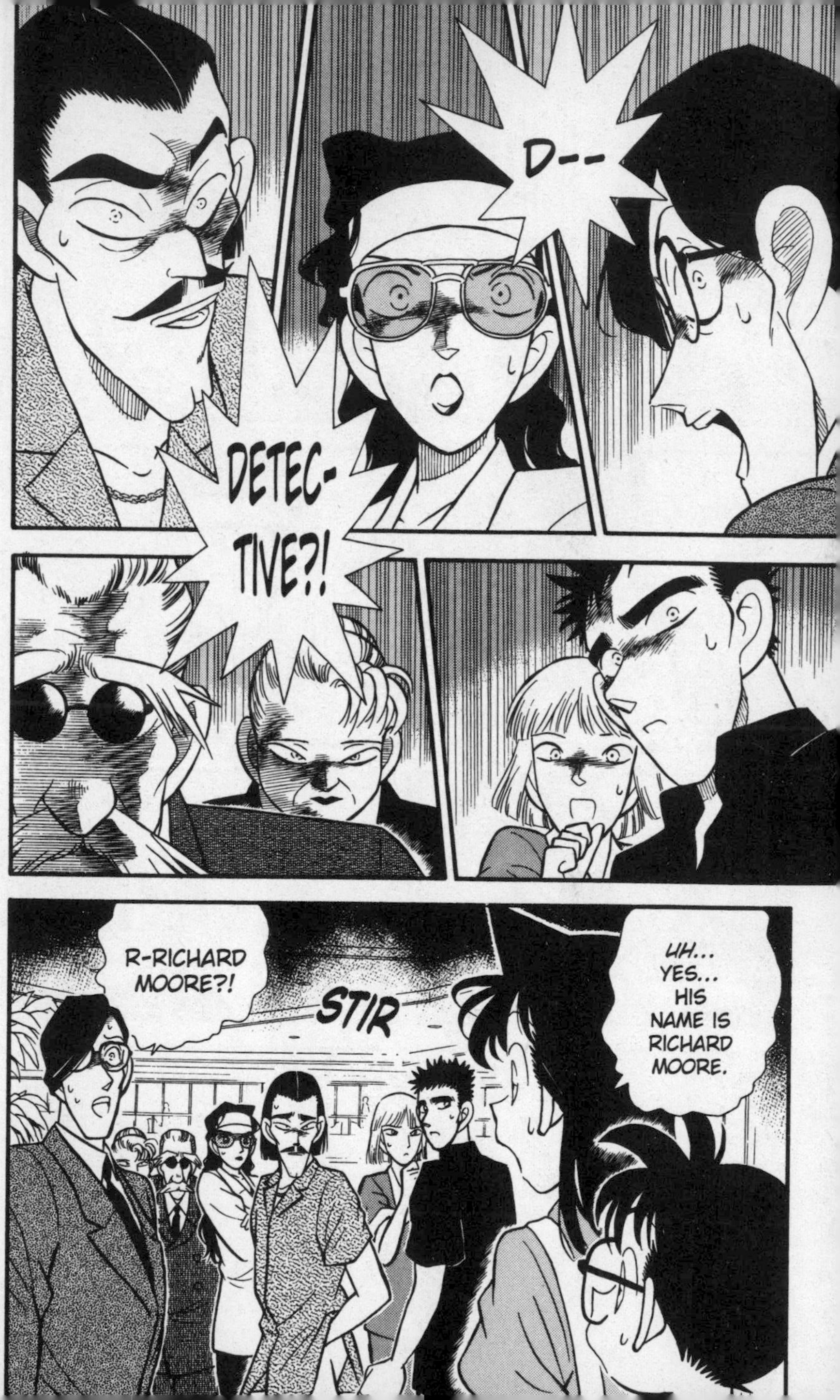
D--
DETEC-TIVE?!
UH... YES... HIS NAME IS RICHARD MOORE.
STIR
R-RICHARD MOORE?!

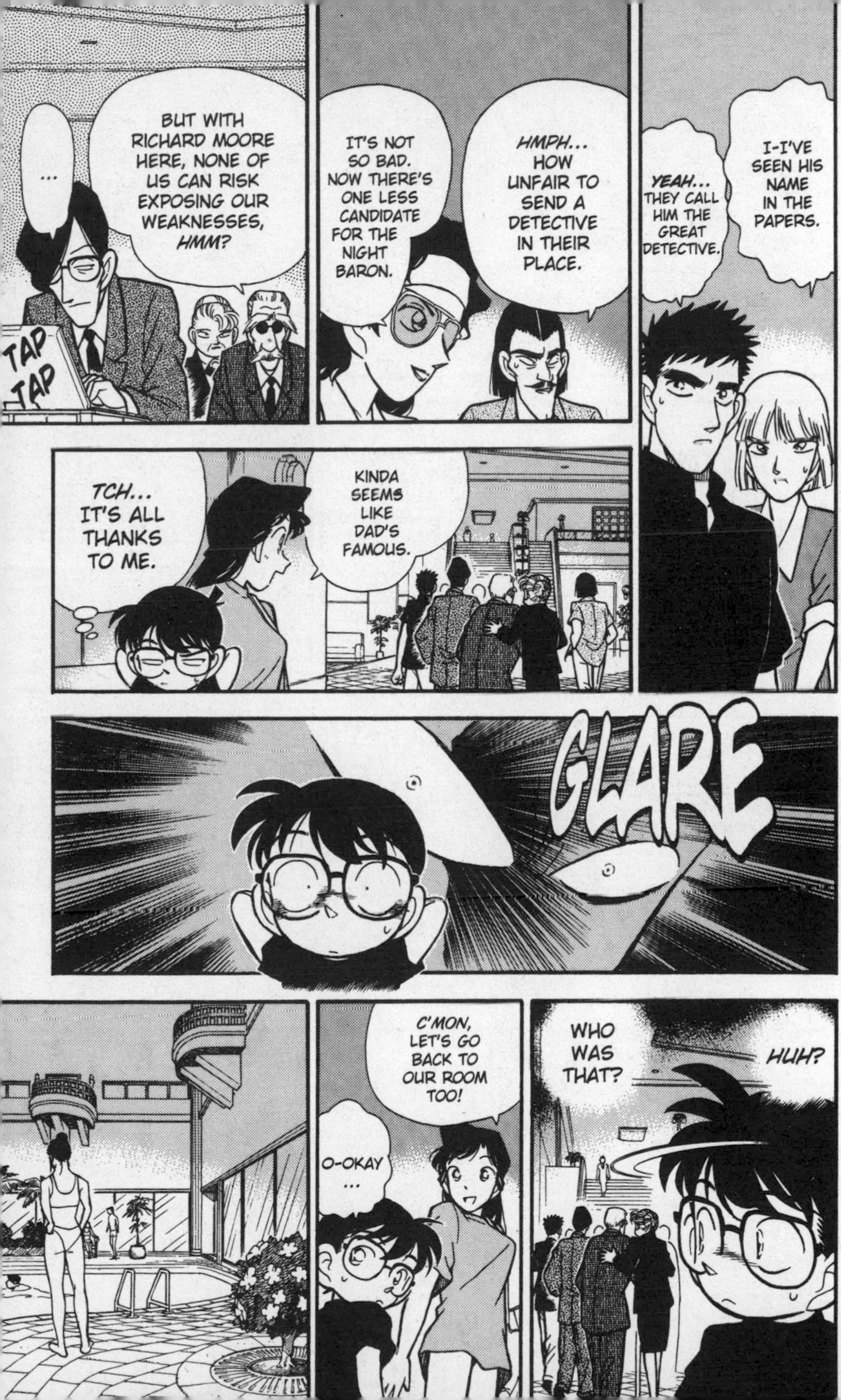
I-I'VE SEEN HIS NAME IN THE PAPERS.
YEAH... THEY CALL HIM THE GREAT DETECTIVE.
HMPH... HOW UNFAIR TO SEND A DETECTIVE IN THEIR PLACE.
IT'S NOT SO BAD. NOW THERE'S ONE LESS CANDIDATE FOR THE NIGHT BARON.
BUT WITH RICHARD MOORE HERE, NONE OF US CAN RISK EXPOSING OUR WEAKNESSES, HMM?
...
TAP TAP
KINDA SEEMS LIKE DAD'S FAMOUS.
TCH... IT'S ALL THANKS TO ME.
GLARE
HUH?
WHO WAS THAT?
C'MON, LET'S GO BACK TO OUR ROOM TOO!
O-OKAY ...

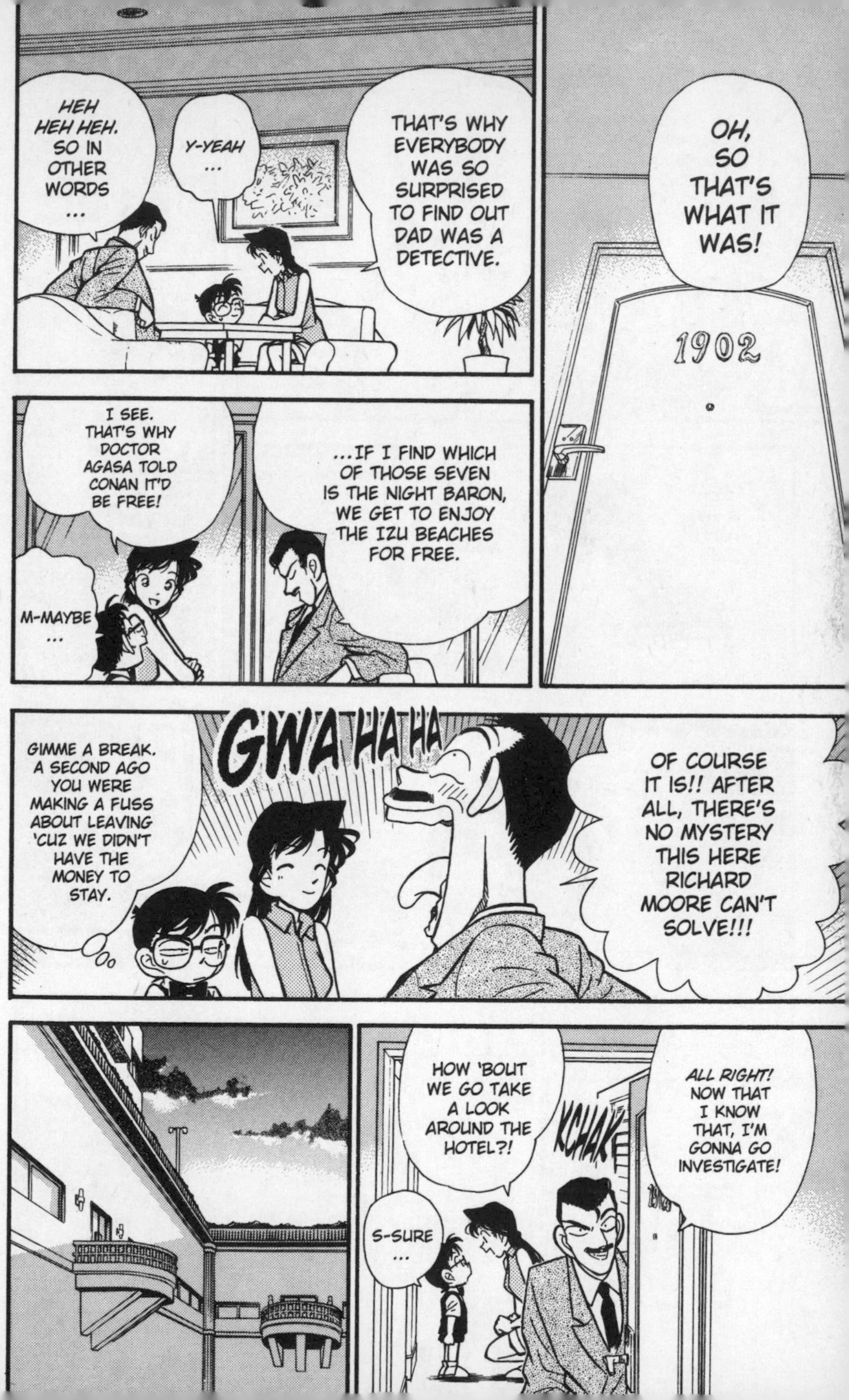
OH, SO THAT'S WHAT IT WAS!
1902
THAT'S WHY EVERYBODY WAS SO SURPRISED TO FIND OUT DAD WAS A DETECTIVE.
Y-YEAH ...
HEH HEH HEH. SO IN OTHER WORDS ...
...IF I FIND WHICH OF THOSE SEVEN IS THE NIGHT BARON, WE GET TO ENJOY THE IZU BEACHES FOR FREE.
I SEE. THAT'S WHY DOCTOR AGASA TOLD CONAN IT'D BE FREE!
M-MAYBE ...
OF COURSE IT IS!! AFTER ALL, THERE'S NO MYSTERY THIS HERE RICHARD MOORE CAN'T SOLVE!!!
GWA HA HA
GIMME A BREAK. A SECOND AGO YOU WERE MAKING A FUSS ABOUT LEAVING 'CUZ WE DIDN'T HAVE THE MONEY TO STAY.
ALL RIGHT! NOW THAT I KNOW THAT, I'M GONNA GO INVESTIGATE!
KCHAK
HOW 'BOUT WE GO TAKE A LOOK AROUND THE HOTEL?!
S-SURE ...

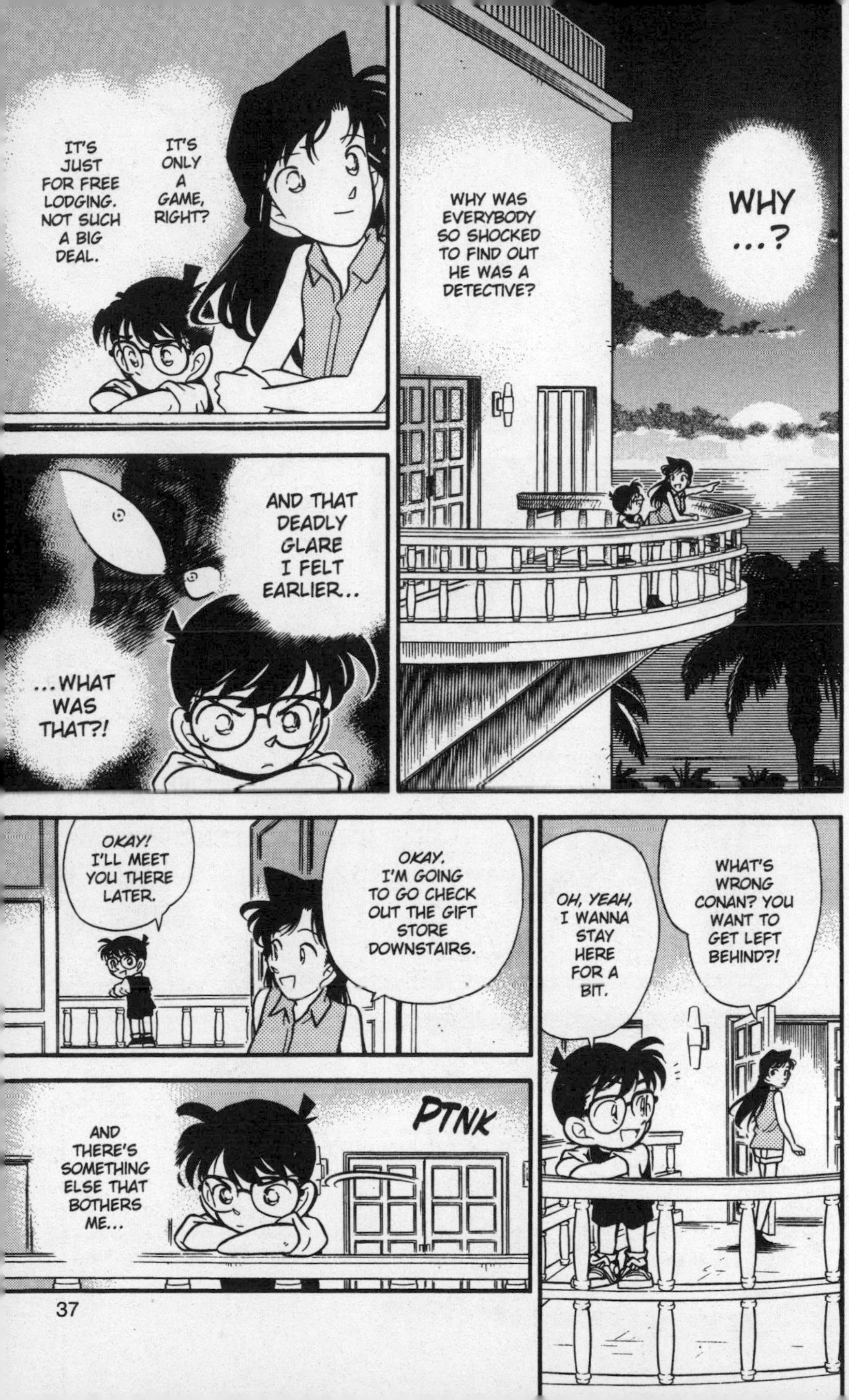
WHY ...?
WHY WAS EVERYBODY SO SHOCKED TO FIND OUT HE WAS A DETECTIVE?
IT'S ONLY A GAME, RIGHT?
IT'S JUST FOR FREE LODGING. NOT SUCH A BIG DEAL.
AND THAT DEADLY GLARE I FELT EARLIER...
...WHAT WAS THAT?!
WHAT'S WRONG CONAN? YOU WANT TO GET LEFT BEHIND?!
OH, YEAH, I WANNA STAY HERE FOR A BIT.
OKAY. I'M GOING TO GO CHECK OUT THE GIFT STORE DOWNSTAIRS.
OKAY! I'LL MEET YOU THERE LATER.
PTNK
AND THERE'S SOMETHING ELSE THAT BOTHERS ME...

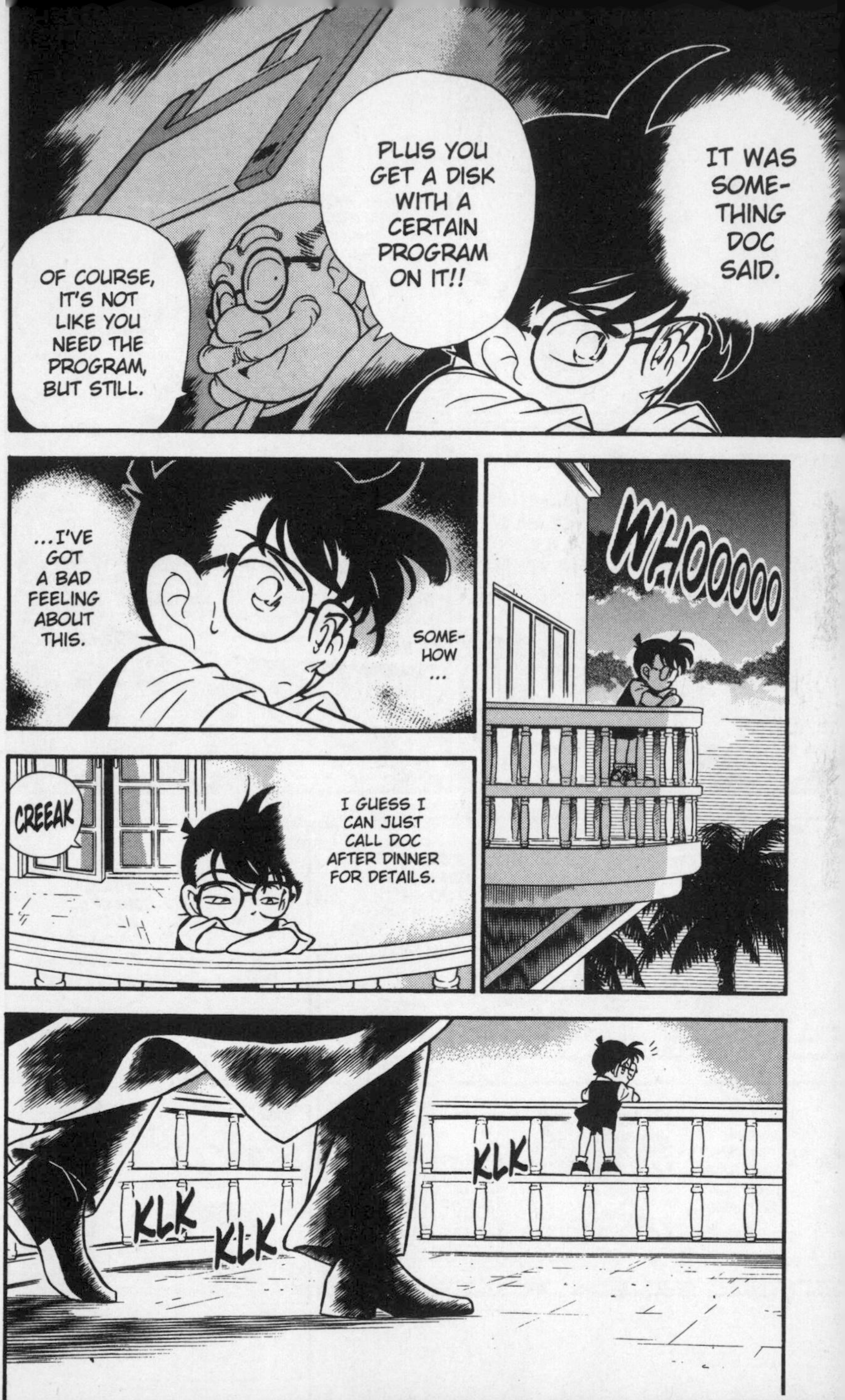
IT WAS SOME-THING DOC SAID.
PLUS YOU GET A DISK WITH A CERTAIN PROGRAM ON IT!!
OF COURSE, IT'S NOT LIKE YOU NEED THE PROGRAM, BUT STILL.
WHOOOOO
SOME-HOW ...
...I'VE GOT A BAD FEELING ABOUT THIS.
I GUESS I CAN JUST CALL DOC AFTER DINNER FOR DETAILS.
CREEAK
KLK
KLK
KLK

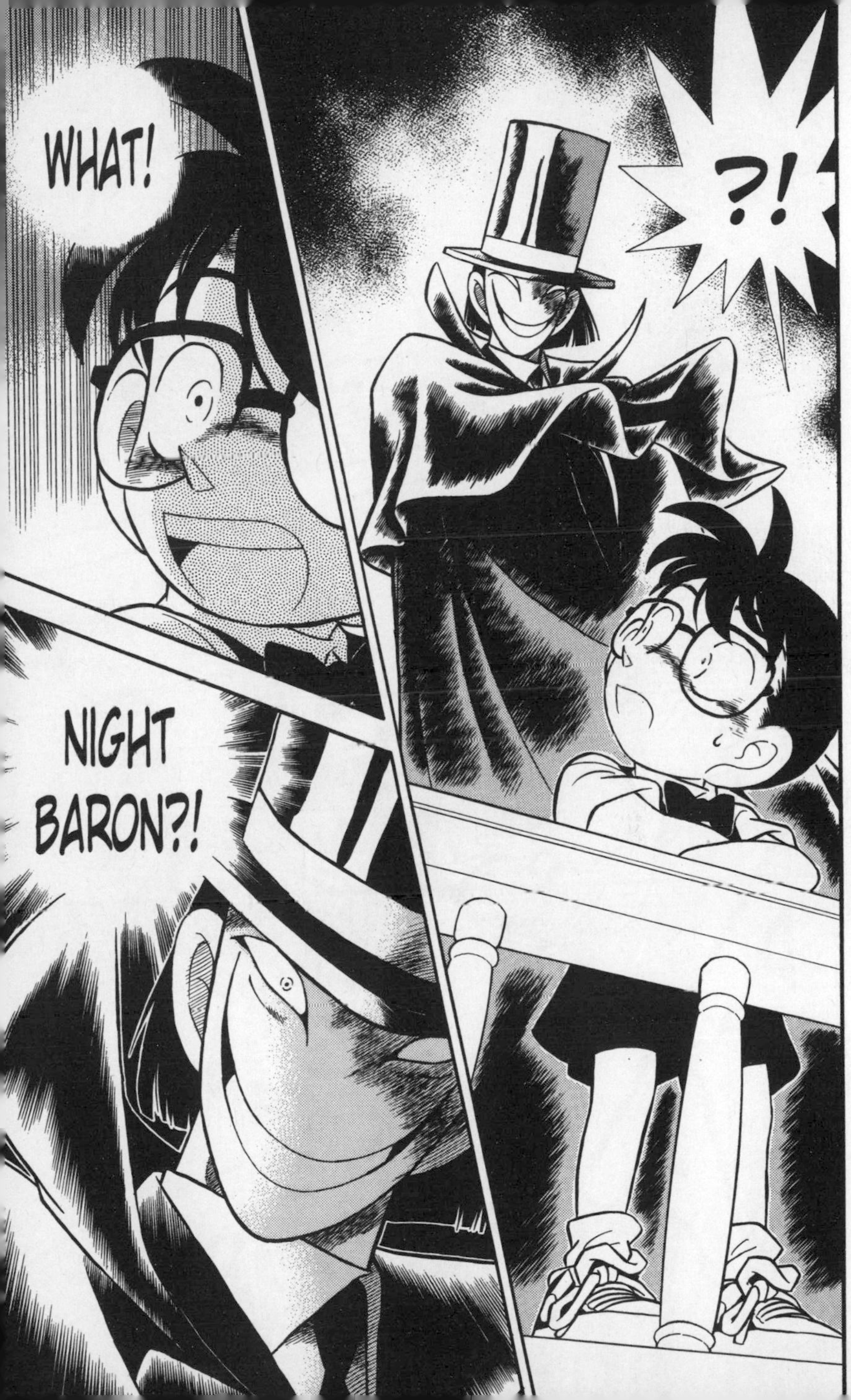
?!
WHAT!
NIGHT BARON?!

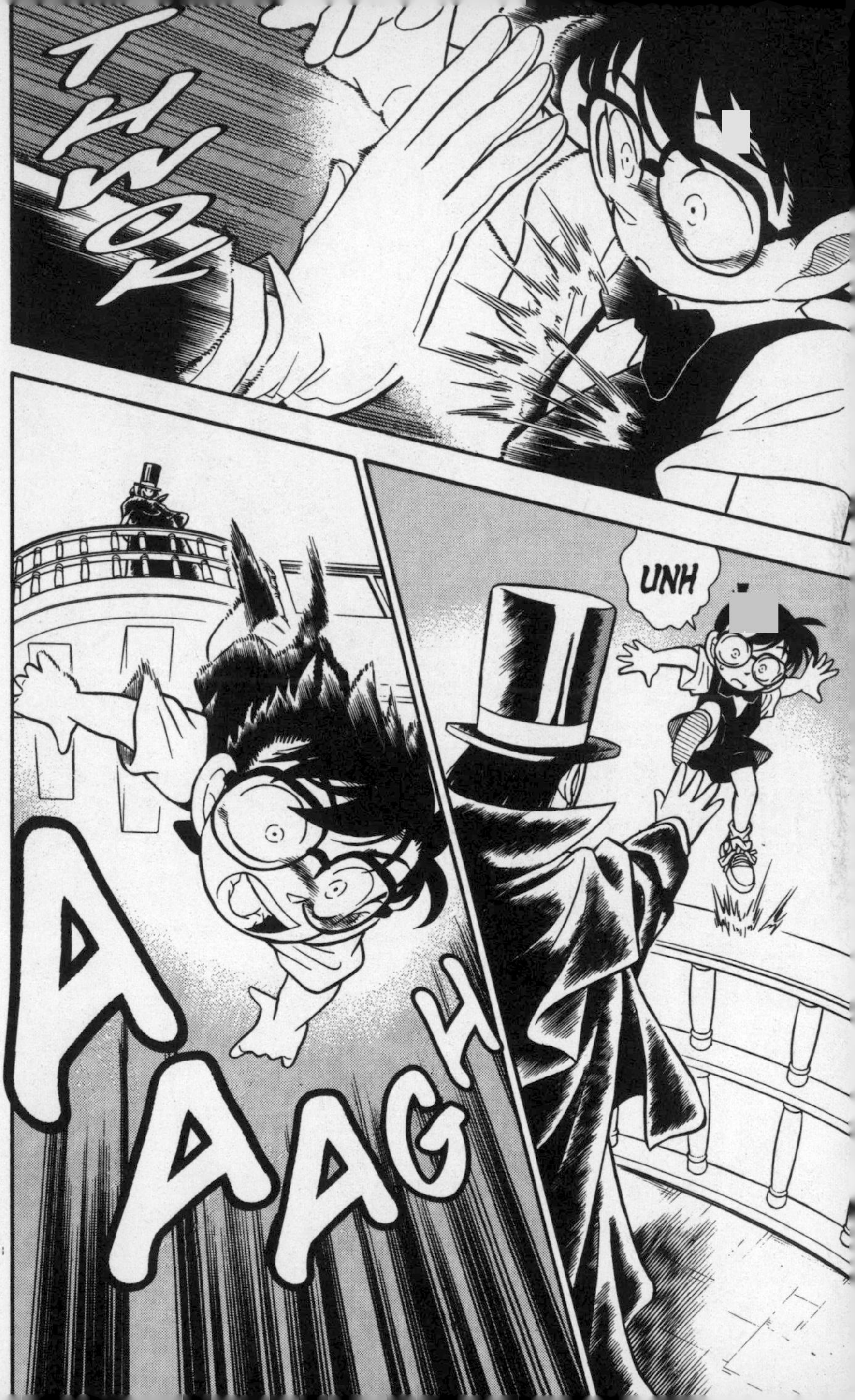
THWOK
UNH
AAAGH

FILE 3: THE VIRUS OF TERROR

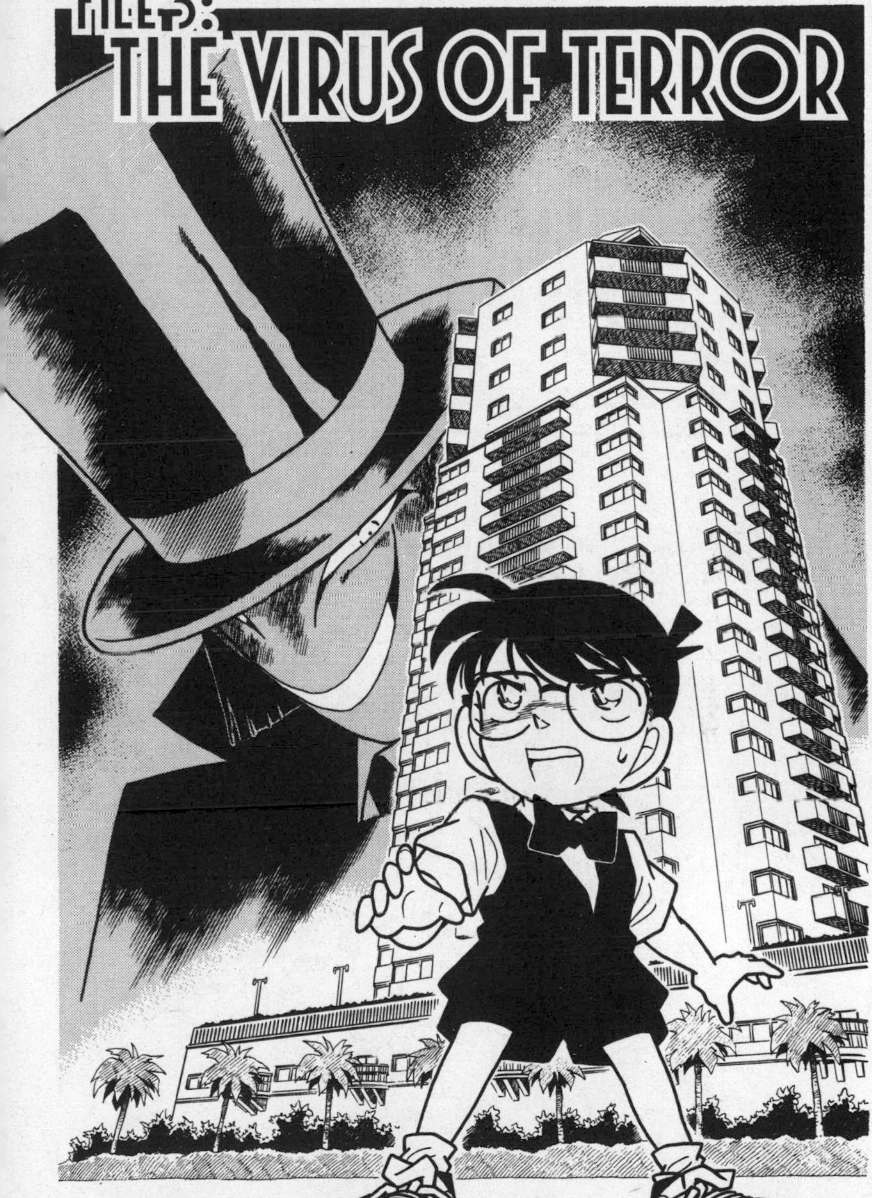

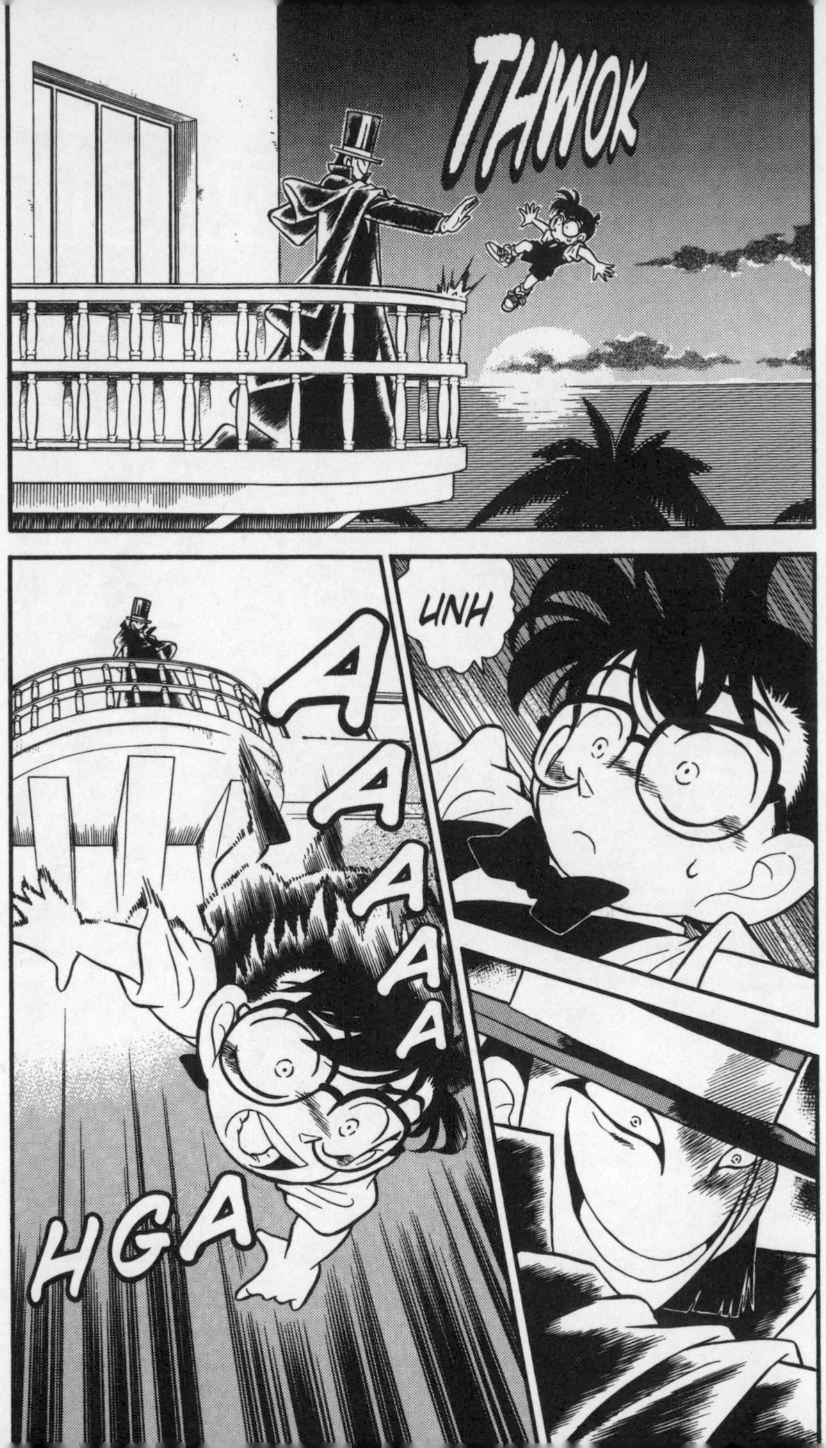
THWOK
UNH
AAAAAA
HGA

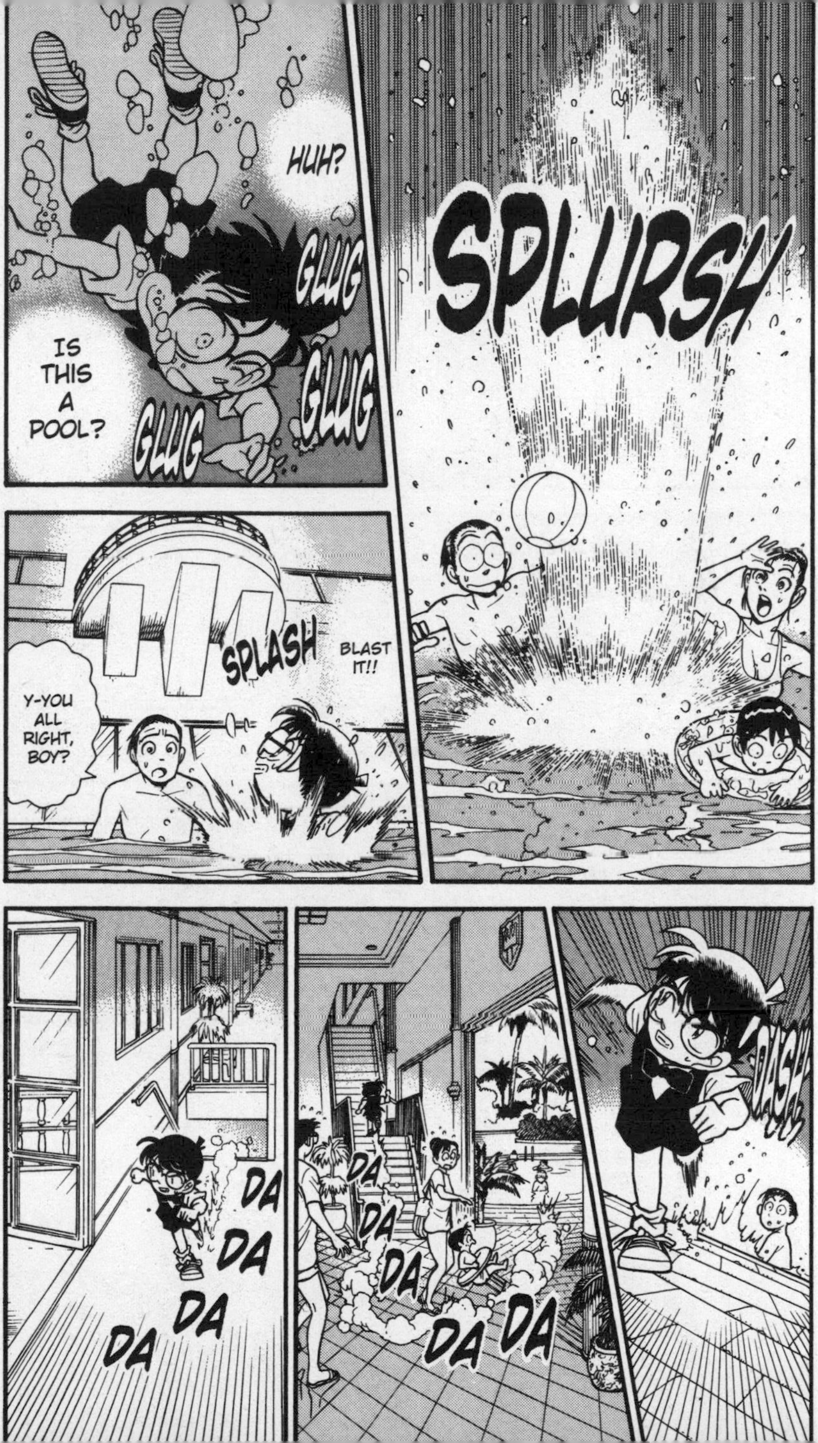
SPLURSH
HUH?
IS THIS A POOL?
GLUG
GLUG
GLUG
BLAST IT!!
SPLASH
Y-YOU ALL RIGHT, BOY?
DASH
DA
DA
DA
DA
DA
DA
DA
DA
DA
DA

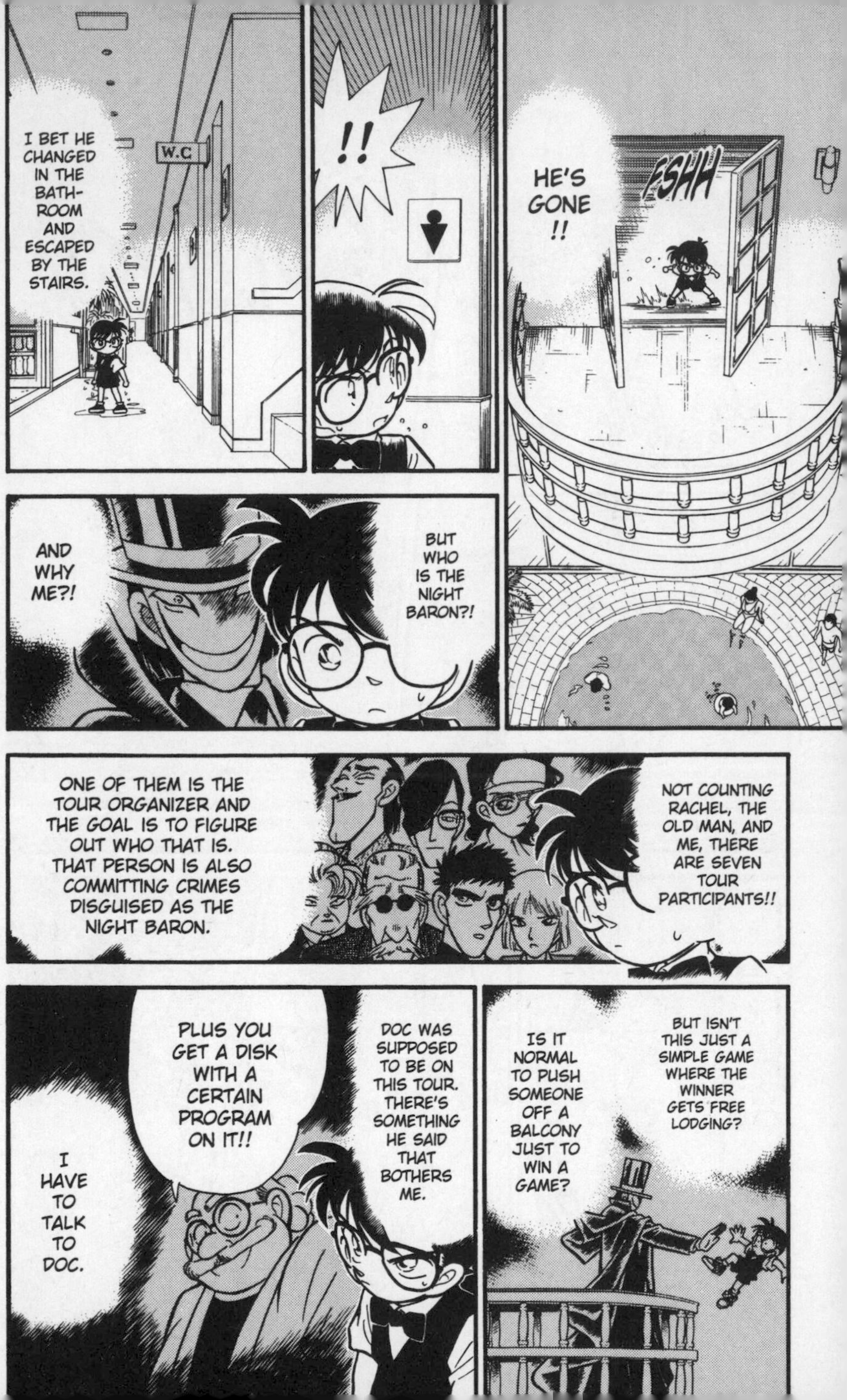
HE'S GONE !!
FSHH
!!
I BET HE CHANGED IN THE BATH-ROOM AND ESCAPED BY THE STAIRS.
W.C
BUT WHO IS THE NIGHT BARON?!
AND WHY ME?!
NOT COUNTING RACHEL, THE OLD MAN, AND ME, THERE ARE SEVEN TOUR PARTICIPANTS!!
ONE OF THEM IS THE TOUR ORGANIZER AND THE GOAL IS TO FIGURE OUT WHO THAT IS. THAT PERSON IS ALSO COMMITTING CRIMES DISGUISED AS THE NIGHT BARON.
BUT ISN'T THIS JUST A SIMPLE GAME WHERE THE WINNER GETS FREE LODGING?
IS IT NORMAL TO PUSH SOMEONE OFF A BALCONY JUST TO WIN A GAME?
DOC WAS SUPPOSED TO BE ON THIS TOUR. THERE'S SOMETHING HE SAID THAT BOTHERS ME.
PLUS YOU GET A DISK WITH A CERTAIN PROGRAM ON IT!!
I HAVE TO TALK TO DOC.

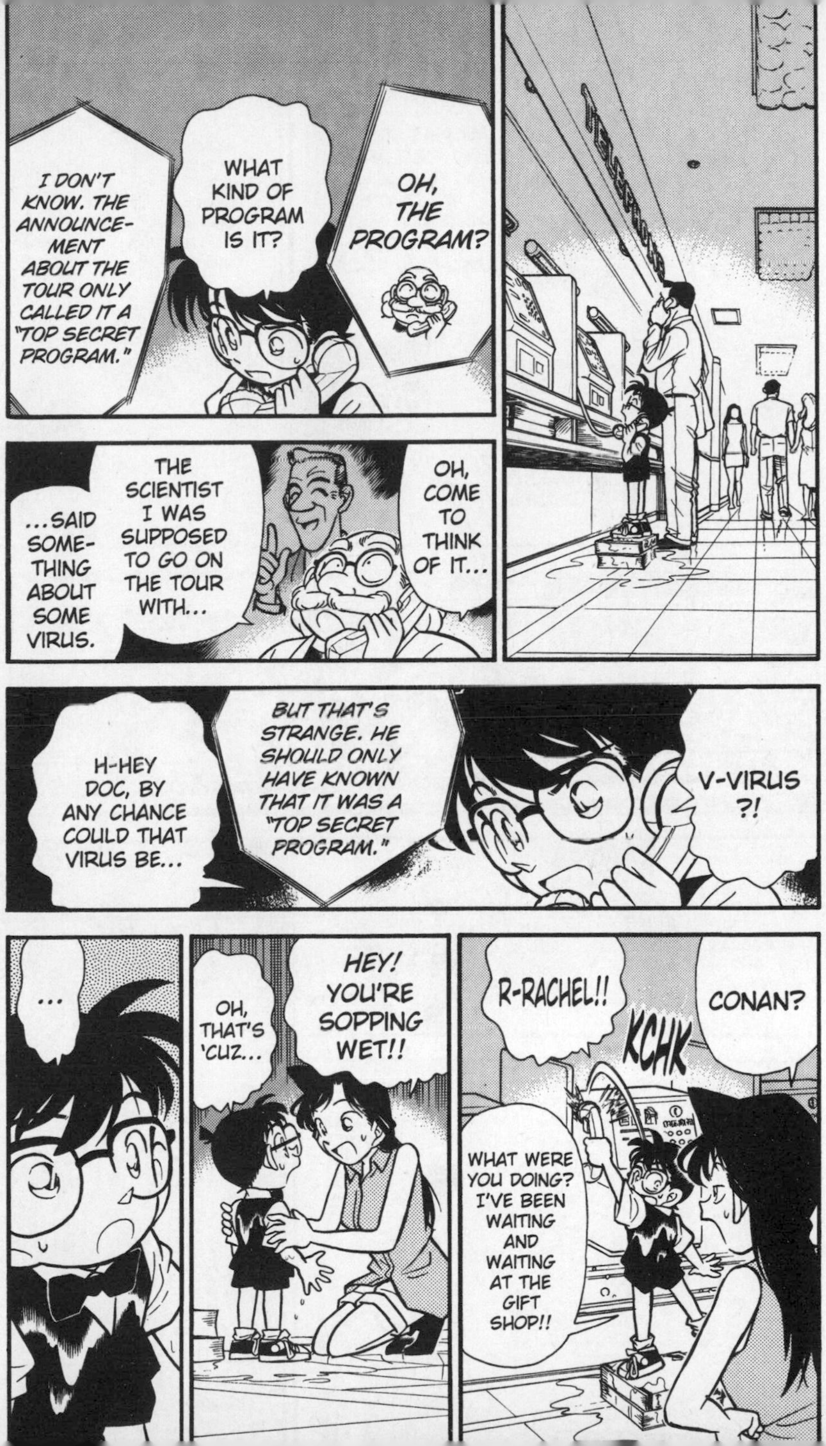
OH, THE PROGRAM?
WHAT KIND OF PROGRAM IS IT?
I DON'T KNOW. THE ANNOUNCEMENT ABOUT THE TOUR ONLY CALLED IT A "TOP SECRET PROGRAM."
OH, COME TO THINK OF IT...
THE SCIENTIST I WAS SUPPOSED TO GO ON THE TOUR WITH...
...SAID SOMETHING ABOUT SOME VIRUS.
V-VIRUS ?!
BUT THAT'S STRANGE. HE SHOULD ONLY HAVE KNOWN THAT IT WAS A "TOP SECRET PROGRAM."
H-HEY DOC, BY ANY CHANCE COULD THAT VIRUS BE...
CONAN?
R-RACHEL!!
KCHK
WHAT WERE YOU DOING? I'VE BEEN WAITING AND WAITING AT THE GIFT SHOP!!
HEY! YOU'RE SOPPING WET!!
OH, THAT'S 'CUZ...
...

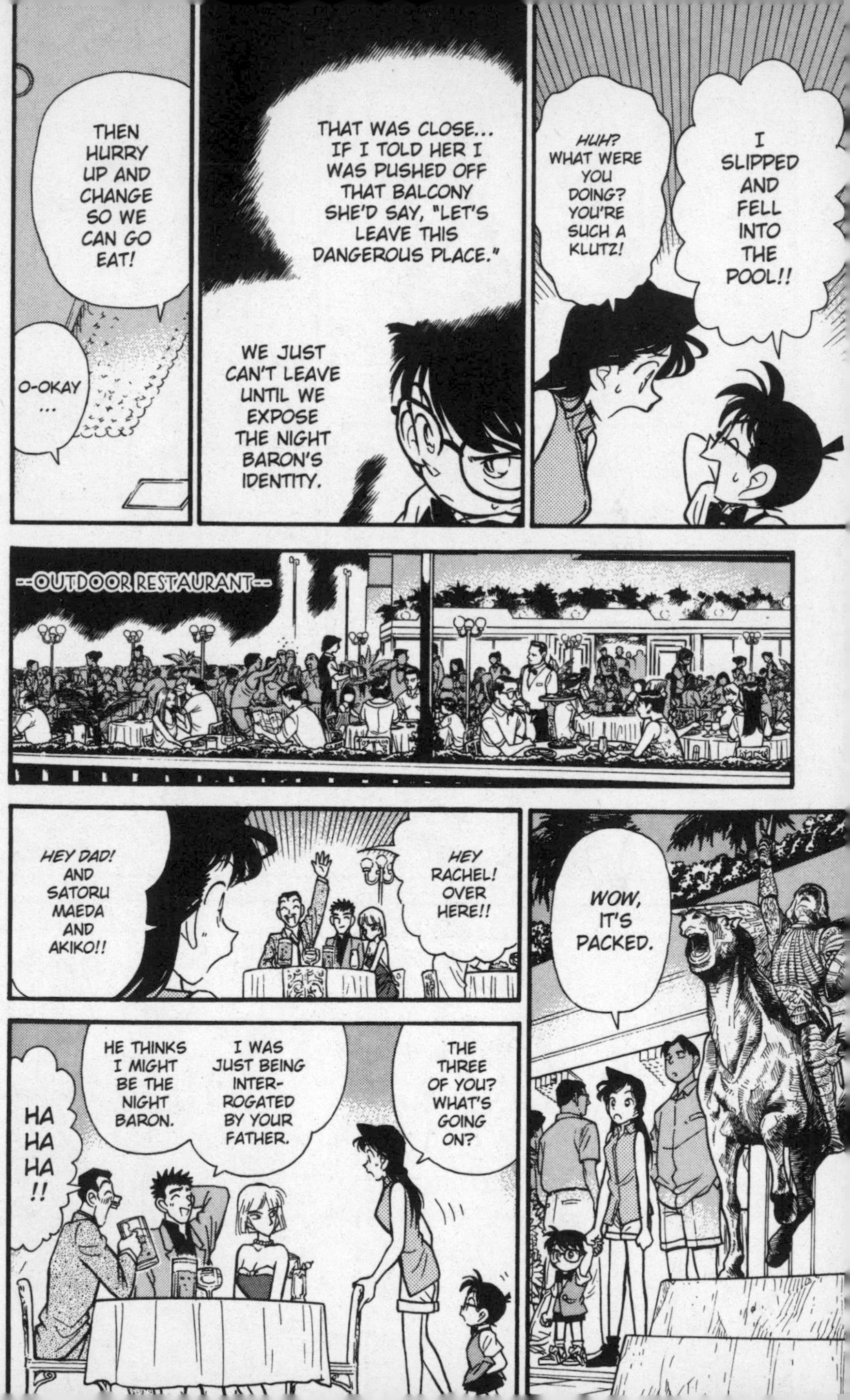
I SLIPPED AND FELL INTO THE POOL!!
HUH? WHAT WERE YOU DOING? YOU'RE SUCH A KLUTZ!
THAT WAS CLOSE... IF I TOLD HER I WAS PUSHED OFF THAT BALCONY SHE'D SAY, "LET'S LEAVE THIS DANGEROUS PLACE."
WE JUST CAN'T LEAVE UNTIL WE EXPOSE THE NIGHT BARON'S IDENTITY.
THEN HURRY UP AND CHANGE SO WE CAN GO EAT!
O-OKAY ...
--OUTDOOR RESTAURANT--
WOW, IT'S PACKED.
HEY RACHEL! OVER HERE!!
HEY DAD! AND SATORU MAEDA AND AKIKO!!
THE THREE OF YOU? WHAT'S GOING ON?
I WAS JUST BEING INTER-ROGATED BY YOUR FATHER.
HE THINKS I MIGHT BE THE NIGHT BARON.
HA HA HA!!

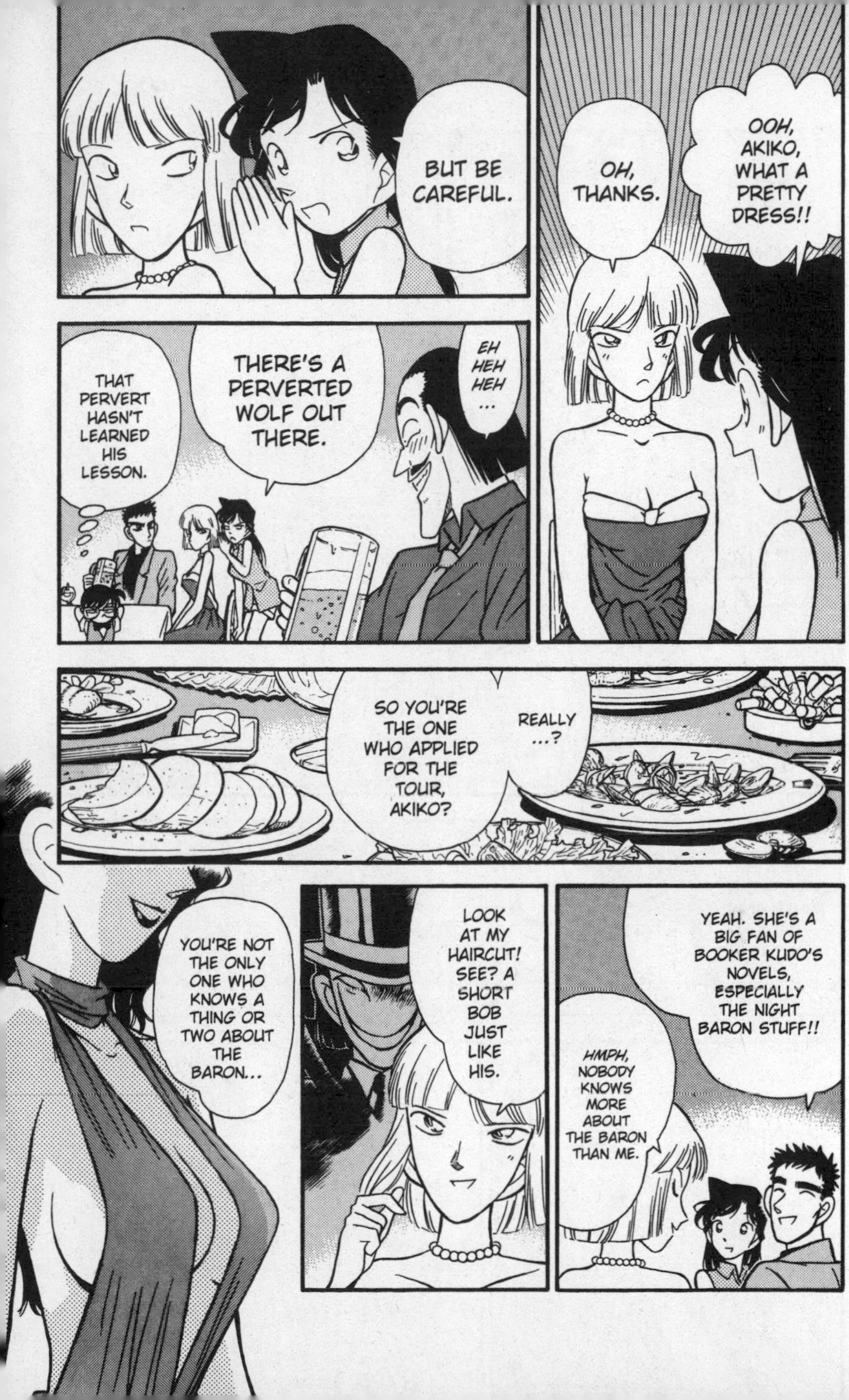
OOH, AKIKO, WHAT A PRETTY DRESS!!
OH, THANKS.
BUT BE CAREFUL.
EH HEH HEH ...
THERE'S A PERVERTED WOLF OUT THERE.
THAT PERVERT HASN'T LEARNED HIS LESSON.
REALLY ...?
SO YOU'RE THE ONE WHO APPLIED FOR THE TOUR, AKIKO?
YEAH. SHE'S A BIG FAN OF BOOKER KUDO'S NOVELS, ESPECIALLY THE NIGHT BARON STUFF!!
HMPH, NOBODY KNOWS MORE ABOUT THE BARON THAN ME.
LOOK AT MY HAIRCUT! SEE? A SHORT BOB JUST LIKE HIS.
YOU'RE NOT THE ONLY ONE WHO KNOWS A THING OR TWO ABOUT THE BARON...

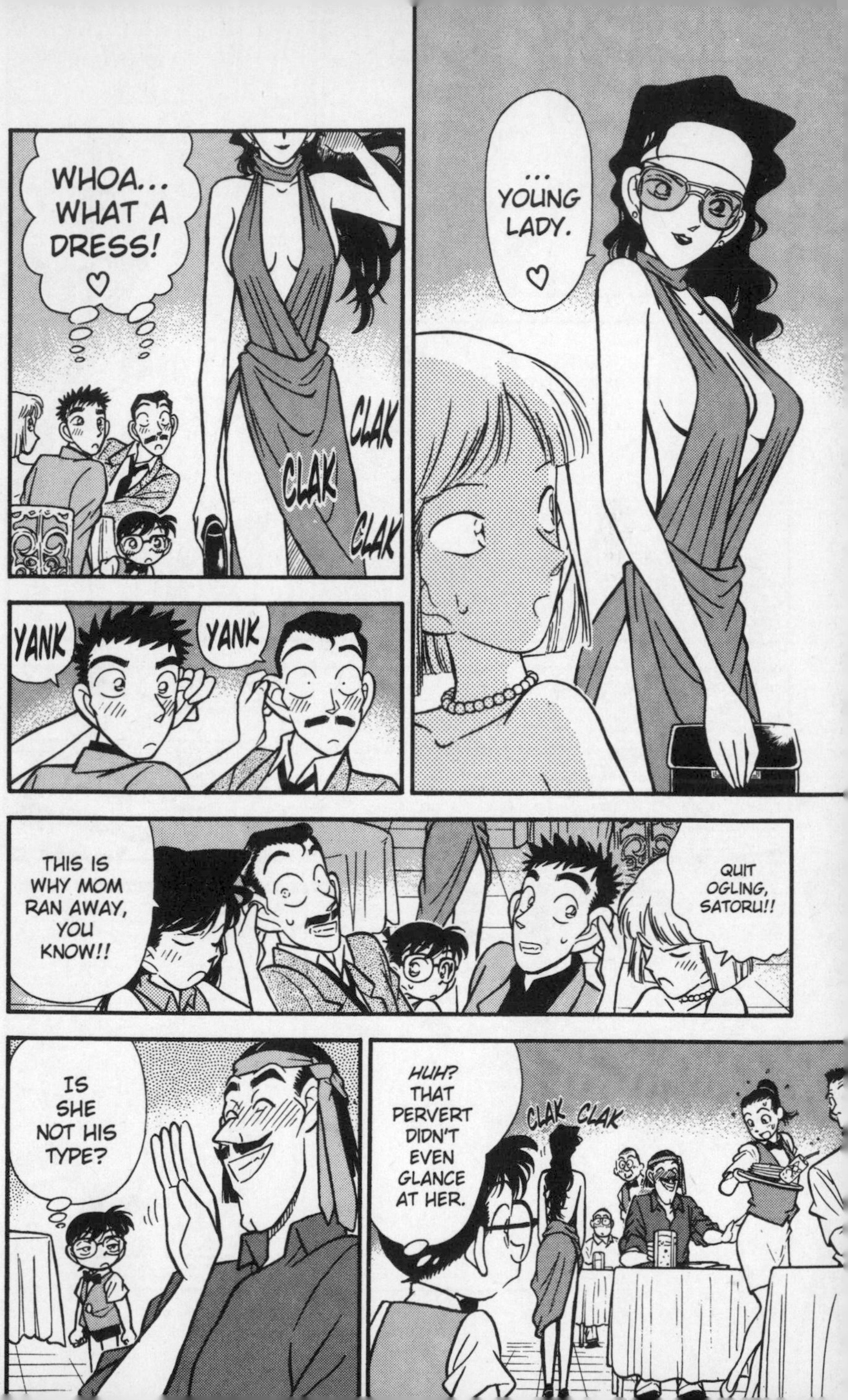
... YOUNG LADY. ♡
WHOA... WHAT A DRESS! ♡
CLAK
CLAK
CLAK
YANK
YANK
QUIT OGLING, SATORU!!
THIS IS WHY MOM RAN AWAY, YOU KNOW!!
CLAK CLAK
HUH? THAT PERVERT DIDN'T EVEN GLANCE AT HER.
IS SHE NOT HIS TYPE?

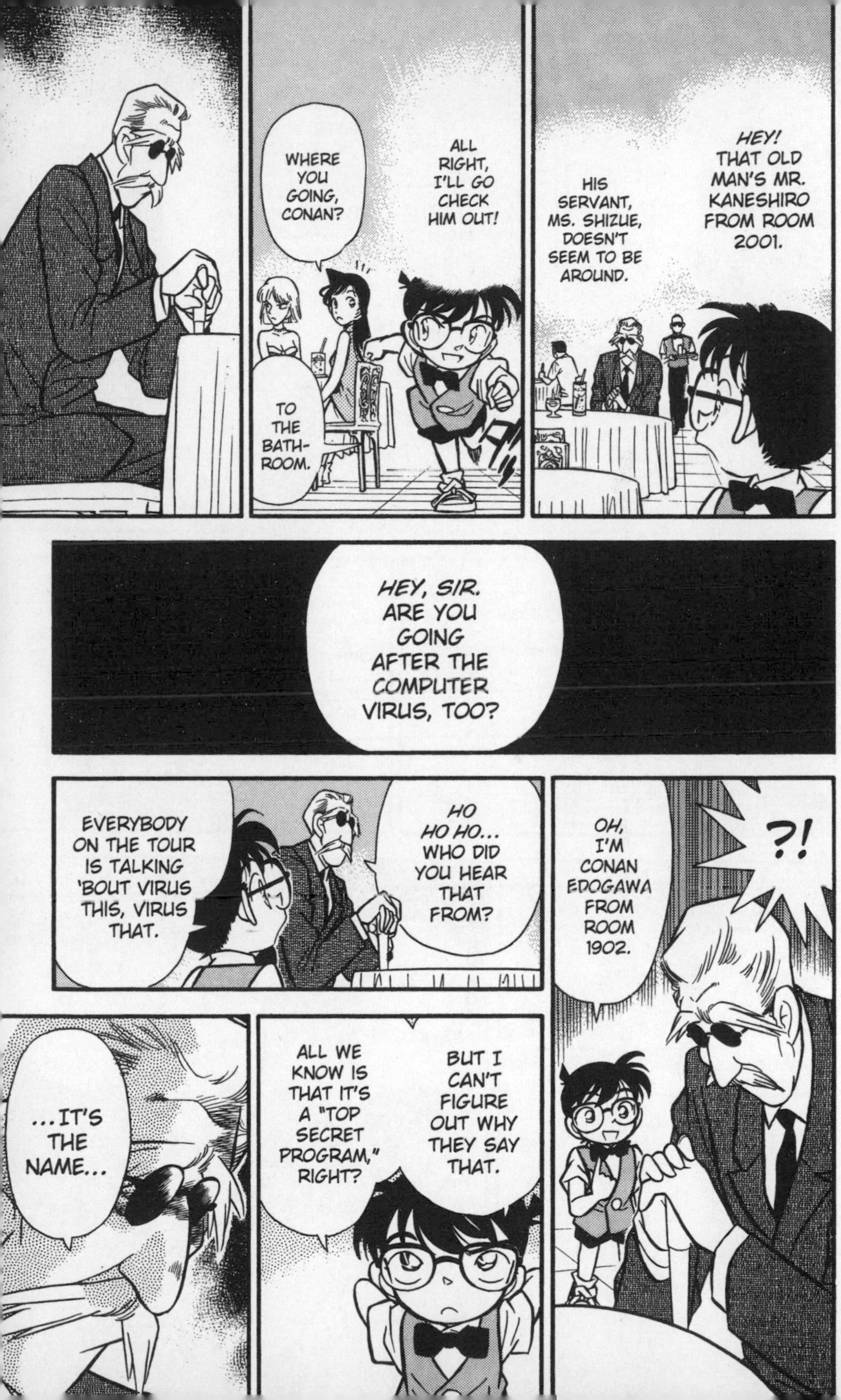
HEY! THAT OLD MAN'S MR. KANESHIRO FROM ROOM 2001.
HIS SERVANT, MS. SHIZUE, DOESN'T SEEM TO BE AROUND.
ALL RIGHT, I'LL GO CHECK HIM OUT!
WHERE YOU GOING, CONAN?
TO THE BATH-ROOM.
HEY, SIR. ARE YOU GOING AFTER THE COMPUTER VIRUS, TOO?
?!
OH, I'M CONAN EDOGAWA FROM ROOM 1902.
HO HO HO... WHO DID YOU HEAR THAT FROM?
EVERYBODY ON THE TOUR IS TALKING 'BOUT VIRUS THIS, VIRUS THAT.
BUT I CAN'T FIGURE OUT WHY THEY SAY THAT.
ALL WE KNOW IS THAT IT'S A "TOP SECRET PROGRAM," RIGHT?
...IT'S THE NAME...

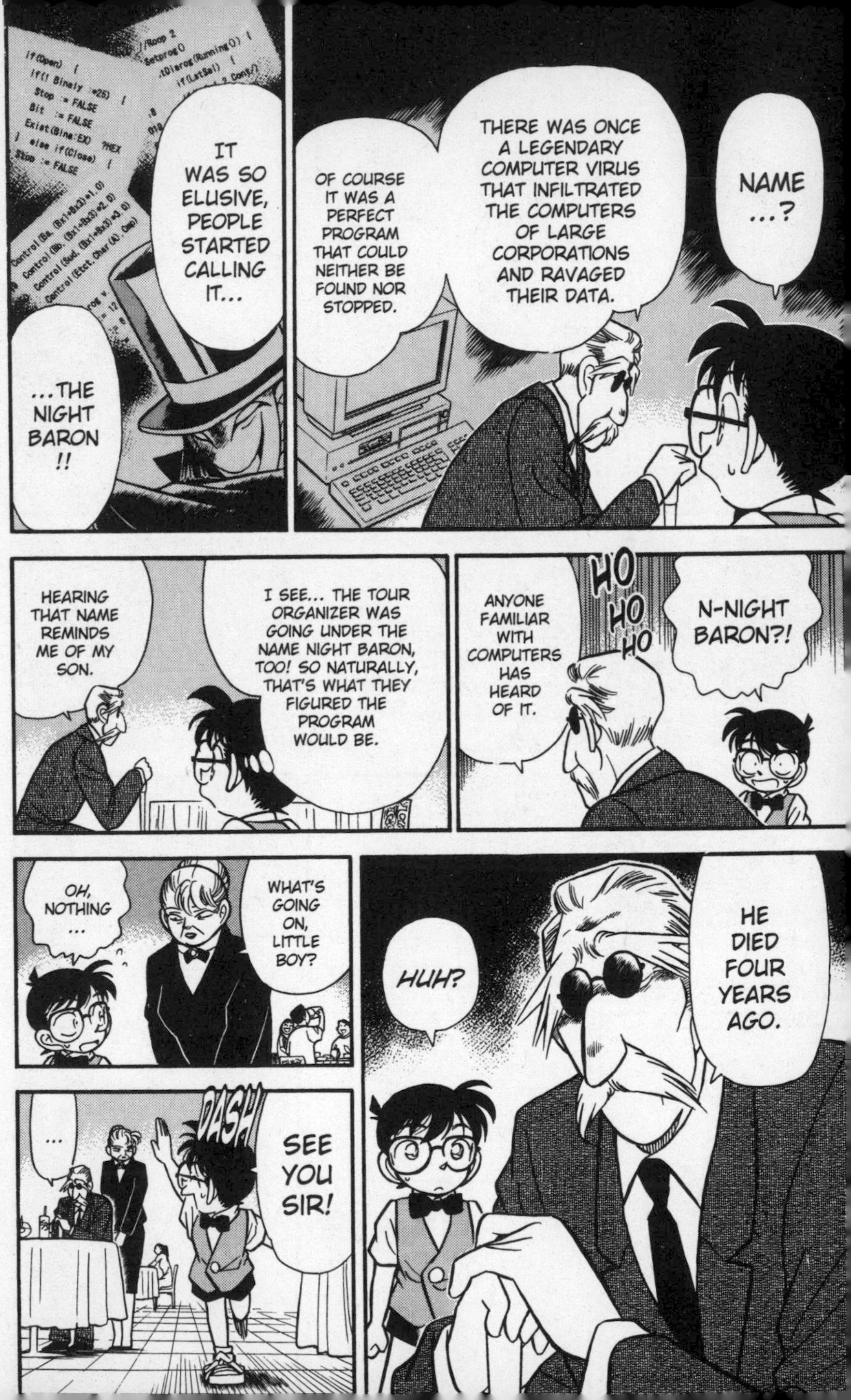
NAME ...?
THERE WAS ONCE A LEGENDARY COMPUTER VIRUS THAT INFILTRATED THE COMPUTERS OF LARGE CORPORATIONS AND RAVAGED THEIR DATA.
OF COURSE IT WAS A PERFECT PROGRAM THAT COULD NEITHER BE FOUND NOR STOPPED.
IT WAS SO ELUSIVE, PEOPLE STARTED CALLING IT...
...THE NIGHT BARON !!
N-NIGHT BARON?!
HO HO HO
ANYONE FAMILIAR WITH COMPUTERS HAS HEARD OF IT.
I SEE... THE TOUR ORGANIZER WAS GOING UNDER THE NAME NIGHT BARON, TOO! SO NATURALLY, THAT'S WHAT THEY FIGURED THE PROGRAM WOULD BE.
HEARING THAT NAME REMINDS ME OF MY SON.
HE DIED FOUR YEARS AGO.
HUH?
WHAT'S GOING ON, LITTLE BOY?
OH, NOTHING ...
SEE YOU SIR!
DASH
...

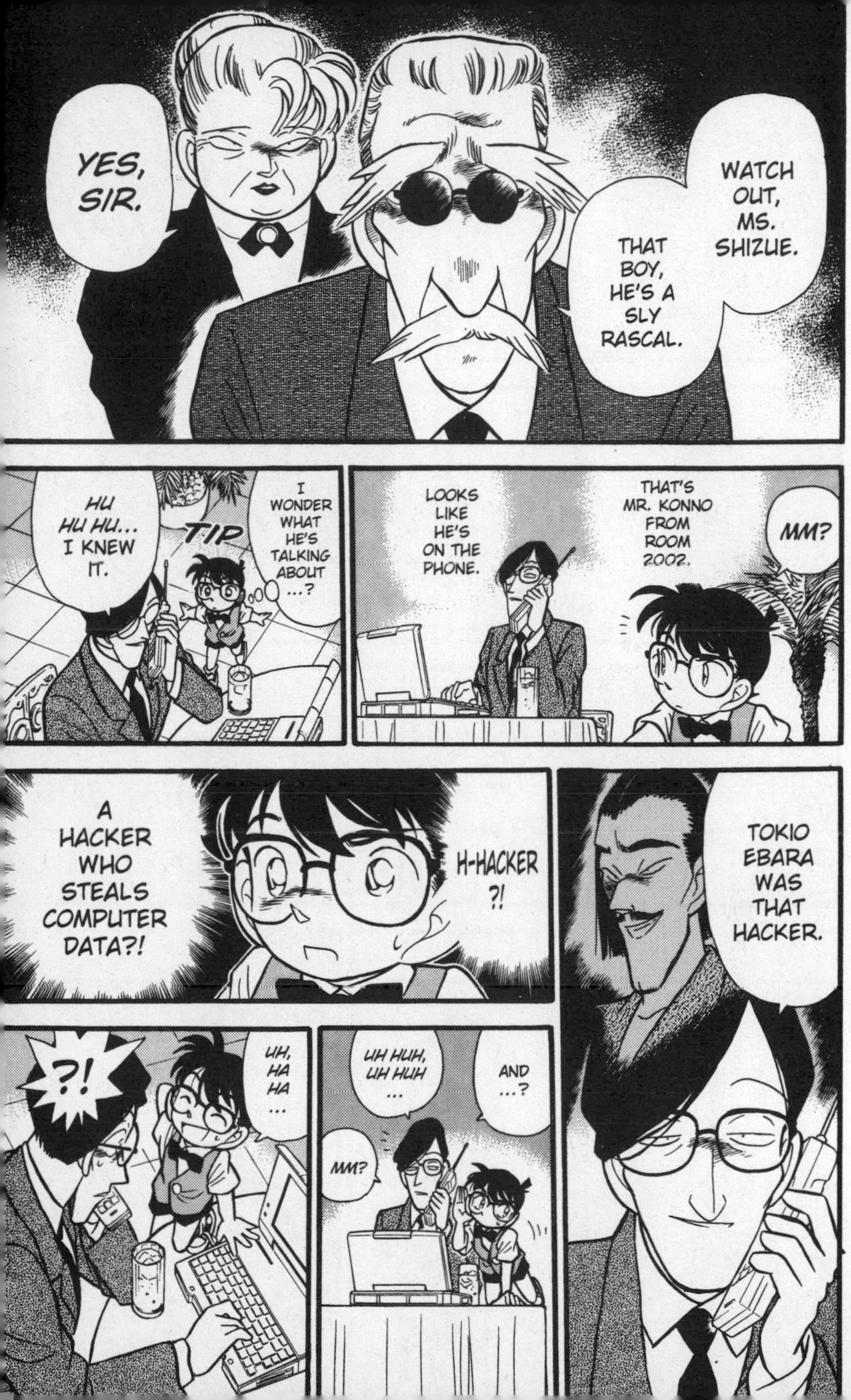
WATCH OUT, MS. SHIZUE.
THAT BOY, HE'S A SLY RASCAL.
YES, SIR.
MM?
THAT'S MR. KONNO FROM ROOM 2002.
LOOKS LIKE HE'S ON THE PHONE.
I WONDER WHAT HE'S TALKING ABOUT ...?
TIP
HU HU HU... I KNEW IT.
H-HACKER ?!
A HACKER WHO STEALS COMPUTER DATA?!
TOKIO EBARA WAS THAT HACKER.
AND ...?
UH HUH, UH HUH ...
MM?
UH, HA HA ...
?!

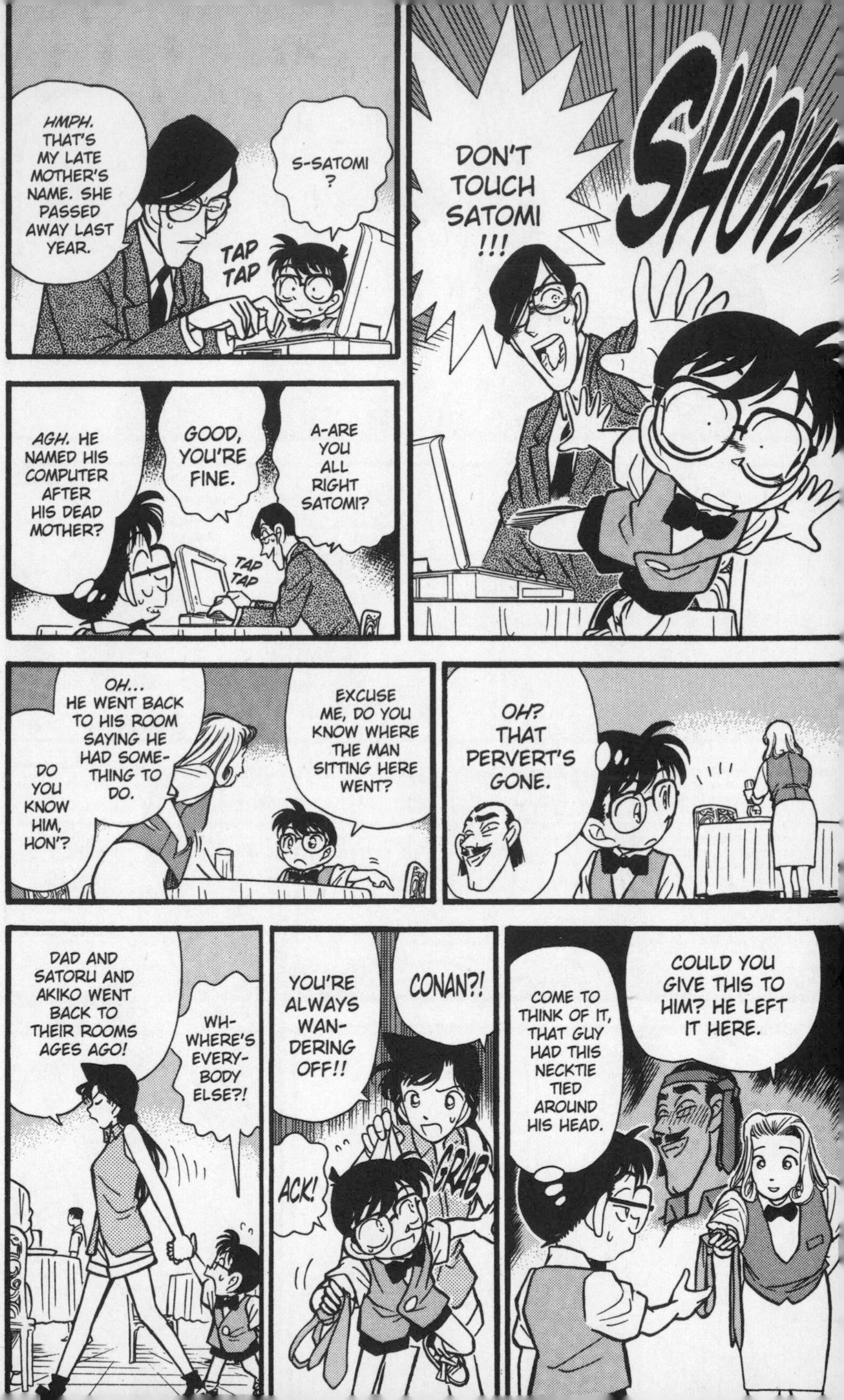
SHOVE
DON'T TOUCH SATOMI !!!
S-SATOMI ?
HMPH. THAT'S MY LATE MOTHER'S NAME. SHE PASSED AWAY LAST YEAR.
TAP TAP
A-ARE YOU ALL RIGHT SATOMI?
GOOD, YOU'RE FINE.
AGH. HE NAMED HIS COMPUTER AFTER HIS DEAD MOTHER?
TAP TAP
OH? THAT PERVERT'S GONE.
EXCUSE ME, DO YOU KNOW WHERE THE MAN SITTING HERE WENT?
OH... HE WENT BACK TO HIS ROOM SAYING HE HAD SOME-THING TO DO.
DO YOU KNOW HIM, HON'?
COULD YOU GIVE THIS TO HIM? HE LEFT IT HERE.
COME TO THINK OF IT, THAT GUY HAD THIS NECKTIE TIED AROUND HIS HEAD.
CONAN?!
YOU'RE ALWAYS WAN-DERING OFF!!
GRAB
ACK!
WH-WHERE'S EVERY-BODY ELSE?!
DAD AND SATORU AND AKIKO WENT BACK TO THEIR ROOMS AGES AGO!

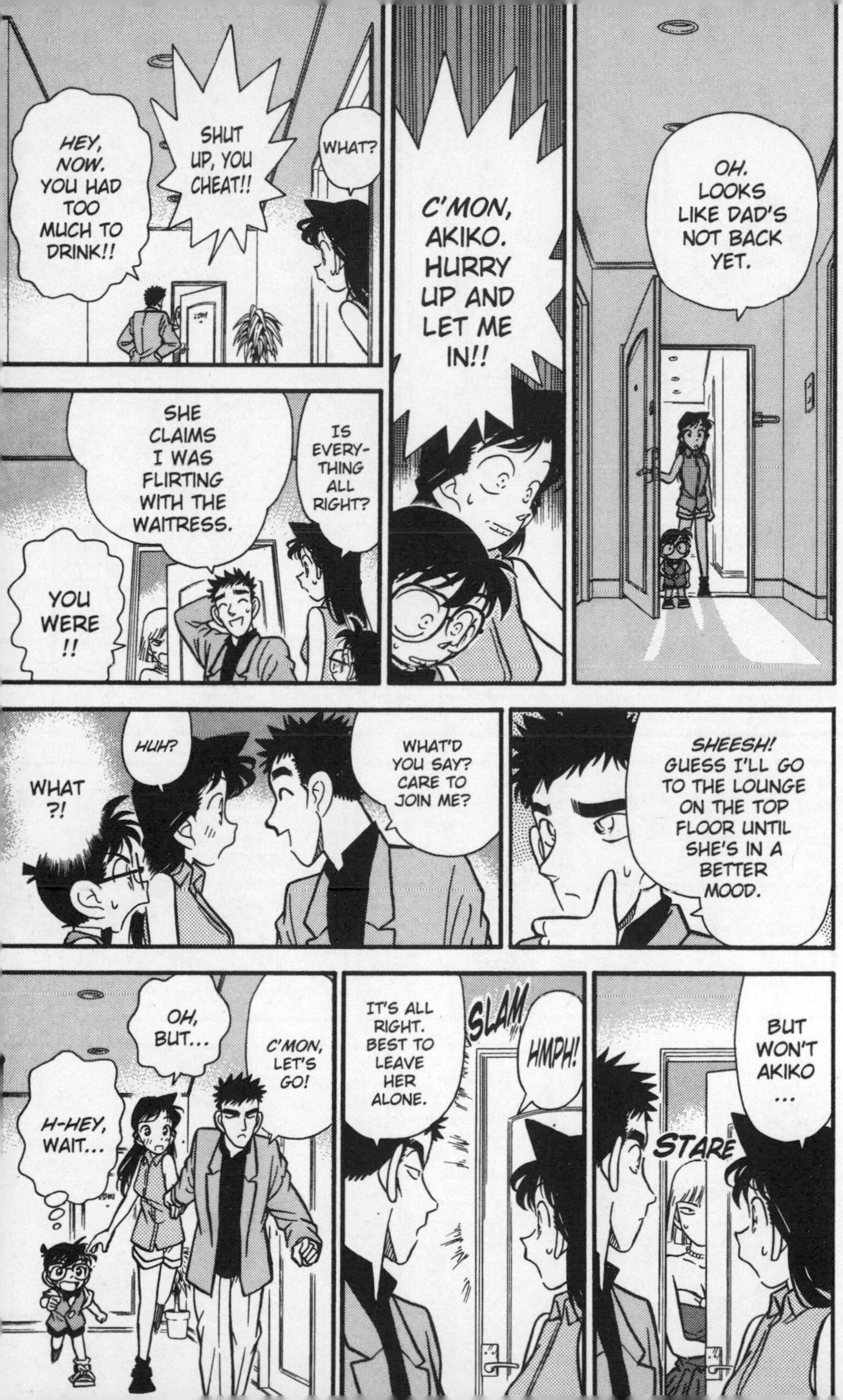

OH. LOOKS LIKE DAD'S NOT BACK YET.
C'MON, AKIKO. HURRY UP AND LET ME IN!!
WHAT?
SHUT UP, YOU CHEAT!!
HEY, NOW. YOU HAD TOO MUCH TO DRINK!!
IS EVERY-THING ALL RIGHT?
SHE CLAIMS I WAS FLIRTING WITH THE WAITRESS.
YOU WERE !!
SHEESH! GUESS I'LL GO TO THE LOUNGE ON THE TOP FLOOR UNTIL SHE'S IN A BETTER MOOD.
WHAT'D YOU SAY? CARE TO JOIN ME?
HUH?
WHAT ?!
BUT WON'T AKIKO ...
STARE
HMPH!
SLAM
IT'S ALL RIGHT. BEST TO LEAVE HER ALONE.
C'MON, LET'S GO!
OH, BUT...
H-HEY, WAIT...

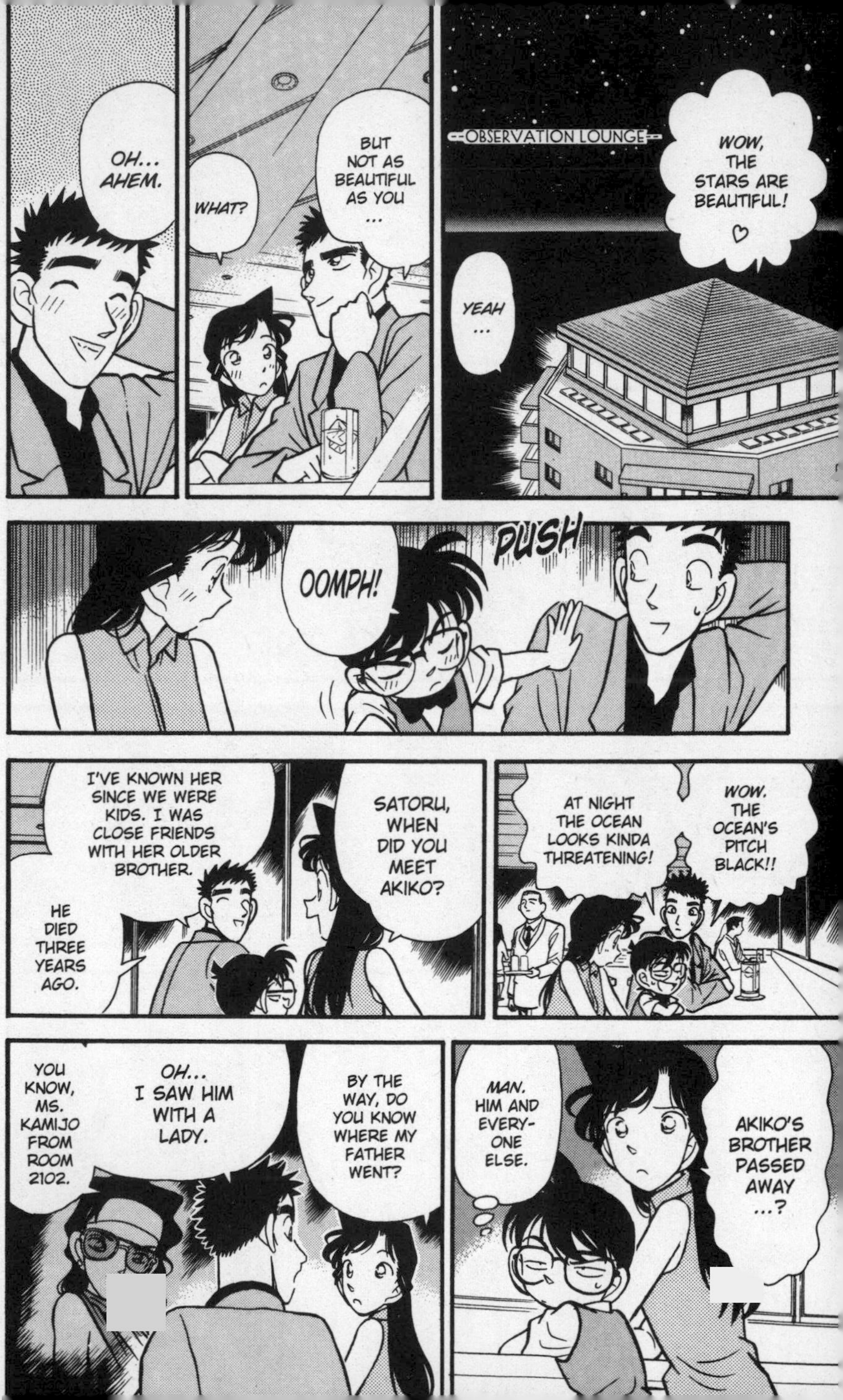
OBSERVATION LOUNGE
WOW, THE STARS ARE BEAUTIFUL! ♡
YEAH ...
BUT NOT AS BEAUTIFUL AS YOU ...
WHAT?
OH... AHEM.
PUSH
OOMPH!
WOW. THE OCEAN'S PITCH BLACK!!
AT NIGHT THE OCEAN LOOKS KINDA THREATENING!
SATORU, WHEN DID YOU MEET AKIKO?
I'VE KNOWN HER SINCE WE WERE KIDS. I WAS CLOSE FRIENDS WITH HER OLDER BROTHER.
HE DIED THREE YEARS AGO.
AKIKO'S BROTHER PASSED AWAY ...?
MAN. HIM AND EVERY-ONE ELSE.
BY THE WAY, DO YOU KNOW WHERE MY FATHER WENT?
OH... I SAW HIM WITH A LADY.
YOU KNOW, MS. KAMIJO FROM ROOM 2102.

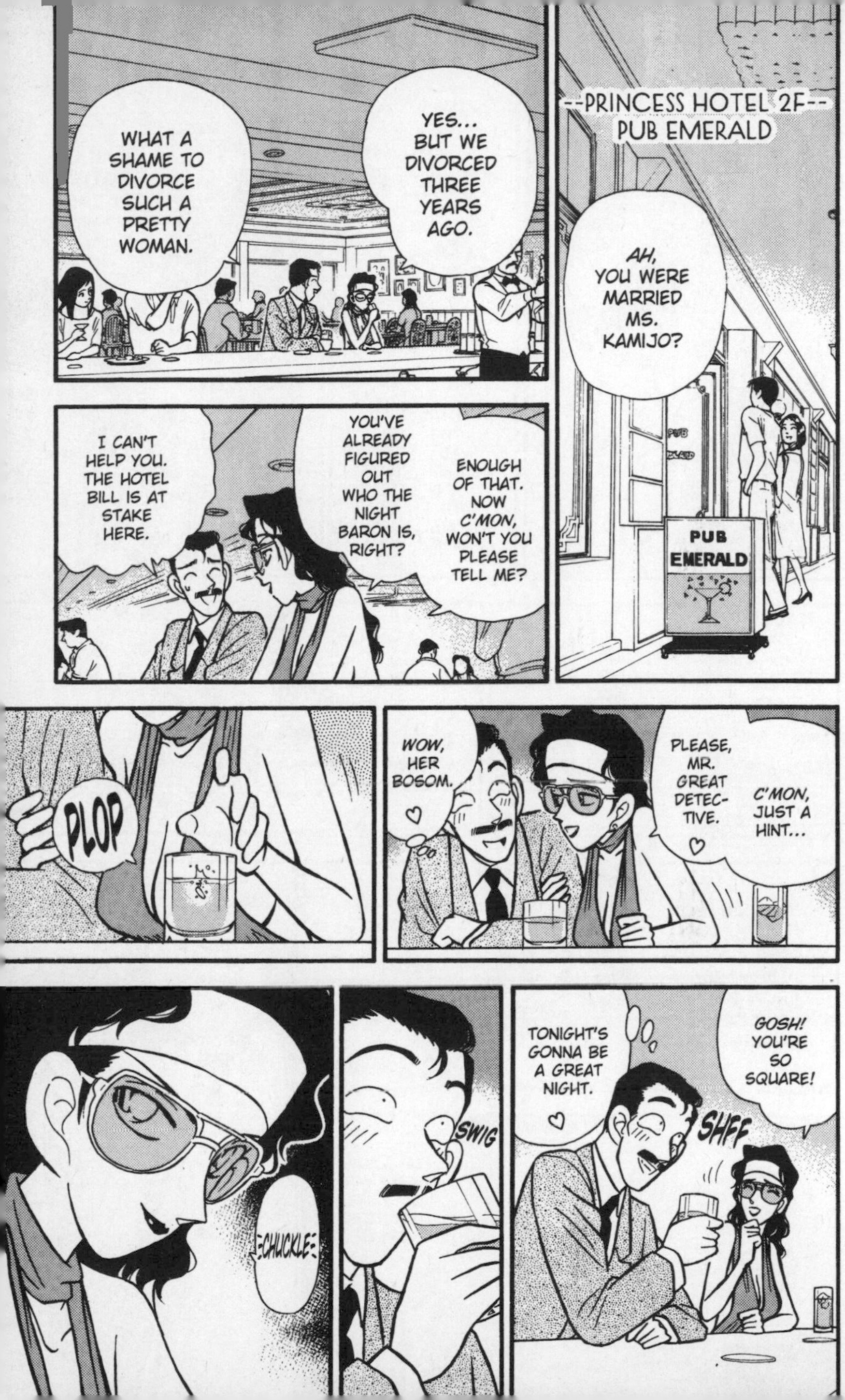
--PRINCESS HOTEL 2F--
PUB EMERALD
AH, YOU WERE MARRIED MS. KAMIJO?
PUB
PUB EMERALD
YES... BUT WE DIVORCED THREE YEARS AGO.
WHAT A SHAME TO DIVORCE SUCH A PRETTY WOMAN.
ENOUGH OF THAT. NOW C'MON, WON'T YOU PLEASE TELL ME?
YOU'VE ALREADY FIGURED OUT WHO THE NIGHT BARON IS, RIGHT?
I CAN'T HELP YOU. THE HOTEL BILL IS AT STAKE HERE.
C'MON, JUST A HINT...
PLEASE, MR. GREAT DETECTIVE.
WOW, HER BOSOM.
PLOP
GOSH! YOU'RE SO SQUARE!
SHFF
TONIGHT'S GONNA BE A GREAT NIGHT.
SWIG
CHUCKLE

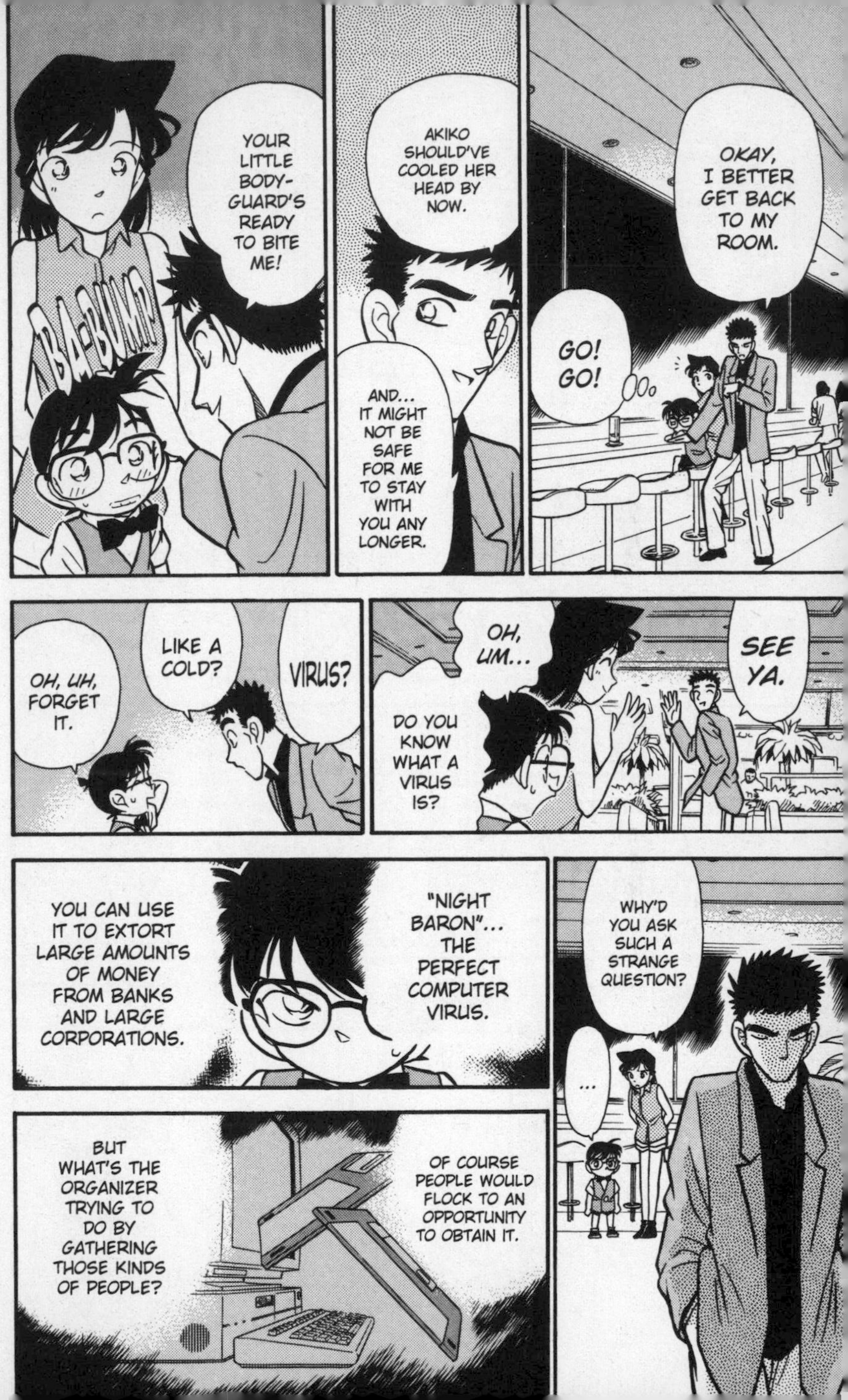
OKAY, I BETTER GET BACK TO MY ROOM.
GO! GO!
AKIKO SHOULD'VE COOLED HER HEAD BY NOW.
AND... IT MIGHT NOT BE SAFE FOR ME TO STAY WITH YOU ANY LONGER.
YOUR LITTLE BODY-GUARD'S READY TO BITE ME!
BA-BUMP
SEE YA.
OH, UM...
DO YOU KNOW WHAT A VIRUS IS?
VIRUS?
LIKE A COLD?
OH, UH, FORGET IT.
WHY'D YOU ASK SUCH A STRANGE QUESTION?
...
"NIGHT BARON"... THE PERFECT COMPUTER VIRUS.
YOU CAN USE IT TO EXTORT LARGE AMOUNTS OF MONEY FROM BANKS AND LARGE CORPORATIONS.
OF COURSE PEOPLE WOULD FLOCK TO AN OPPORTUNITY TO OBTAIN IT.
BUT WHAT'S THE ORGANIZER TRYING TO DO BY GATHERING THOSE KINDS OF PEOPLE?

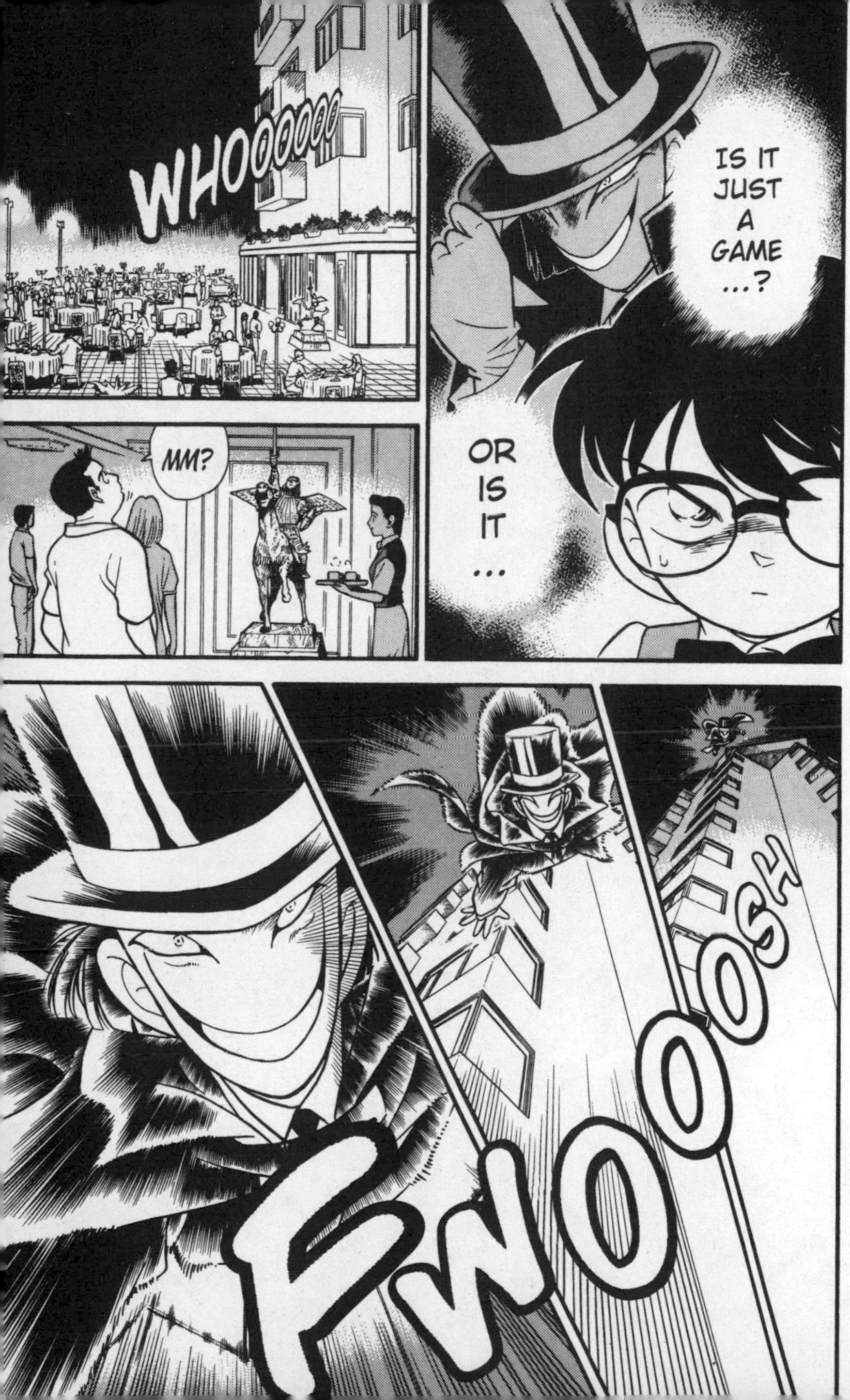
IS IT JUST A GAME ...?
OR IS IT ...
WHOOOOOO
MM?
FWOOOOSH

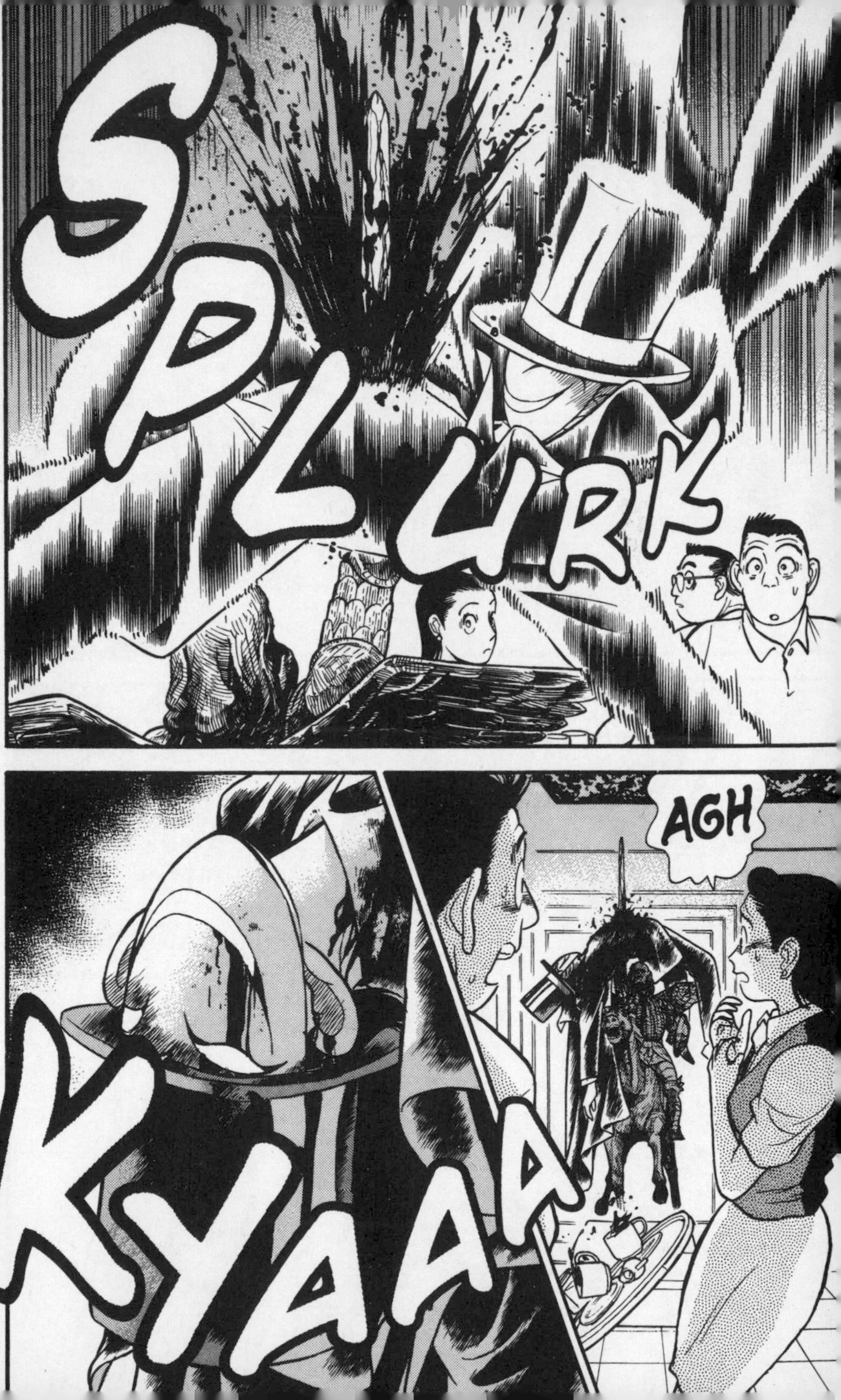
SPLURK
AGH
KYAAA

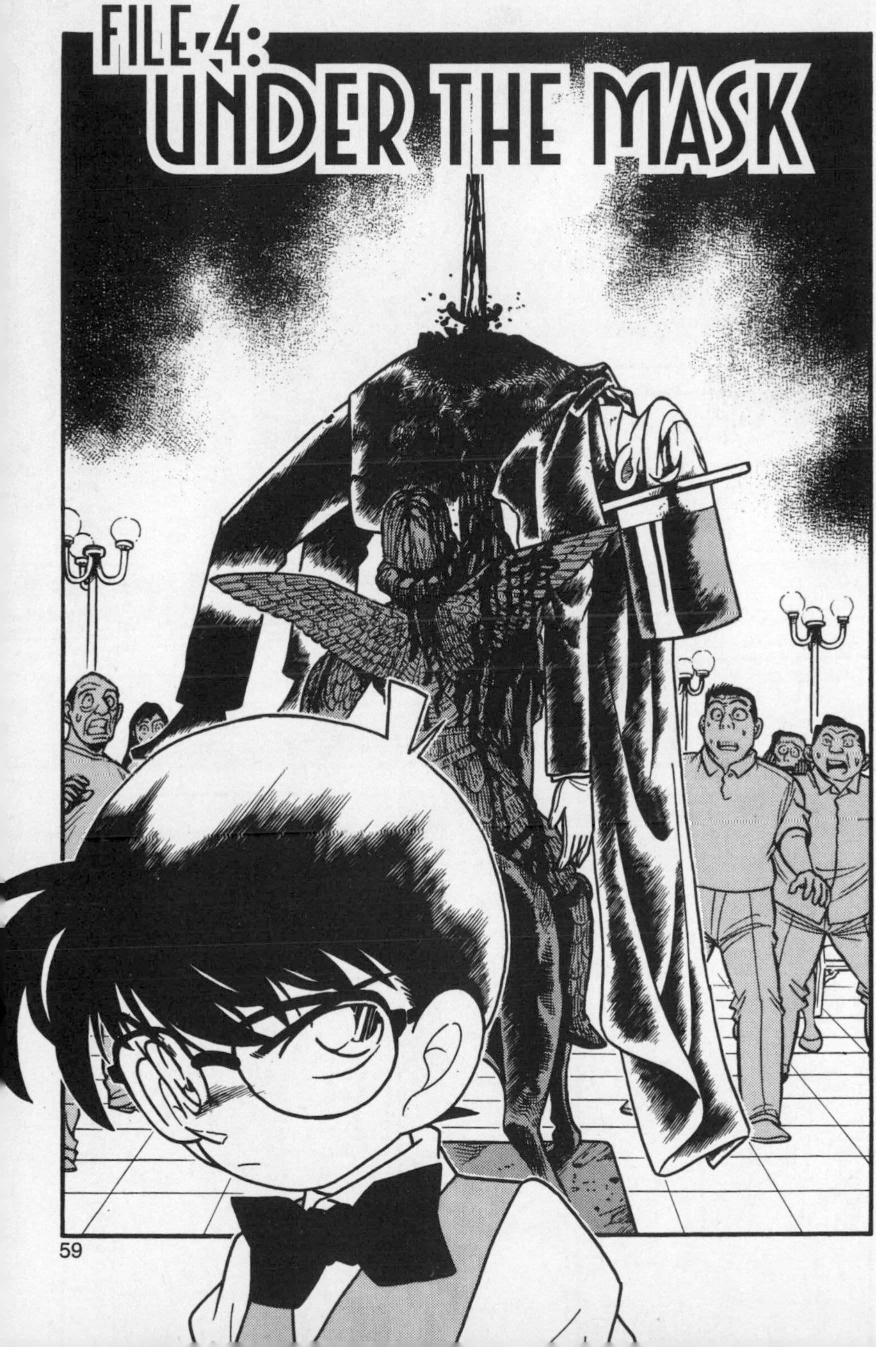
FILE 4:
UNDER THE MASK

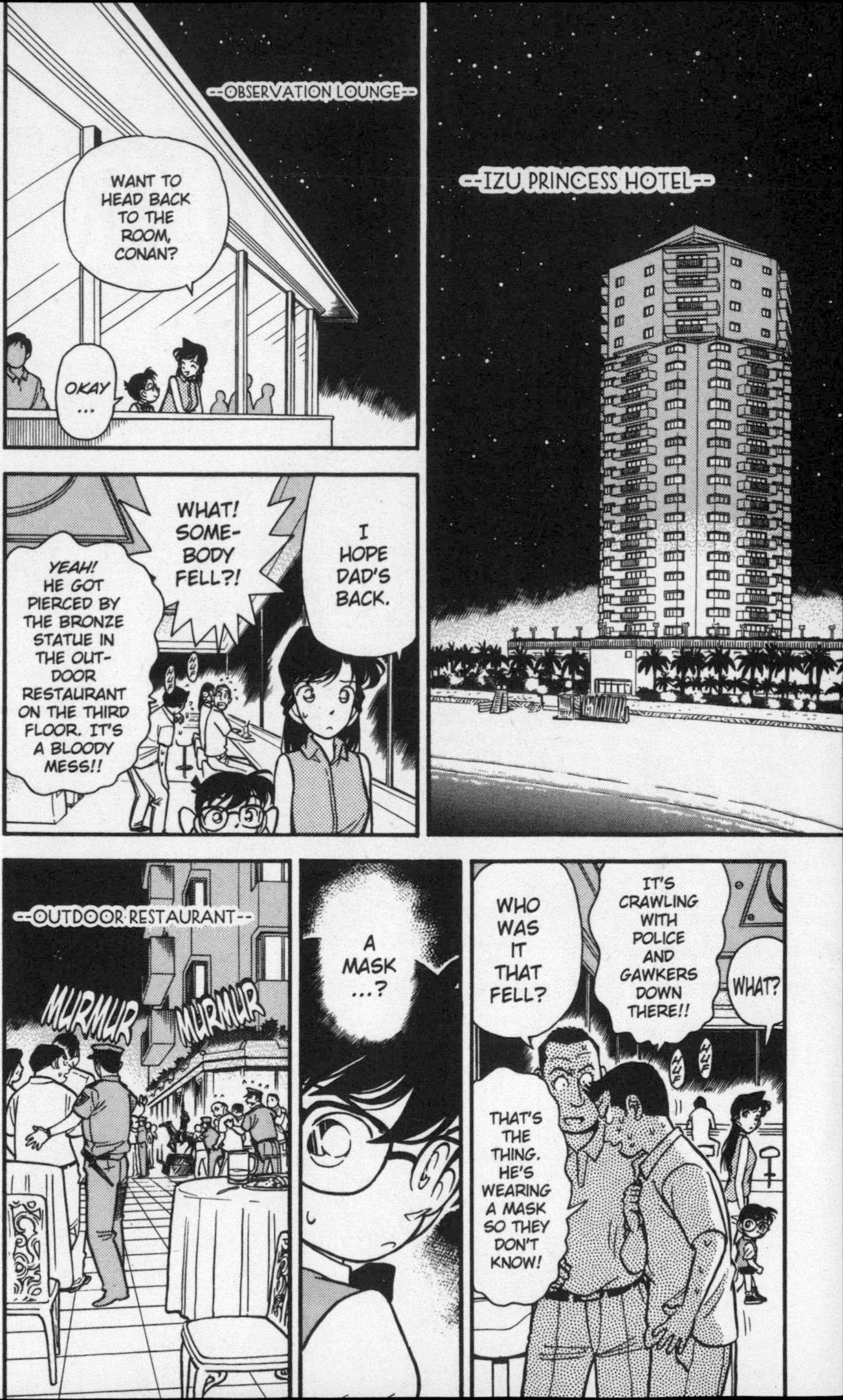
--IZU PRINCESS HOTEL--
--OBSERVATION LOUNGE--
WANT TO HEAD BACK TO THE ROOM, CONAN?
OKAY ...
I HOPE DAD'S BACK.
WHAT! SOME-BODY FELL?!
YEAH! HE GOT PIERCED BY THE BRONZE STATUE IN THE OUT-DOOR RESTAURANT ON THE THIRD FLOOR. IT'S A BLOODY MESS!!
HUF HUF
IT'S CRAWLING WITH POLICE AND GAWKERS DOWN THERE!!
WHO WAS IT THAT FELL?
WHAT?
HUF HUF
THAT'S THE THING. HE'S WEARING A MASK SO THEY DON'T KNOW!
A MASK ...?
--OUTDOOR RESTAURANT--
MURMUR
MURMUR

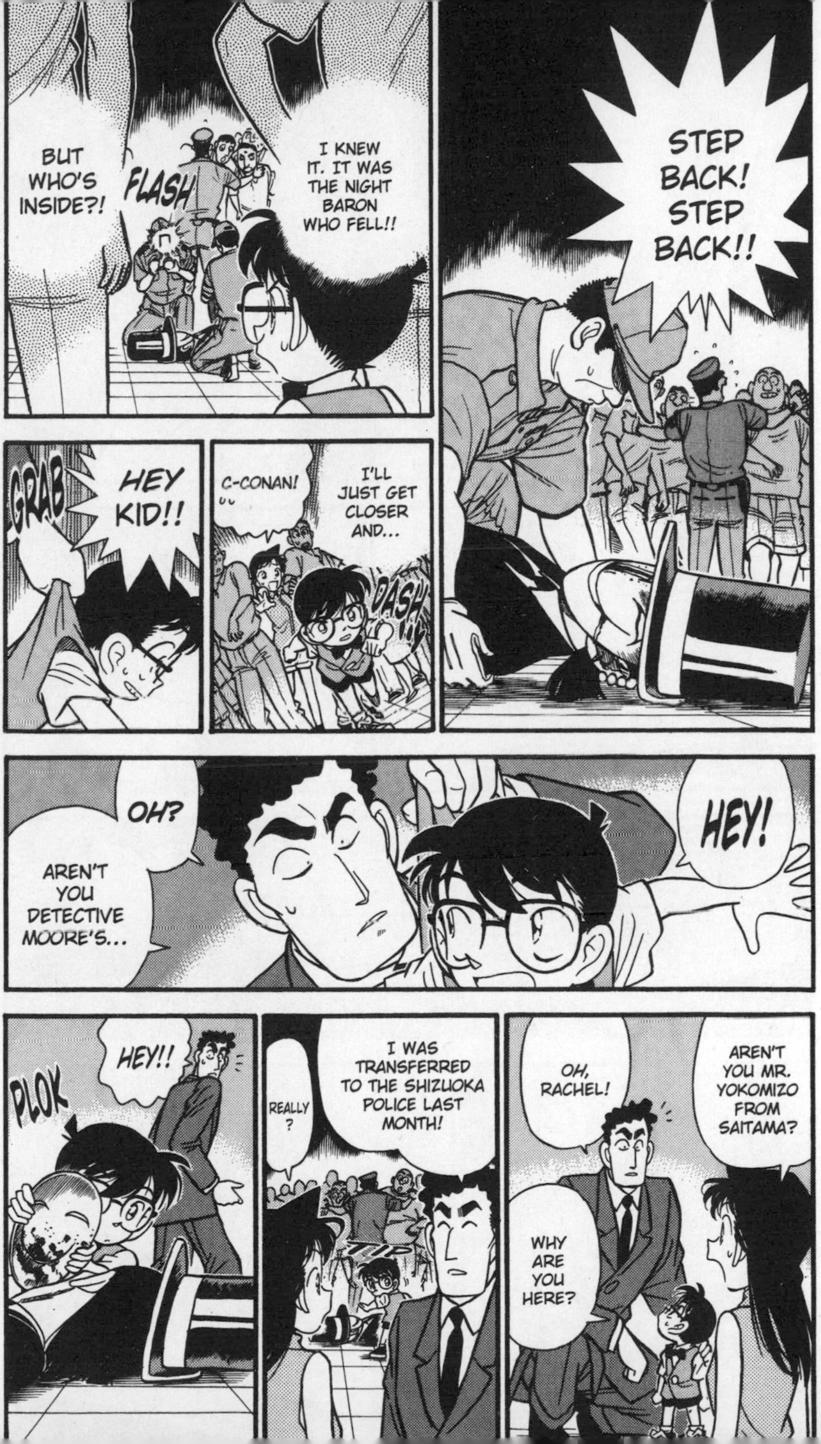
STEP BACK! STEP BACK!!
I KNEW IT. IT WAS THE NIGHT BARON WHO FELL!!
BUT WHO'S INSIDE?!
FLASH
I'LL JUST GET CLOSER AND...
C-CONAN!
DASH
HEY KID!!
GRAB
HEY!
OH?
AREN'T YOU DETECTIVE MOORE'S...
AREN'T YOU MR. YOKOMIZO FROM SAITAMA?
OH, RACHEL!
WHY ARE YOU HERE?
I WAS TRANSFERRED TO THE SHIZUOKA POLICE LAST MONTH!
REALLY?
TIP
HEY!!
PLOK

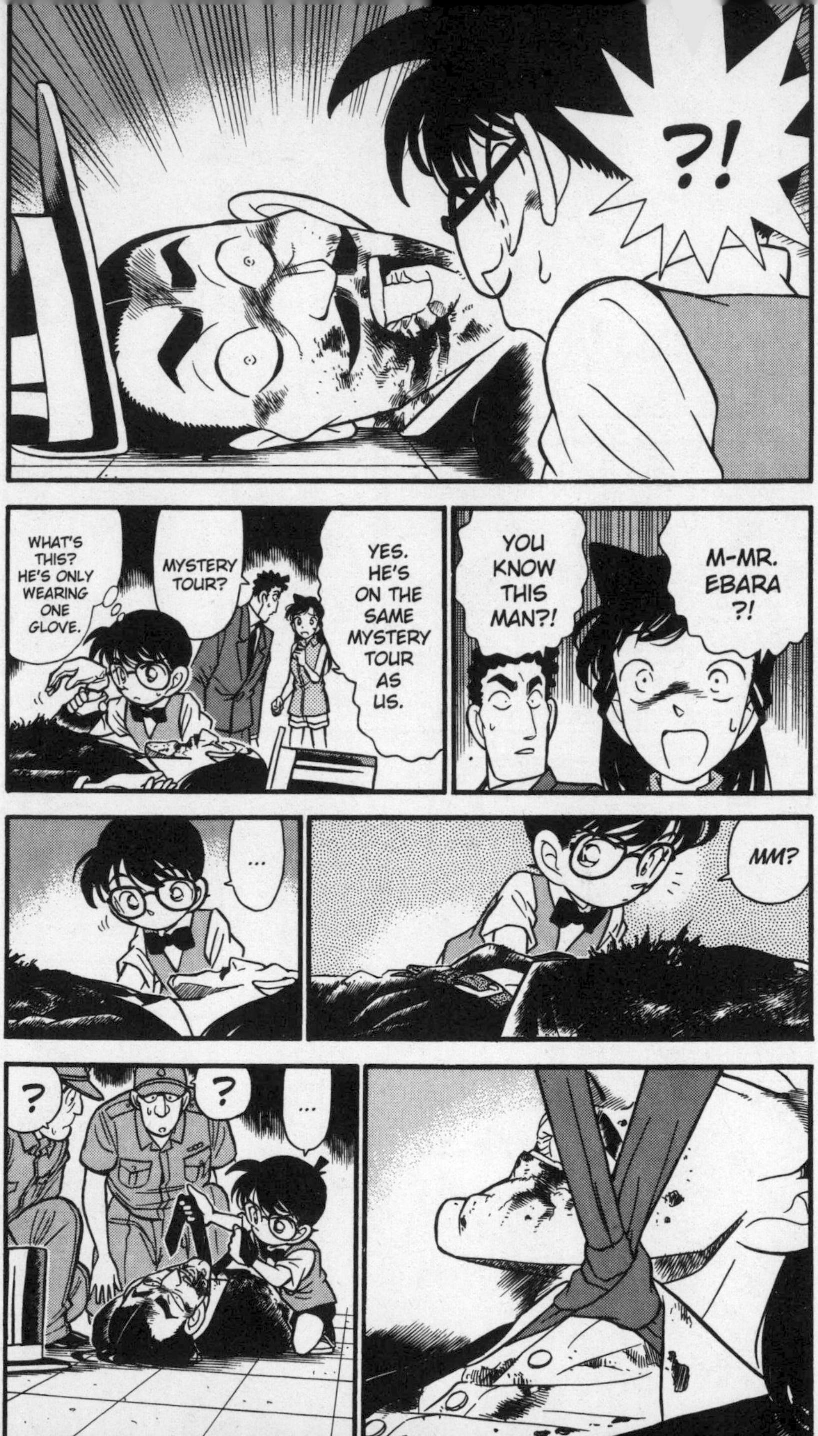
?!
M-MR. EBARA ?!
YOU KNOW THIS MAN?!
YES. HE'S ON THE SAME MYSTERY TOUR AS US.
MYSTERY TOUR?
WHAT'S THIS? HE'S ONLY WEARING ONE GLOVE.
MM?
...
...
?
?

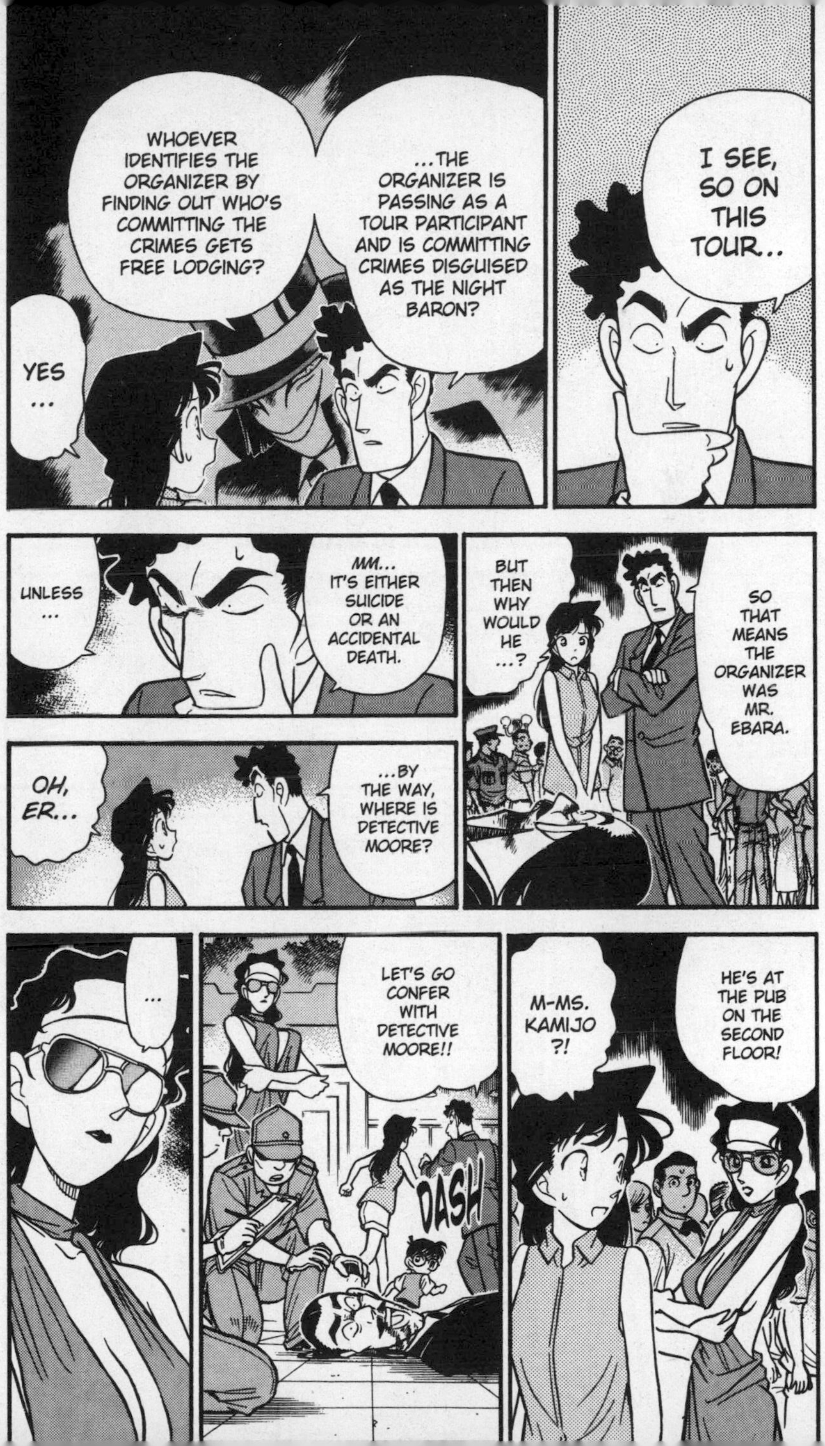
I SEE, SO ON THIS TOUR...
...THE ORGANIZER IS PASSING AS A TOUR PARTICIPANT AND IS COMMITTING CRIMES DISGUISED AS THE NIGHT BARON?
WHOEVER IDENTIFIES THE ORGANIZER BY FINDING OUT WHO'S COMMITTING THE CRIMES GETS FREE LODGING?
YES ...
SO THAT MEANS THE ORGANIZER WAS MR. EBARA.
BUT THEN WHY WOULD HE ...?
MM... IT'S EITHER SUICIDE OR AN ACCIDENTAL DEATH.
UNLESS ...
...BY THE WAY, WHERE IS DETECTIVE MOORE?
OH, ER...
HE'S AT THE PUB ON THE SECOND FLOOR!
M-MS. KAMIJO ?!
LET'S GO CONFER WITH DETECTIVE MOORE!!
DASH
...

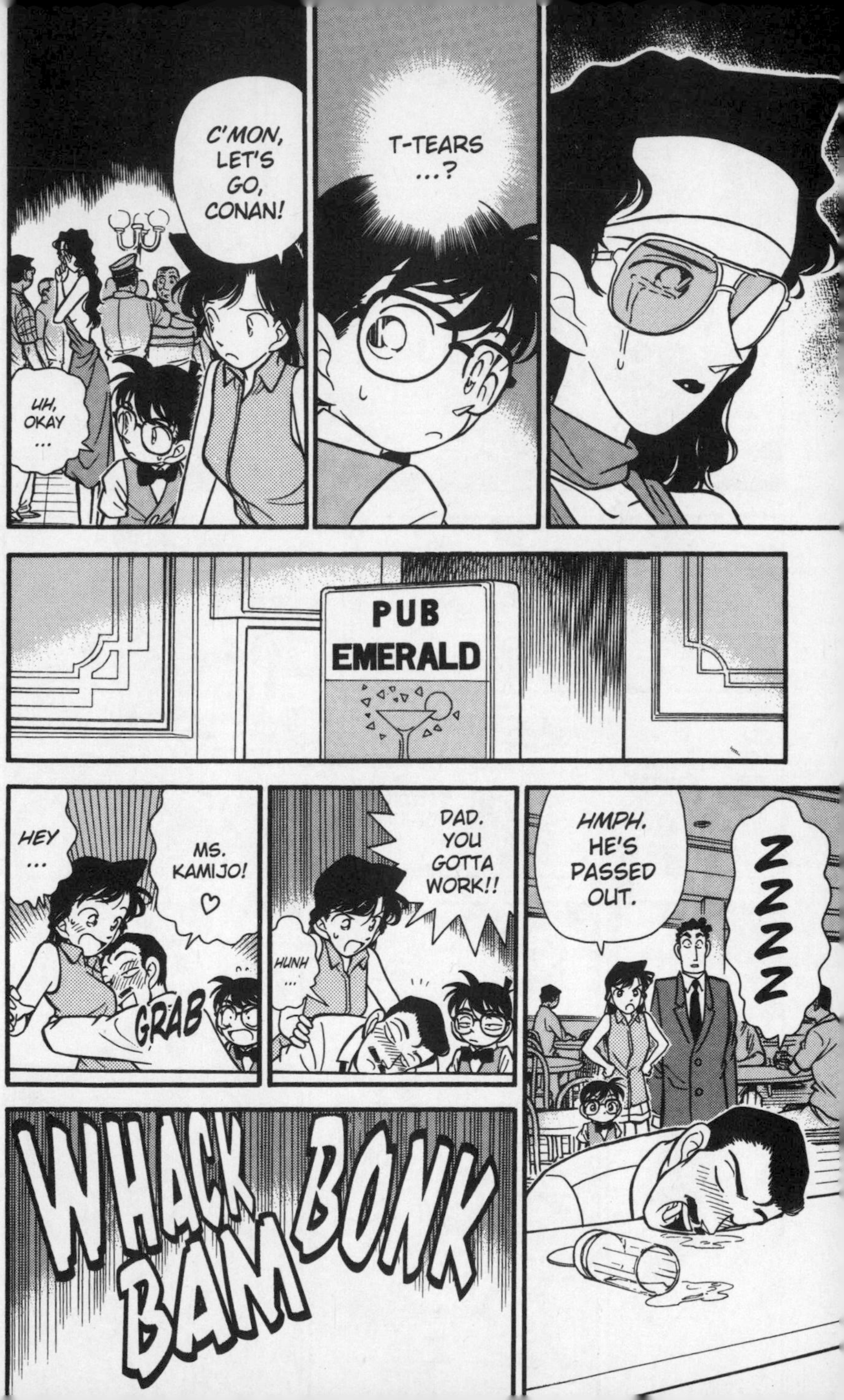
T-TEARS ...?
C'MON, LET'S GO, CONAN!
UH, OKAY ...
PUB EMERALD
HMPH. HE'S PASSED OUT.
ZZZZ
DAD. YOU GOTTA WORK!!
HUNH ...
HEY ...
MS. KAMIJO! ♡
GRAB
WHACK
BONK
BAM

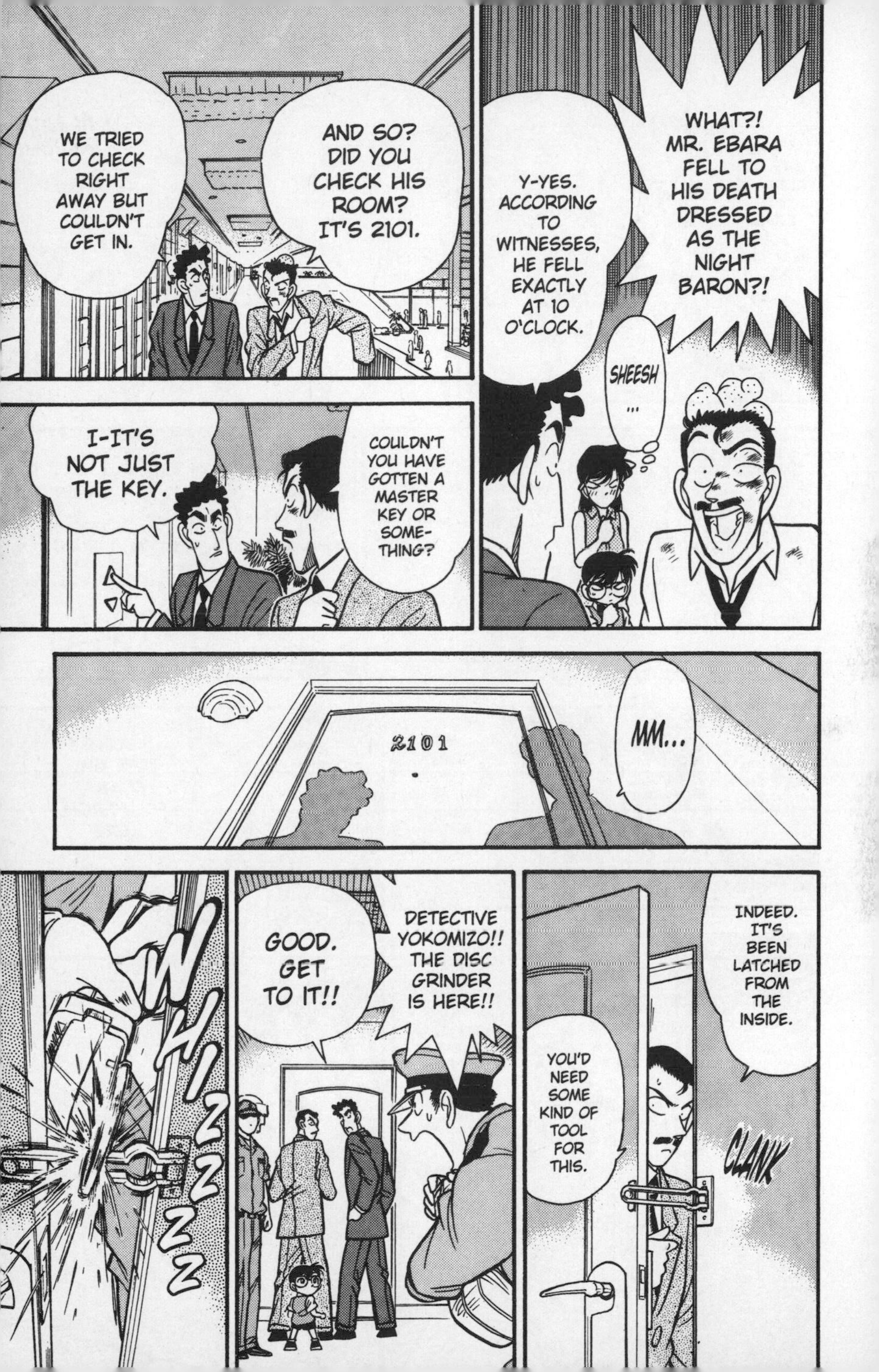
WHAT?! MR. EBARA FELL TO HIS DEATH DRESSED AS THE NIGHT BARON?!
Y-YES. ACCORDING TO WITNESSES, HE FELL EXACTLY AT 10 O'CLOCK.
SHEESH...
AND SO? DID YOU CHECK HIS ROOM? IT'S 2101.
WE TRIED TO CHECK RIGHT AWAY BUT COULDN'T GET IN.
COULDN'T YOU HAVE GOTTEN A MASTER KEY OR SOME-THING?
I-IT'S NOT JUST THE KEY.
MM...
2101
INDEED. IT'S BEEN LATCHED FROM THE INSIDE.
CLANK
YOU'D NEED SOME KIND OF TOOL FOR THIS.
DETECTIVE YOKOMIZO!! THE DISC GRINDER IS HERE!!
GOOD. GET TO IT!!
WHIZZZZ

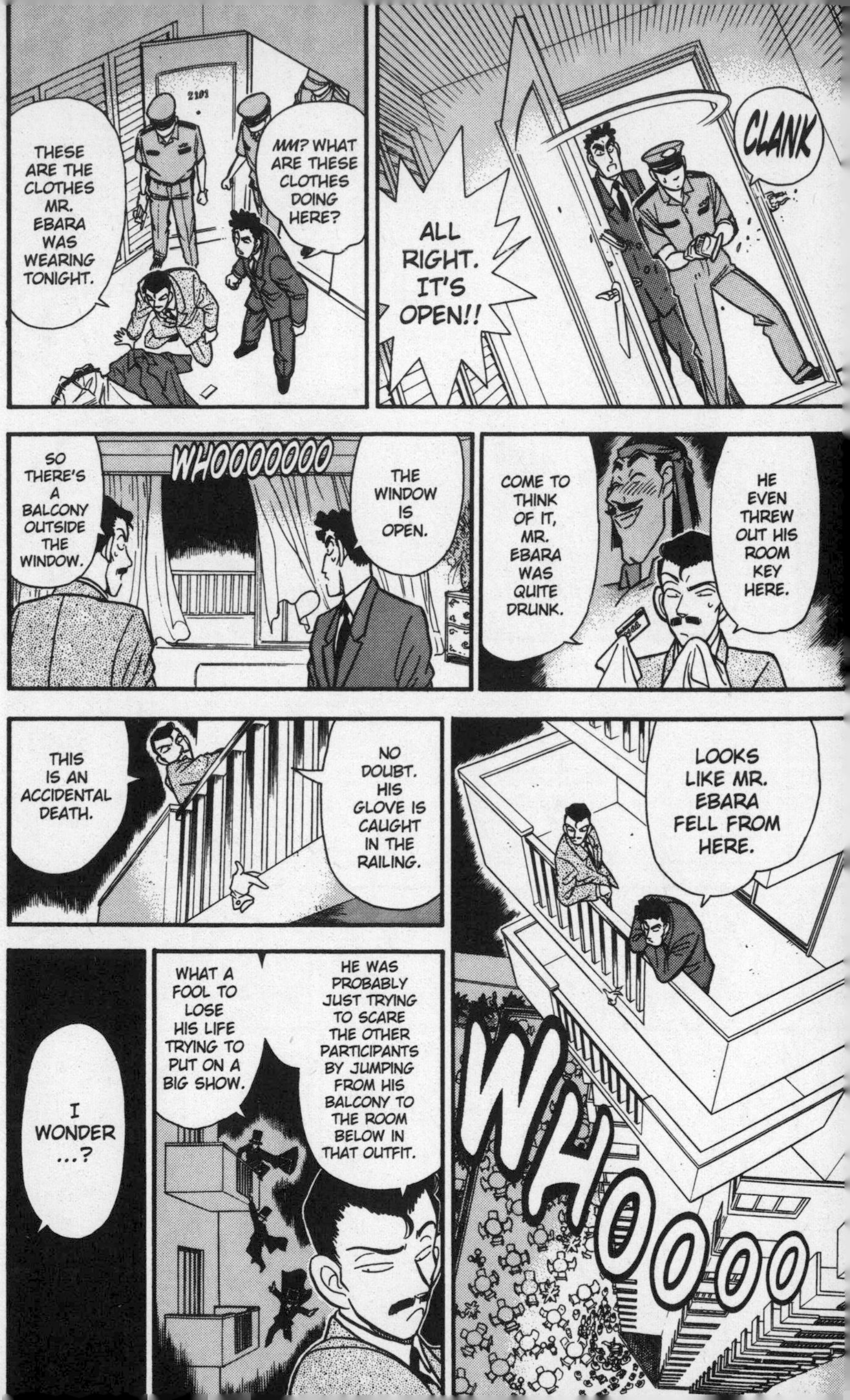
CLANK
ALL RIGHT. IT'S OPEN!!
MM? WHAT ARE THESE CLOTHES DOING HERE?
THESE ARE THE CLOTHES MR. EBARA WAS WEARING TONIGHT.
HE EVEN THREW OUT HIS ROOM KEY HERE.
COME TO THINK OF IT, MR. EBARA WAS QUITE DRUNK.
WHOOOOOOO
THE WINDOW IS OPEN.
SO THERE'S A BALCONY OUTSIDE THE WINDOW.
LOOKS LIKE MR. EBARA FELL FROM HERE.
WHOOOOO
NO DOUBT. HIS GLOVE IS CAUGHT IN THE RAILING.
THIS IS AN ACCIDENTAL DEATH.
HE WAS PROBABLY JUST TRYING TO SCARE THE OTHER PARTICIPANTS BY JUMPING FROM HIS BALCONY TO THE ROOM BELOW IN THAT OUTFIT.
WHAT A FOOL TO LOSE HIS LIFE TRYING TO PUT ON A BIG SHOW.
I WONDER ...?

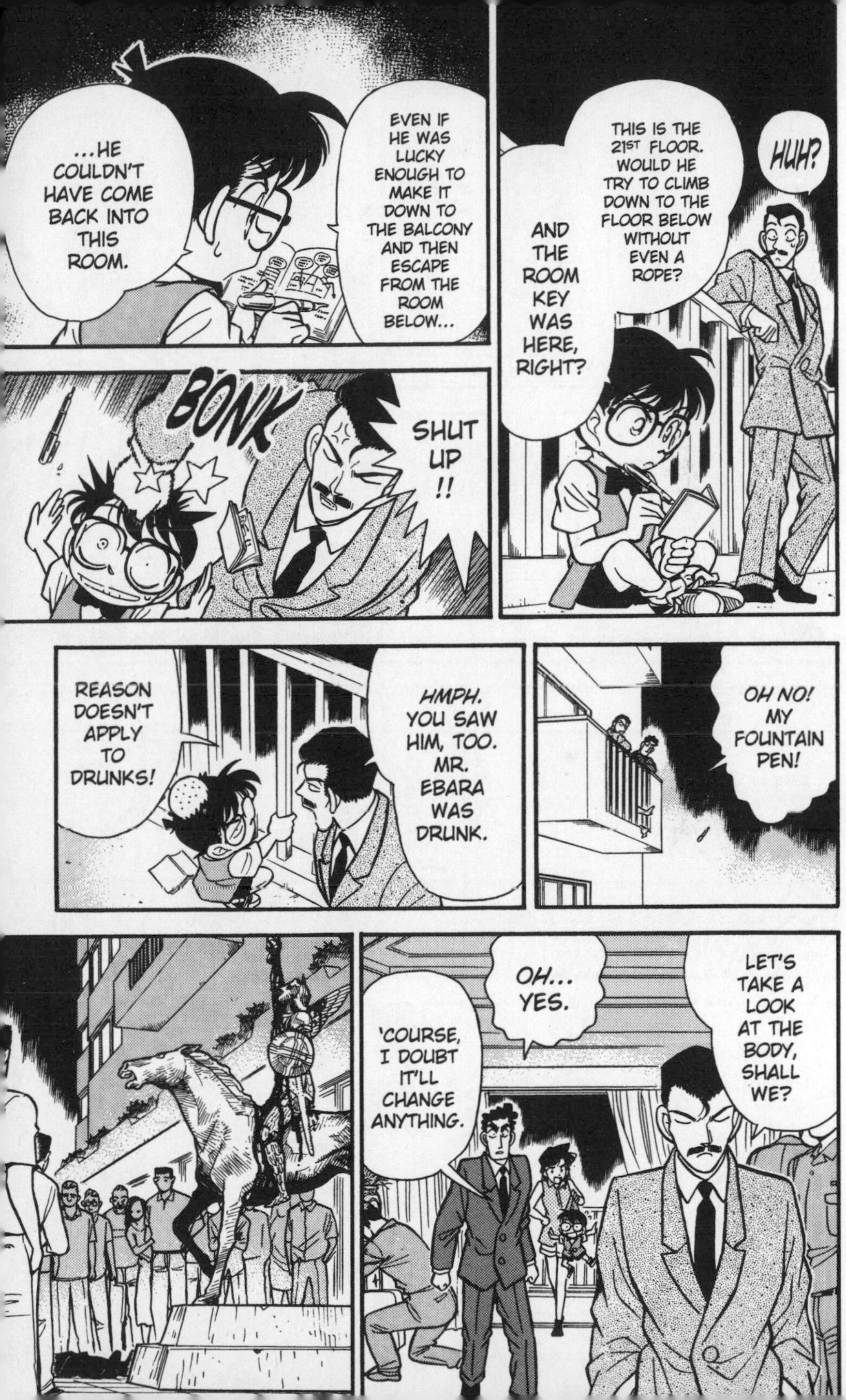

HUH?
THIS IS THE 21ST FLOOR. WOULD HE TRY TO CLIMB DOWN TO THE FLOOR BELOW WITHOUT EVEN A ROPE?
AND THE ROOM KEY WAS HERE, RIGHT?
EVEN IF HE WAS LUCKY ENOUGH TO MAKE IT DOWN TO THE BALCONY AND THEN ESCAPE FROM THE ROOM BELOW...
...HE COULDN'T HAVE COME BACK INTO THIS ROOM.
BONK
SHUT UP!!
OH NO! MY FOUNTAIN PEN!
HMPH. YOU SAW HIM, TOO. MR. EBARA WAS DRUNK.
REASON DOESN'T APPLY TO DRUNKS!
LET'S TAKE A LOOK AT THE BODY, SHALL WE?
OH... YES.
'COURSE, I DOUBT IT'LL CHANGE ANYTHING.

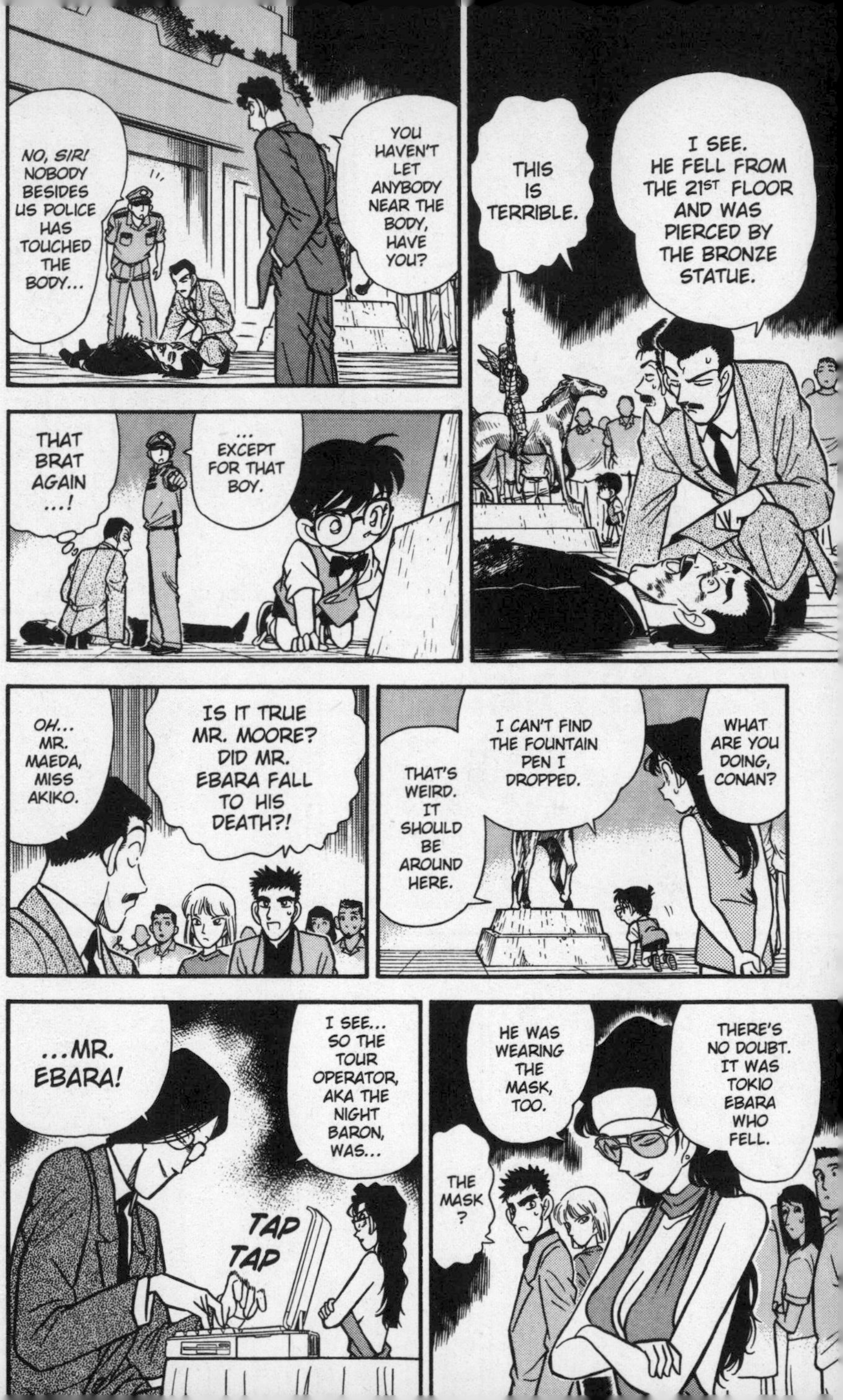
I SEE. HE FELL FROM THE 21ST FLOOR AND WAS PIERCED BY THE BRONZE STATUE.
THIS IS TERRIBLE.
YOU HAVEN'T LET ANYBODY NEAR THE BODY, HAVE YOU?
NO, SIR! NOBODY BESIDES US POLICE HAS TOUCHED THE BODY...
... EXCEPT FOR THAT BOY.
THAT BRAT AGAIN ...!
WHAT ARE YOU DOING, CONAN?
I CAN'T FIND THE FOUNTAIN PEN I DROPPED.
THAT'S WEIRD. IT SHOULD BE AROUND HERE.
IS IT TRUE MR. MOORE? DID MR. EBARA FALL TO HIS DEATH?!
OH... MR. MAEDA, MISS AKIKO.
THERE'S NO DOUBT. IT WAS TOKIO EBARA WHO FELL.
HE WAS WEARING THE MASK, TOO.
THE MASK?
I SEE... SO THE TOUR OPERATOR, AKA THE NIGHT BARON, WAS...
...MR. EBARA!
TAP TAP

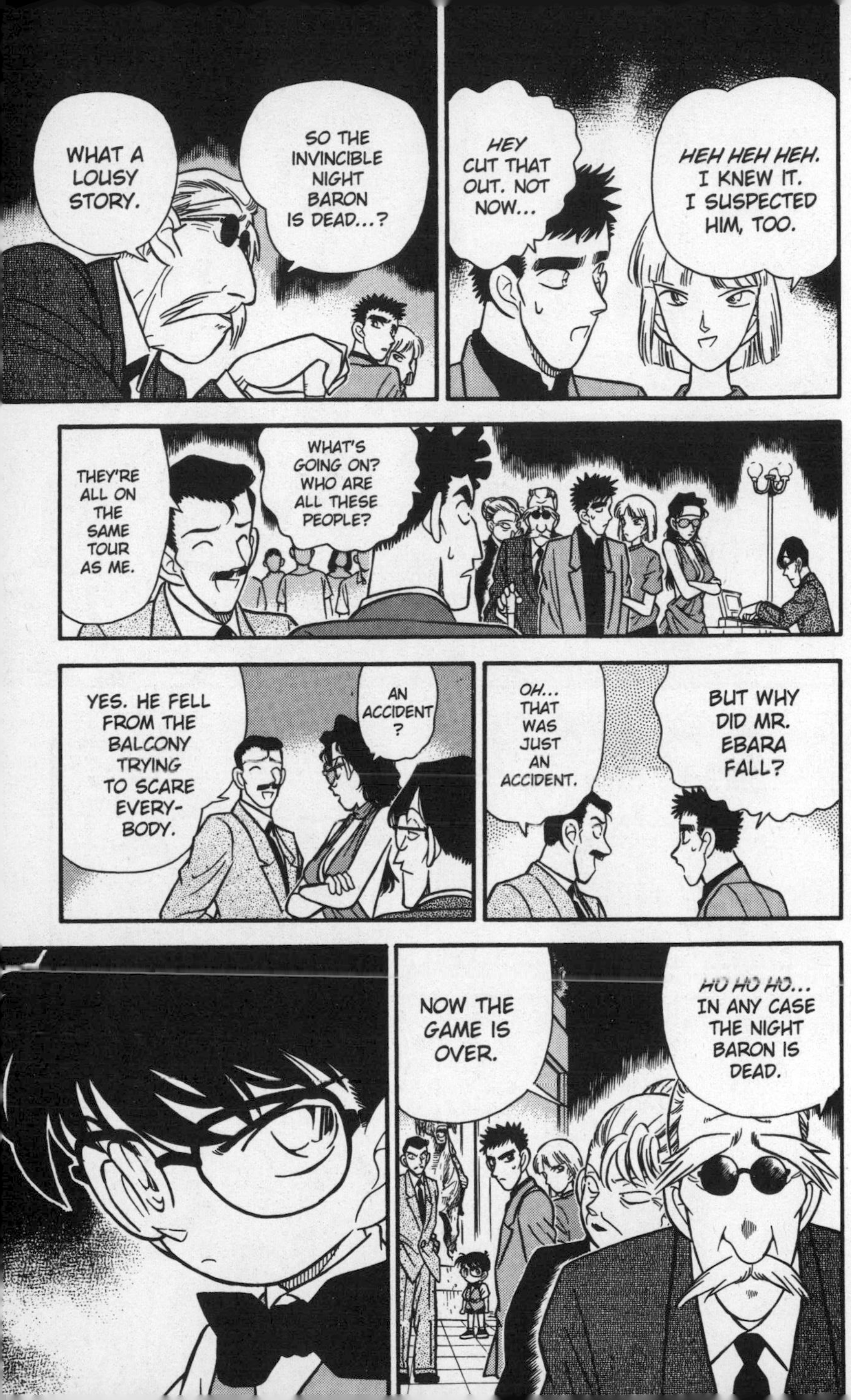
HEH HEH HEH. I KNEW IT. I SUSPECTED HIM, TOO.
HEY CUT THAT OUT. NOT NOW...
SO THE INVINCIBLE NIGHT BARON IS DEAD...?
WHAT A LOUSY STORY.
WHAT'S GOING ON? WHO ARE ALL THESE PEOPLE?
THEY'RE ALL ON THE SAME TOUR AS ME.
BUT WHY DID MR. EBARA FALL?
OH... THAT WAS JUST AN ACCIDENT.
AN ACCIDENT?
YES. HE FELL FROM THE BALCONY TRYING TO SCARE EVERYBODY.
HO HO HO... IN ANY CASE THE NIGHT BARON IS DEAD.
NOW THE GAME IS OVER.

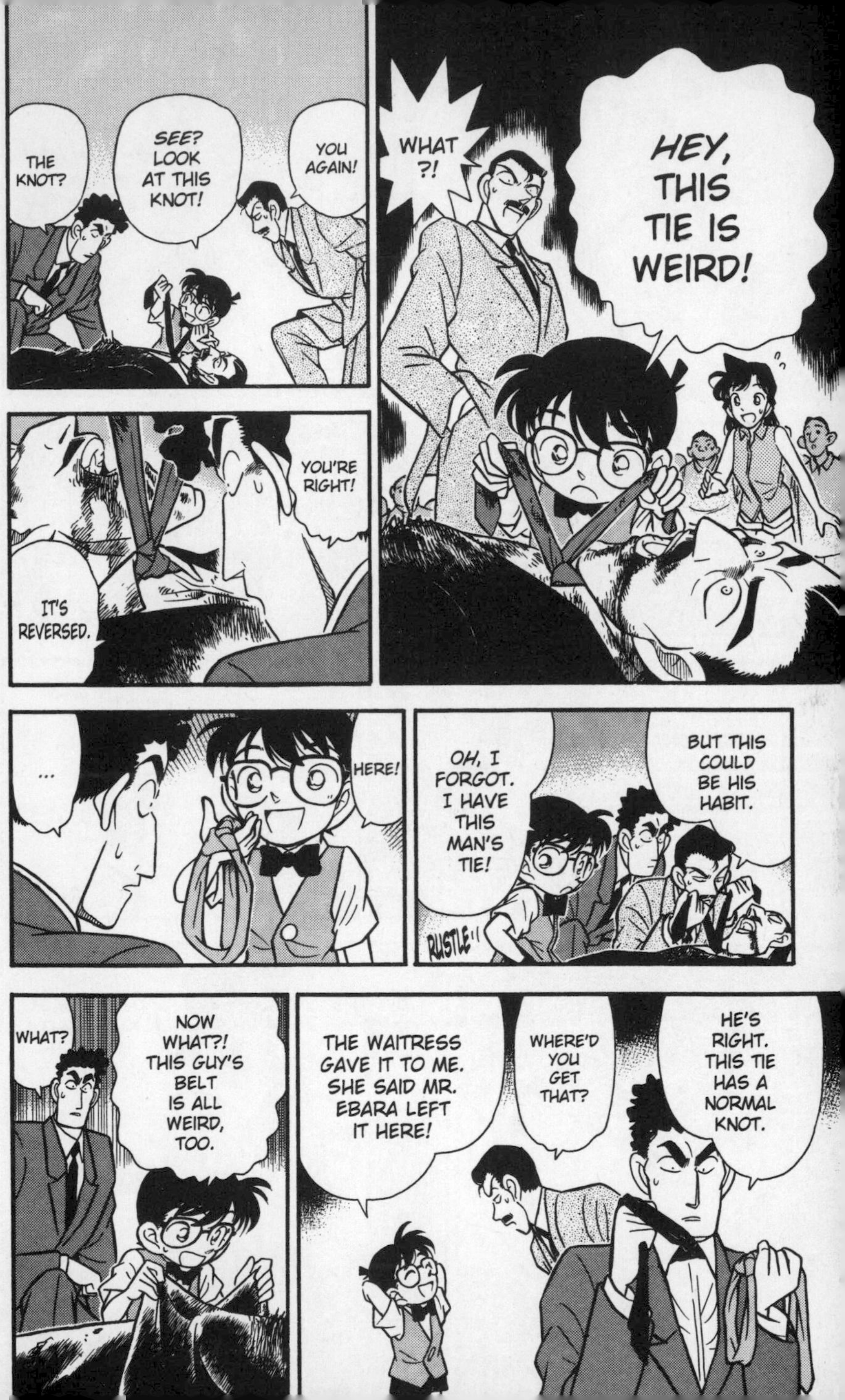
HEY, THIS TIE IS WEIRD!
WHAT ?!
YOU AGAIN!
SEE? LOOK AT THIS KNOT!
THE KNOT?
YOU'RE RIGHT!
IT'S REVERSED.
BUT THIS COULD BE HIS HABIT.
OH, I FORGOT. I HAVE THIS MAN'S TIE!
RUSTLE
HERE!
...
HE'S RIGHT. THIS TIE HAS A NORMAL KNOT.
WHERE'D YOU GET THAT?
THE WAITRESS GAVE IT TO ME. SHE SAID MR. EBARA LEFT IT HERE!
NOW WHAT?! THIS GUY'S BELT IS ALL WEIRD, TOO.
WHAT?

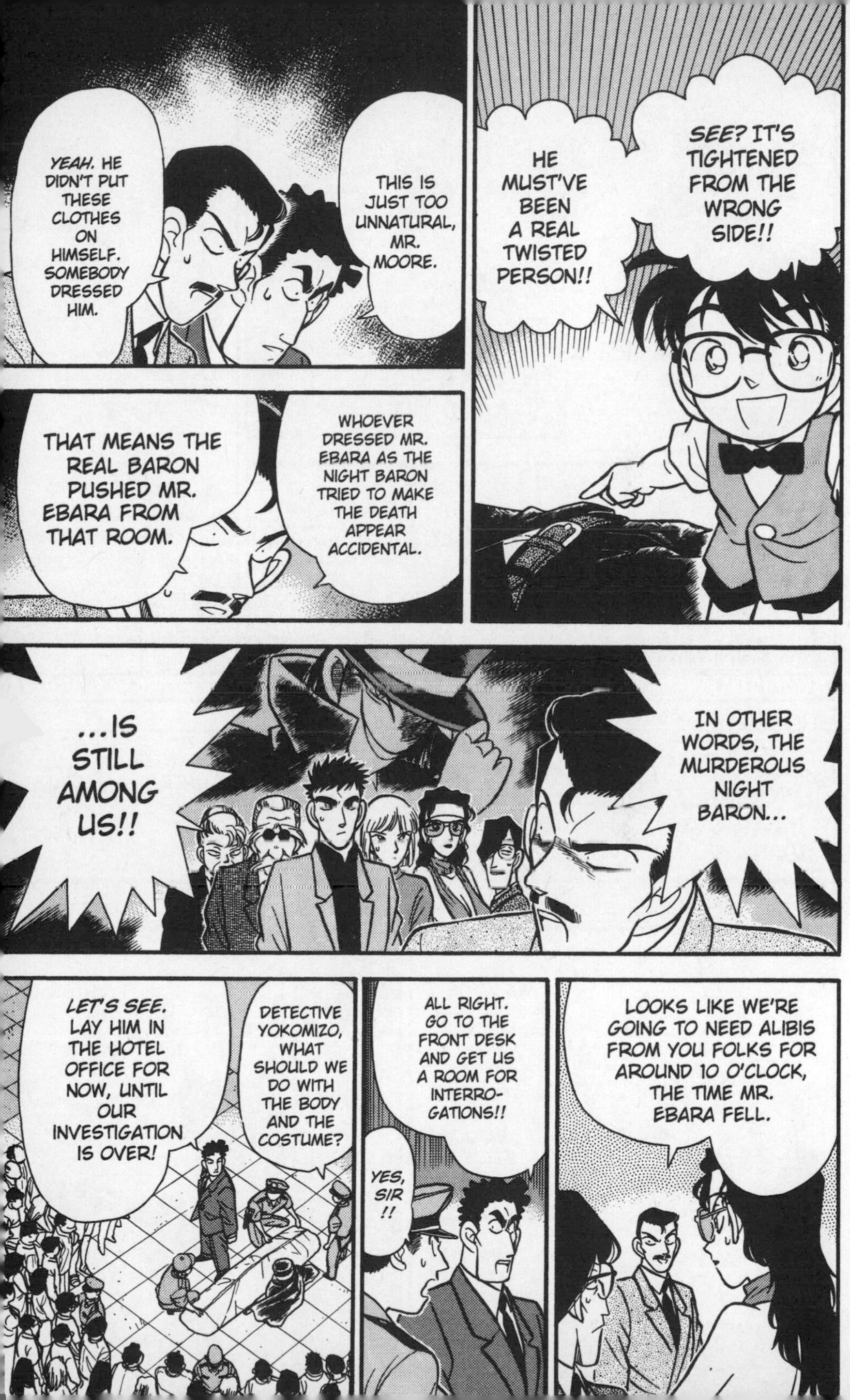
SEE? IT'S TIGHTENED FROM THE WRONG SIDE!!
HE MUST'VE BEEN A REAL TWISTED PERSON!!
THIS IS JUST TOO UNNATURAL, MR. MOORE.
YEAH. HE DIDN'T PUT THESE CLOTHES ON HIMSELF. SOMEBODY DRESSED HIM.
WHOEVER DRESSED MR. EBARA AS THE NIGHT BARON TRIED TO MAKE THE DEATH APPEAR ACCIDENTAL.
THAT MEANS THE REAL BARON PUSHED MR. EBARA FROM THAT ROOM.
IN OTHER WORDS, THE MURDEROUS NIGHT BARON...
...IS STILL AMONG US!!
LOOKS LIKE WE'RE GOING TO NEED ALIBIS FROM YOU FOLKS FOR AROUND 10 O'CLOCK, THE TIME MR. EBARA FELL.
ALL RIGHT. GO TO THE FRONT DESK AND GET US A ROOM FOR INTERRO-GATIONS!!
YES, SIR!!
DETECTIVE YOKOMIZO, WHAT SHOULD WE DO WITH THE BODY AND THE COSTUME?
LET'S SEE. LAY HIM IN THE HOTEL OFFICE FOR NOW, UNTIL OUR INVESTIGATION IS OVER!

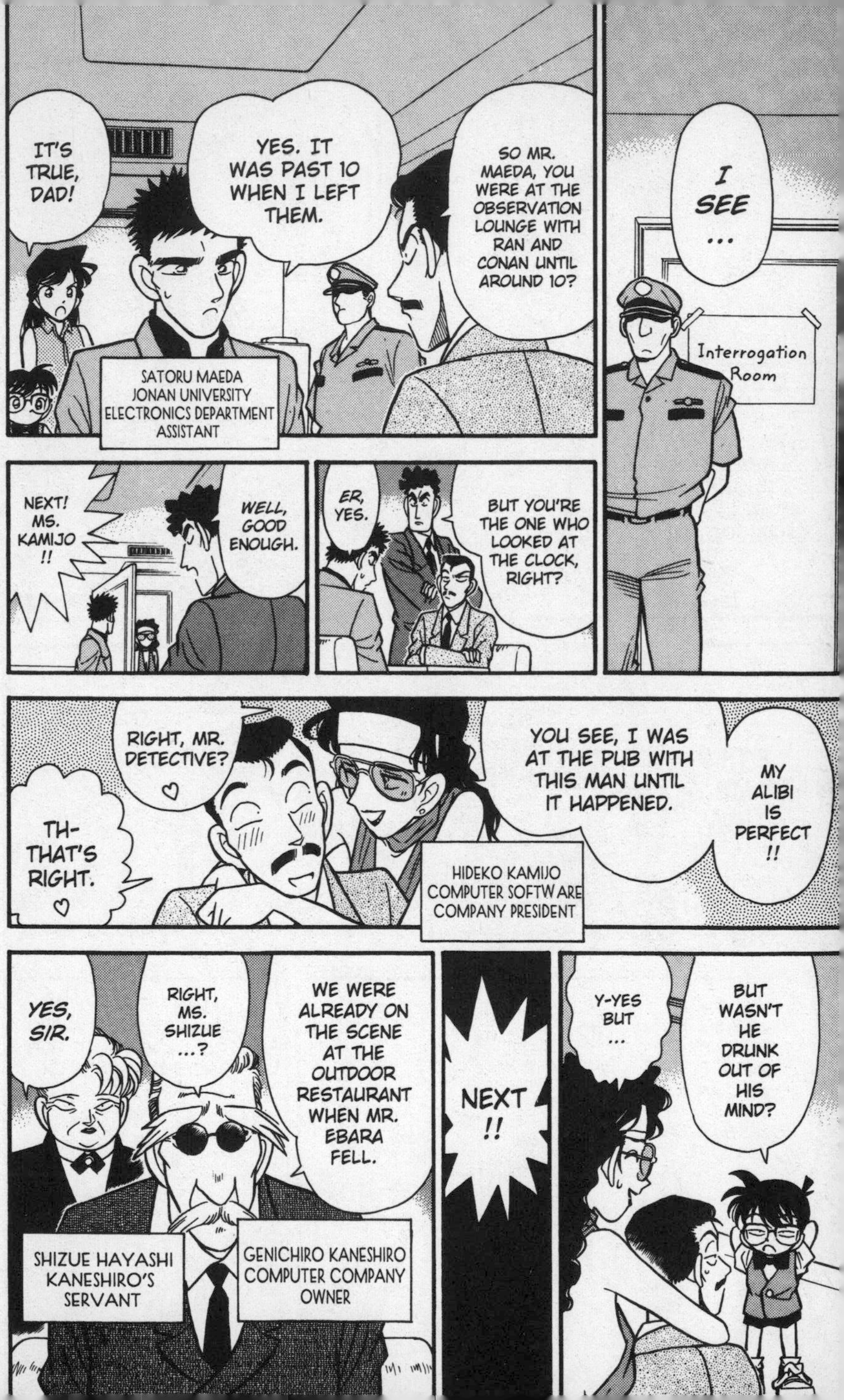
I SEE ...
Interrogation Room
SO MR. MAEDA, YOU WERE AT THE OBSERVATION LOUNGE WITH RAN AND CONAN UNTIL AROUND 10?
YES. IT WAS PAST 10 WHEN I LEFT THEM.
IT'S TRUE, DAD!
SATORU MAEDA JONAN UNIVERSITY ELECTRONICS DEPARTMENT ASSISTANT
BUT YOU'RE THE ONE WHO LOOKED AT THE CLOCK, RIGHT?
ER, YES.
WELL, GOOD ENOUGH.
NEXT! MS. KAMIJO !!
MY ALIBI IS PERFECT !!
YOU SEE, I WAS AT THE PUB WITH THIS MAN UNTIL IT HAPPENED.
HIDEKO KAMIJO COMPUTER SOFTWARE COMPANY PRESIDENT
RIGHT, MR. DETECTIVE? ♡
TH-THAT'S RIGHT. ♡
BUT WASN'T HE DRUNK OUT OF HIS MIND?
Y-YES BUT ...
NEXT !!
WE WERE ALREADY ON THE SCENE AT THE OUTDOOR RESTAURANT WHEN MR. EBARA FELL.
RIGHT, MS. SHIZUE ...?
YES, SIR.
GENICHIRO KANESHIRO COMPUTER COMPANY OWNER
SHIZUE HAYASHI KANESHIRO'S SERVANT

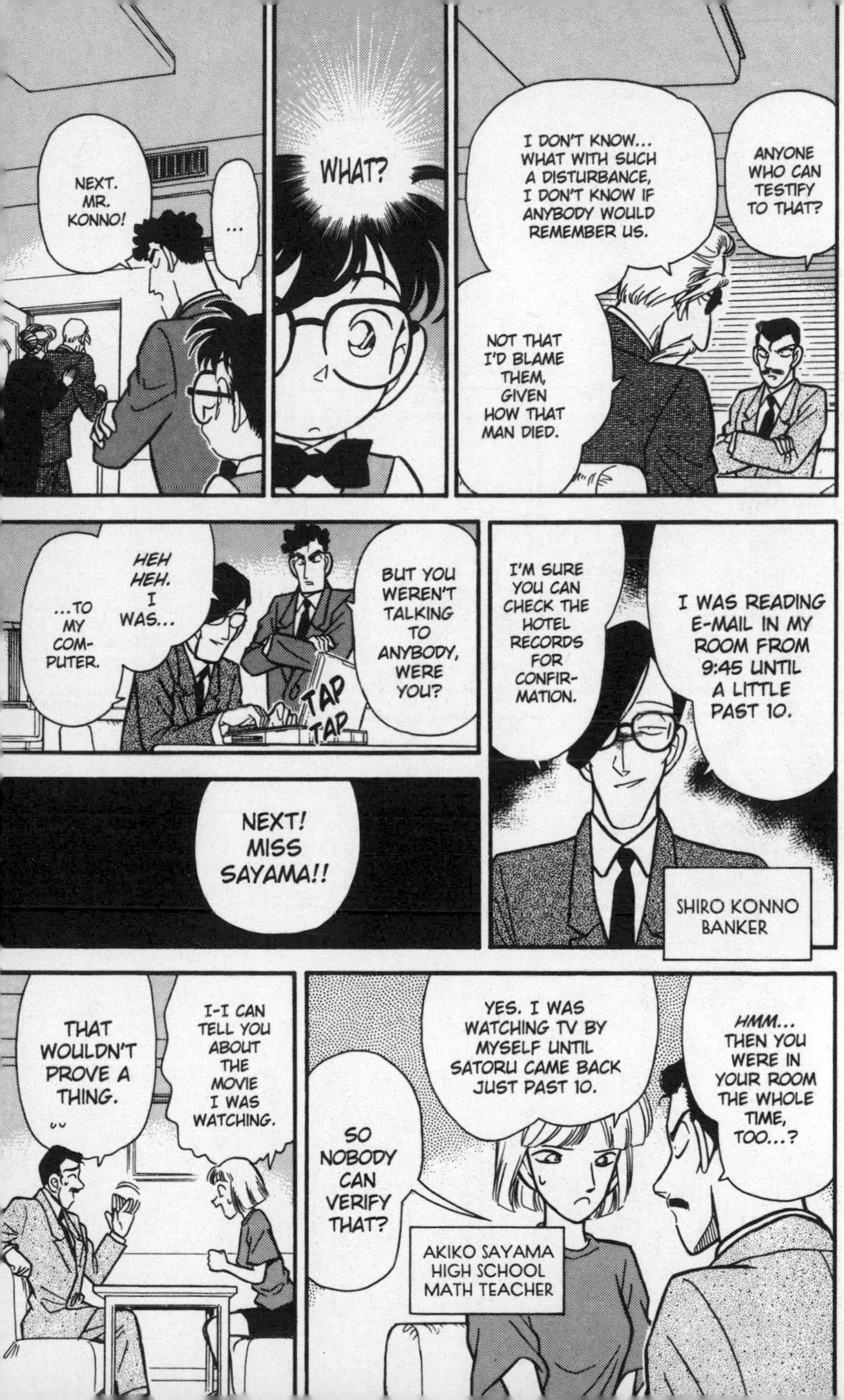
ANYONE WHO CAN TESTIFY TO THAT?
I DON'T KNOW... WHAT WITH SUCH A DISTURBANCE, I DON'T KNOW IF ANYBODY WOULD REMEMBER US.
NOT THAT I'D BLAME THEM, GIVEN HOW THAT MAN DIED.
WHAT?
...
NEXT. MR. KONNO!
I WAS READING E-MAIL IN MY ROOM FROM 9:45 UNTIL A LITTLE PAST 10.
I'M SURE YOU CAN CHECK THE HOTEL RECORDS FOR CONFIRMATION.
SHIRO KONNO BANKER
BUT YOU WEREN'T TALKING TO ANYBODY, WERE YOU?
TAP TAP
HEH HEH. I WAS...
...TO MY COMPUTER.
NEXT! MISS SAYAMA!!
HMM... THEN YOU WERE IN YOUR ROOM THE WHOLE TIME, TOO...?
YES. I WAS WATCHING TV BY MYSELF UNTIL SATORU CAME BACK JUST PAST 10.
SO NOBODY CAN VERIFY THAT?
AKIKO SAYAMA HIGH SCHOOL MATH TEACHER
I-I CAN TELL YOU ABOUT THE MOVIE I WAS WATCHING.
THAT WOULDN'T PROVE A THING.

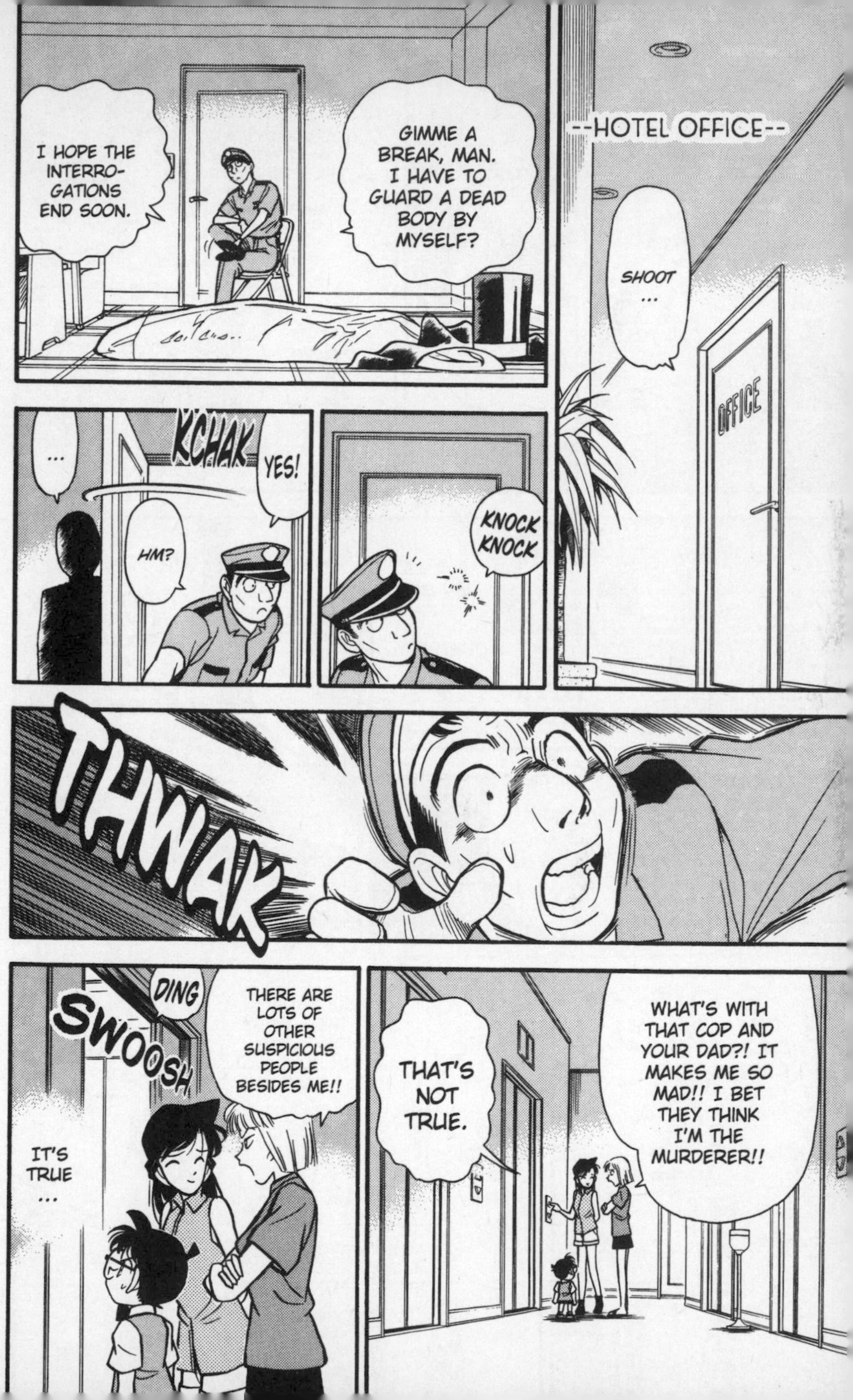
--HOTEL OFFICE--
SHOOT ...
OFFICE
GIMME A BREAK, MAN. I HAVE TO GUARD A DEAD BODY BY MYSELF?
I HOPE THE INTERRO-GATIONS END SOON.
KNOCK KNOCK
KCHAK
YES!
...
HM?
THWAK
WHAT'S WITH THAT COP AND YOUR DAD?! IT MAKES ME SO MAD!! I BET THEY THINK I'M THE MURDERER!!
THAT'S NOT TRUE.
THERE ARE LOTS OF OTHER SUSPICIOUS PEOPLE BESIDES ME!!
DING
SWOOSH
IT'S TRUE ...

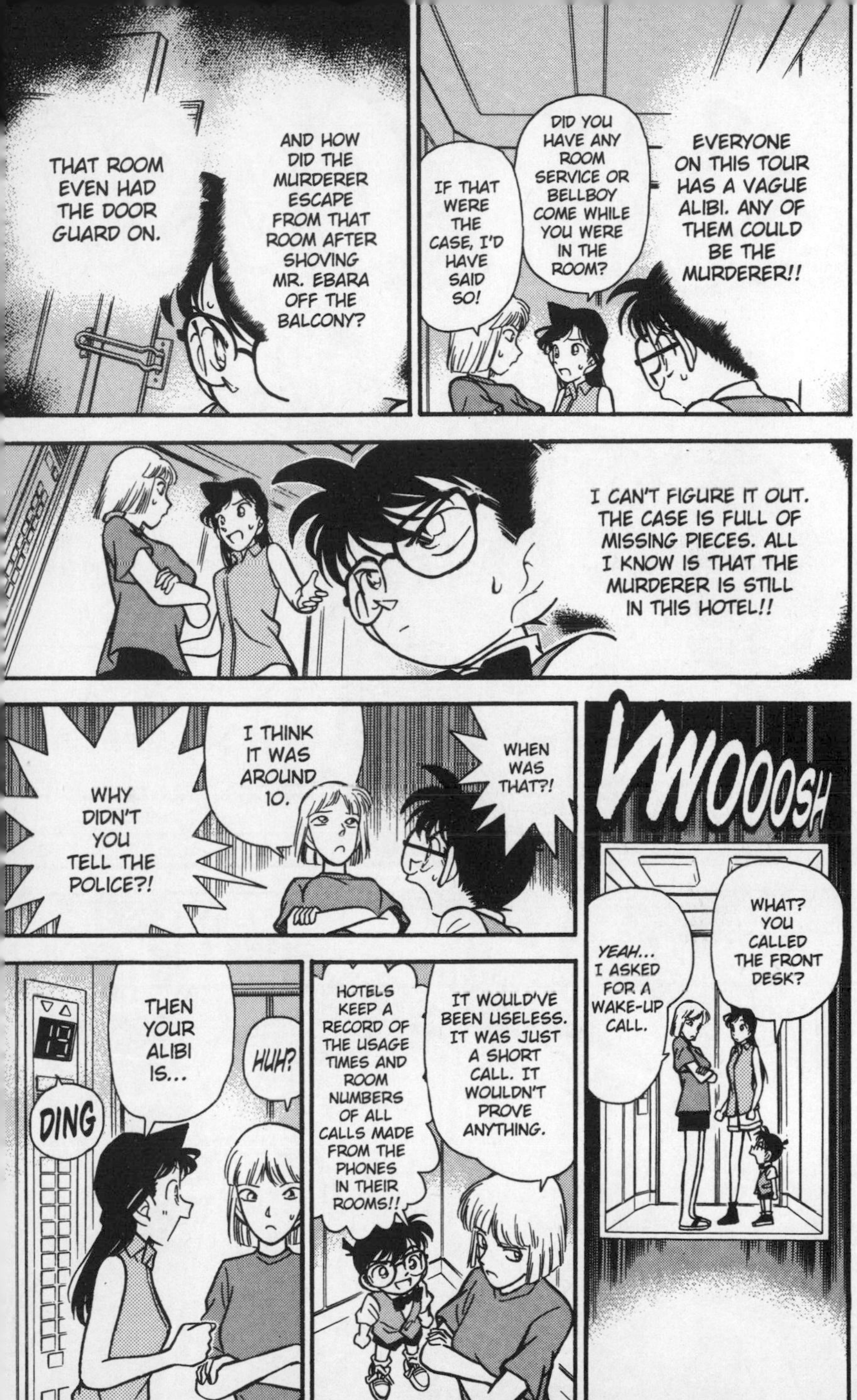
EVERYONE ON THIS TOUR HAS A VAGUE ALIBI. ANY OF THEM COULD BE THE MURDERER!!
DID YOU HAVE ANY ROOM SERVICE OR BELLBOY COME WHILE YOU WERE IN THE ROOM?
IF THAT WERE THE CASE, I'D HAVE SAID SO!
AND HOW DID THE MURDERER ESCAPE FROM THAT ROOM AFTER SHOVING MR. EBARA OFF THE BALCONY?
THAT ROOM EVEN HAD THE DOOR GUARD ON.
I CAN'T FIGURE IT OUT. THE CASE IS FULL OF MISSING PIECES. ALL I KNOW IS THAT THE MURDERER IS STILL IN THIS HOTEL!!
VWOOOSH
WHAT? YOU CALLED THE FRONT DESK?
YEAH... I ASKED FOR A WAKE-UP CALL.
WHEN WAS THAT?!
I THINK IT WAS AROUND 10.
WHY DIDN'T YOU TELL THE POLICE?!
IT WOULD'VE BEEN USELESS. IT WAS JUST A SHORT CALL. IT WOULDN'T PROVE ANYTHING.
HOTELS KEEP A RECORD OF THE USAGE TIMES AND ROOM NUMBERS OF ALL CALLS MADE FROM THE PHONES IN THEIR ROOMS!!
HUH?
THEN YOUR ALIBI IS...
DING

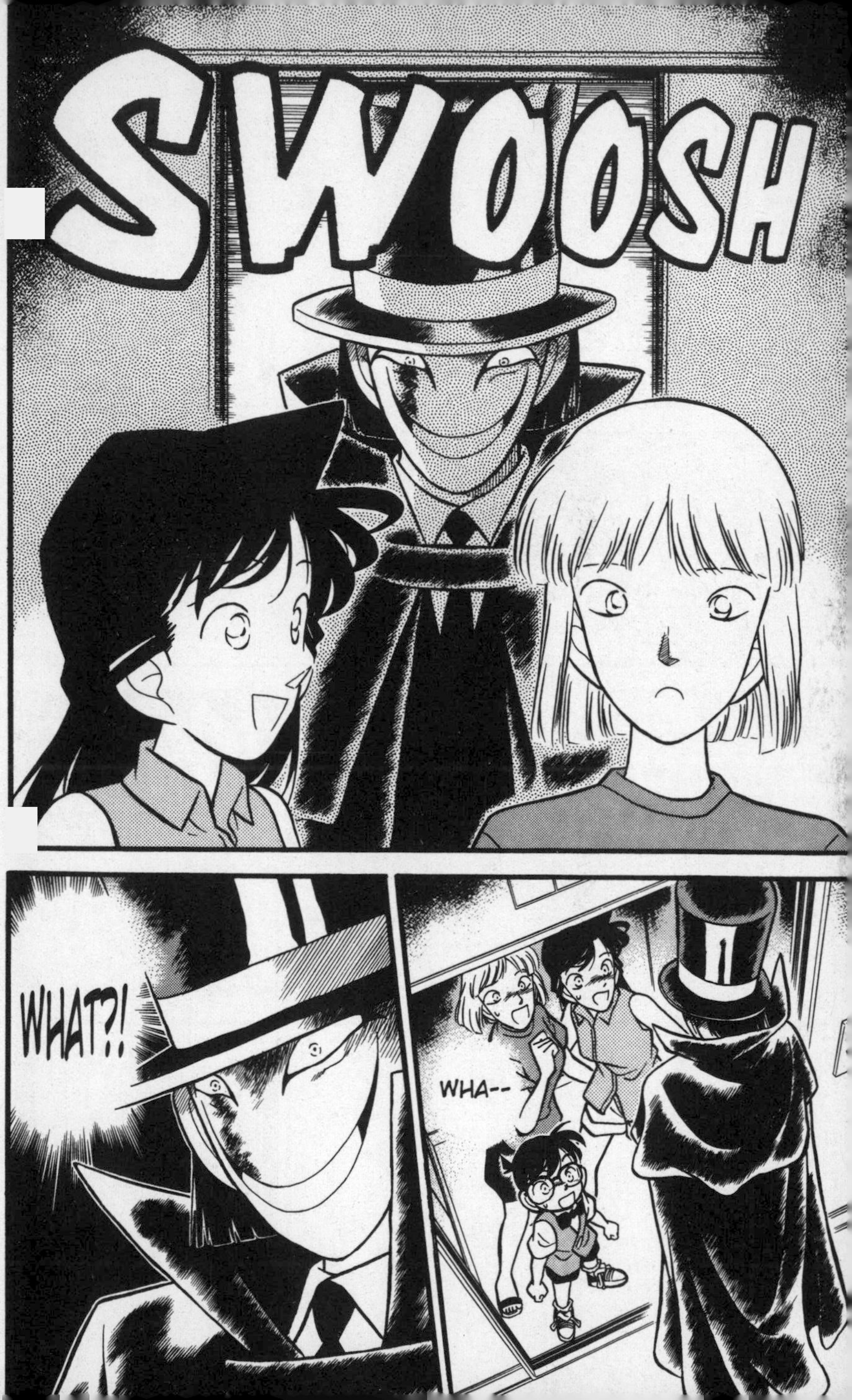
SWOOSH
WHA--
WHAT?!

FILE 5:

RACHEL'S TEARS

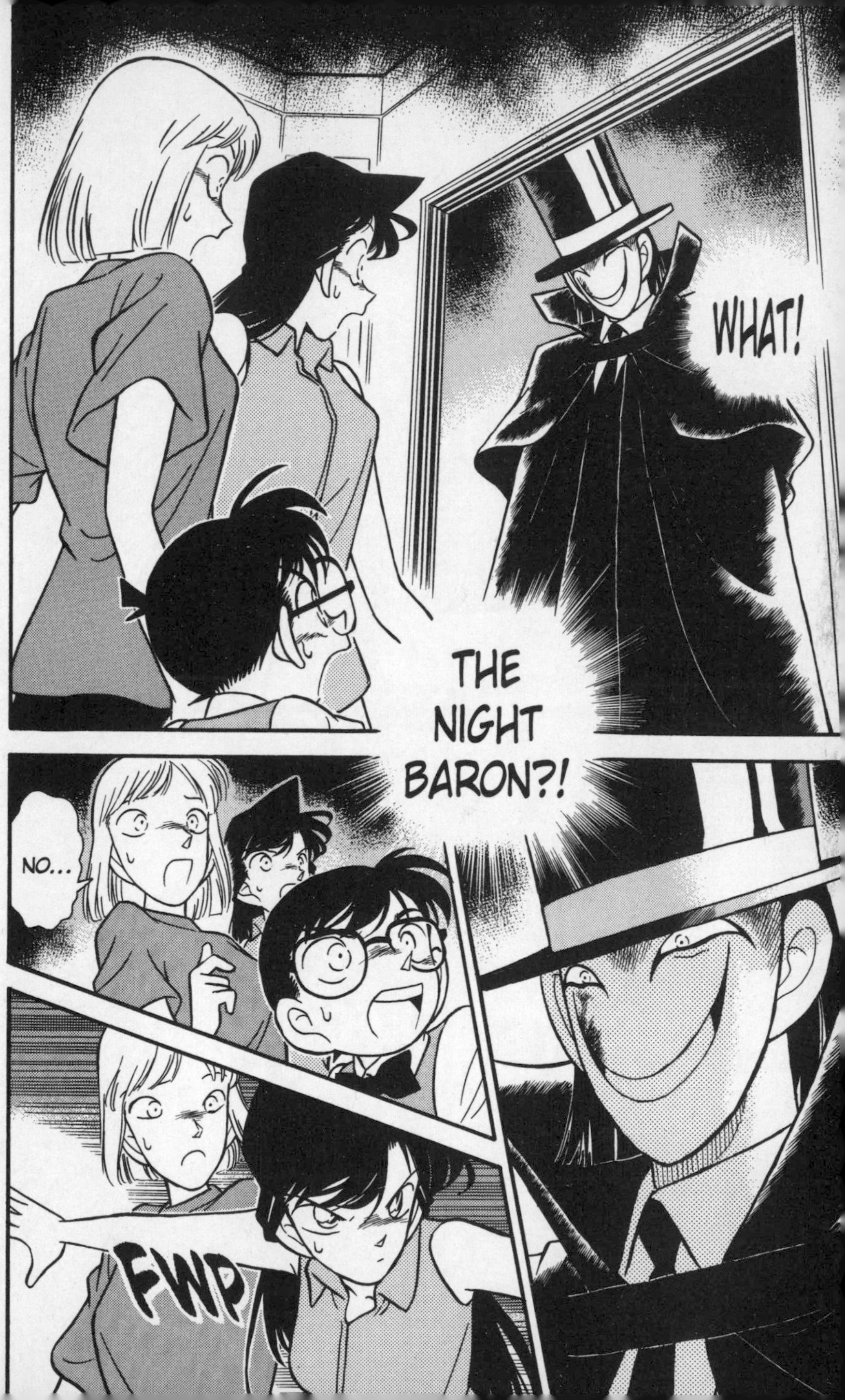
WHAT!
THE NIGHT BARON?!
NO...
FWP

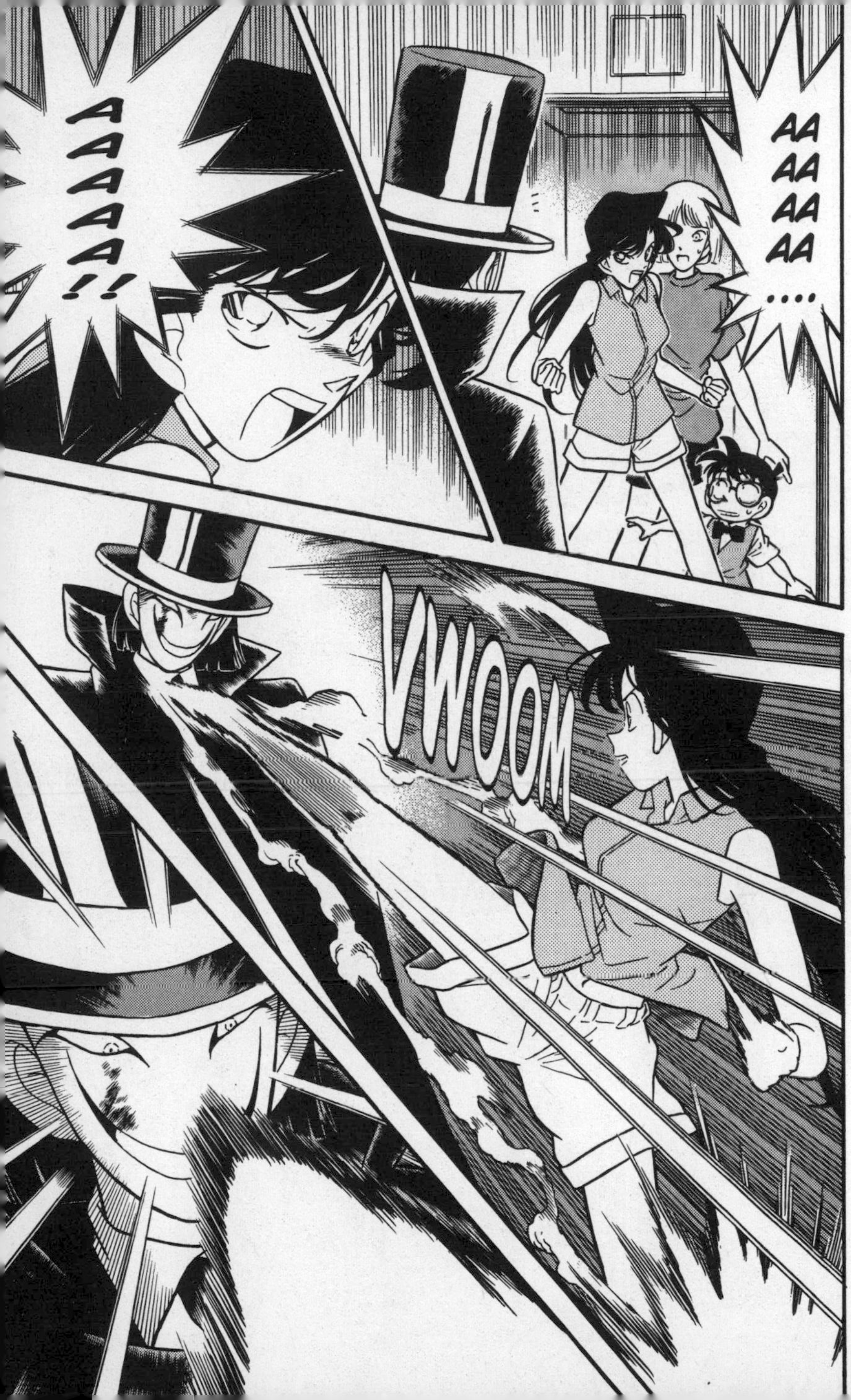
AAAAAAAA....
AAAAAA!!
VWOOM

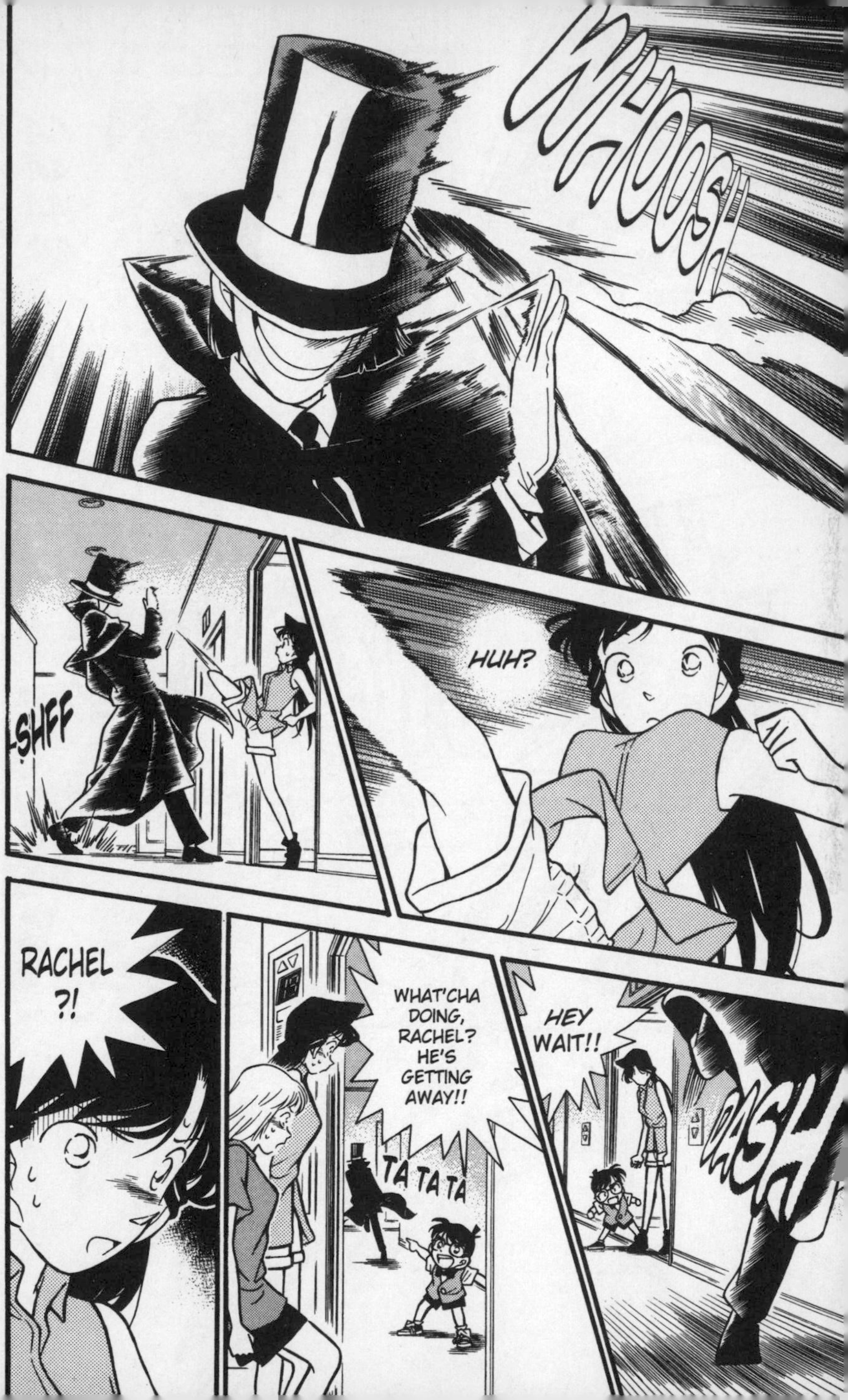
WHOOSH
HUH?
SHFF
HEY WAIT!!
WHAT'CHA DOING, RACHEL? HE'S GETTING AWAY!!
TA TA TA
RACHEL ?!

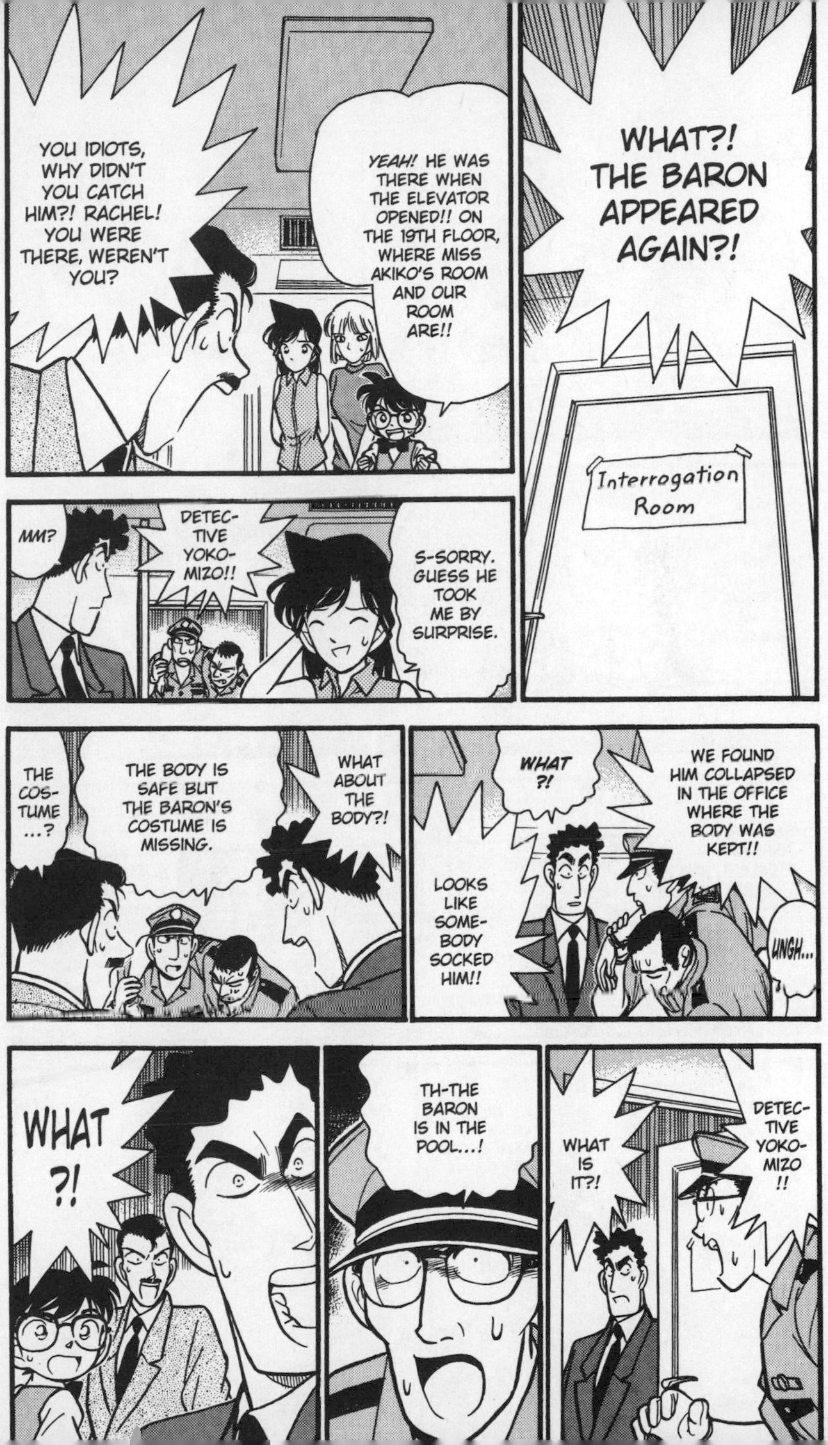
WHAT?! THE BARON APPEARED AGAIN?!
Interrogation Room
YEAH! HE WAS THERE WHEN THE ELEVATOR OPENED!! ON THE 19TH FLOOR, WHERE MISS AKIKO'S ROOM AND OUR ROOM ARE!!
YOU IDIOTS, WHY DIDN'T YOU CATCH HIM?! RACHEL! YOU WERE THERE, WEREN'T YOU?
S-SORRY. GUESS HE TOOK ME BY SURPRISE.
DETECTIVE YOKOMIZO!!
MM?
WE FOUND HIM COLLAPSED IN THE OFFICE WHERE THE BODY WAS KEPT!!
WHAT ?!
LOOKS LIKE SOMEBODY SOCKED HIM!!
UNGH...
WHAT ABOUT THE BODY?!
THE BODY IS SAFE BUT THE BARON'S COSTUME IS MISSING.
THE COSTUME ...?
DETECTIVE YOKOMIZO !!
WHAT IS IT?!
TH-THE BARON IS IN THE POOL...!
WHAT ?!

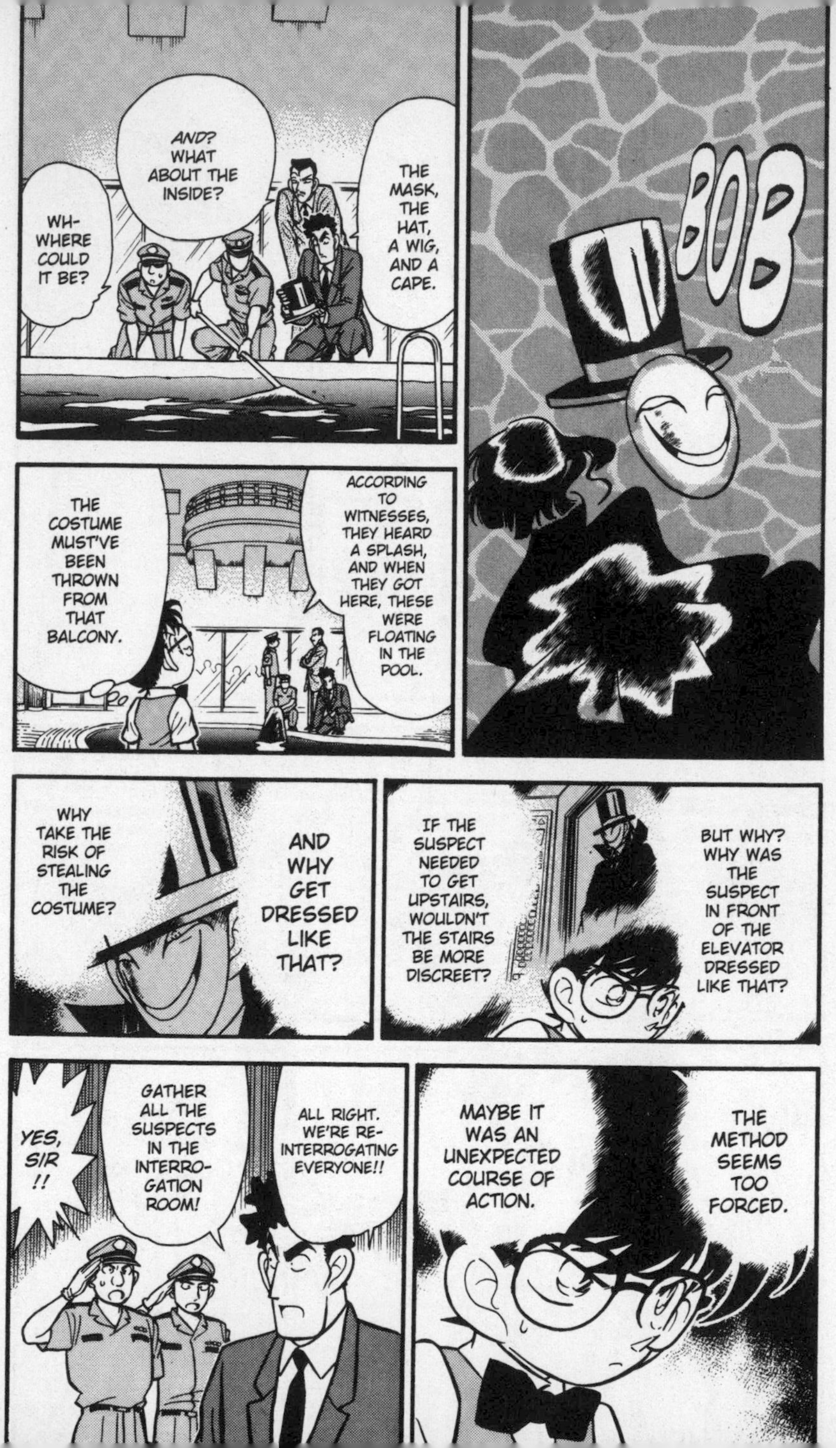
BOB
THE MASK, THE HAT, A WIG, AND A CAPE.
AND? WHAT ABOUT THE INSIDE?
WH-WHERE COULD IT BE?
ACCORDING TO WITNESSES, THEY HEARD A SPLASH, AND WHEN THEY GOT HERE, THESE WERE FLOATING IN THE POOL.
THE COSTUME MUST'VE BEEN THROWN FROM THAT BALCONY.
BUT WHY? WHY WAS THE SUSPECT IN FRONT OF THE ELEVATOR DRESSED LIKE THAT?
IF THE SUSPECT NEEDED TO GET UPSTAIRS, WOULDN'T THE STAIRS BE MORE DISCREET?
AND WHY GET DRESSED LIKE THAT?
WHY TAKE THE RISK OF STEALING THE COSTUME?
THE METHOD SEEMS TOO FORCED.
MAYBE IT WAS AN UNEXPECTED COURSE OF ACTION.
ALL RIGHT. WE'RE RE-INTERROGATING EVERYONE!!
GATHER ALL THE SUSPECTS IN THE INTERRO-GATION ROOM!
YES, SIR!!

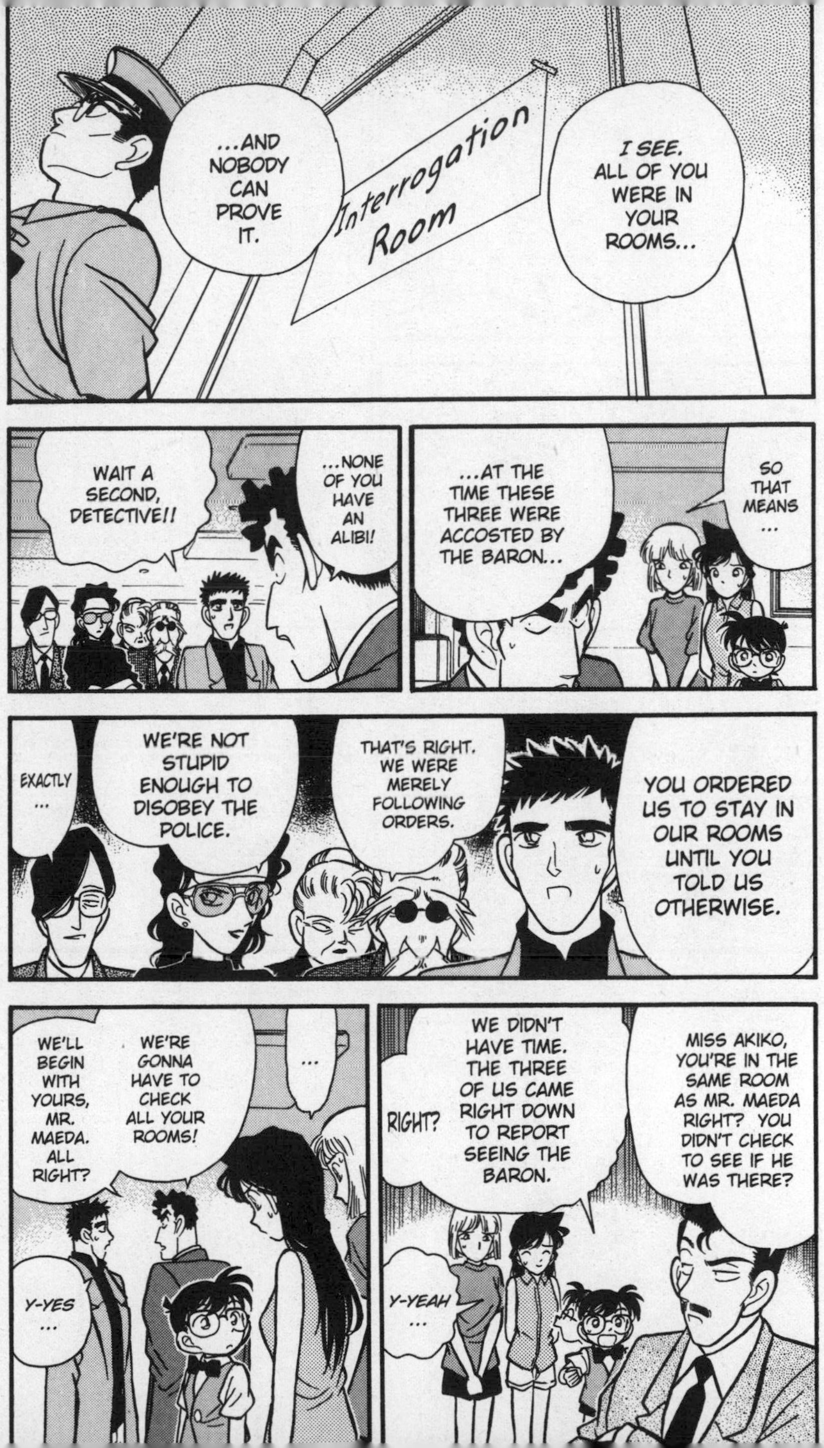
I SEE. ALL OF YOU WERE IN YOUR ROOMS...
Interrogation Room
...AND NOBODY CAN PROVE IT.
SO THAT MEANS...
...AT THE TIME THESE THREE WERE ACCOSTED BY THE BARON...
...NONE OF YOU HAVE AN ALIBI!
WAIT A SECOND, DETECTIVE!!
YOU ORDERED US TO STAY IN OUR ROOMS UNTIL YOU TOLD US OTHERWISE.
THAT'S RIGHT. WE WERE MERELY FOLLOWING ORDERS.
WE'RE NOT STUPID ENOUGH TO DISOBEY THE POLICE.
EXACTLY...
MISS AKIKO, YOU'RE IN THE SAME ROOM AS MR. MAEDA RIGHT? YOU DIDN'T CHECK TO SEE IF HE WAS THERE?
WE DIDN'T HAVE TIME. THE THREE OF US CAME RIGHT DOWN TO REPORT SEEING THE BARON.
RIGHT?
Y-YEAH...
...
WE'RE GONNA HAVE TO CHECK ALL YOUR ROOMS!
WE'LL BEGIN WITH YOURS, MR. MAEDA. ALL RIGHT?
Y-YES...

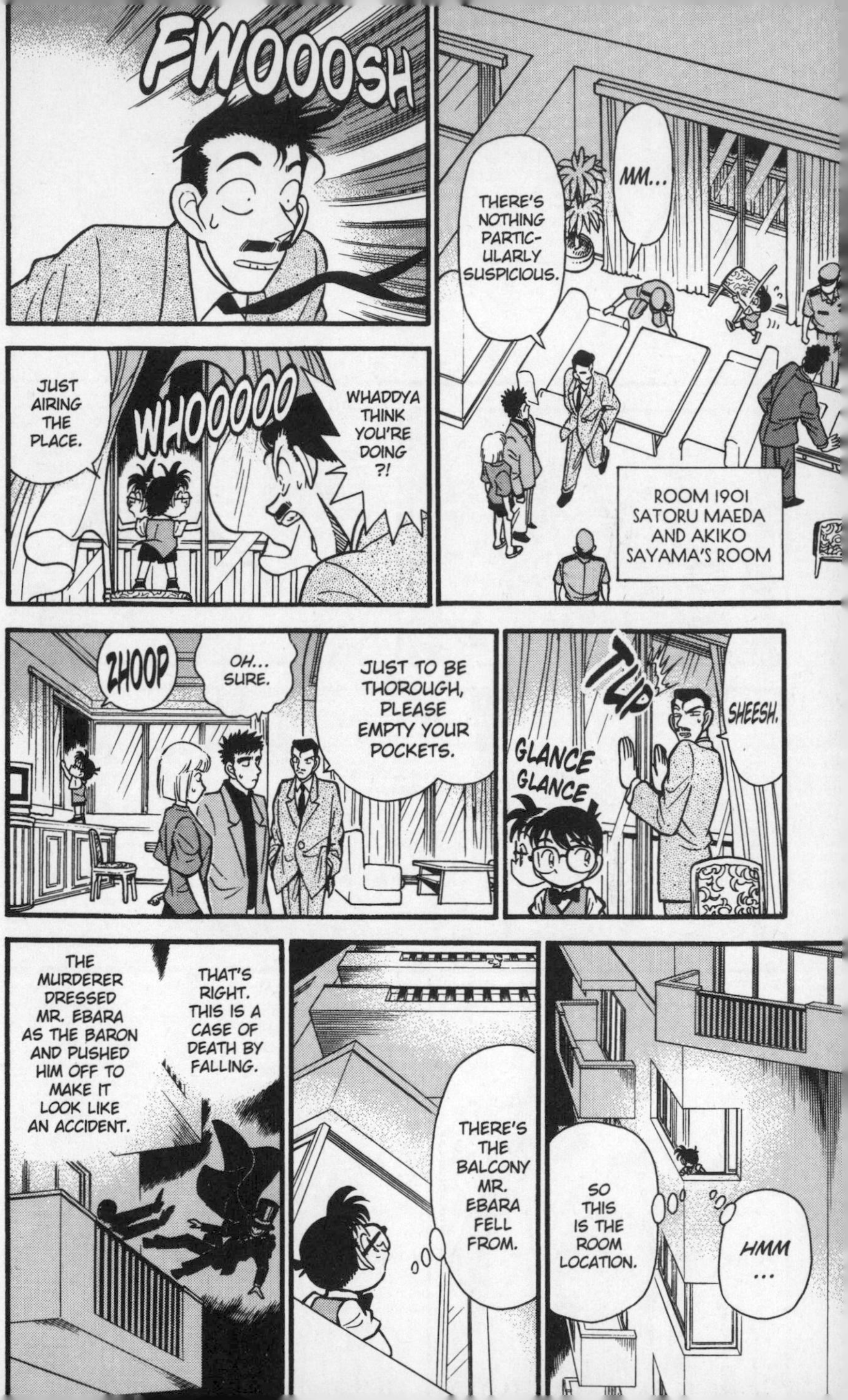
MM...
THERE'S NOTHING PARTICULARLY SUSPICIOUS.
ROOM 1901 SATORU MAEDA AND AKIKO SAYAMA'S ROOM
FWOOOSH
WHADDYA THINK YOU'RE DOING ?!
WHOOOOO
JUST AIRING THE PLACE.
TUP
SHEESH.
GLANCE GLANCE
JUST TO BE THOROUGH, PLEASE EMPTY YOUR POCKETS.
OH... SURE.
ZHOOP
HMM ...
SO THIS IS THE ROOM LOCATION.
THERE'S THE BALCONY MR. EBARA FELL FROM.
THAT'S RIGHT. THIS IS A CASE OF DEATH BY FALLING.
THE MURDERER DRESSED MR. EBARA AS THE BARON AND PUSHED HIM OFF TO MAKE IT LOOK LIKE AN ACCIDENT.

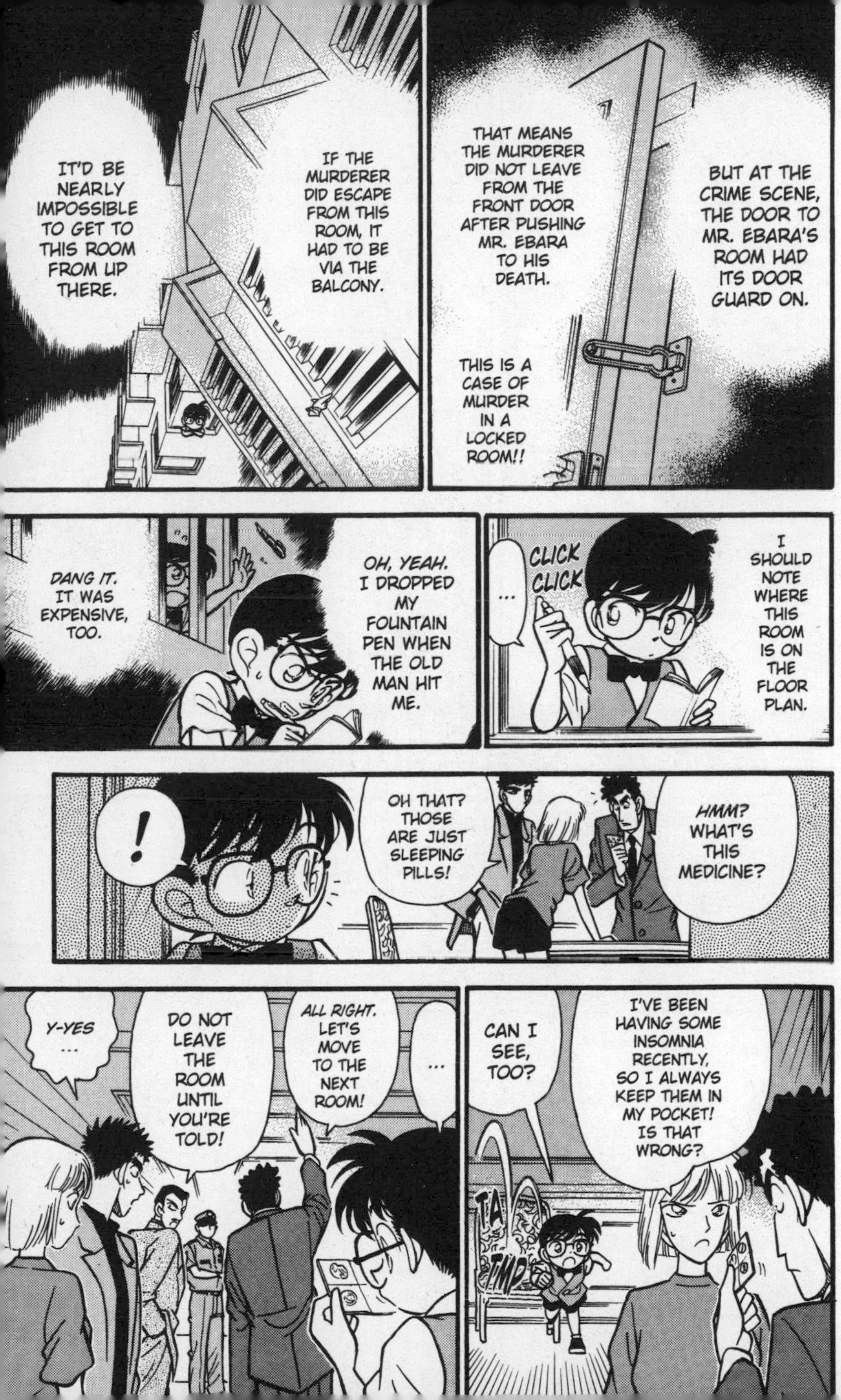
BUT AT THE CRIME SCENE, THE DOOR TO MR. EBARA'S ROOM HAD ITS DOOR GUARD ON.
THAT MEANS THE MURDERER DID NOT LEAVE FROM THE FRONT DOOR AFTER PUSHING MR. EBARA TO HIS DEATH.
THIS IS A CASE OF MURDER IN A LOCKED ROOM!!
IF THE MURDERER DID ESCAPE FROM THIS ROOM, IT HAD TO BE VIA THE BALCONY.
IT'D BE NEARLY IMPOSSIBLE TO GET TO THIS ROOM FROM UP THERE.
I SHOULD NOTE WHERE THIS ROOM IS ON THE FLOOR PLAN.
CLICK CLICK
...
OH, YEAH. I DROPPED MY FOUNTAIN PEN WHEN THE OLD MAN HIT ME.
DANG IT. IT WAS EXPENSIVE, TOO.
HMM? WHAT'S THIS MEDICINE?
OH THAT? THOSE ARE JUST SLEEPING PILLS!
!
I'VE BEEN HAVING SOME INSOMNIA RECENTLY, SO I ALWAYS KEEP THEM IN MY POCKET! IS THAT WRONG?
CAN I SEE, TOO?
TA
TMP
...
ALL RIGHT. LET'S MOVE TO THE NEXT ROOM!
DO NOT LEAVE THE ROOM UNTIL YOU'RE TOLD!
Y-YES ...

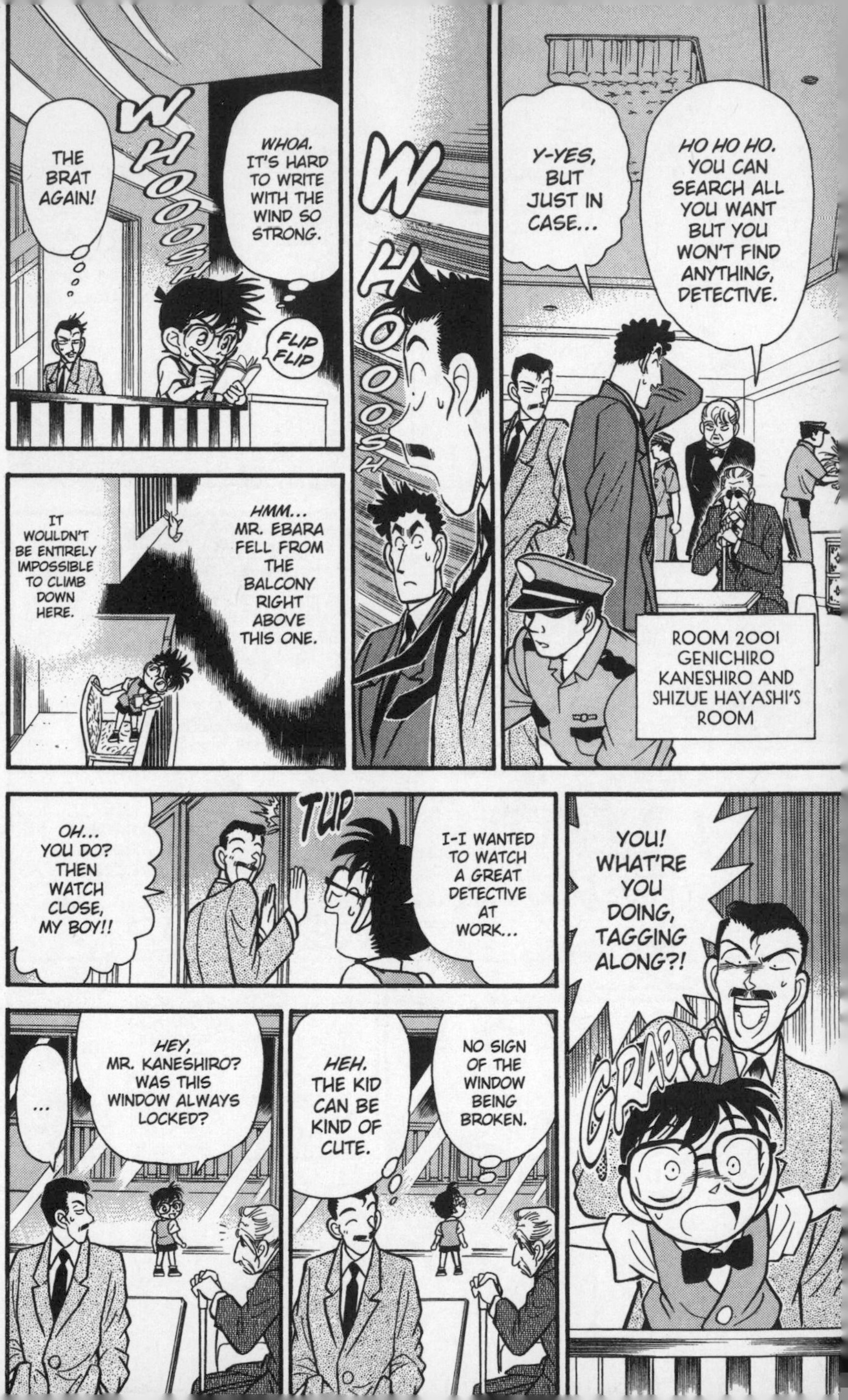
HO HO HO. YOU CAN SEARCH ALL YOU WANT BUT YOU WON'T FIND ANYTHING, DETECTIVE.
Y-YES, BUT JUST IN CASE...
ROOM 2001 GENICHIRO KANESHIRO AND SHIZUE HAYASHI'S ROOM
WHOOOOSH
WHOA. IT'S HARD TO WRITE WITH THE WIND SO STRONG.
WHOOOOSH
FLIP FLIP
THE BRAT AGAIN!
HMM... MR. EBARA FELL FROM THE BALCONY RIGHT ABOVE THIS ONE.
IT WOULDN'T BE ENTIRELY IMPOSSIBLE TO CLIMB DOWN HERE.
YOU! WHAT'RE YOU DOING, TAGGING ALONG?!
GRAB
TUP
I-I WANTED TO WATCH A GREAT DETECTIVE AT WORK...
OH... YOU DO? THEN WATCH CLOSE, MY BOY!!
NO SIGN OF THE WINDOW BEING BROKEN.
HEH. THE KID CAN BE KIND OF CUTE.
HEY, MR. KANESHIRO? WAS THIS WINDOW ALWAYS LOCKED?
...

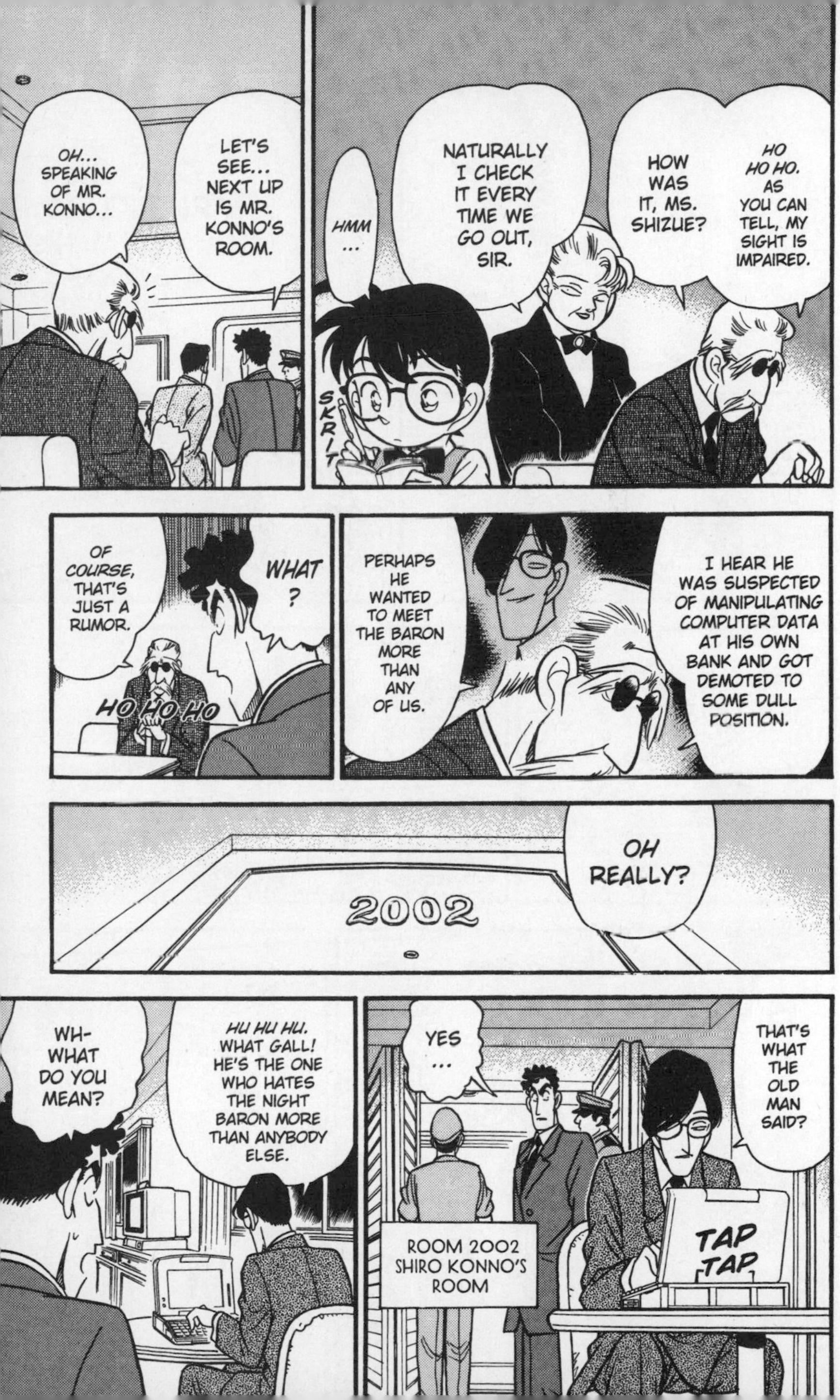
HO HO HO. AS YOU CAN TELL, MY SIGHT IS IMPAIRED.
HOW WAS IT, MS. SHIZUE?
NATURALLY I CHECK IT EVERY TIME WE GO OUT, SIR.
HMM...
SKRIT
LET'S SEE... NEXT UP IS MR. KONNO'S ROOM.
OH... SPEAKING OF MR. KONNO...
I HEAR HE WAS SUSPECTED OF MANIPULATING COMPUTER DATA AT HIS OWN BANK AND GOT DEMOTED TO SOME DULL POSITION.
PERHAPS HE WANTED TO MEET THE BARON MORE THAN ANY OF US.
WHAT?
OF COURSE, THAT'S JUST A RUMOR.
HO HO HO
OH REALLY?
2002
THAT'S WHAT THE OLD MAN SAID?
YES...
TAP TAP
ROOM 2002 SHIRO KONNO'S ROOM
HU HU HU. WHAT GALL! HE'S THE ONE WHO HATES THE NIGHT BARON MORE THAN ANYBODY ELSE.
WH- WHAT DO YOU MEAN?

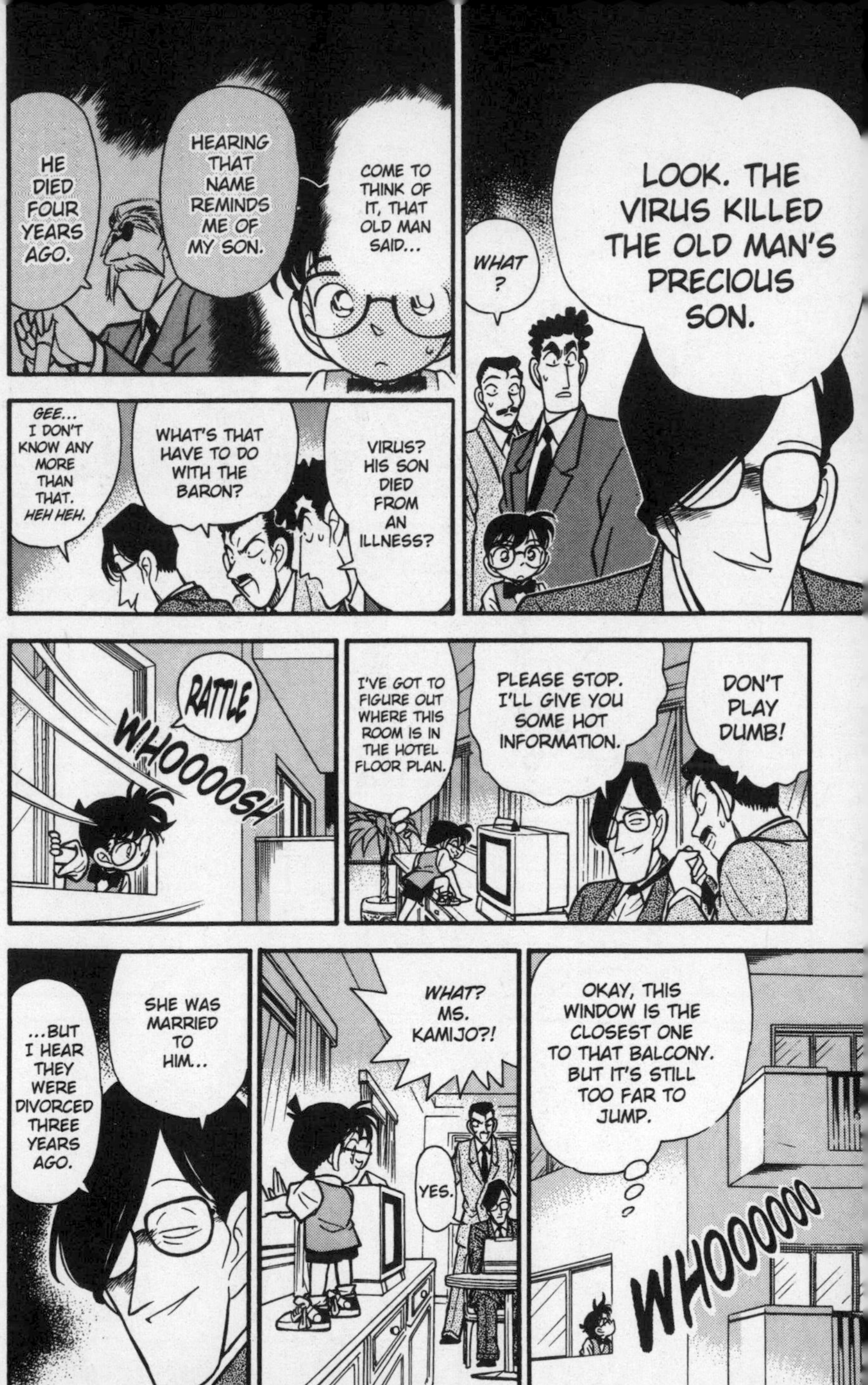
LOOK. THE VIRUS KILLED THE OLD MAN'S PRECIOUS SON.
WHAT?
COME TO THINK OF IT, THAT OLD MAN SAID...
HEARING THAT NAME REMINDS ME OF MY SON.
HE DIED FOUR YEARS AGO.
VIRUS? HIS SON DIED FROM AN ILLNESS?
WHAT'S THAT HAVE TO DO WITH THE BARON?
GEE... I DON'T KNOW ANY MORE THAN THAT. HEH HEH.
DON'T PLAY DUMB!
PLEASE STOP. I'LL GIVE YOU SOME HOT INFORMATION.
I'VE GOT TO FIGURE OUT WHERE THIS ROOM IS IN THE HOTEL FLOOR PLAN.
RATTLE
WHOOOOOSH
OKAY, THIS WINDOW IS THE CLOSEST ONE TO THAT BALCONY. BUT IT'S STILL TOO FAR TO JUMP.
WHOOOOOO
WHAT? MS. KAMIJO?!
YES.
SHE WAS MARRIED TO HIM...
...BUT I HEAR THEY WERE DIVORCED THREE YEARS AGO.

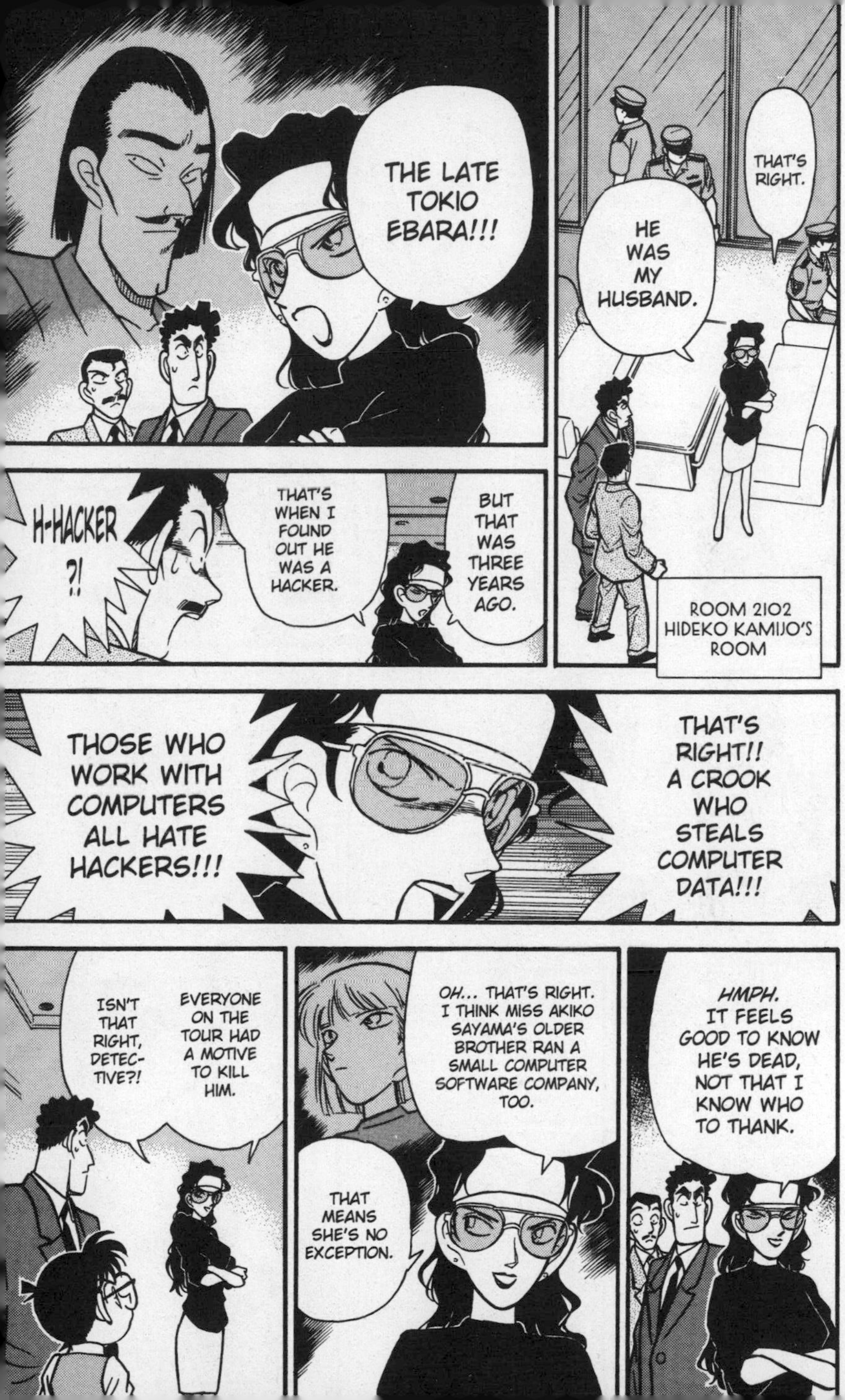
ROOM 2102 HIDEKO KAMIJO'S ROOM
THAT'S RIGHT.
HE WAS MY HUSBAND.
THE LATE TOKIO EBARA!!!
BUT THAT WAS THREE YEARS AGO.
THAT'S WHEN I FOUND OUT HE WAS A HACKER.
H-HACKER ?!
THAT'S RIGHT!! A CROOK WHO STEALS COMPUTER DATA!!!
THOSE WHO WORK WITH COMPUTERS ALL HATE HACKERS!!!
HMPH. IT FEELS GOOD TO KNOW HE'S DEAD, NOT THAT I KNOW WHO TO THANK.
OH... THAT'S RIGHT. I THINK MISS AKIKO SAYAMA'S OLDER BROTHER RAN A SMALL COMPUTER SOFTWARE COMPANY, TOO.
THAT MEANS SHE'S NO EXCEPTION.
EVERYONE ON THE TOUR HAD A MOTIVE TO KILL HIM.
ISN'T THAT RIGHT, DETECTIVE?!

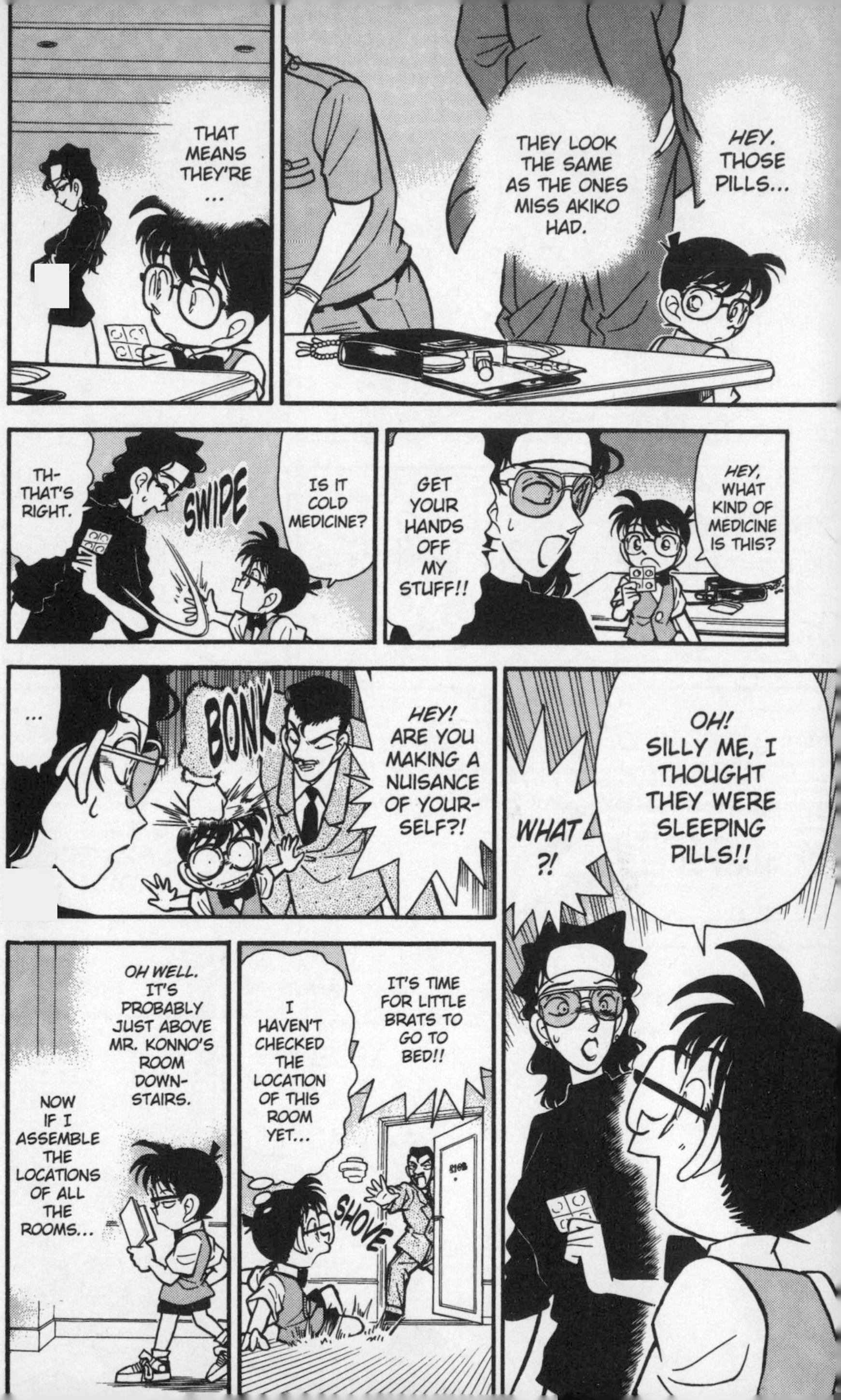
HEY. THOSE PILLS...
THEY LOOK THE SAME AS THE ONES MISS AKIKO HAD.
THAT MEANS THEY'RE ...
HEY, WHAT KIND OF MEDICINE IS THIS?
GET YOUR HANDS OFF MY STUFF!!
IS IT COLD MEDICINE?
SWIPE
TH-THAT'S RIGHT.
OH! SILLY ME, I THOUGHT THEY WERE SLEEPING PILLS!!
WHAT ?!
HEY! ARE YOU MAKING A NUISANCE OF YOUR-SELF?!
BONK
...
IT'S TIME FOR LITTLE BRATS TO GO TO BED!!
I HAVEN'T CHECKED THE LOCATION OF THIS ROOM YET...
SHOVE
OH WELL. IT'S PROBABLY JUST ABOVE MR. KONNO'S ROOM DOWN-STAIRS.
NOW IF I ASSEMBLE THE LOCATIONS OF ALL THE ROOMS...

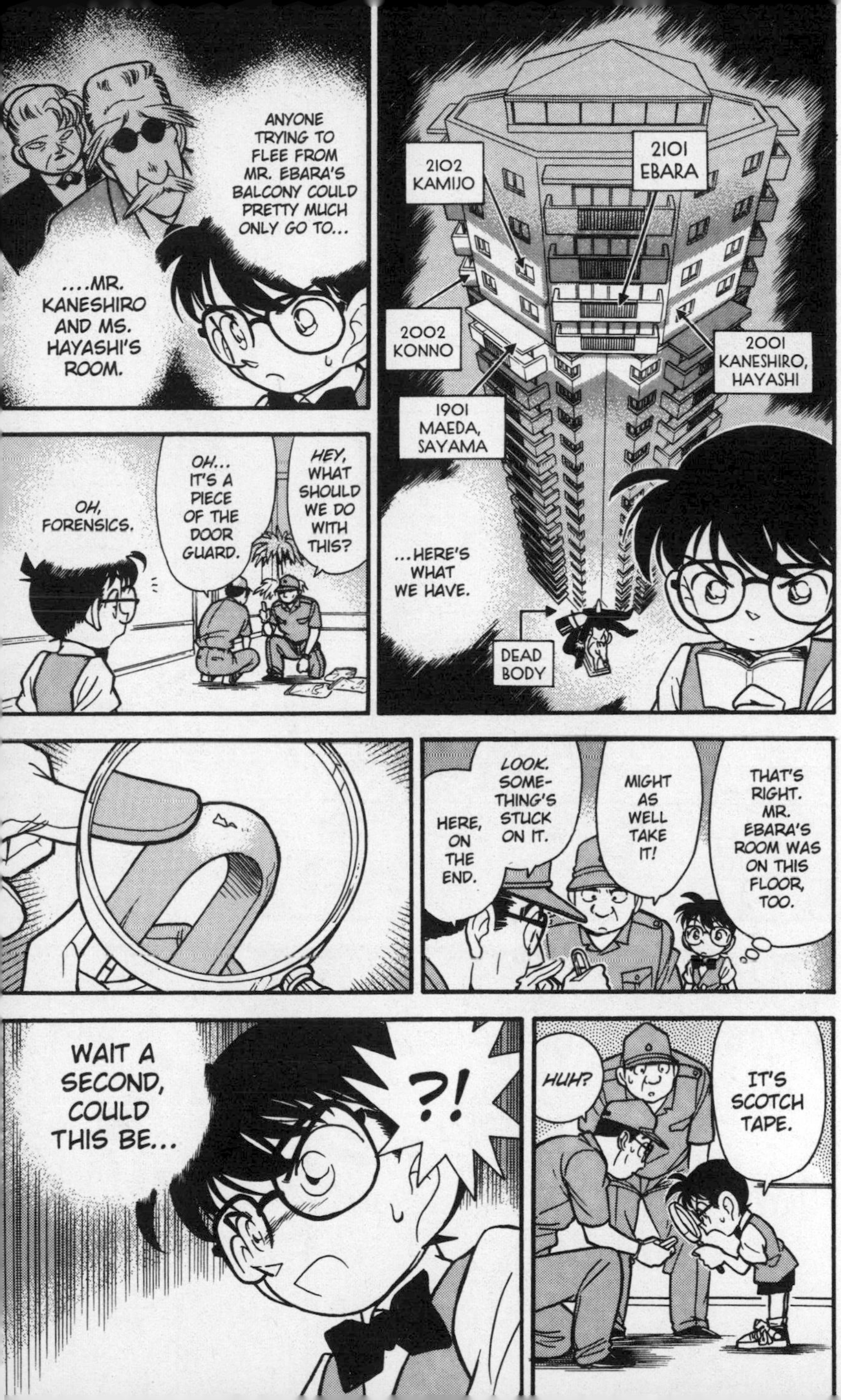
2101 EBARA
2102 KAMIJO
2001 KANESHIRO, HAYASHI
2002 KONNO
1901 MAEDA, SAYAMA
...HERE'S WHAT WE HAVE.
DEAD BODY
ANYONE TRYING TO FLEE FROM MR. EBARA'S BALCONY COULD PRETTY MUCH ONLY GO TO...
....MR. KANESHIRO AND MS. HAYASHI'S ROOM.
HEY, WHAT SHOULD WE DO WITH THIS?
OH... IT'S A PIECE OF THE DOOR GUARD.
OH, FORENSICS.
THAT'S RIGHT. MR. EBARA'S ROOM WAS ON THIS FLOOR, TOO.
MIGHT AS WELL TAKE IT!
LOOK. SOMETHING'S STUCK ON IT.
HERE, ON THE END.
IT'S SCOTCH TAPE.
HUH?
?!
WAIT A SECOND, COULD THIS BE...

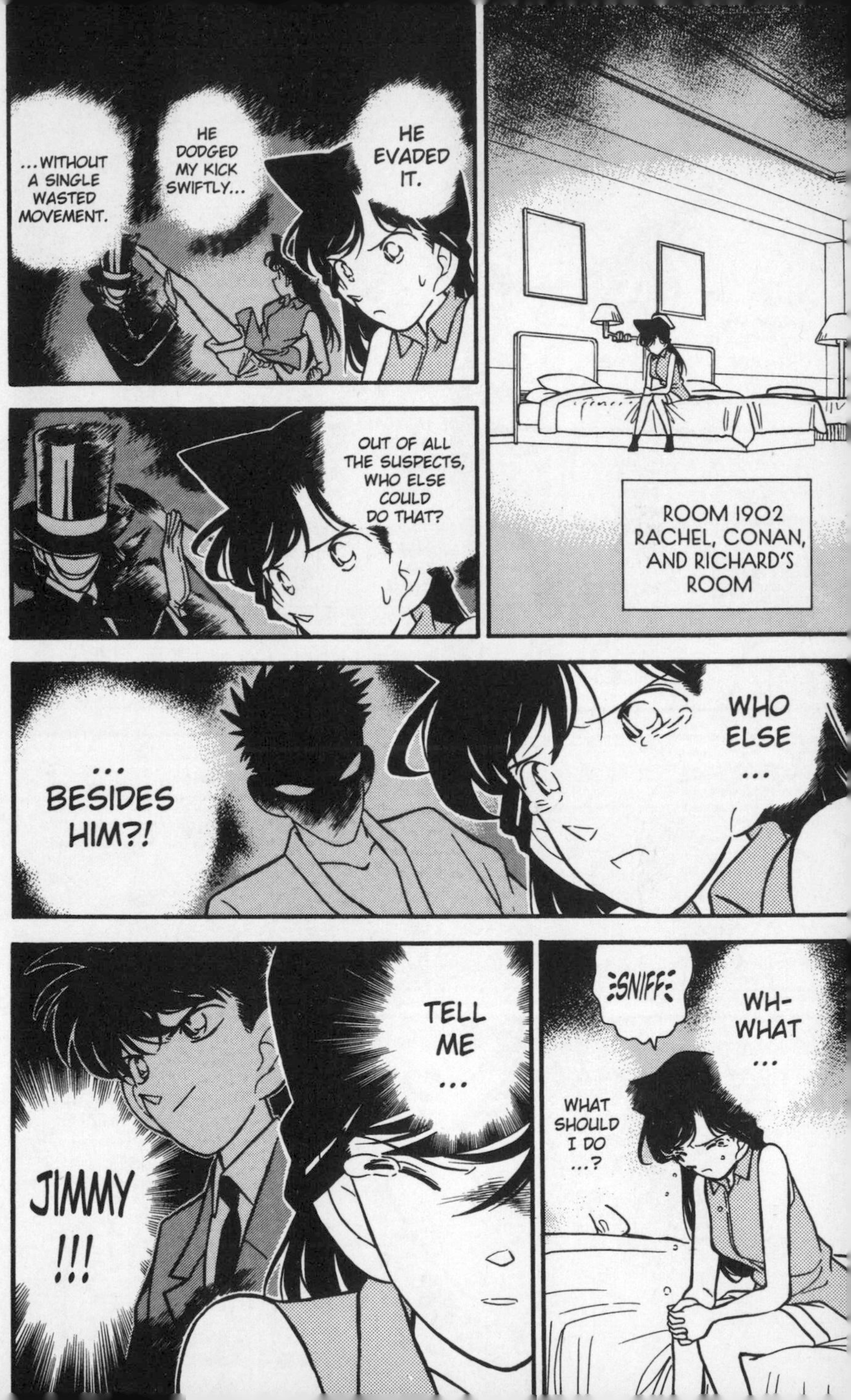
ROOM 1902 RACHEL, CONAN, AND RICHARD'S ROOM
HE EVADED IT.
HE DODGED MY KICK SWIFTLY...
...WITHOUT A SINGLE WASTED MOVEMENT.
OUT OF ALL THE SUSPECTS, WHO ELSE COULD DO THAT?
WHO ELSE ...
... BESIDES HIM?!
SNIFF
WH- WHAT ...
WHAT SHOULD I DO ...?
TELL ME ...
JIMMY !!!

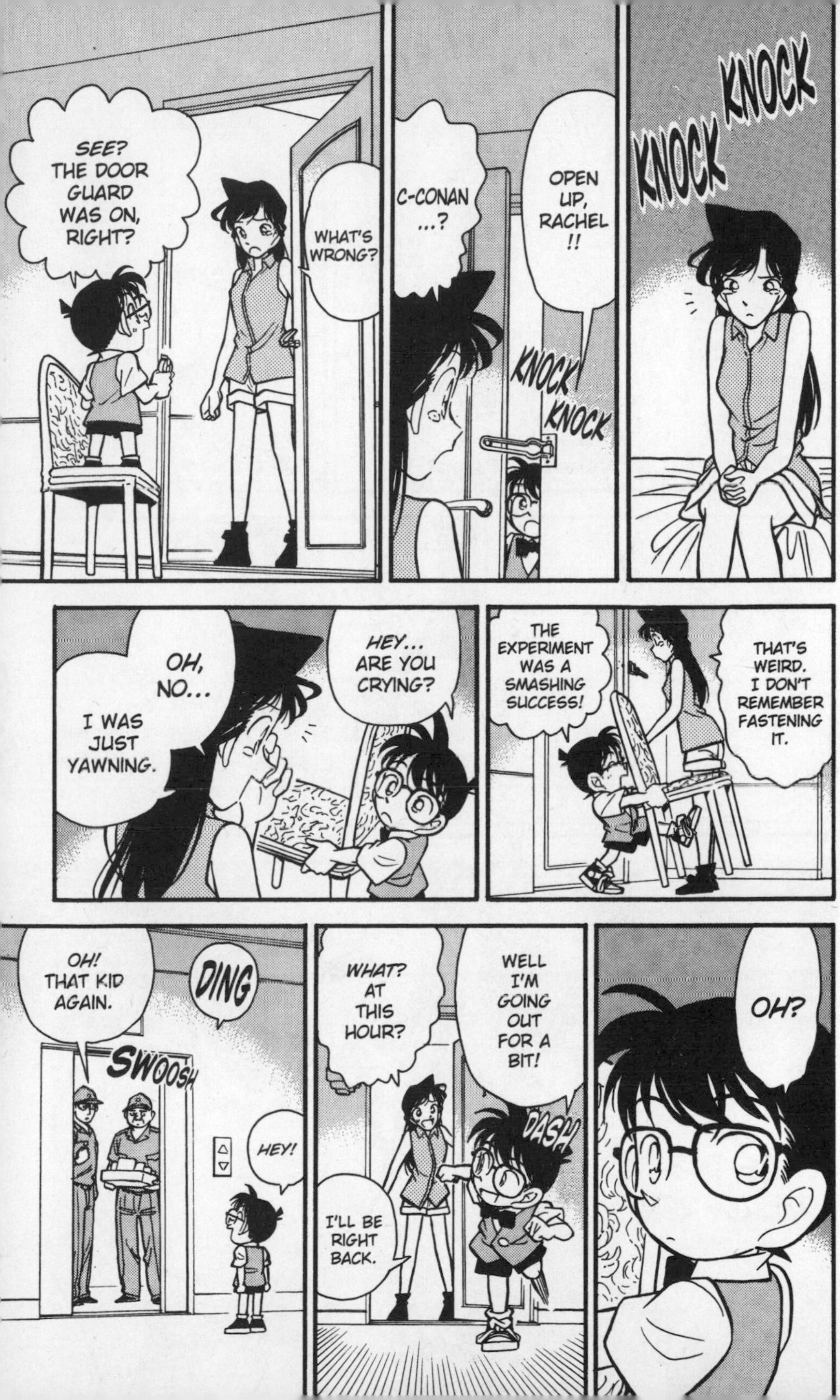
KNOCK
KNOCK
OPEN UP, RACHEL!!
C-CONAN ...?
KNOCK
KNOCK
WHAT'S WRONG?
SEE? THE DOOR GUARD WAS ON, RIGHT?
THAT'S WEIRD. I DON'T REMEMBER FASTENING IT.
THE EXPERIMENT WAS A SMASHING SUCCESS!
HEY... ARE YOU CRYING?
OH, NO...
I WAS JUST YAWNING.
OH?
WELL I'M GOING OUT FOR A BIT!
WHAT? AT THIS HOUR?
DASH
I'LL BE RIGHT BACK.
DING
OH! THAT KID AGAIN.
SWOOSH
HEY!

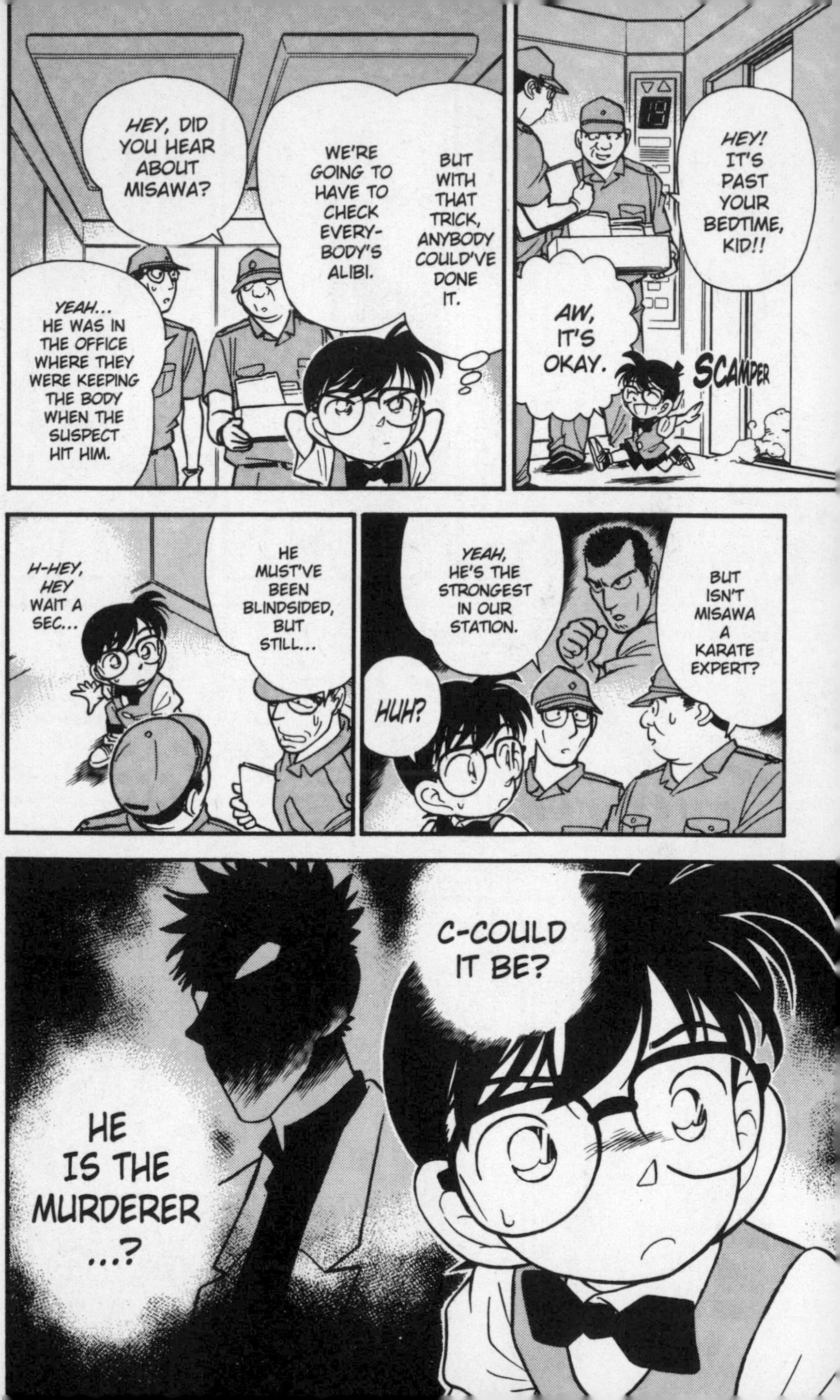
HEY! IT'S PAST YOUR BEDTIME, KID!!
AW, IT'S OKAY.
SCAMPER
BUT WITH THAT TRICK, ANYBODY COULD'VE DONE IT.
WE'RE GOING TO HAVE TO CHECK EVERY-BODY'S ALIBI.
HEY, DID YOU HEAR ABOUT MISAWA?
YEAH... HE WAS IN THE OFFICE WHERE THEY WERE KEEPING THE BODY WHEN THE SUSPECT HIT HIM.
BUT ISN'T MISAWA A KARATE EXPERT?
YEAH, HE'S THE STRONGEST IN OUR STATION.
HUH?
HE MUST'VE BEEN BLINDSIDED, BUT STILL...
H-HEY, HEY WAIT A SEC...
C-COULD IT BE?
HE IS THE MURDERER ...?

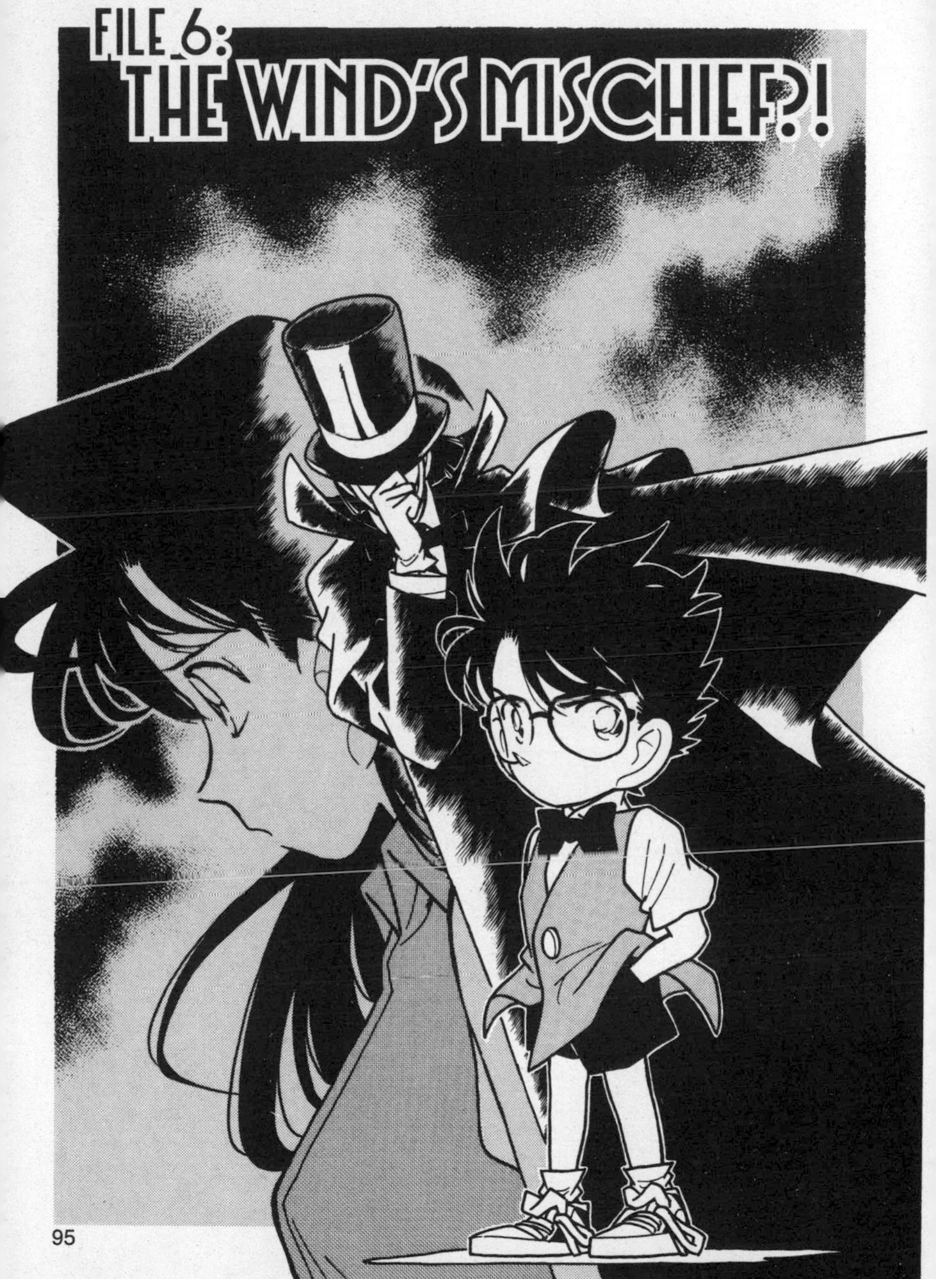
FILE 6:
THE WIND'S MISCHIEF?!

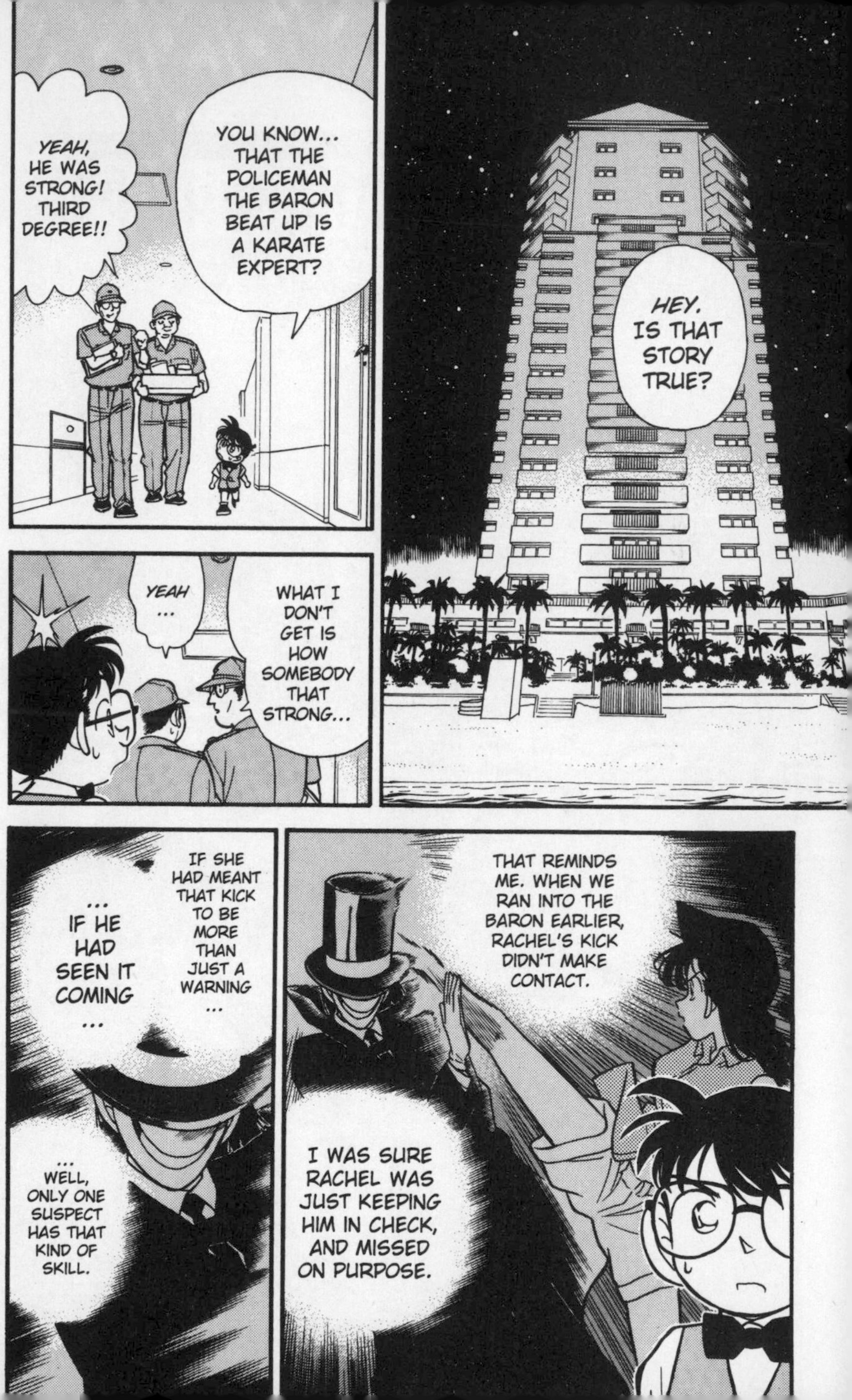
HEY. IS THAT STORY TRUE?
YOU KNOW... THAT THE POLICEMAN THE BARON BEAT UP IS A KARATE EXPERT?
YEAH, HE WAS STRONG! THIRD DEGREE!!
WHAT I DON'T GET IS HOW SOMEBODY THAT STRONG...
YEAH ...
THAT REMINDS ME. WHEN WE RAN INTO THE BARON EARLIER, RACHEL'S KICK DIDN'T MAKE CONTACT.
I WAS SURE RACHEL WAS JUST KEEPING HIM IN CHECK, AND MISSED ON PURPOSE.
IF SHE HAD MEANT THAT KICK TO BE MORE THAN JUST A WARNING ...
... IF HE HAD SEEN IT COMING ...
... WELL, ONLY ONE SUSPECT HAS THAT KIND OF SKILL.

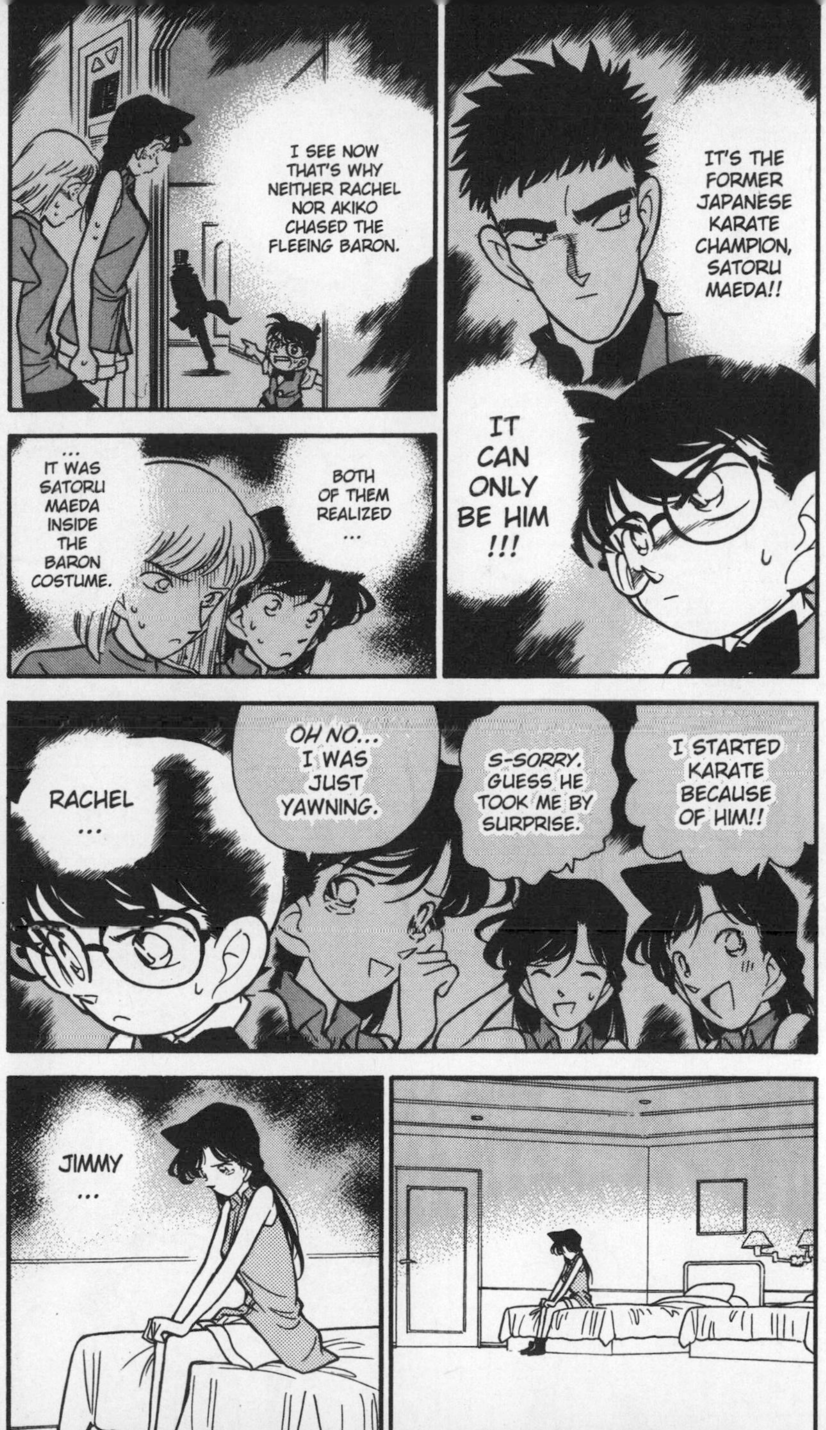
IT'S THE FORMER JAPANESE KARATE CHAMPION, SATORU MAEDA!!
IT CAN ONLY BE HIM !!!
I SEE NOW THAT'S WHY NEITHER RACHEL NOR AKIKO CHASED THE FLEEING BARON.
BOTH OF THEM REALIZED ...
... IT WAS SATORU MAEDA INSIDE THE BARON COSTUME.
I STARTED KARATE BECAUSE OF HIM!!
S-SORRY. GUESS HE TOOK ME BY SURPRISE.
OH NO... I WAS JUST YAWNING.
RACHEL ...
JIMMY ...

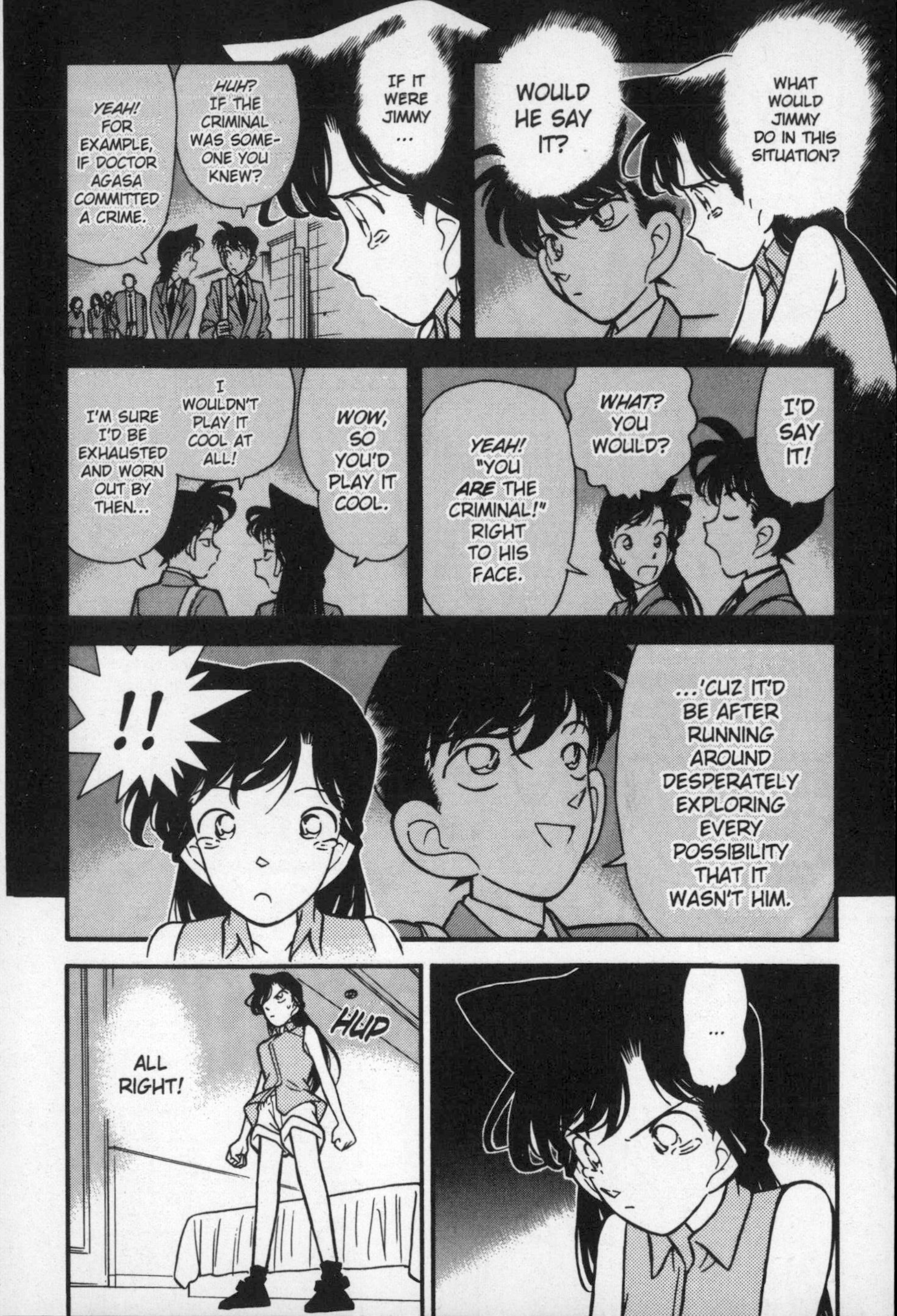
WHAT WOULD JIMMY DO IN THIS SITUATION?
WOULD HE SAY IT?
IF IT WERE JIMMY ...
HUH? IF THE CRIMINAL WAS SOME-ONE YOU KNEW?
YEAH! FOR EXAMPLE, IF DOCTOR AGASA COMMITTED A CRIME.
I'D SAY IT!
WHAT? YOU WOULD?
YEAH! "YOU ARE THE CRIMINAL!" RIGHT TO HIS FACE.
WOW, SO YOU'D PLAY IT COOL.
I WOULDN'T PLAY IT COOL AT ALL!
I'M SURE I'D BE EXHAUSTED AND WORN OUT BY THEN...
...'CUZ IT'D BE AFTER RUNNING AROUND DESPERATELY EXPLORING EVERY POSSIBILITY THAT IT WASN'T HIM.
!!
...
HUP
ALL RIGHT!

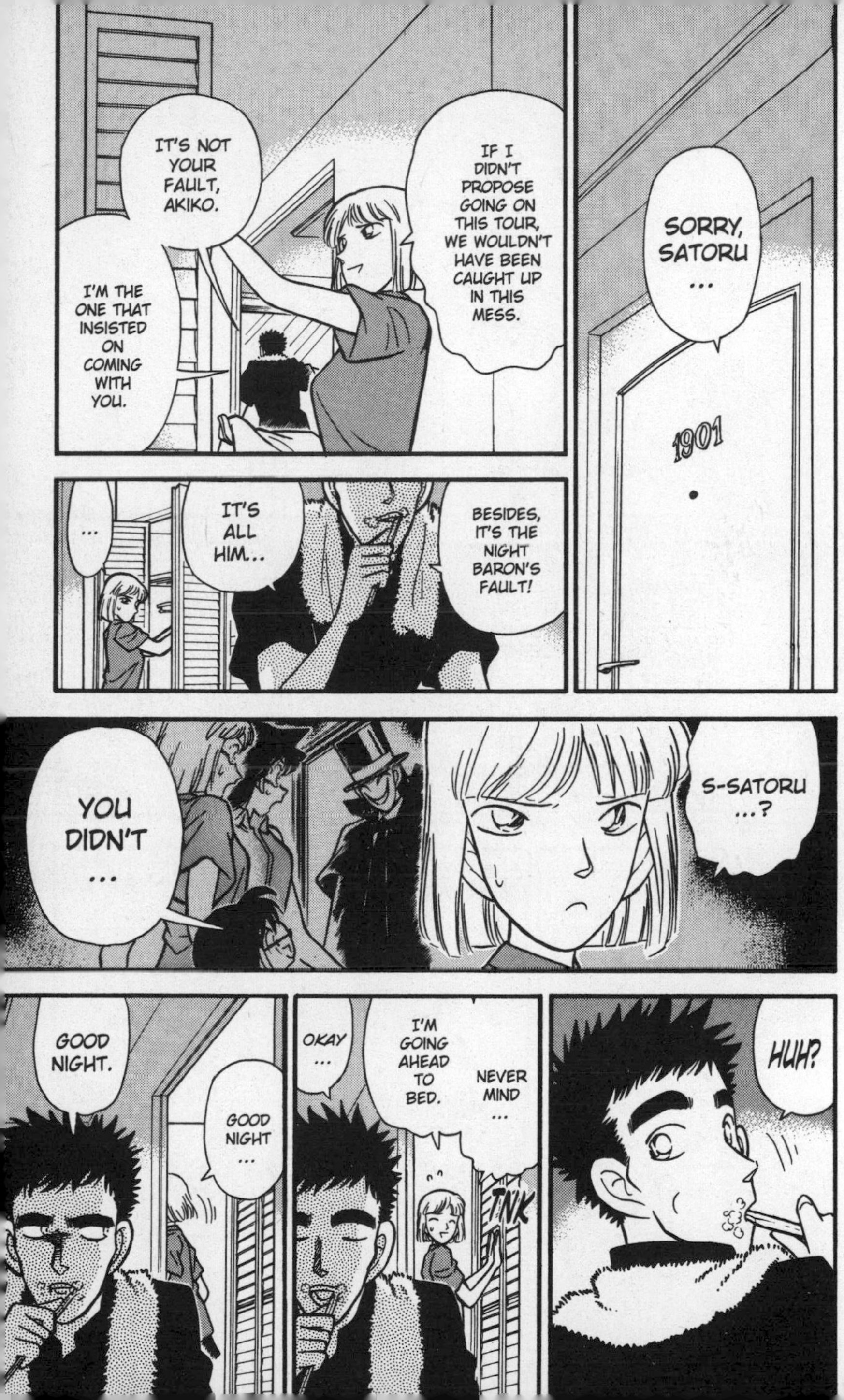
SORRY, SATORU ...
IF I DIDN'T PROPOSE GOING ON THIS TOUR, WE WOULDN'T HAVE BEEN CAUGHT UP IN THIS MESS.
IT'S NOT YOUR FAULT, AKIKO.
I'M THE ONE THAT INSISTED ON COMING WITH YOU.
BESIDES, IT'S THE NIGHT BARON'S FAULT!
IT'S ALL HIM...
...
S-SATORU ...?
YOU DIDN'T ...
HUH?
NEVER MIND ...
I'M GOING AHEAD TO BED.
OKAY ...
TNK
GOOD NIGHT.
GOOD NIGHT ...

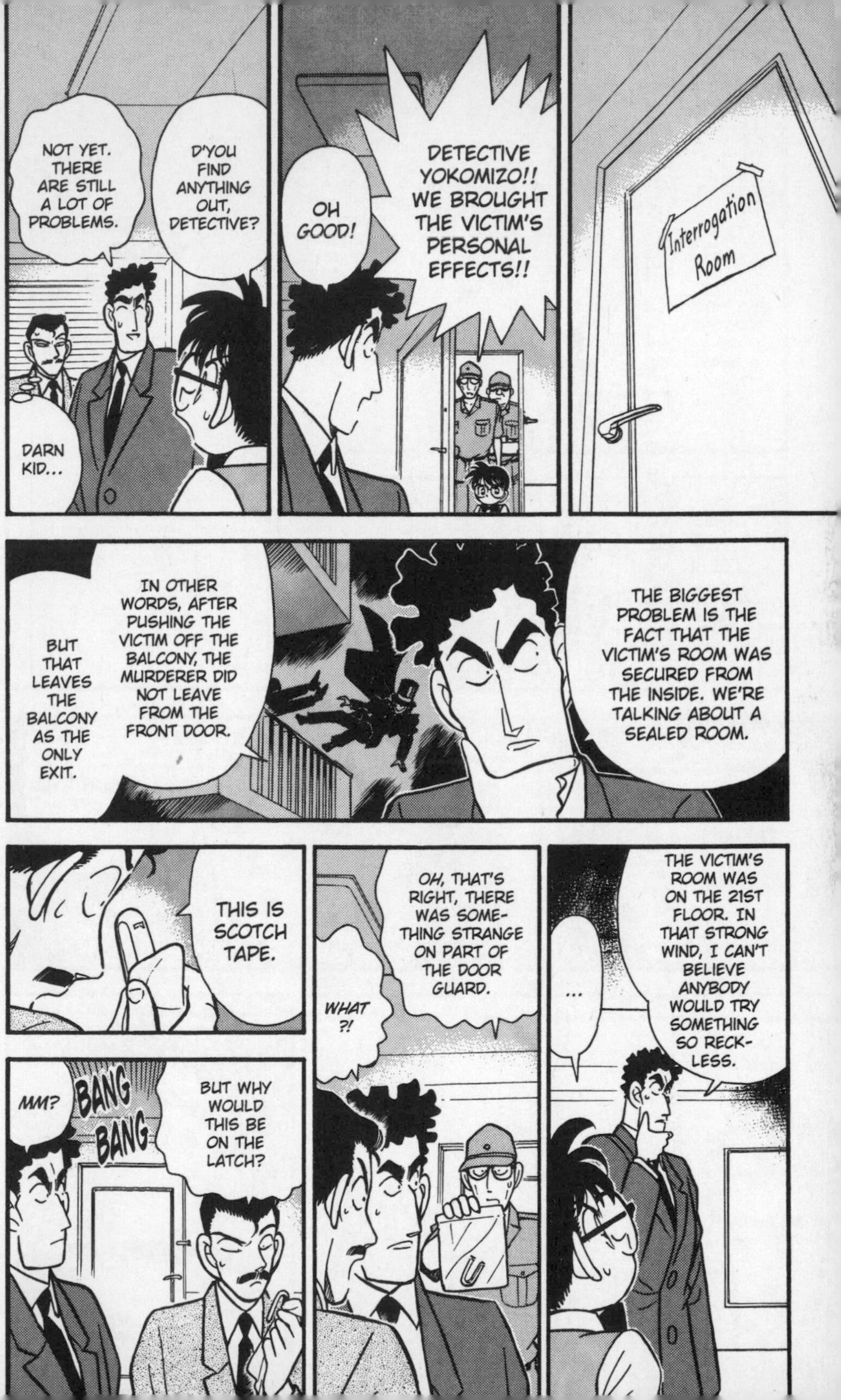
Interrogation Room
DETECTIVE YOKOMIZO!! WE BROUGHT THE VICTIM'S PERSONAL EFFECTS!!
OH GOOD!
D'YOU FIND ANYTHING OUT, DETECTIVE?
NOT YET. THERE ARE STILL A LOT OF PROBLEMS.
DARN KID...
THE BIGGEST PROBLEM IS THE FACT THAT THE VICTIM'S ROOM WAS SECURED FROM THE INSIDE. WE'RE TALKING ABOUT A SEALED ROOM.
IN OTHER WORDS, AFTER PUSHING THE VICTIM OFF THE BALCONY, THE MURDERER DID NOT LEAVE FROM THE FRONT DOOR.
BUT THAT LEAVES THE BALCONY AS THE ONLY EXIT.
THE VICTIM'S ROOM WAS ON THE 21ST FLOOR. IN THAT STRONG WIND, I CAN'T BELIEVE ANYBODY WOULD TRY SOMETHING SO RECK-LESS.
...
OH, THAT'S RIGHT, THERE WAS SOME-THING STRANGE ON PART OF THE DOOR GUARD.
WHAT ?!
THIS IS SCOTCH TAPE.
BUT WHY WOULD THIS BE ON THE LATCH?
BANG BANG
MM?

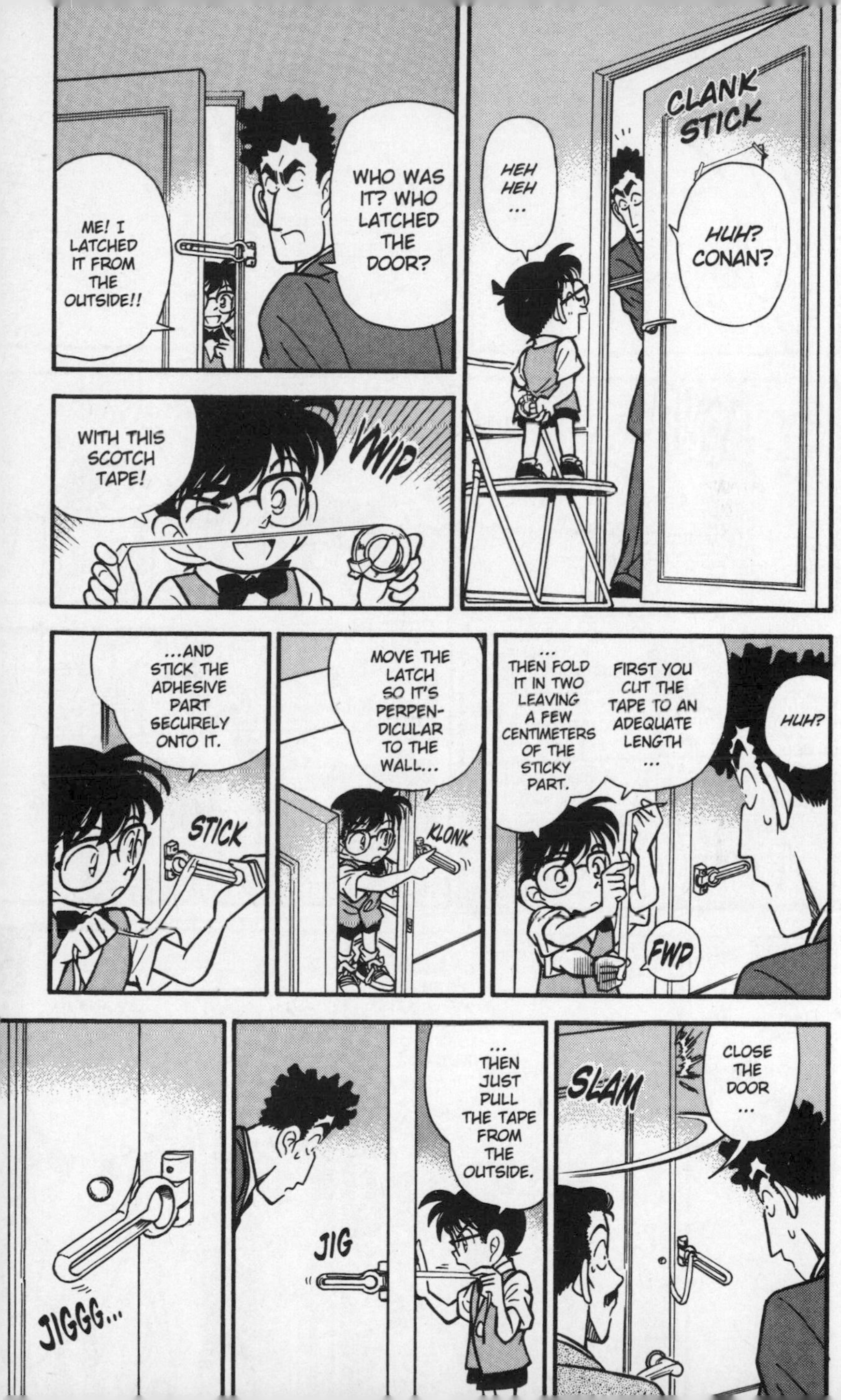
CLANK
STICK
HUH? CONAN?
HEH HEH ...
WHO WAS IT? WHO LATCHED THE DOOR?
ME! I LATCHED IT FROM THE OUTSIDE!!
VWIP
WITH THIS SCOTCH TAPE!
HUH?
FIRST YOU CUT THE TAPE TO AN ADEQUATE LENGTH ...
... THEN FOLD IT IN TWO LEAVING A FEW CENTIMETERS OF THE STICKY PART.
FWP
MOVE THE LATCH SO IT'S PERPEN-DICULAR TO THE WALL...
KLONK
...AND STICK THE ADHESIVE PART SECURELY ONTO IT.
STICK
CLOSE THE DOOR ...
SLAM
... THEN JUST PULL THE TAPE FROM THE OUTSIDE.
JIG
JIGGG...

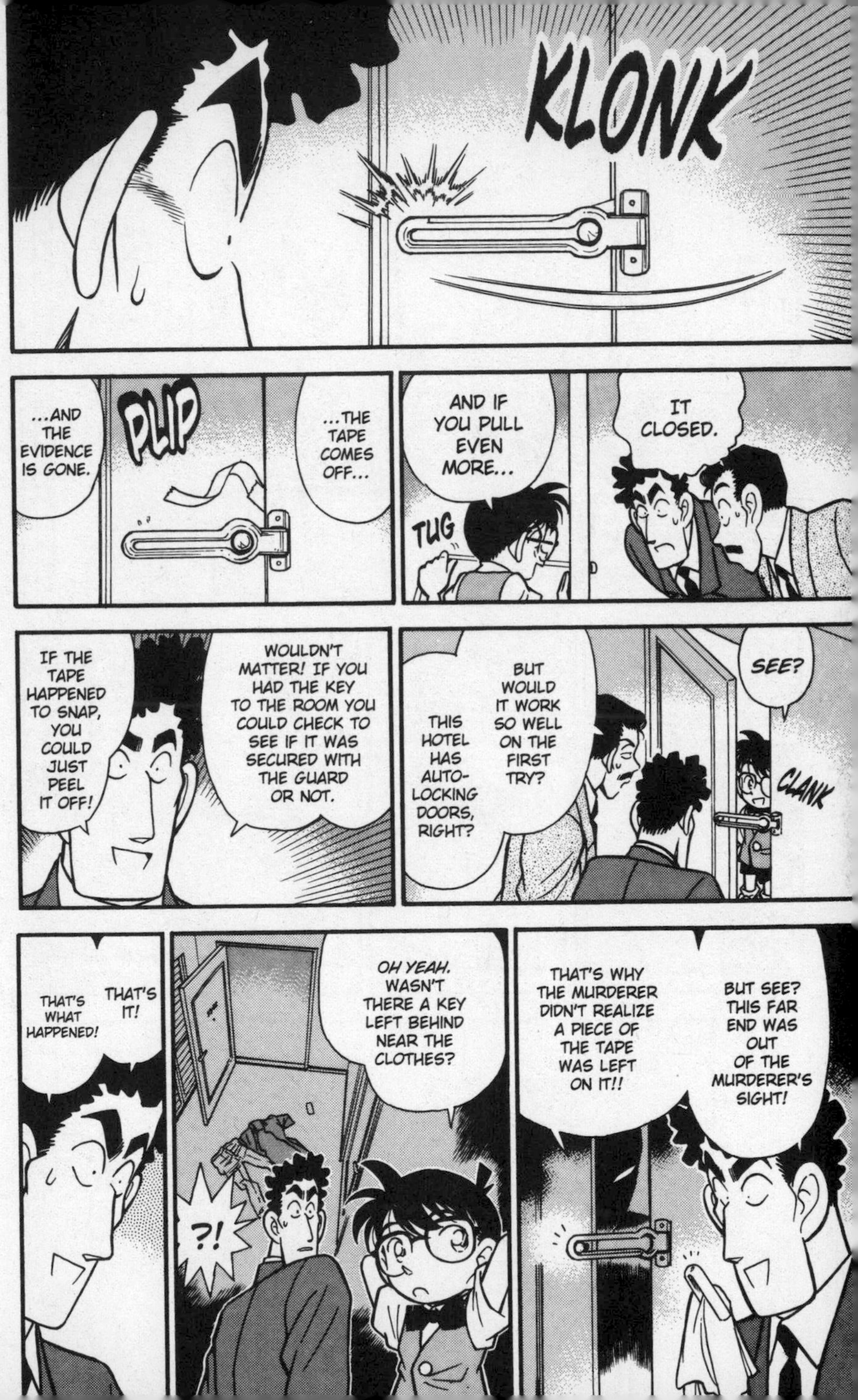
KLONK
IT CLOSED.
AND IF YOU PULL EVEN MORE...
TUG
...THE TAPE COMES OFF...
PLIP
...AND THE EVIDENCE IS GONE.
SEE?
CLANK
BUT WOULD IT WORK SO WELL ON THE FIRST TRY?
THIS HOTEL HAS AUTO-LOCKING DOORS, RIGHT?
WOULDN'T MATTER! IF YOU HAD THE KEY TO THE ROOM YOU COULD CHECK TO SEE IF IT WAS SECURED WITH THE GUARD OR NOT.
IF THE TAPE HAPPENED TO SNAP, YOU COULD JUST PEEL IT OFF!
BUT SEE? THIS FAR END WAS OUT OF THE MURDERER'S SIGHT!
THAT'S WHY THE MURDERER DIDN'T REALIZE A PIECE OF THE TAPE WAS LEFT ON IT!!
OH YEAH. WASN'T THERE A KEY LEFT BEHIND NEAR THE CLOTHES?
?!
THAT'S IT!
THAT'S WHAT HAPPENED!

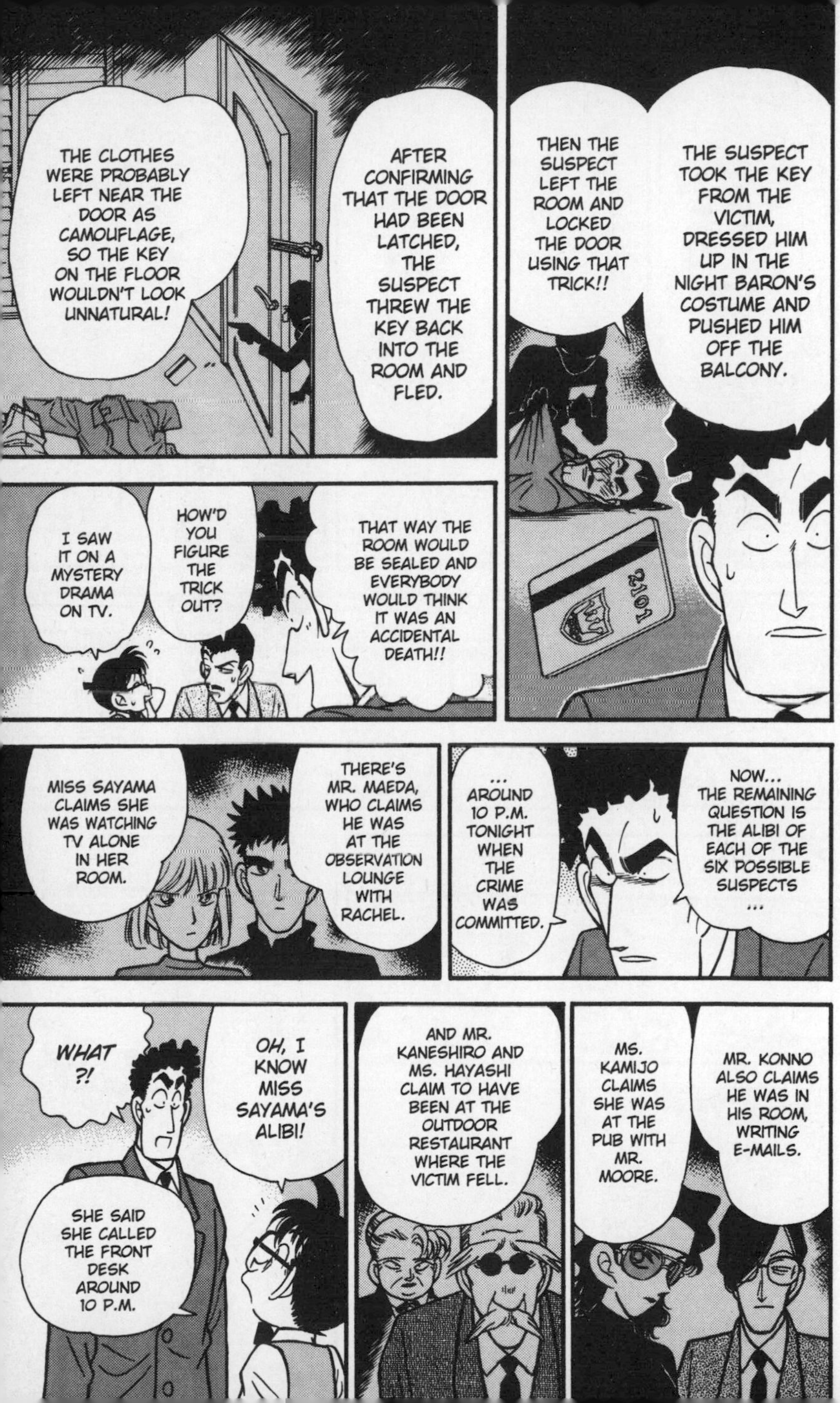
THE SUSPECT TOOK THE KEY FROM THE VICTIM, DRESSED HIM UP IN THE NIGHT BARON'S COSTUME AND PUSHED HIM OFF THE BALCONY.
THEN THE SUSPECT LEFT THE ROOM AND LOCKED THE DOOR USING THAT TRICK!!
2101
AFTER CONFIRMING THAT THE DOOR HAD BEEN LATCHED, THE SUSPECT THREW THE KEY BACK INTO THE ROOM AND FLED.
THE CLOTHES WERE PROBABLY LEFT NEAR THE DOOR AS CAMOUFLAGE, SO THE KEY ON THE FLOOR WOULDN'T LOOK UNNATURAL!
THAT WAY THE ROOM WOULD BE SEALED AND EVERYBODY WOULD THINK IT WAS AN ACCIDENTAL DEATH!!
HOW'D YOU FIGURE THE TRICK OUT?
I SAW IT ON A MYSTERY DRAMA ON TV.
NOW... THE REMAINING QUESTION IS THE ALIBI OF EACH OF THE SIX POSSIBLE SUSPECTS ...
... AROUND 10 P.M. TONIGHT WHEN THE CRIME WAS COMMITTED.
THERE'S MR. MAEDA, WHO CLAIMS HE WAS AT THE OBSERVATION LOUNGE WITH RACHEL.
MISS SAYAMA CLAIMS SHE WAS WATCHING TV ALONE IN HER ROOM.
MR. KONNO ALSO CLAIMS HE WAS IN HIS ROOM, WRITING E-MAILS.
MS. KAMIJO CLAIMS SHE WAS AT THE PUB WITH MR. MOORE.
AND MR. KANESHIRO AND MS. HAYASHI CLAIM TO HAVE BEEN AT THE OUTDOOR RESTAURANT WHERE THE VICTIM FELL.
OH, I KNOW MISS SAYAMA'S ALIBI!
WHAT ?!
SHE SAID SHE CALLED THE FRONT DESK AROUND 10 P.M.

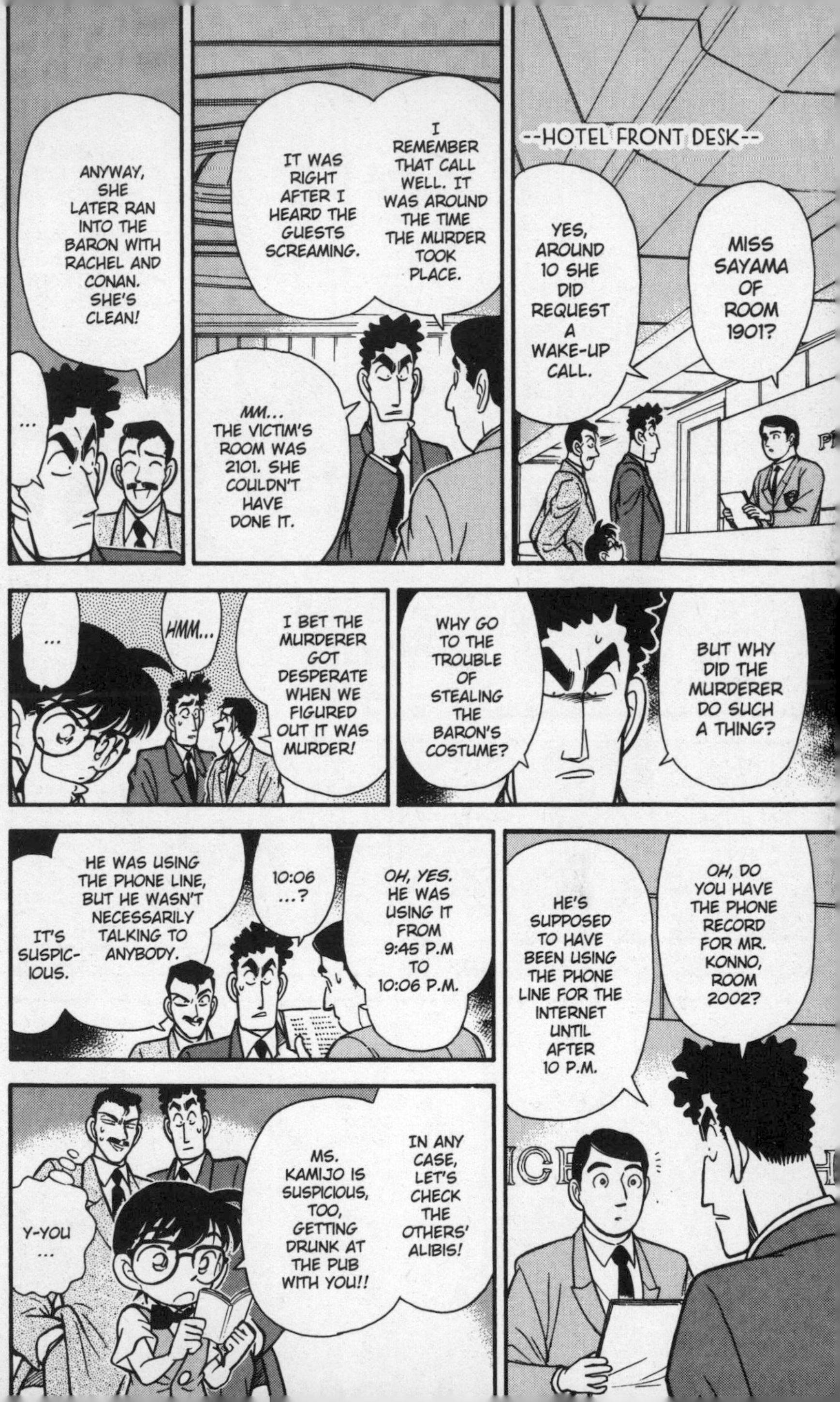
--HOTEL FRONT DESK--
MISS SAYAMA OF ROOM 1901?
YES, AROUND 10 SHE DID REQUEST A WAKE-UP CALL.
I REMEMBER THAT CALL WELL. IT WAS AROUND THE TIME THE MURDER TOOK PLACE.
IT WAS RIGHT AFTER I HEARD THE GUESTS SCREAMING.
MM... THE VICTIM'S ROOM WAS 2101. SHE COULDN'T HAVE DONE IT.
ANYWAY, SHE LATER RAN INTO THE BARON WITH RACHEL AND CONAN. SHE'S CLEAN!
...
BUT WHY DID THE MURDERER DO SUCH A THING?
WHY GO TO THE TROUBLE OF STEALING THE BARON'S COSTUME?
I BET THE MURDERER GOT DESPERATE WHEN WE FIGURED OUT IT WAS MURDER!
HMM...
...
OH, DO YOU HAVE THE PHONE RECORD FOR MR. KONNO, ROOM 2002?
HE'S SUPPOSED TO HAVE BEEN USING THE PHONE LINE FOR THE INTERNET UNTIL AFTER 10 P.M.
OH, YES. HE WAS USING IT FROM 9:45 P.M TO 10:06 P.M.
10:06 ...?
HE WAS USING THE PHONE LINE, BUT HE WASN'T NECESSARILY TALKING TO ANYBODY.
IT'S SUSPIC-IOUS.
IN ANY CASE, LET'S CHECK THE OTHERS' ALIBIS!
MS. KAMIJO IS SUSPICIOUS, TOO, GETTING DRUNK AT THE PUB WITH YOU!!
Y-YOU ...

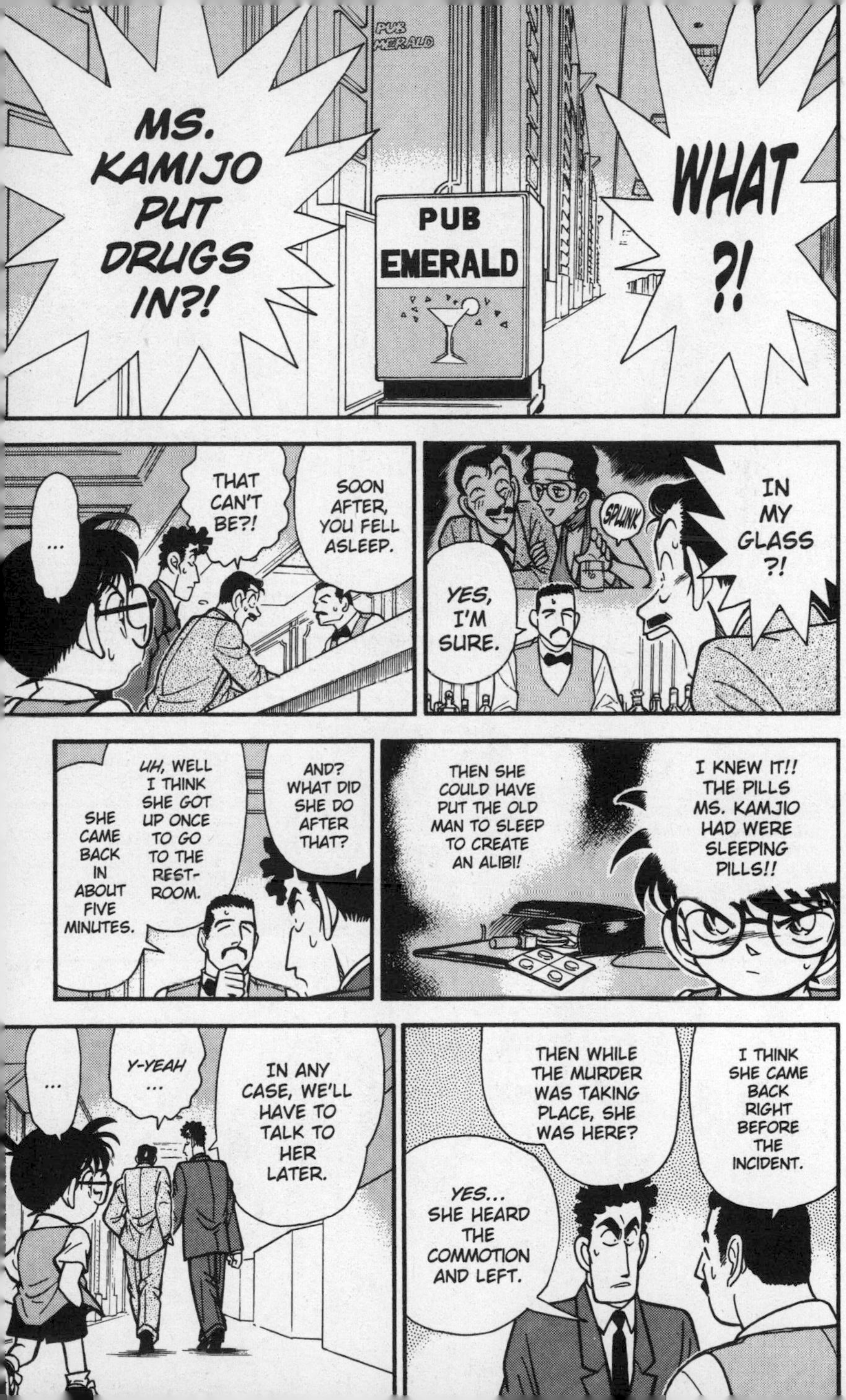
PUB MERALD
WHAT ?!
MS. KAMIJO PUT DRUGS IN?!
PUB EMERALD
IN MY GLASS ?!
SPLUNK
YES, I'M SURE.
SOON AFTER, YOU FELL ASLEEP.
THAT CAN'T BE?!
...
I KNEW IT!! THE PILLS MS. KAMJIO HAD WERE SLEEPING PILLS!!
THEN SHE COULD HAVE PUT THE OLD MAN TO SLEEP TO CREATE AN ALIBI!
AND? WHAT DID SHE DO AFTER THAT?
UH, WELL I THINK SHE GOT UP ONCE TO GO TO THE REST-ROOM.
SHE CAME BACK IN ABOUT FIVE MINUTES.
I THINK SHE CAME BACK RIGHT BEFORE THE INCIDENT.
THEN WHILE THE MURDER WAS TAKING PLACE, SHE WAS HERE?
YES... SHE HEARD THE COMMOTION AND LEFT.
IN ANY CASE, WE'LL HAVE TO TALK TO HER LATER.
Y-YEAH ...
...

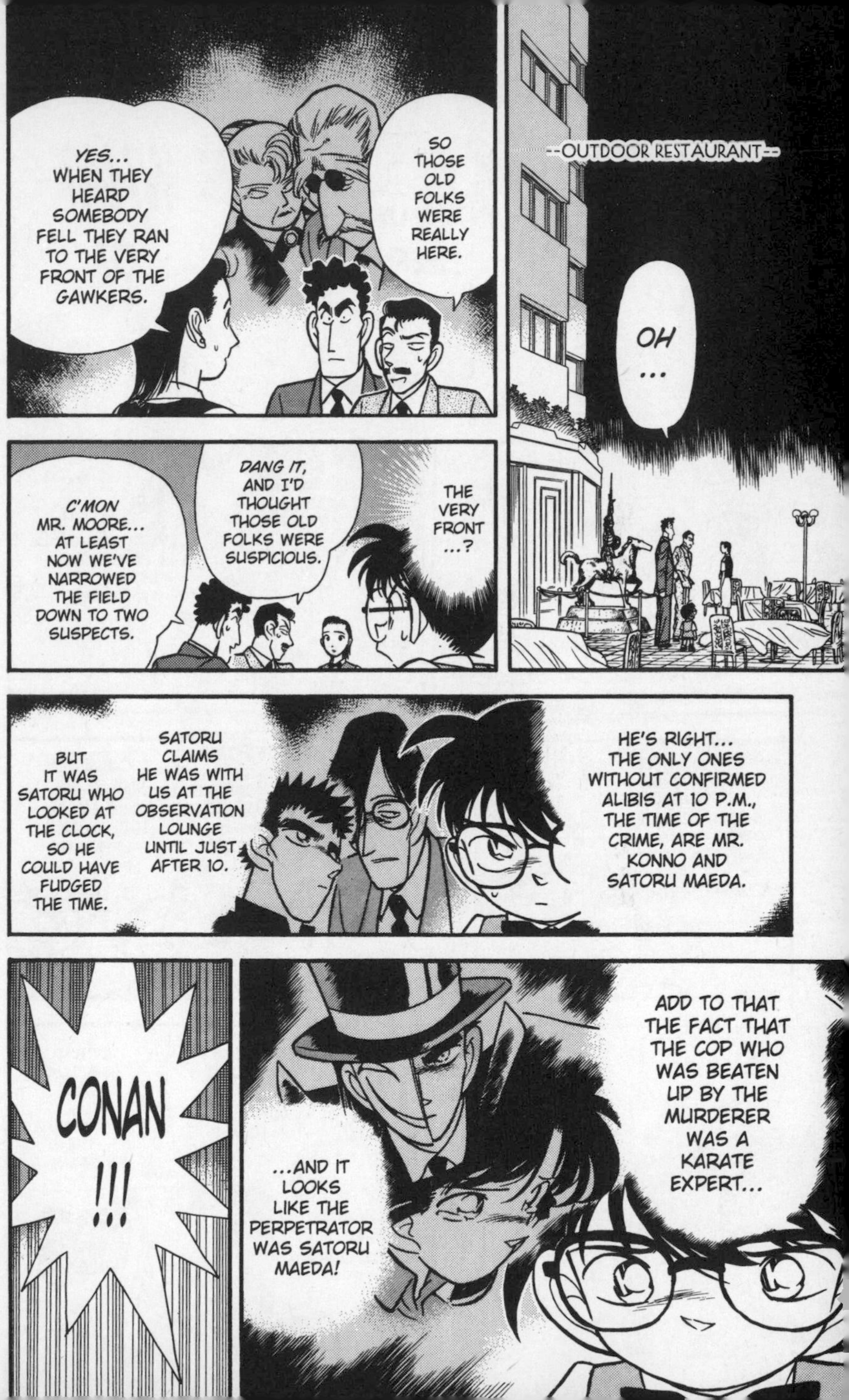
--OUTDOOR RESTAURANT--
OH ...
SO THOSE OLD FOLKS WERE REALLY HERE.
YES... WHEN THEY HEARD SOMEBODY FELL THEY RAN TO THE VERY FRONT OF THE GAWKERS.
THE VERY FRONT ...?
DANG IT, AND I'D THOUGHT THOSE OLD FOLKS WERE SUSPICIOUS.
C'MON MR. MOORE... AT LEAST NOW WE'VE NARROWED THE FIELD DOWN TO TWO SUSPECTS.
HE'S RIGHT... THE ONLY ONES WITHOUT CONFIRMED ALIBIS AT 10 P.M., THE TIME OF THE CRIME, ARE MR. KONNO AND SATORU MAEDA.
SATORU CLAIMS HE WAS WITH US AT THE OBSERVATION LOUNGE UNTIL JUST AFTER 10.
BUT IT WAS SATORU WHO LOOKED AT THE CLOCK, SO HE COULD HAVE FUDGED THE TIME.
ADD TO THAT THE FACT THAT THE COP WHO WAS BEATEN UP BY THE MURDERER WAS A KARATE EXPERT...
...AND IT LOOKS LIKE THE PERPETRATOR WAS SATORU MAEDA!
CONAN !!!

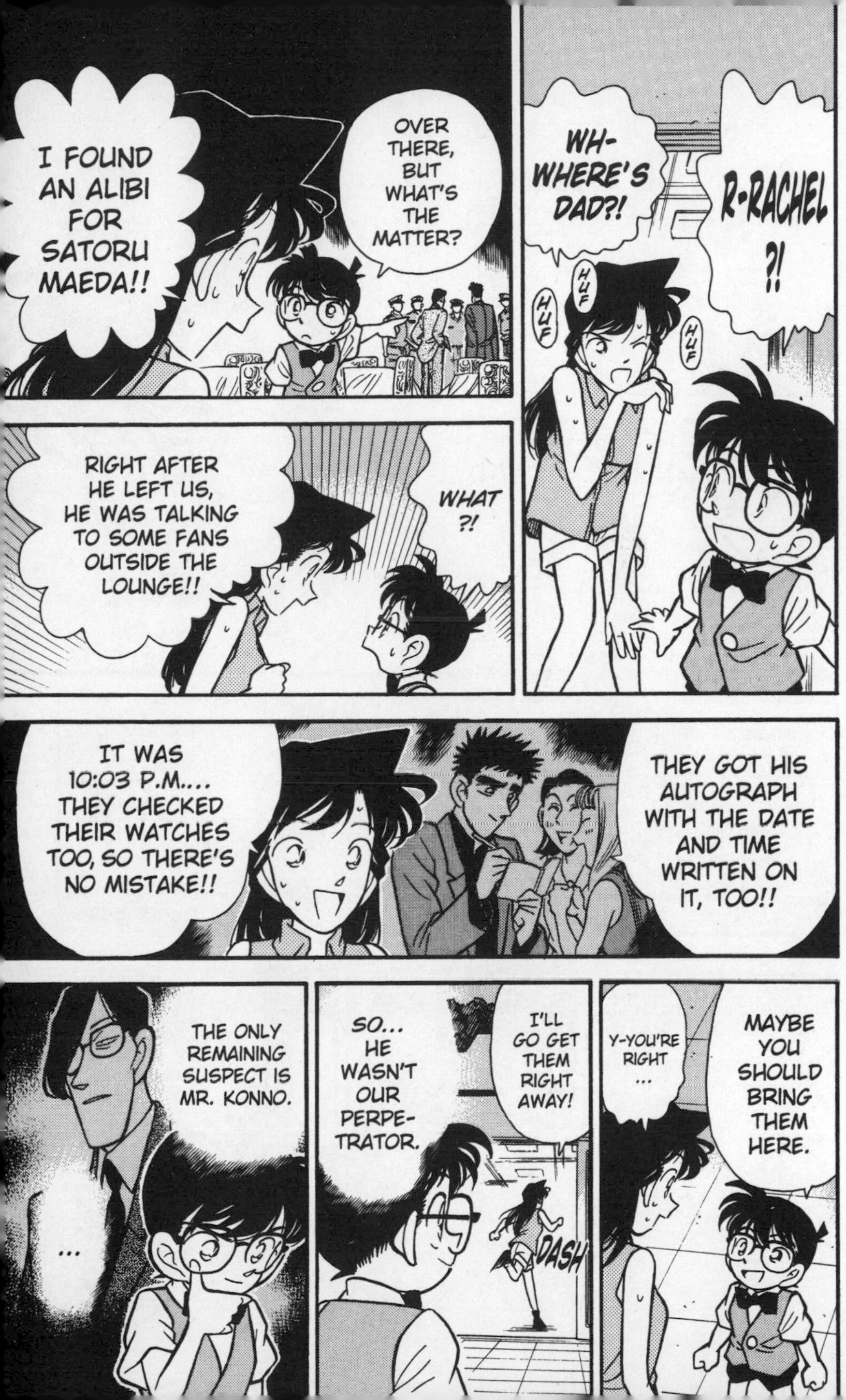

R-RACHEL ?!
WH- WHERE'S DAD?!
HUF
HUF
HUF
OVER THERE, BUT WHAT'S THE MATTER?
I FOUND AN ALIBI FOR SATORU MAEDA!!
WHAT ?!
RIGHT AFTER HE LEFT US, HE WAS TALKING TO SOME FANS OUTSIDE THE LOUNGE!!
THEY GOT HIS AUTOGRAPH WITH THE DATE AND TIME WRITTEN ON IT, TOO!!
IT WAS 10:03 P.M.... THEY CHECKED THEIR WATCHES TOO, SO THERE'S NO MISTAKE!!
MAYBE YOU SHOULD BRING THEM HERE.
Y-YOU'RE RIGHT ...
I'LL GO GET THEM RIGHT AWAY!
SO... HE WASN'T OUR PERPETRATOR.
DASH
THE ONLY REMAINING SUSPECT IS MR. KONNO.
...

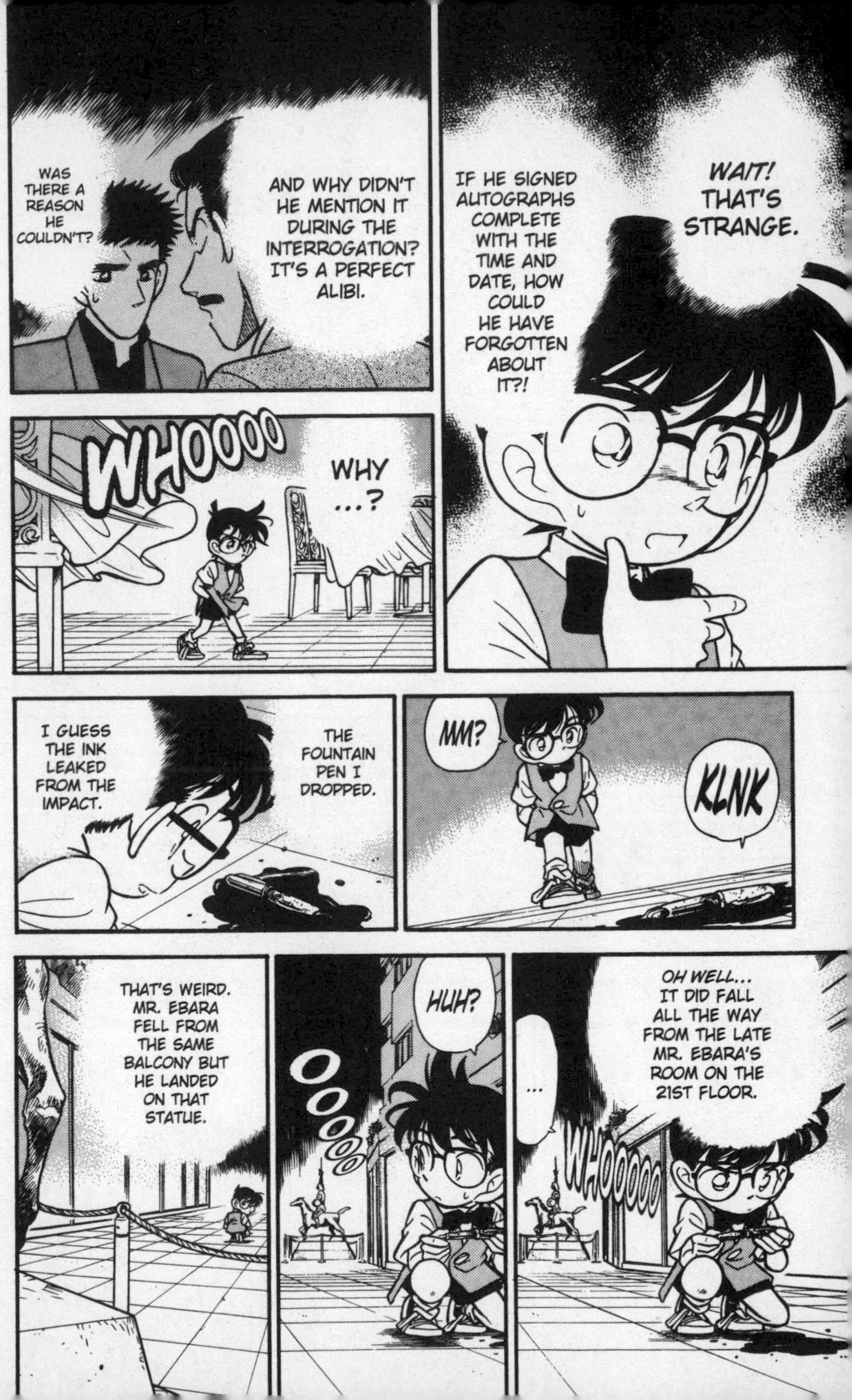
WAIT! THAT'S STRANGE.
IF HE SIGNED AUTOGRAPHS COMPLETE WITH THE TIME AND DATE, HOW COULD HE HAVE FORGOTTEN ABOUT IT?!
AND WHY DIDN'T HE MENTION IT DURING THE INTERROGATION? IT'S A PERFECT ALIBI.
WAS THERE A REASON HE COULDN'T?
WHY ...?
WHOOOO
KLNK
MM?
THE FOUNTAIN PEN I DROPPED.
I GUESS THE INK LEAKED FROM THE IMPACT.
OH WELL... IT DID FALL ALL THE WAY FROM THE LATE MR. EBARA'S ROOM ON THE 21ST FLOOR.
...
WHOOOOOO
HUH?
OOOOOO
THAT'S WEIRD. MR. EBARA FELL FROM THE SAME BALCONY BUT HE LANDED ON THAT STATUE.

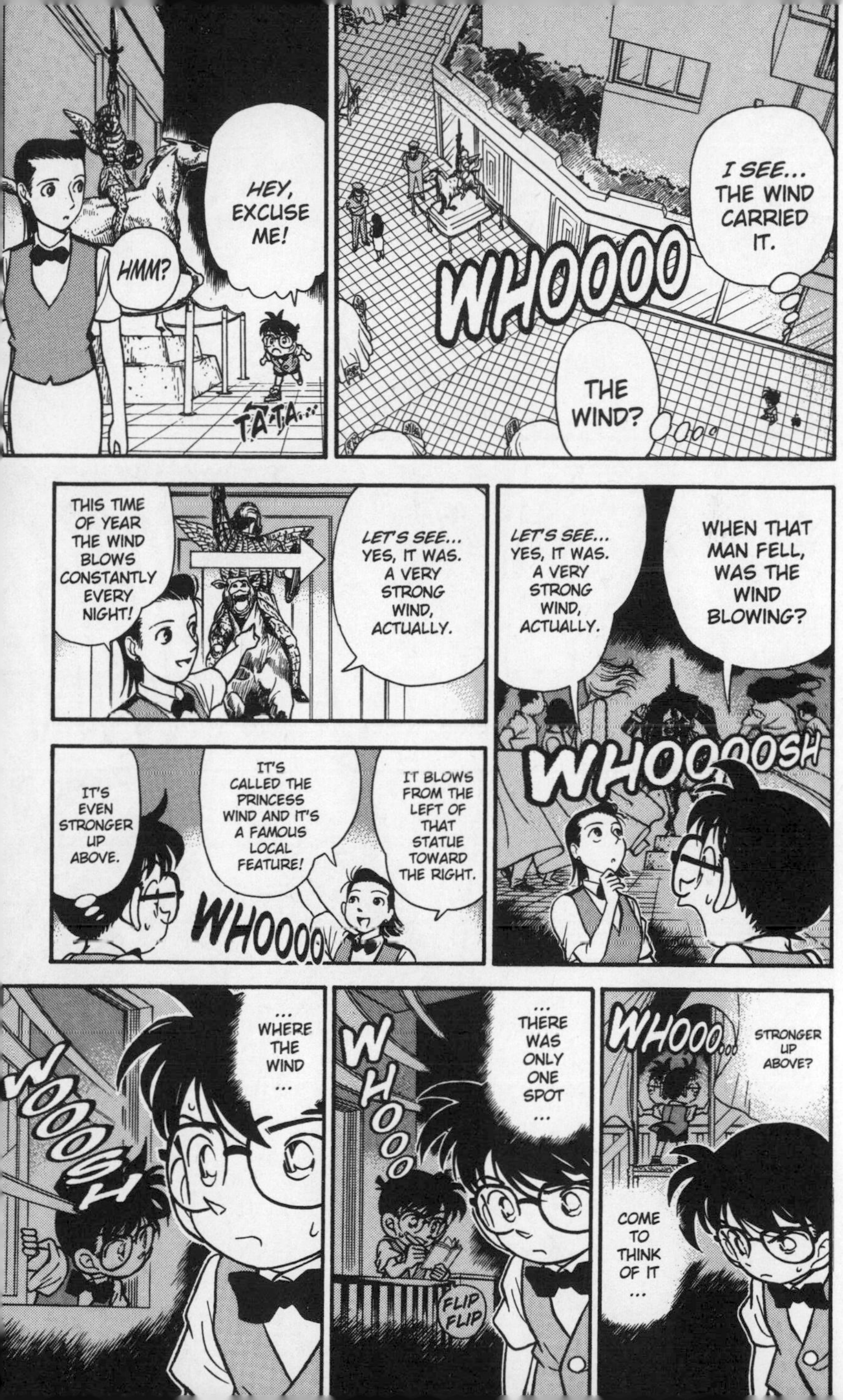
I SEE... THE WIND CARRIED IT.
WHOOOOO
THE WIND?
HEY, EXCUSE ME!
HMM?
TA TA...
WHEN THAT MAN FELL, WAS THE WIND BLOWING?
LET'S SEE... YES, IT WAS. A VERY STRONG WIND, ACTUALLY.
WHOOOOOSH
LET'S SEE... YES, IT WAS. A VERY STRONG WIND, ACTUALLY.
THIS TIME OF YEAR THE WIND BLOWS CONSTANTLY EVERY NIGHT!
IT BLOWS FROM THE LEFT OF THAT STATUE TOWARD THE RIGHT.
IT'S CALLED THE PRINCESS WIND AND IT'S A FAMOUS LOCAL FEATURE!
IT'S EVEN STRONGER UP ABOVE.
WHOOOO
STRONGER UP ABOVE?
WHOOO...
COME TO THINK OF IT ...
... THERE WAS ONLY ONE SPOT ...
WHOOO
FLIP FLIP
... WHERE THE WIND ...

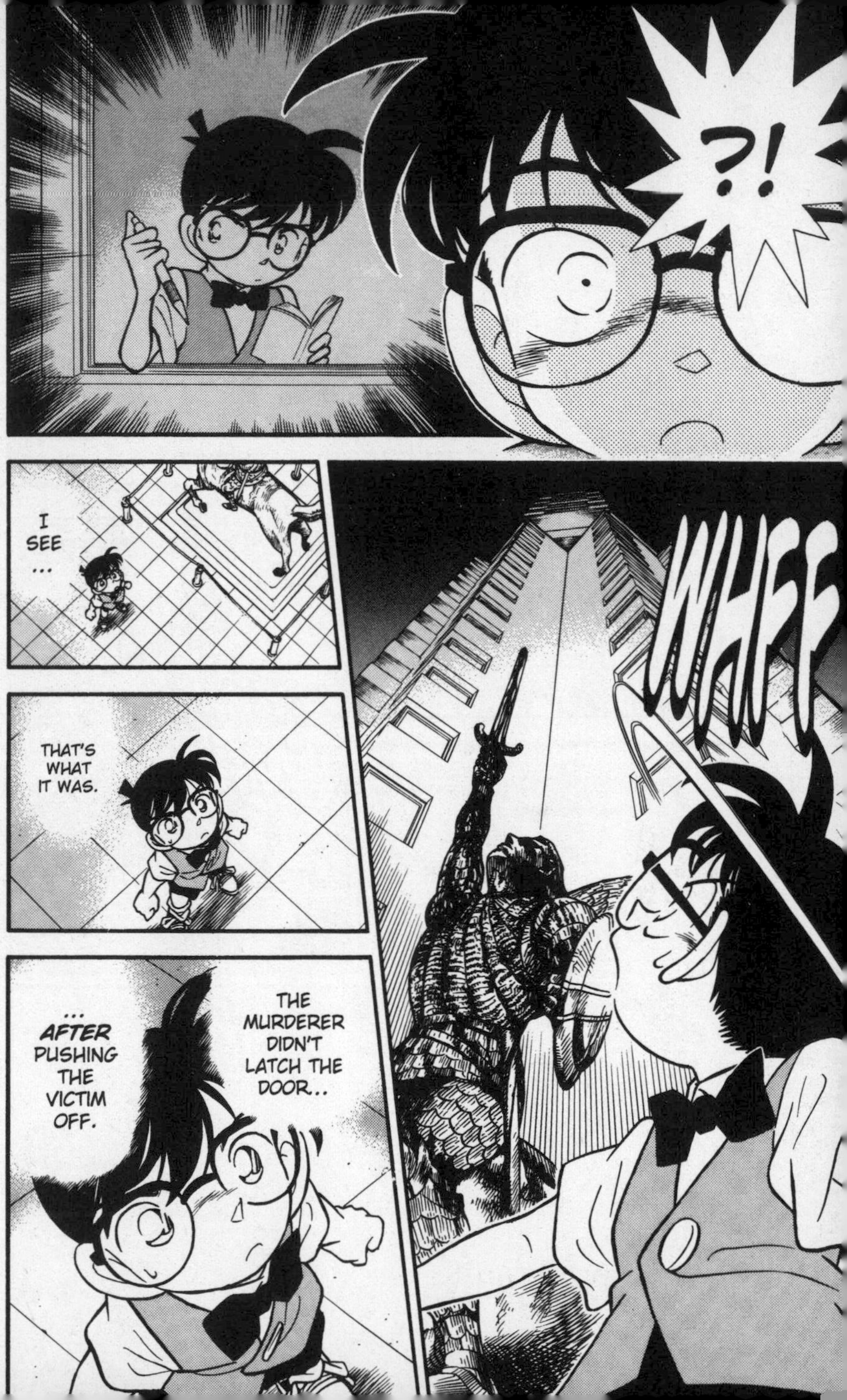
?!
WHEE
I SEE ...
THAT'S WHAT IT WAS.
THE MURDERER DIDN'T LATCH THE DOOR...
... AFTER PUSHING THE VICTIM OFF.

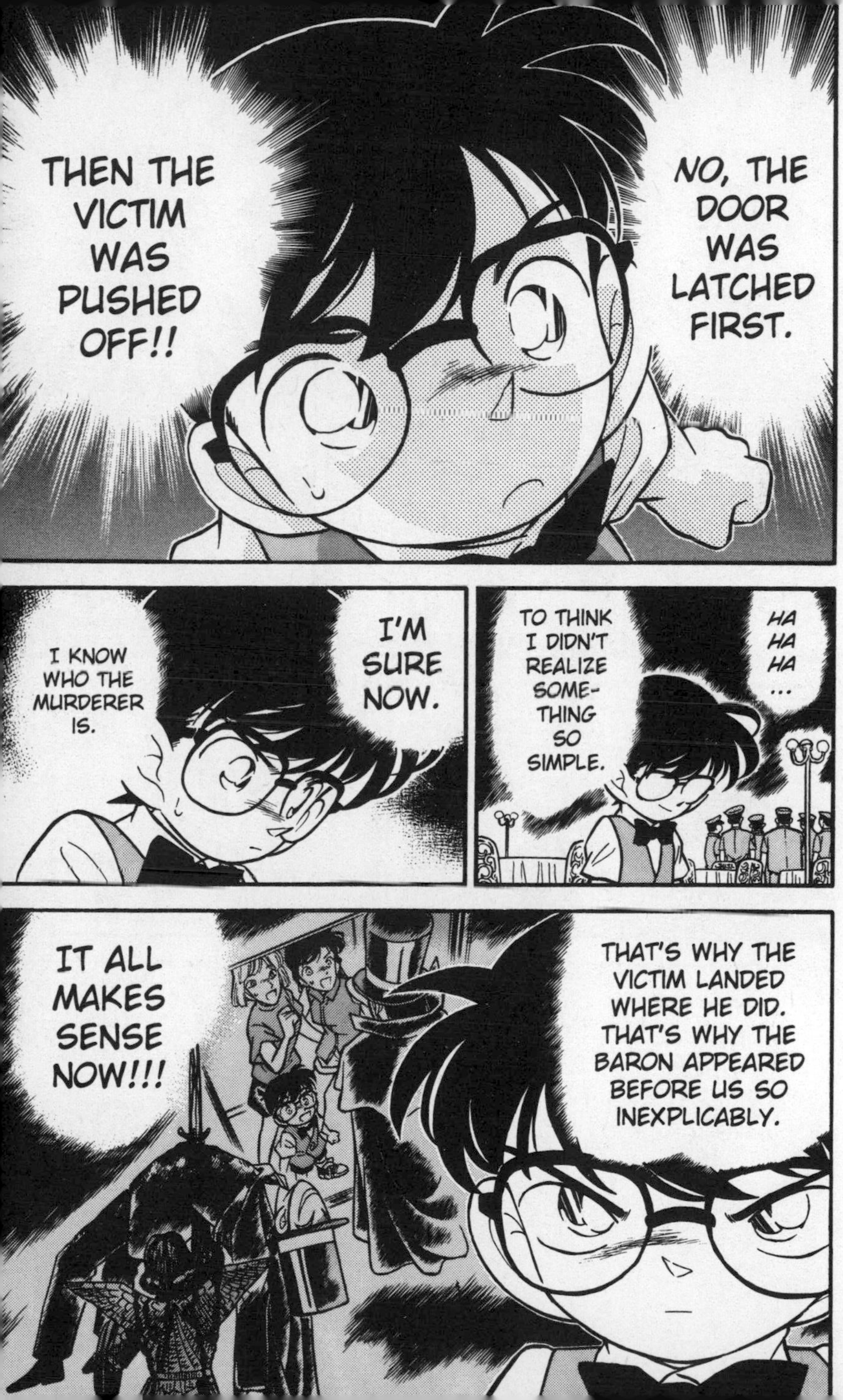
NO, THE DOOR WAS LATCHED FIRST.
THEN THE VICTIM WAS PUSHED OFF!!
HA HA HA ...
TO THINK I DIDN'T REALIZE SOME-THING SO SIMPLE.
I'M SURE NOW.
I KNOW WHO THE MURDERER IS.
THAT'S WHY THE VICTIM LANDED WHERE HE DID. THAT'S WHY THE BARON APPEARED BEFORE US SO INEXPLICABLY.
IT ALL MAKES SENSE NOW!!!

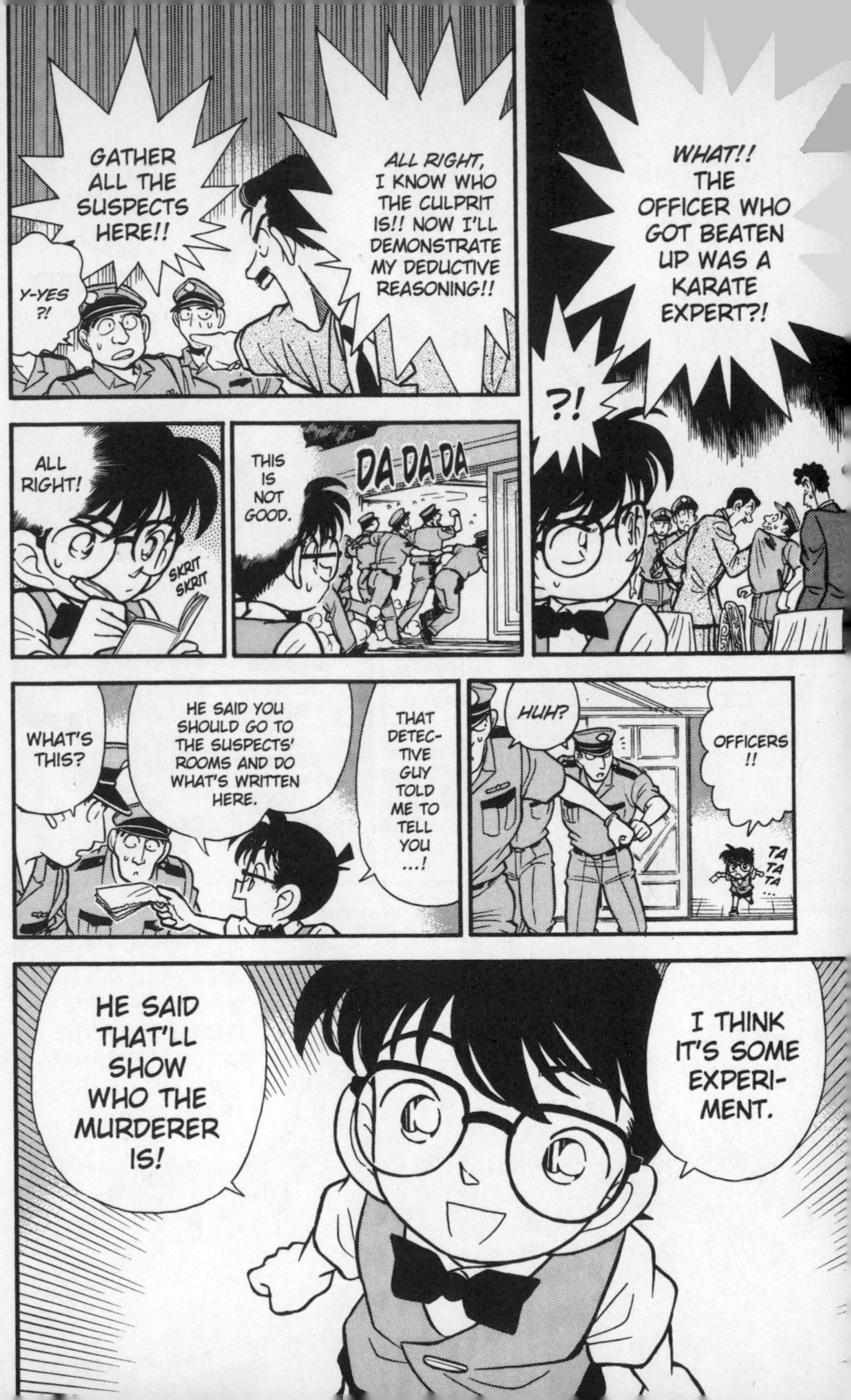
WHAT!! THE OFFICER WHO GOT BEATEN UP WAS A KARATE EXPERT?!
?!
ALL RIGHT, I KNOW WHO THE CULPRIT IS!! NOW I'LL DEMONSTRATE MY DEDUCTIVE REASONING!!
GATHER ALL THE SUSPECTS HERE!!
Y-YES ?!
DA DA DA
THIS IS NOT GOOD.
ALL RIGHT!
SKRIT SKRIT
OFFICERS !!
HUH?
TA TA TA ...
THAT DETEC-TIVE GUY TOLD ME TO TELL YOU ...!
HE SAID YOU SHOULD GO TO THE SUSPECTS' ROOMS AND DO WHAT'S WRITTEN HERE.
WHAT'S THIS?
I THINK IT'S SOME EXPERI-MENT.
HE SAID THAT'LL SHOW WHO THE MURDERER IS!

FILE 7: THE SECRET OF THE LANDING SPOT

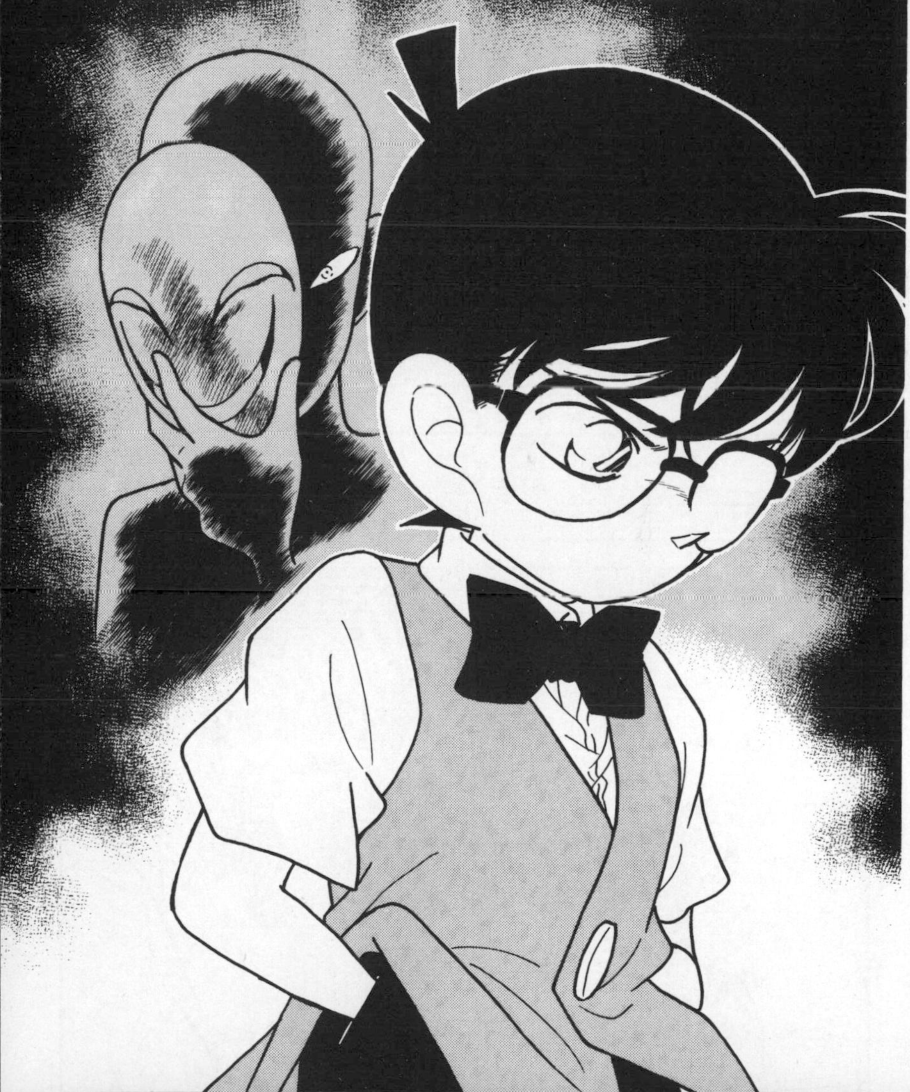

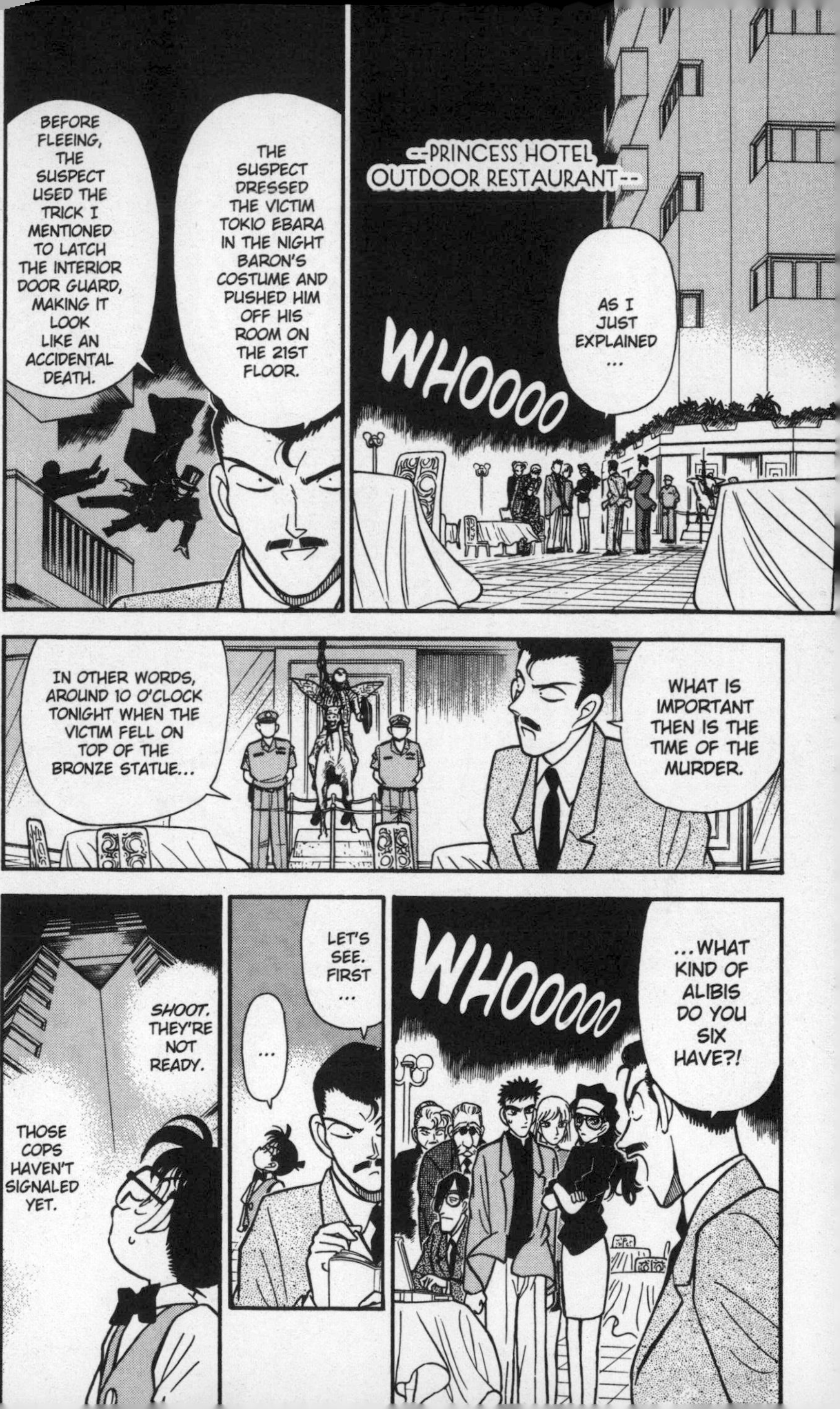
--PRINCESS HOTEL OUTDOOR RESTAURANT--
WHOOOO
AS I JUST EXPLAINED ...
THE SUSPECT DRESSED THE VICTIM TOKIO EBARA IN THE NIGHT BARON'S COSTUME AND PUSHED HIM OFF HIS ROOM ON THE 21ST FLOOR.
BEFORE FLEEING, THE SUSPECT USED THE TRICK I MENTIONED TO LATCH THE INTERIOR DOOR GUARD, MAKING IT LOOK LIKE AN ACCIDENTAL DEATH.
WHAT IS IMPORTANT THEN IS THE TIME OF THE MURDER.
IN OTHER WORDS, AROUND 10 O'CLOCK TONIGHT WHEN THE VICTIM FELL ON TOP OF THE BRONZE STATUE...
...WHAT KIND OF ALIBIS DO YOU SIX HAVE?!
WHOOOOOO
LET'S SEE. FIRST ...
...
SHOOT. THEY'RE NOT READY.
THOSE COPS HAVEN'T SIGNALED YET.

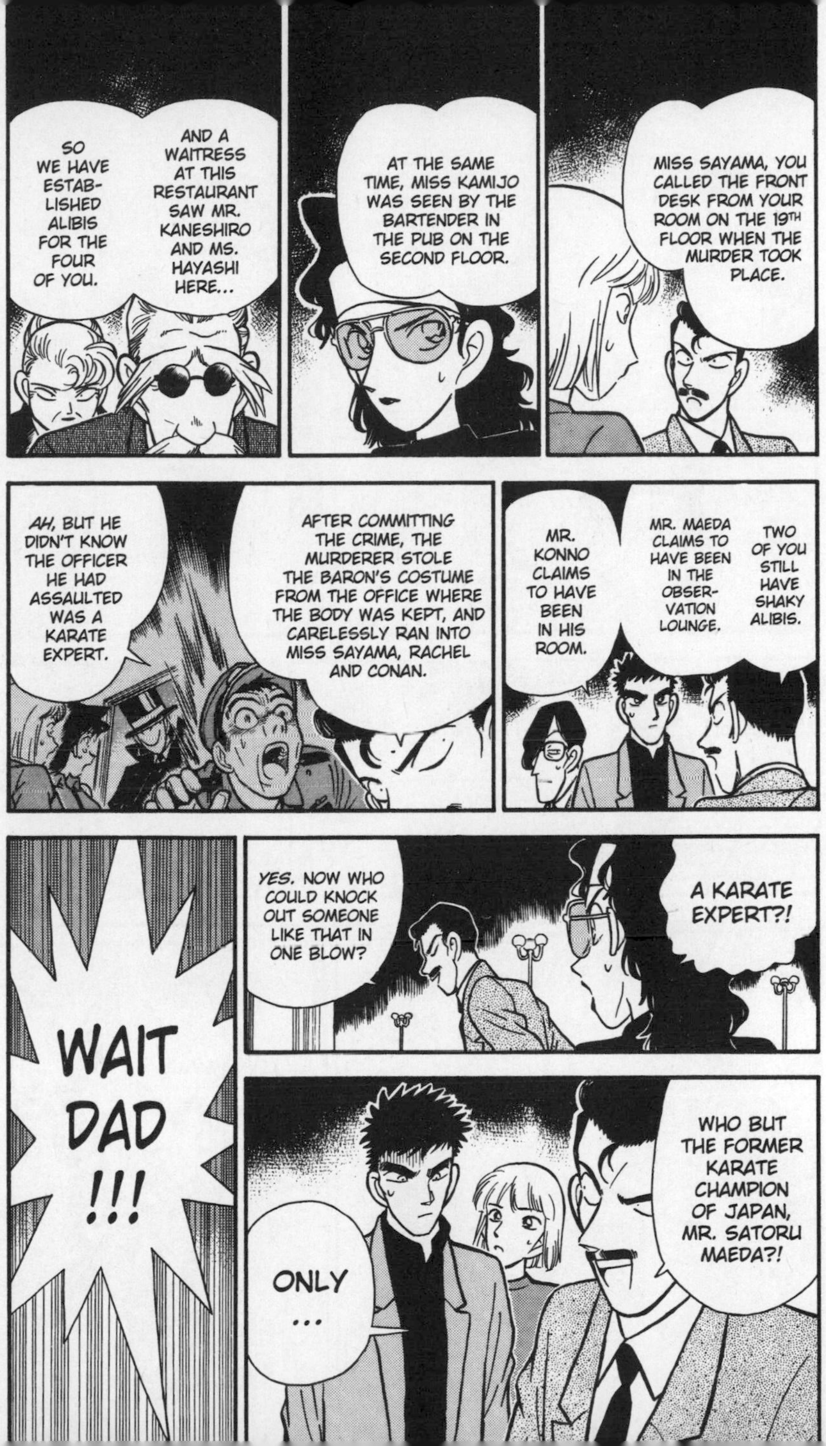
MISS SAYAMA, YOU CALLED THE FRONT DESK FROM YOUR ROOM ON THE 19TH FLOOR WHEN THE MURDER TOOK PLACE.
AT THE SAME TIME, MISS KAMIJO WAS SEEN BY THE BARTENDER IN THE PUB ON THE SECOND FLOOR.
AND A WAITRESS AT THIS RESTAURANT SAW MR. KANESHIRO AND MS. HAYASHI HERE...
SO WE HAVE ESTABLISHED ALIBIS FOR THE FOUR OF YOU.
TWO OF YOU STILL HAVE SHAKY ALIBIS.
MR. MAEDA CLAIMS TO HAVE BEEN IN THE OBSERVATION LOUNGE.
MR. KONNO CLAIMS TO HAVE BEEN IN HIS ROOM.
AFTER COMMITTING THE CRIME, THE MURDERER STOLE THE BARON'S COSTUME FROM THE OFFICE WHERE THE BODY WAS KEPT, AND CARELESSLY RAN INTO MISS SAYAMA, RACHEL AND CONAN.
AH, BUT HE DIDN'T KNOW THE OFFICER HE HAD ASSAULTED WAS A KARATE EXPERT.
A KARATE EXPERT?!
YES. NOW WHO COULD KNOCK OUT SOMEONE LIKE THAT IN ONE BLOW?
WHO BUT THE FORMER KARATE CHAMPION OF JAPAN, MR. SATORU MAEDA?!
ONLY ...
WAIT DAD !!!

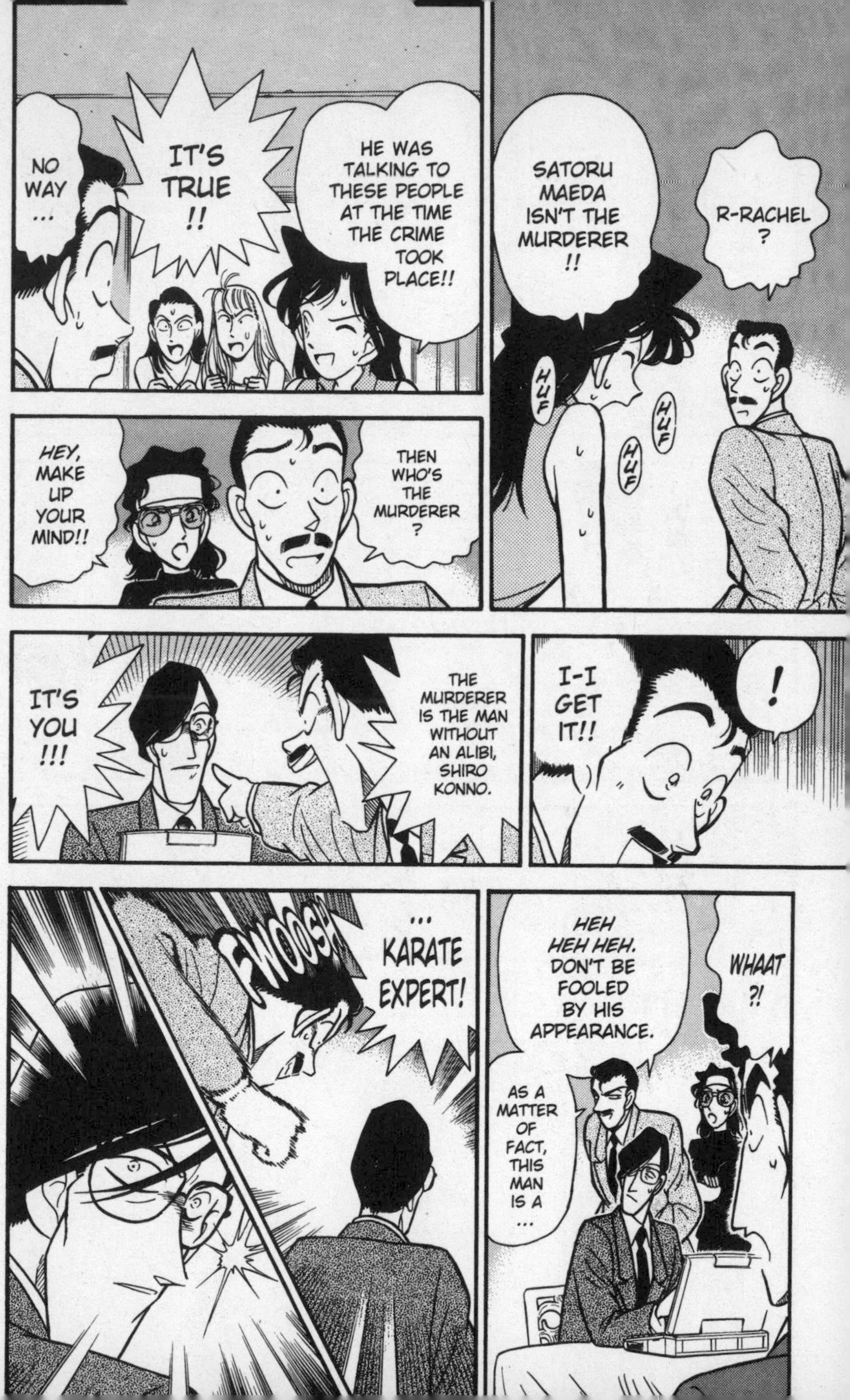
R-RACHEL ?
SATORU MAEDA ISN'T THE MURDERER !!
HUF
HUF
HUF
HE WAS TALKING TO THESE PEOPLE AT THE TIME THE CRIME TOOK PLACE!!
IT'S TRUE !!
NO WAY ...
THEN WHO'S THE MURDERER ?
HEY, MAKE UP YOUR MIND!!
!
I-I GET IT!!
THE MURDERER IS THE MAN WITHOUT AN ALIBI, SHIRO KONNO.
IT'S YOU !!!
WHAAT ?!
HEH HEH HEH. DON'T BE FOOLED BY HIS APPEARANCE.
AS A MATTER OF FACT, THIS MAN IS A ...
... KARATE EXPERT!
WOOSH

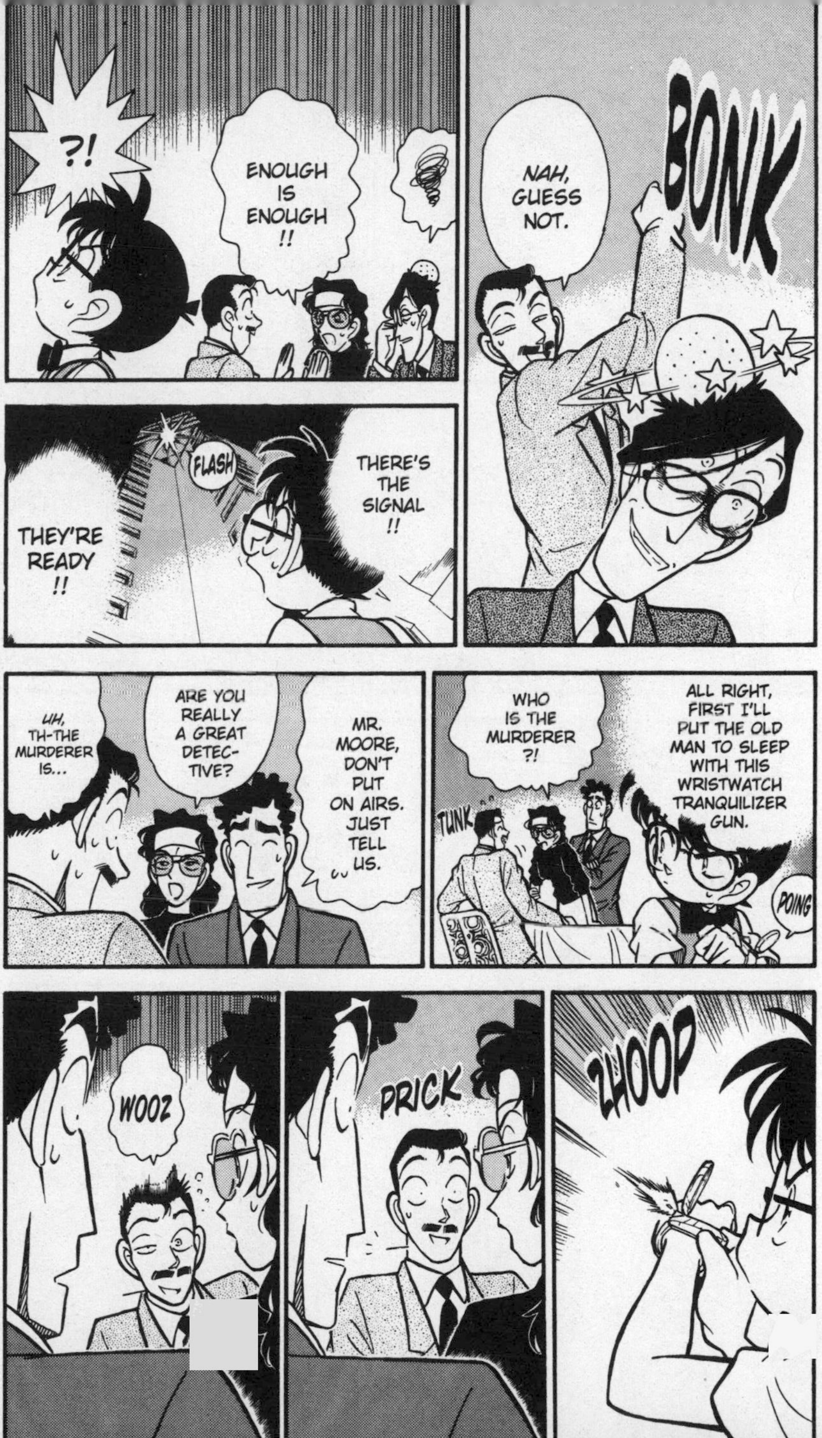
BONK
NAH, GUESS NOT.
ENOUGH IS ENOUGH!!
?!
THERE'S THE SIGNAL!!
FLASH
THEY'RE READY!!
ALL RIGHT, FIRST I'LL PUT THE OLD MAN TO SLEEP WITH THIS WRISTWATCH TRANQUILIZER GUN.
WHO IS THE MURDERER?!
POING
TUNK
MR. MOORE, DON'T PUT ON AIRS. JUST TELL US.
ARE YOU REALLY A GREAT DETECTIVE?
UH, TH-THE MURDERER IS...
ZHOOP
PRICK
WOOZ

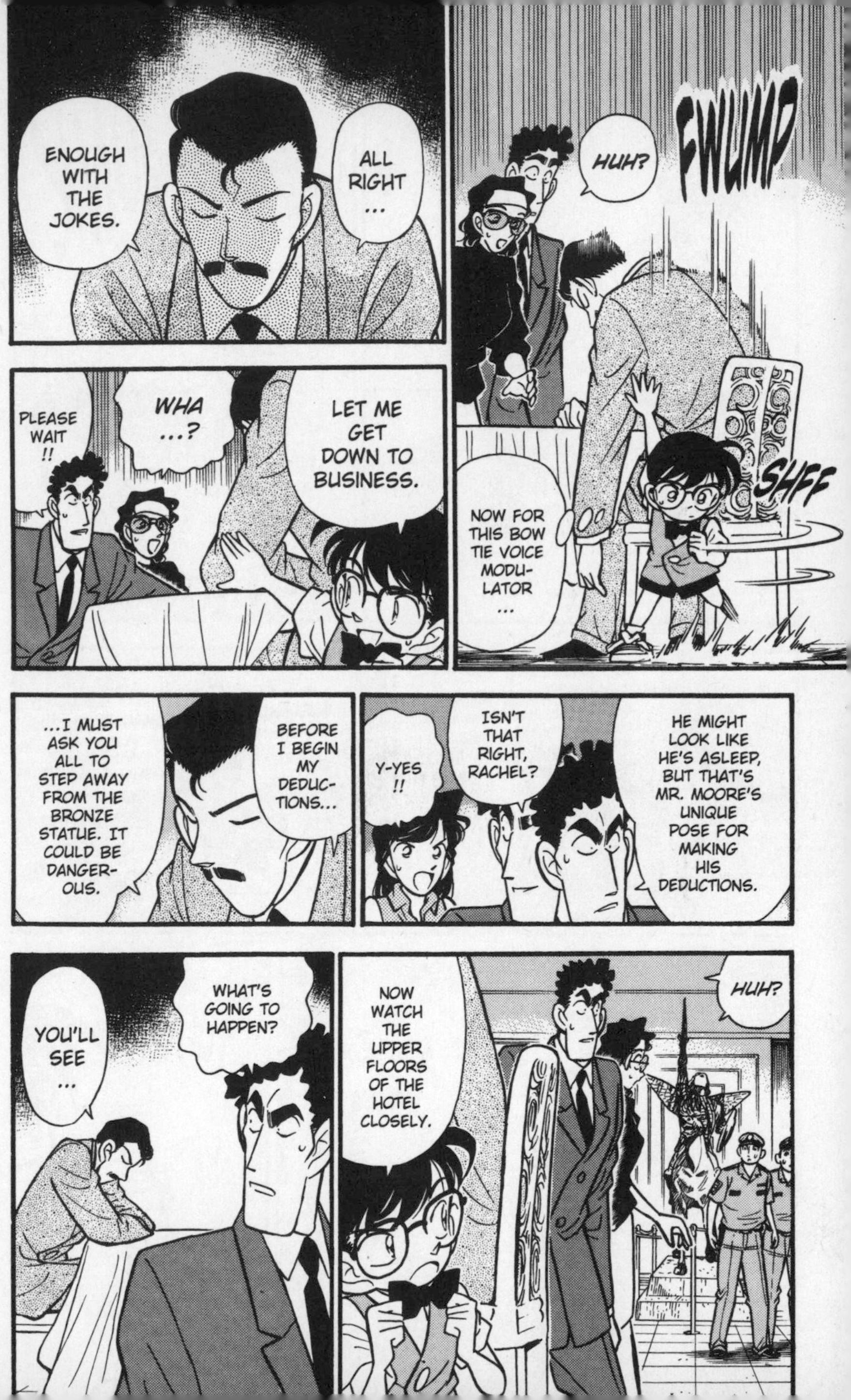
HUH?
FWUMP
NOW FOR THIS BOW TIE VOICE MODULATOR ...
SHFF
ALL RIGHT ...
ENOUGH WITH THE JOKES.
LET ME GET DOWN TO BUSINESS.
WHA ...?
PLEASE WAIT !!
HE MIGHT LOOK LIKE HE'S ASLEEP, BUT THAT'S MR. MOORE'S UNIQUE POSE FOR MAKING HIS DEDUCTIONS.
ISN'T THAT RIGHT, RACHEL?
Y-YES !!
BEFORE I BEGIN MY DEDUCTIONS...
...I MUST ASK YOU ALL TO STEP AWAY FROM THE BRONZE STATUE. IT COULD BE DANGEROUS.
HUH?
NOW WATCH THE UPPER FLOORS OF THE HOTEL CLOSELY.
WHAT'S GOING TO HAPPEN?
YOU'LL SEE ...

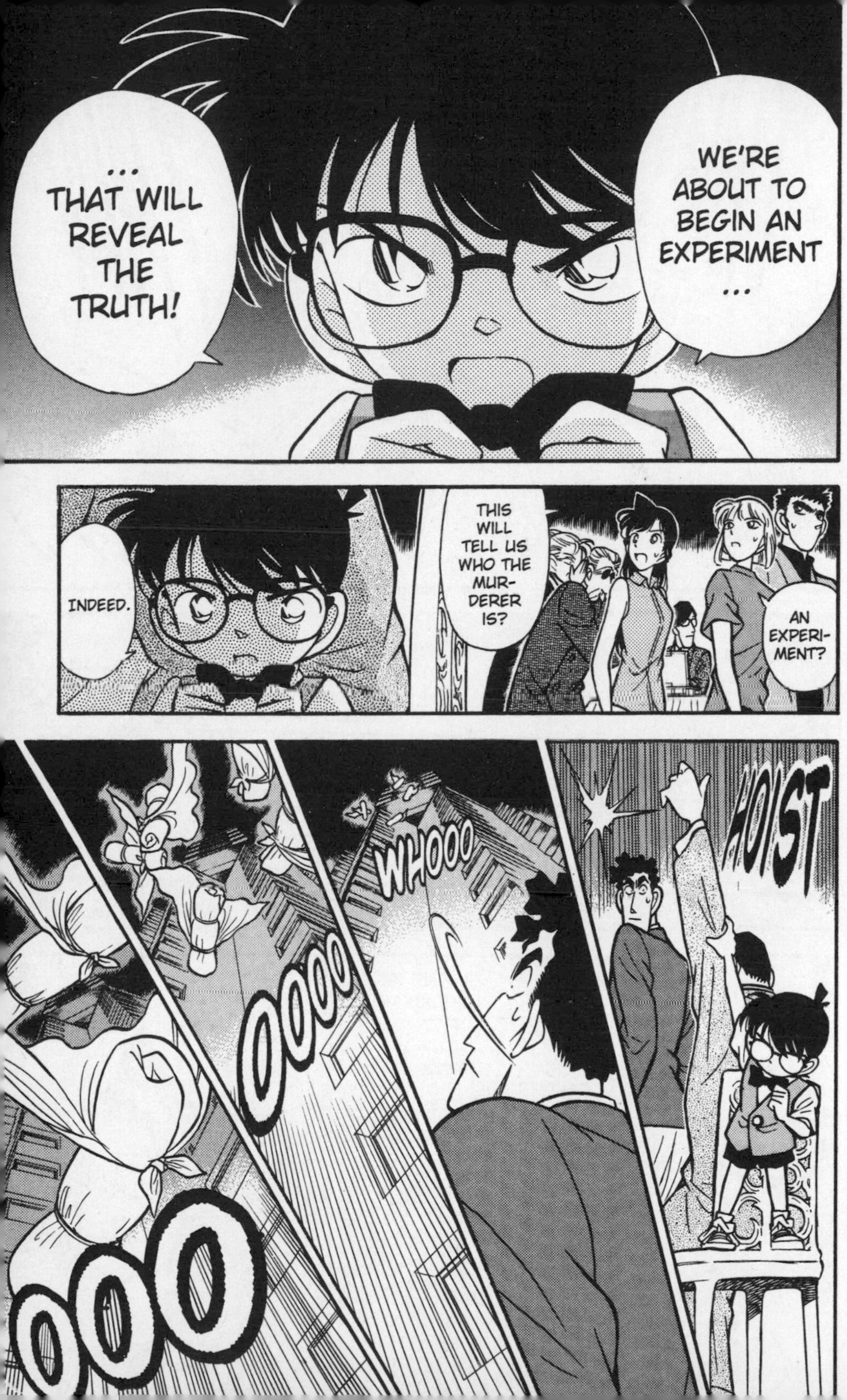
WE'RE ABOUT TO BEGIN AN EXPERIMENT ...
... THAT WILL REVEAL THE TRUTH!
AN EXPERIMENT?
THIS WILL TELL US WHO THE MURDERER IS?
INDEED.
HOIST
WHOOO
OOOO
OOO

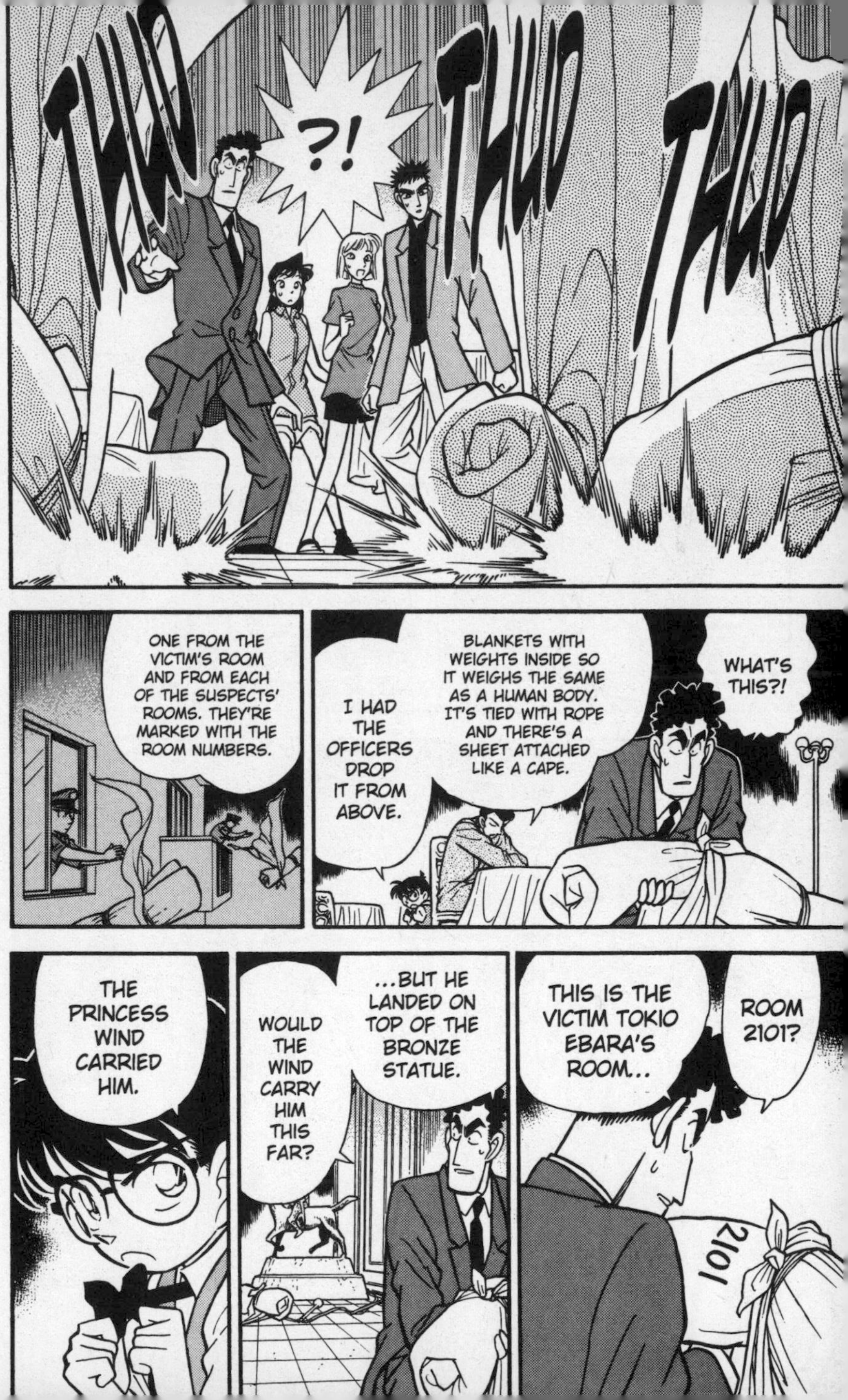
THUD
THUD
?!
THUD
WHAT'S THIS?!
BLANKETS WITH WEIGHTS INSIDE SO IT WEIGHS THE SAME AS A HUMAN BODY. IT'S TIED WITH ROPE AND THERE'S A SHEET ATTACHED LIKE A CAPE.
I HAD THE OFFICERS DROP IT FROM ABOVE.
ONE FROM THE VICTIM'S ROOM AND FROM EACH OF THE SUSPECTS' ROOMS. THEY'RE MARKED WITH THE ROOM NUMBERS.
ROOM 2101?
THIS IS THE VICTIM TOKIO EBARA'S ROOM...
2101
...BUT HE LANDED ON TOP OF THE BRONZE STATUE.
WOULD THE WIND CARRY HIM THIS FAR?
THE PRINCESS WIND CARRIED HIM.

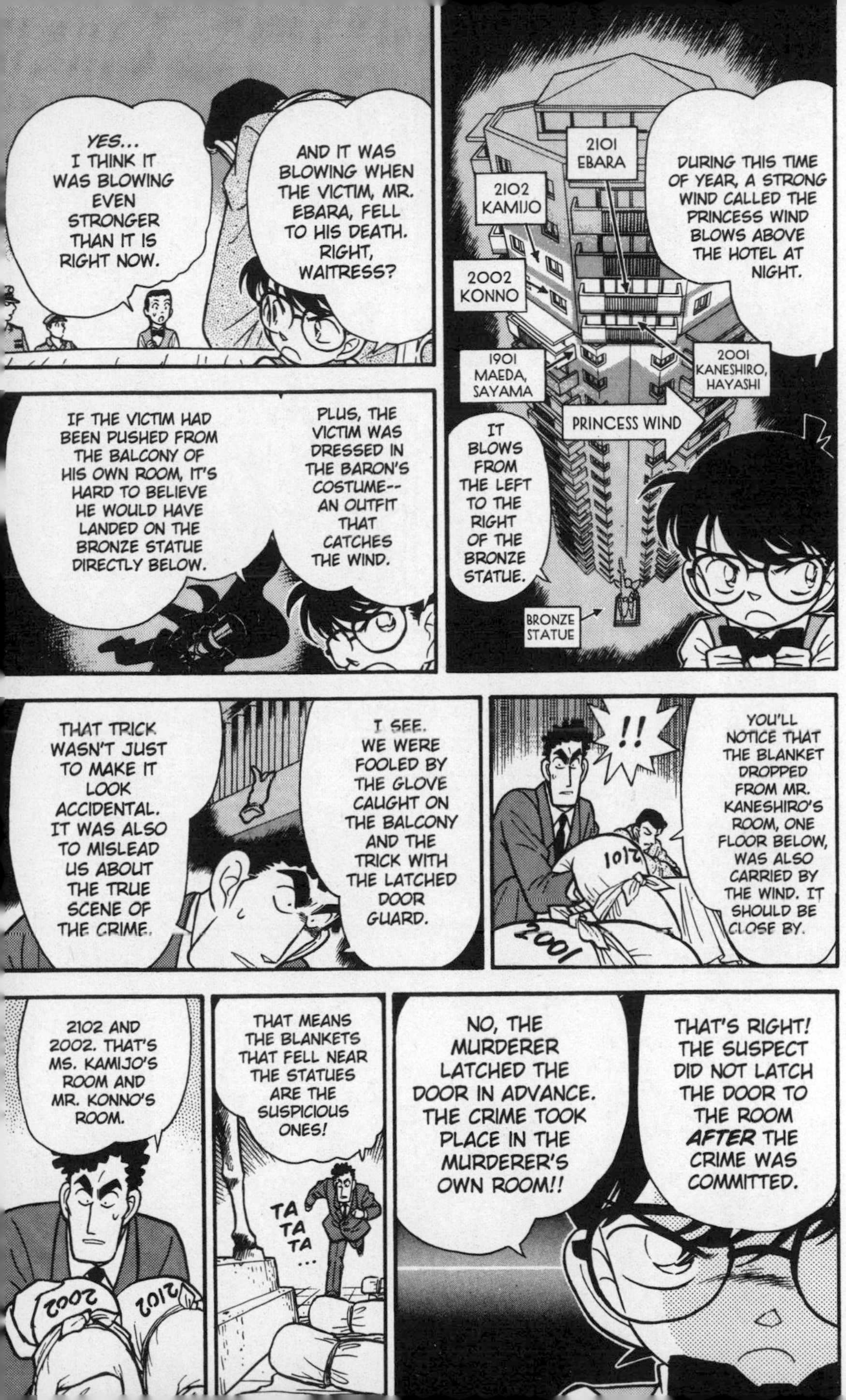
DURING THIS TIME OF YEAR, A STRONG WIND CALLED THE PRINCESS WIND BLOWS ABOVE THE HOTEL AT NIGHT.
2101 EBARA
2102 KAMIJO
2002 KONNO
2001 KANESHIRO, HAYASHI
1901 MAEDA, SAYAMA
PRINCESS WIND
IT BLOWS FROM THE LEFT TO THE RIGHT OF THE BRONZE STATUE.
BRONZE STATUE
AND IT WAS BLOWING WHEN THE VICTIM, MR. EBARA, FELL TO HIS DEATH. RIGHT, WAITRESS?
YES... I THINK IT WAS BLOWING EVEN STRONGER THAN IT IS RIGHT NOW.
PLUS, THE VICTIM WAS DRESSED IN THE BARON'S COSTUME-- AN OUTFIT THAT CATCHES THE WIND.
IF THE VICTIM HAD BEEN PUSHED FROM THE BALCONY OF HIS OWN ROOM, IT'S HARD TO BELIEVE HE WOULD HAVE LANDED ON THE BRONZE STATUE DIRECTLY BELOW.
!!
YOU'LL NOTICE THAT THE BLANKET DROPPED FROM MR. KANESHIRO'S ROOM, ONE FLOOR BELOW, WAS ALSO CARRIED BY THE WIND. IT SHOULD BE CLOSE BY.
2001
I SEE. WE WERE FOOLED BY THE GLOVE CAUGHT ON THE BALCONY AND THE TRICK WITH THE LATCHED DOOR GUARD.
THAT TRICK WASN'T JUST TO MAKE IT LOOK ACCIDENTAL. IT WAS ALSO TO MISLEAD US ABOUT THE TRUE SCENE OF THE CRIME.
THAT'S RIGHT! THE SUSPECT DID NOT LATCH THE DOOR TO THE ROOM AFTER THE CRIME WAS COMMITTED.
NO, THE MURDERER LATCHED THE DOOR IN ADVANCE. THE CRIME TOOK PLACE IN THE MURDERER'S OWN ROOM!!
THAT MEANS THE BLANKETS THAT FELL NEAR THE STATUES ARE THE SUSPICIOUS ONES!
TA TA TA ...
2102 AND 2002. THAT'S MS. KAMIJO'S ROOM AND MR. KONNO'S ROOM.
2002
2102

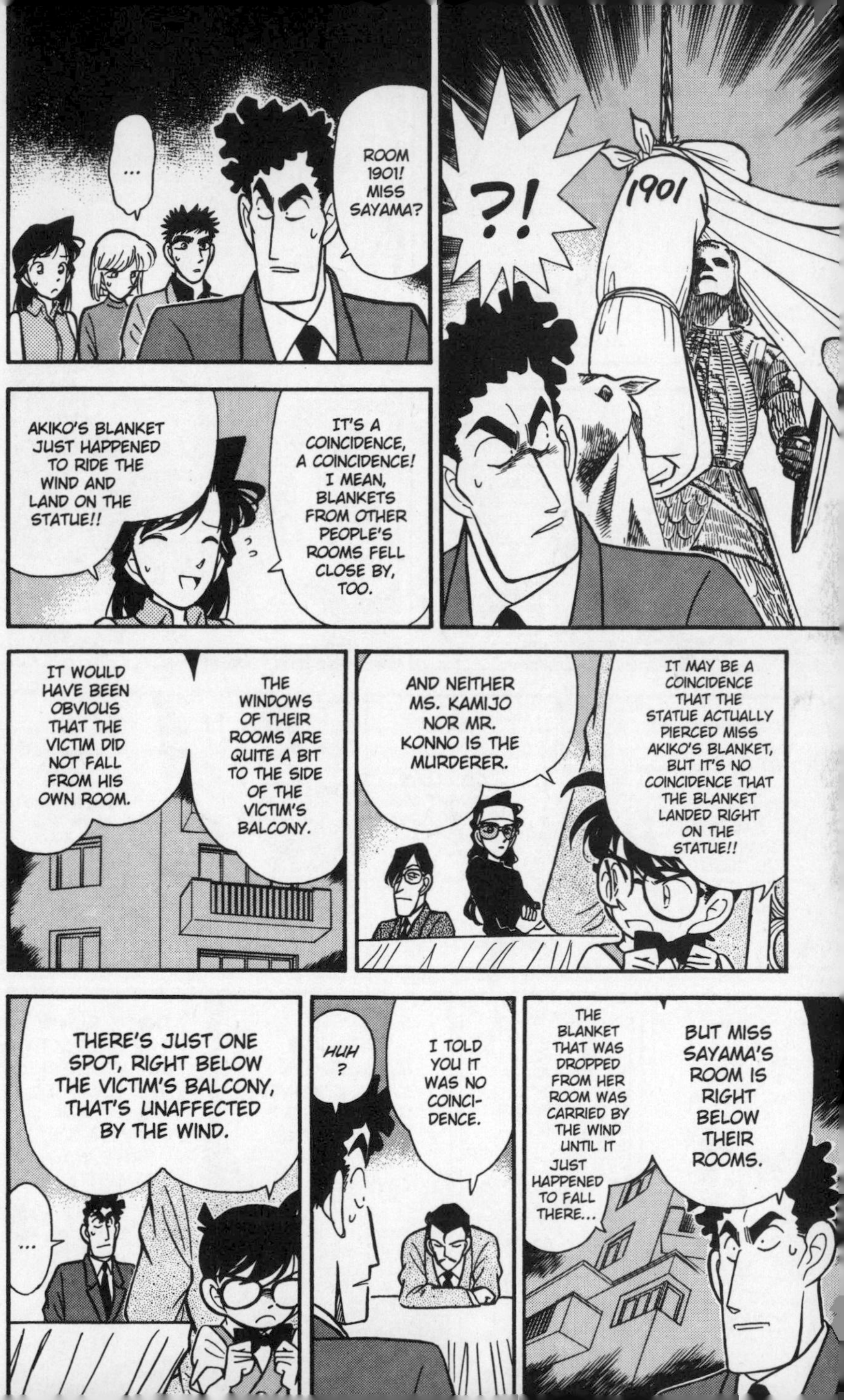
?!
1901
ROOM 1901! MISS SAYAMA?
...
IT'S A COINCIDENCE, A COINCIDENCE! I MEAN, BLANKETS FROM OTHER PEOPLE'S ROOMS FELL CLOSE BY, TOO.
AKIKO'S BLANKET JUST HAPPENED TO RIDE THE WIND AND LAND ON THE STATUE!!
IT MAY BE A COINCIDENCE THAT THE STATUE ACTUALLY PIERCED MISS AKIKO'S BLANKET, BUT IT'S NO COINCIDENCE THAT THE BLANKET LANDED RIGHT ON THE STATUE!!
AND NEITHER MS. KAMIJO NOR MR. KONNO IS THE MURDERER.
THE WINDOWS OF THEIR ROOMS ARE QUITE A BIT TO THE SIDE OF THE VICTIM'S BALCONY.
IT WOULD HAVE BEEN OBVIOUS THAT THE VICTIM DID NOT FALL FROM HIS OWN ROOM.
BUT MISS SAYAMA'S ROOM IS RIGHT BELOW THEIR ROOMS.
THE BLANKET THAT WAS DROPPED FROM HER ROOM WAS CARRIED BY THE WIND UNTIL IT JUST HAPPENED TO FALL THERE...
I TOLD YOU IT WAS NO COINCIDENCE.
HUH?
THERE'S JUST ONE SPOT, RIGHT BELOW THE VICTIM'S BALCONY, THAT'S UNAFFECTED BY THE WIND.
...

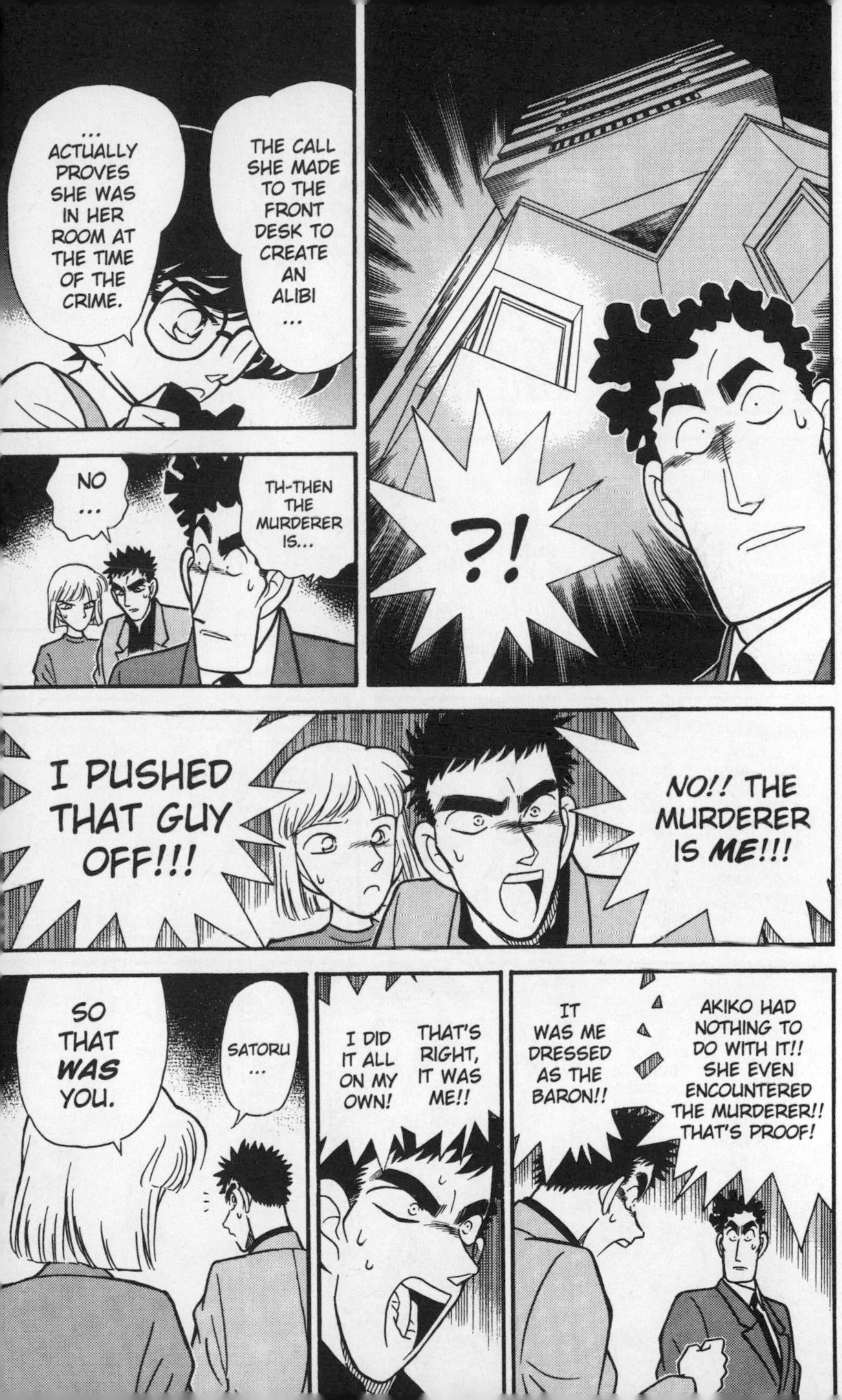
?!
THE CALL SHE MADE TO THE FRONT DESK TO CREATE AN ALIBI ...
... ACTUALLY PROVES SHE WAS IN HER ROOM AT THE TIME OF THE CRIME.
TH-THEN THE MURDERER IS...
NO ...
NO!! THE MURDERER IS *ME!!!*
I PUSHED THAT GUY OFF!!!
AKIKO HAD NOTHING TO DO WITH IT!! SHE EVEN ENCOUNTERED THE MURDERER!! THAT'S PROOF!
IT WAS ME DRESSED AS THE BARON!!
THAT'S RIGHT, IT WAS ME!!
I DID IT ALL ON MY OWN!
SATORU ...
SO THAT **WAS** YOU.

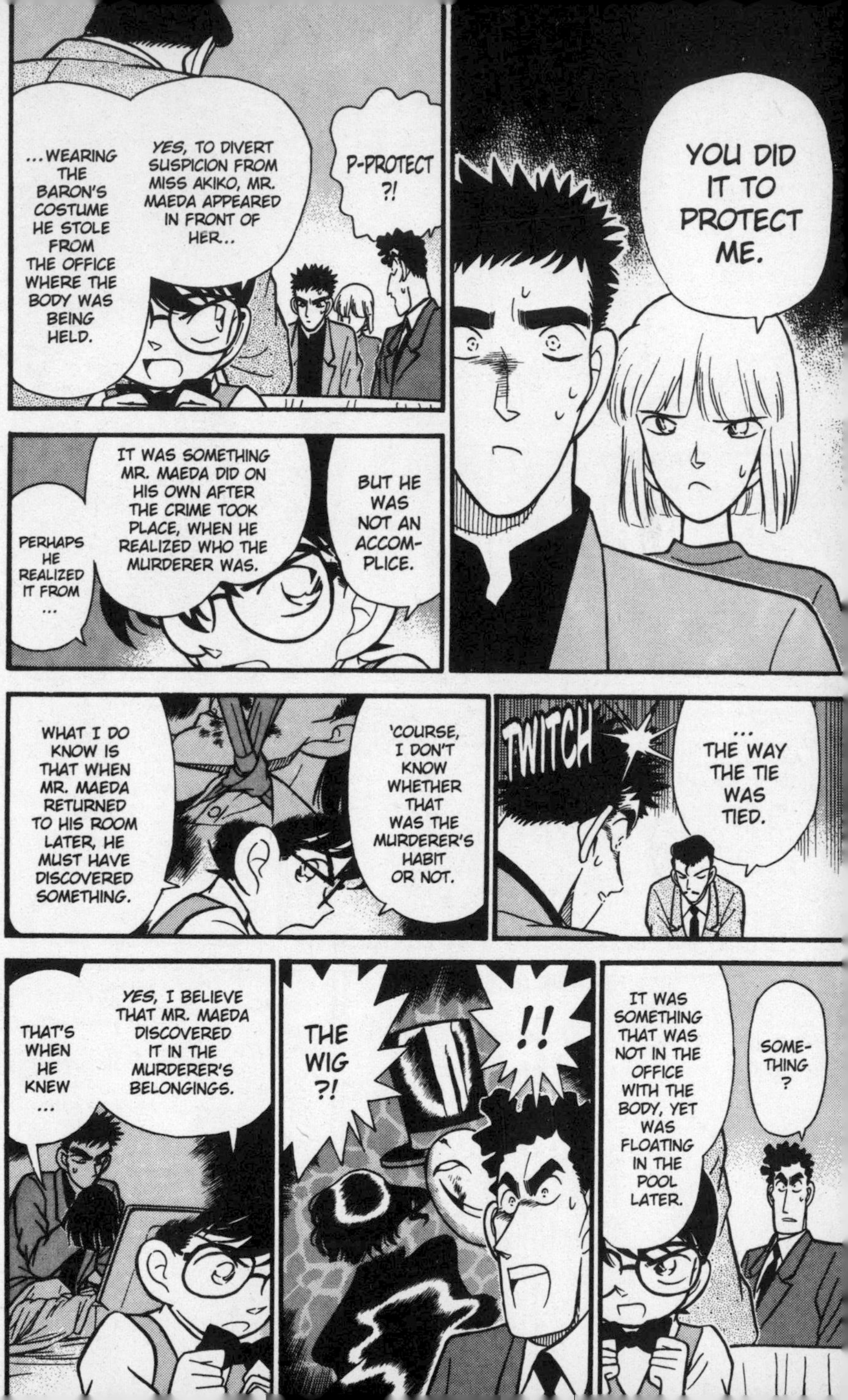
YOU DID IT TO PROTECT ME.
P-PROTECT ?!
YES, TO DIVERT SUSPICION FROM MISS AKIKO, MR. MAEDA APPEARED IN FRONT OF HER...
...WEARING THE BARON'S COSTUME HE STOLE FROM THE OFFICE WHERE THE BODY WAS BEING HELD.
BUT HE WAS NOT AN ACCOMPLICE.
IT WAS SOMETHING MR. MAEDA DID ON HIS OWN AFTER THE CRIME TOOK PLACE, WHEN HE REALIZED WHO THE MURDERER WAS.
PERHAPS HE REALIZED IT FROM ...
... THE WAY THE TIE WAS TIED.
TWITCH
'COURSE, I DON'T KNOW WHETHER THAT WAS THE MURDERER'S HABIT OR NOT.
WHAT I DO KNOW IS THAT WHEN MR. MAEDA RETURNED TO HIS ROOM LATER, HE MUST HAVE DISCOVERED SOMETHING.
SOME-THING ?
IT WAS SOMETHING THAT WAS NOT IN THE OFFICE WITH THE BODY, YET WAS FLOATING IN THE POOL LATER.
!!
THE WIG ?!
YES, I BELIEVE THAT MR. MAEDA DISCOVERED IT IN THE MURDERER'S BELONGINGS.
THAT'S WHEN HE KNEW ...

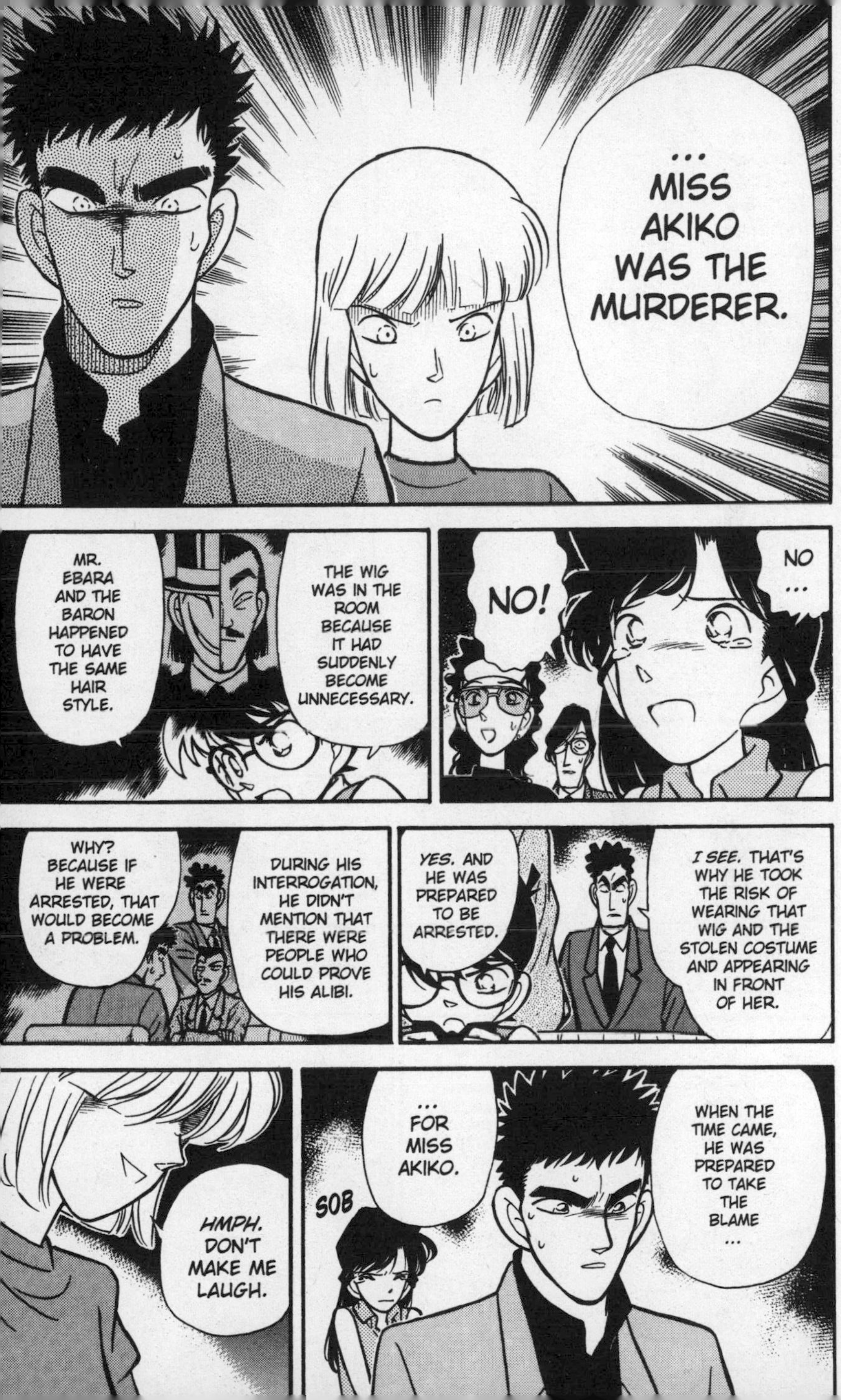
... MISS AKIKO WAS THE MURDERER.
NO ...
NO!
THE WIG WAS IN THE ROOM BECAUSE IT HAD SUDDENLY BECOME UNNECESSARY.
MR. EBARA AND THE BARON HAPPENED TO HAVE THE SAME HAIR STYLE.
I SEE. THAT'S WHY HE TOOK THE RISK OF WEARING THAT WIG AND THE STOLEN COSTUME AND APPEARING IN FRONT OF HER.
YES. AND HE WAS PREPARED TO BE ARRESTED.
DURING HIS INTERROGATION, HE DIDN'T MENTION THAT THERE WERE PEOPLE WHO COULD PROVE HIS ALIBI.
WHY? BECAUSE IF HE WERE ARRESTED, THAT WOULD BECOME A PROBLEM.
WHEN THE TIME CAME, HE WAS PREPARED TO TAKE THE BLAME ...
... FOR MISS AKIKO.
SOB
HMPH. DON'T MAKE ME LAUGH.

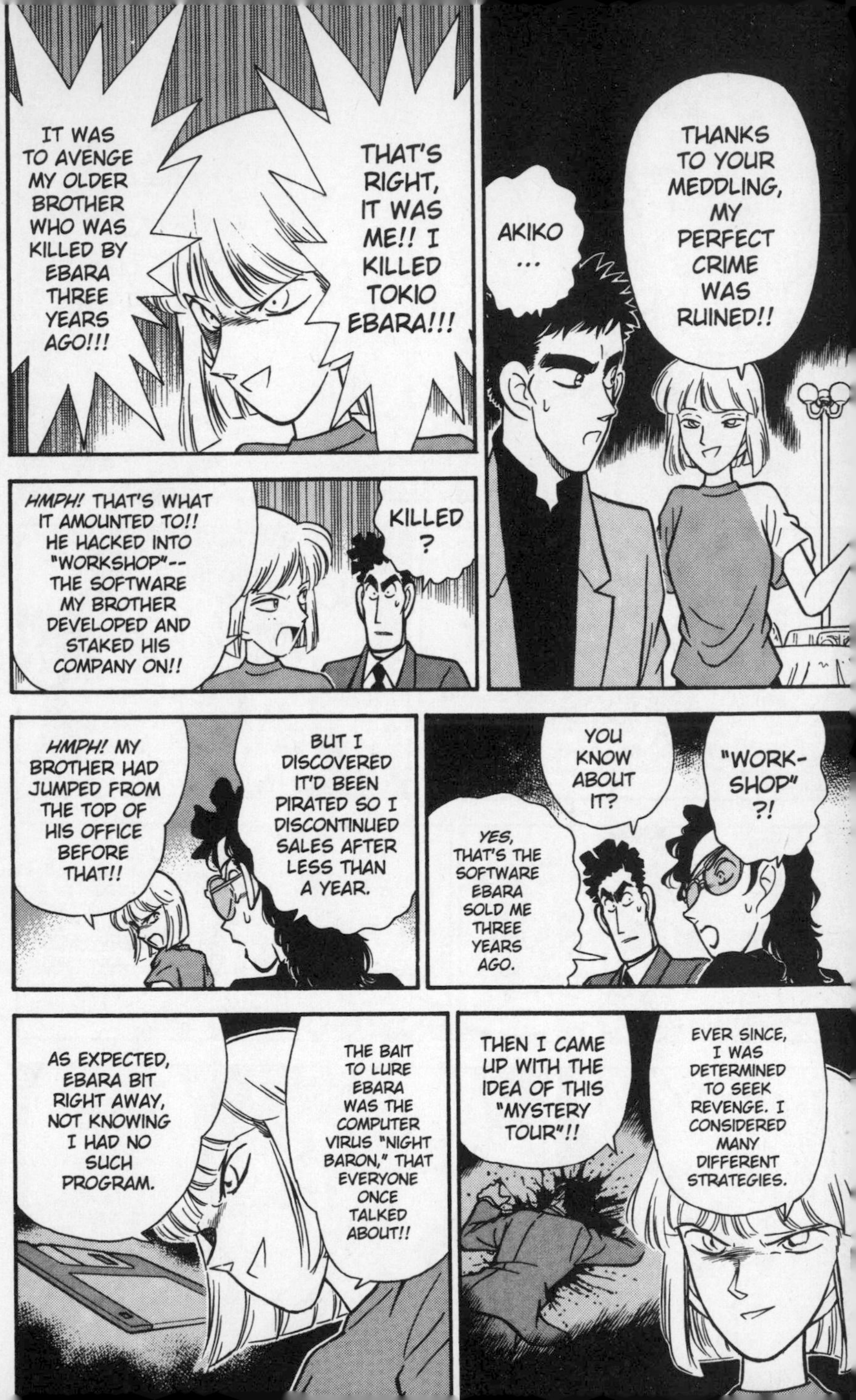
THANKS TO YOUR MEDDLING, MY PERFECT CRIME WAS RUINED!!
AKIKO ...
THAT'S RIGHT, IT WAS ME!! I KILLED TOKIO EBARA!!!
IT WAS TO AVENGE MY OLDER BROTHER WHO WAS KILLED BY EBARA THREE YEARS AGO!!!
KILLED ?
HMPH! THAT'S WHAT IT AMOUNTED TO!! HE HACKED INTO "WORKSHOP"-- THE SOFTWARE MY BROTHER DEVELOPED AND STAKED HIS COMPANY ON!!
"WORK-SHOP" ?!
YOU KNOW ABOUT IT?
YES, THAT'S THE SOFTWARE EBARA SOLD ME THREE YEARS AGO.
BUT I DISCOVERED IT'D BEEN PIRATED SO I DISCONTINUED SALES AFTER LESS THAN A YEAR.
HMPH! MY BROTHER HAD JUMPED FROM THE TOP OF HIS OFFICE BEFORE THAT!!
EVER SINCE, I WAS DETERMINED TO SEEK REVENGE. I CONSIDERED MANY DIFFERENT STRATEGIES.
THEN I CAME UP WITH THE IDEA OF THIS "MYSTERY TOUR"!!
THE BAIT TO LURE EBARA WAS THE COMPUTER VIRUS "NIGHT BARON," THAT EVERYONE ONCE TALKED ABOUT!!
AS EXPECTED, EBARA BIT RIGHT AWAY, NOT KNOWING I HAD NO SUCH PROGRAM.

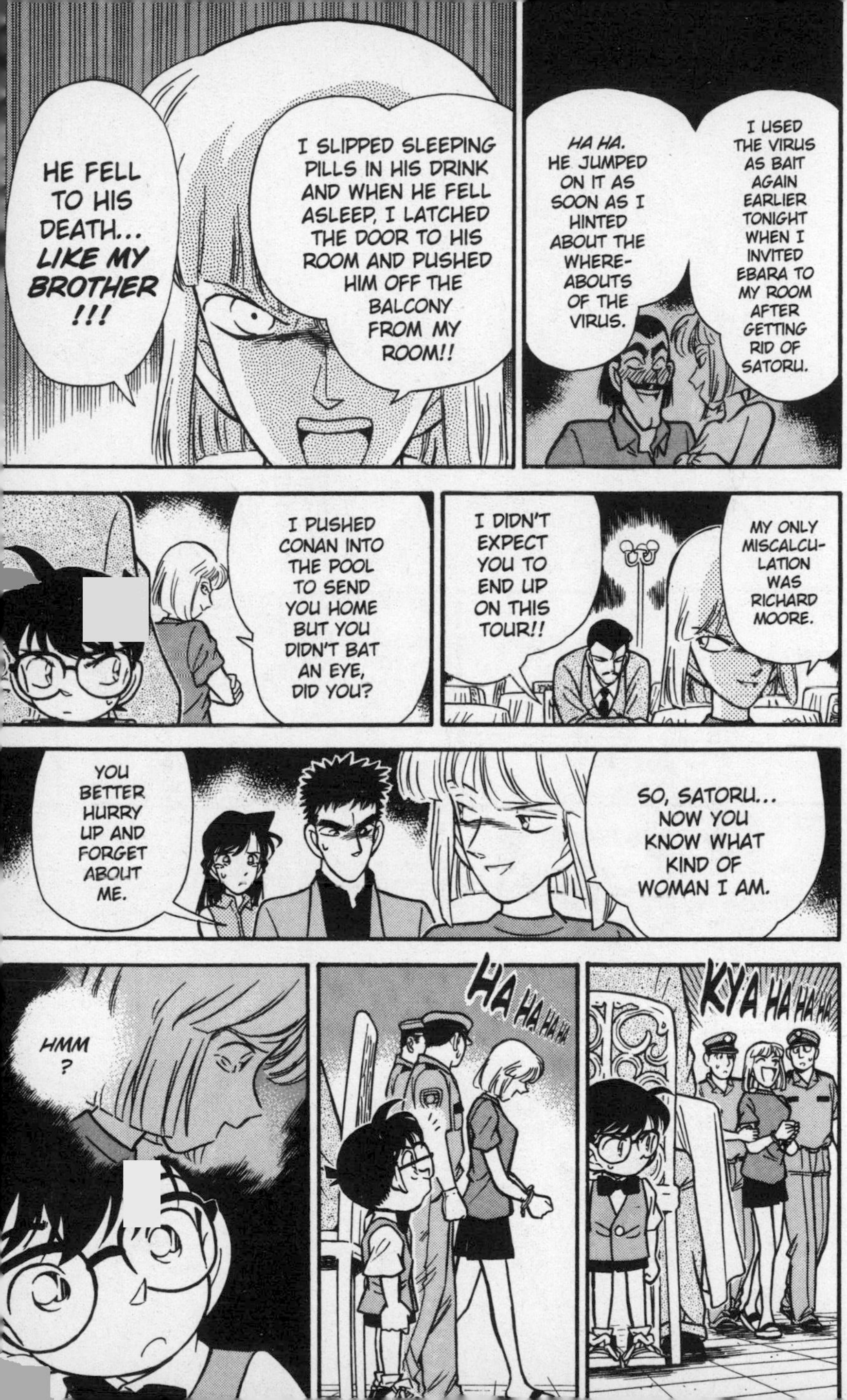
I USED THE VIRUS AS BAIT AGAIN EARLIER TONIGHT WHEN I INVITED EBARA TO MY ROOM AFTER GETTING RID OF SATORU.
HA HA. HE JUMPED ON IT AS SOON AS I HINTED ABOUT THE WHERE-ABOUTS OF THE VIRUS.
I SLIPPED SLEEPING PILLS IN HIS DRINK AND WHEN HE FELL ASLEEP, I LATCHED THE DOOR TO HIS ROOM AND PUSHED HIM OFF THE BALCONY FROM MY ROOM!!
HE FELL TO HIS DEATH... LIKE MY BROTHER!!!
MY ONLY MISCALCU-LATION WAS RICHARD MOORE.
I DIDN'T EXPECT YOU TO END UP ON THIS TOUR!!
I PUSHED CONAN INTO THE POOL TO SEND YOU HOME BUT YOU DIDN'T BAT AN EYE, DID YOU?
SO, SATORU... NOW YOU KNOW WHAT KIND OF WOMAN I AM.
YOU BETTER HURRY UP AND FORGET ABOUT ME.
KYA HA HA HA HA
HA HA HA HA HA
HMM ?

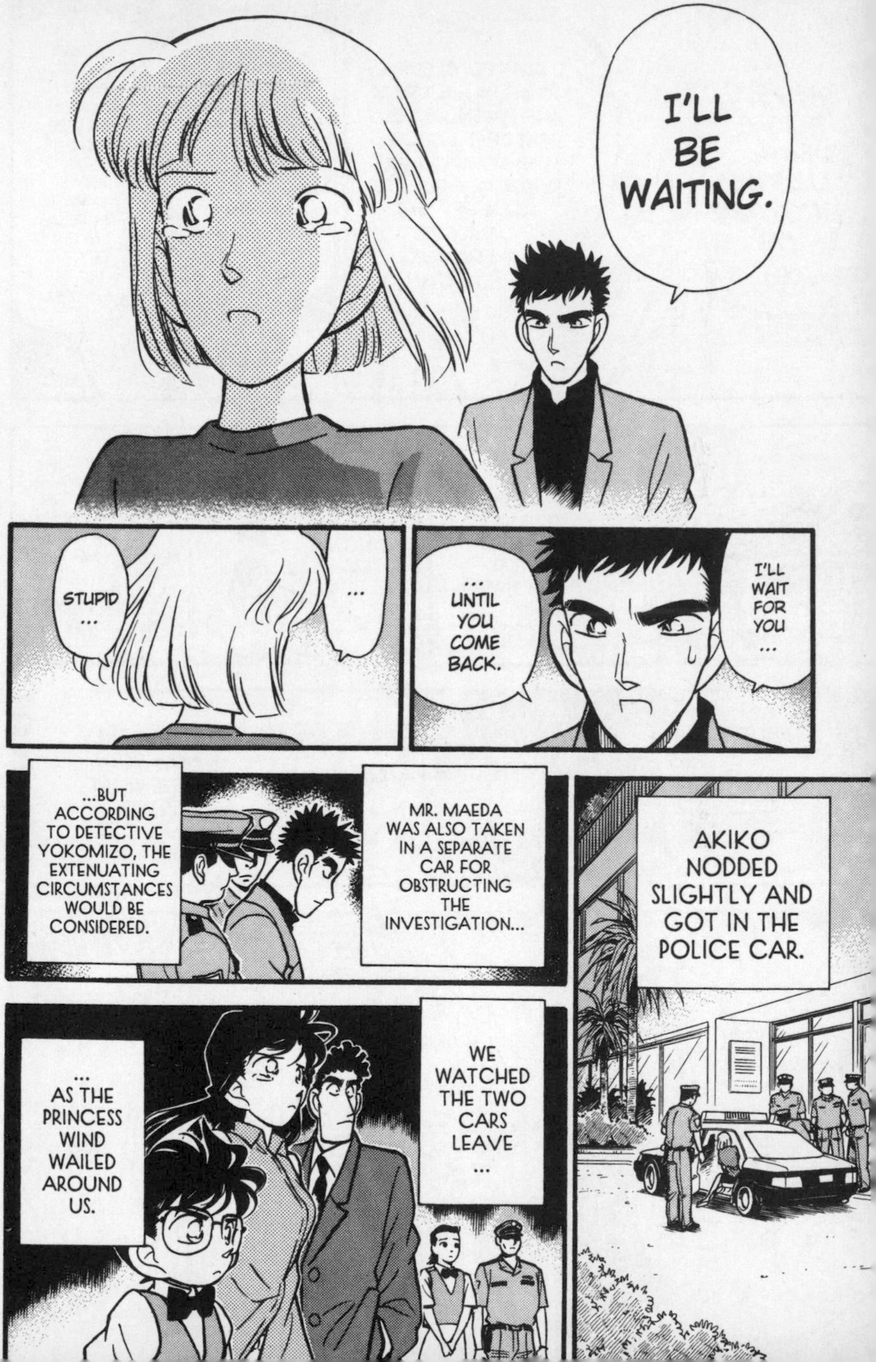
I'LL BE WAITING.
I'LL WAIT FOR YOU...
...UNTIL YOU COME BACK.
...
STUPID...
AKIKO NODDED SLIGHTLY AND GOT IN THE POLICE CAR.
MR. MAEDA WAS ALSO TAKEN IN A SEPARATE CAR FOR OBSTRUCTING THE INVESTIGATION...
...BUT ACCORDING TO DETECTIVE YOKOMIZO, THE EXTENUATING CIRCUMSTANCES WOULD BE CONSIDERED.
WE WATCHED THE TWO CARS LEAVE...
...AS THE PRINCESS WIND WAILED AROUND US.

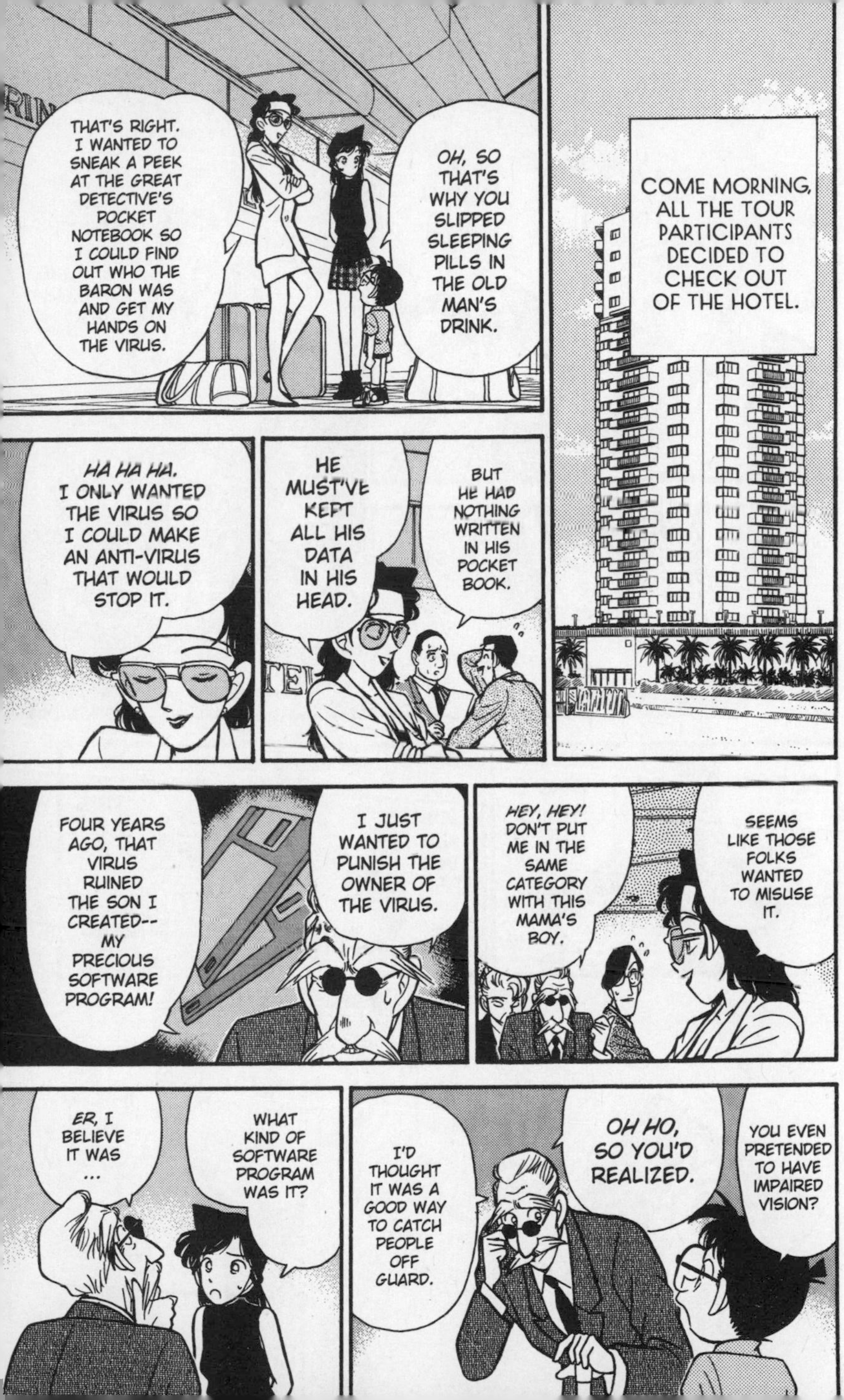
COME MORNING, ALL THE TOUR PARTICIPANTS DECIDED TO CHECK OUT OF THE HOTEL.
OH, SO THAT'S WHY YOU SLIPPED SLEEPING PILLS IN THE OLD MAN'S DRINK.
THAT'S RIGHT. I WANTED TO SNEAK A PEEK AT THE GREAT DETECTIVE'S POCKET NOTEBOOK SO I COULD FIND OUT WHO THE BARON WAS AND GET MY HANDS ON THE VIRUS.
BUT HE HAD NOTHING WRITTEN IN HIS POCKET BOOK.
HE MUST'VE KEPT ALL HIS DATA IN HIS HEAD.
HA HA HA. I ONLY WANTED THE VIRUS SO I COULD MAKE AN ANTI-VIRUS THAT WOULD STOP IT.
SEEMS LIKE THOSE FOLKS WANTED TO MISUSE IT.
HEY, HEY! DON'T PUT ME IN THE SAME CATEGORY WITH THIS MAMA'S BOY.
I JUST WANTED TO PUNISH THE OWNER OF THE VIRUS.
FOUR YEARS AGO, THAT VIRUS RUINED THE SON I CREATED-- MY PRECIOUS SOFTWARE PROGRAM!
YOU EVEN PRETENDED TO HAVE IMPAIRED VISION?
OH HO, SO YOU'D REALIZED.
I'D THOUGHT IT WAS A GOOD WAY TO CATCH PEOPLE OFF GUARD.
WHAT KIND OF SOFTWARE PROGRAM WAS IT?
ER, I BELIEVE IT WAS ...

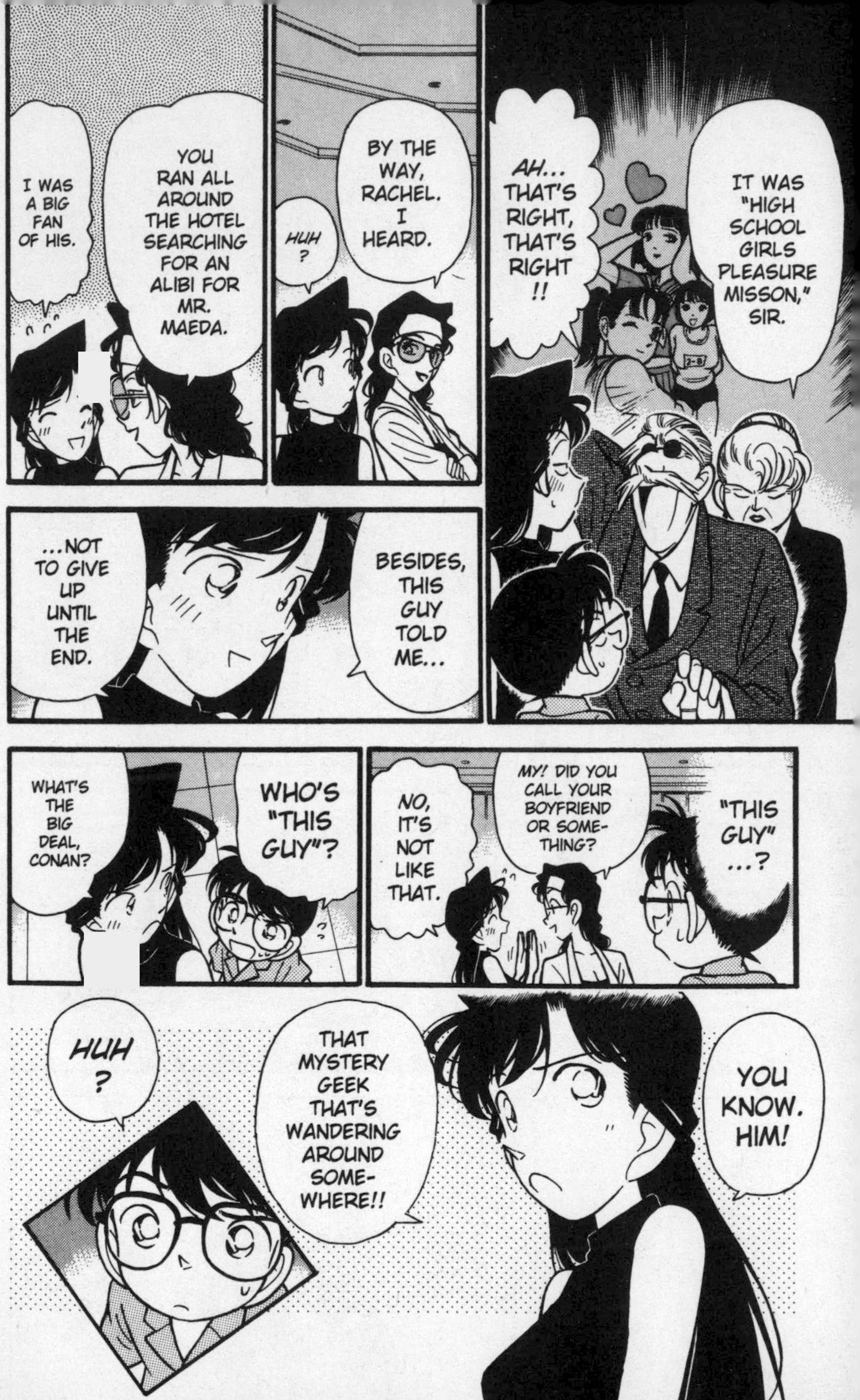
IT WAS "HIGH SCHOOL GIRLS PLEASURE MISSON," SIR.
AH... THAT'S RIGHT, THAT'S RIGHT!!
BY THE WAY, RACHEL. I HEARD.
HUH?
YOU RAN ALL AROUND THE HOTEL SEARCHING FOR AN ALIBI FOR MR. MAEDA.
I WAS A BIG FAN OF HIS.
BESIDES, THIS GUY TOLD ME...
...NOT TO GIVE UP UNTIL THE END.
"THIS GUY" ...?
MY! DID YOU CALL YOUR BOYFRIEND OR SOME-THING?
NO, IT'S NOT LIKE THAT.
WHO'S "THIS GUY"?
WHAT'S THE BIG DEAL, CONAN?
YOU KNOW. HIM!
THAT MYSTERY GEEK THAT'S WANDERING AROUND SOME-WHERE!!
HUH?

FILE 8: THE BRIDE'S TRAGEDY

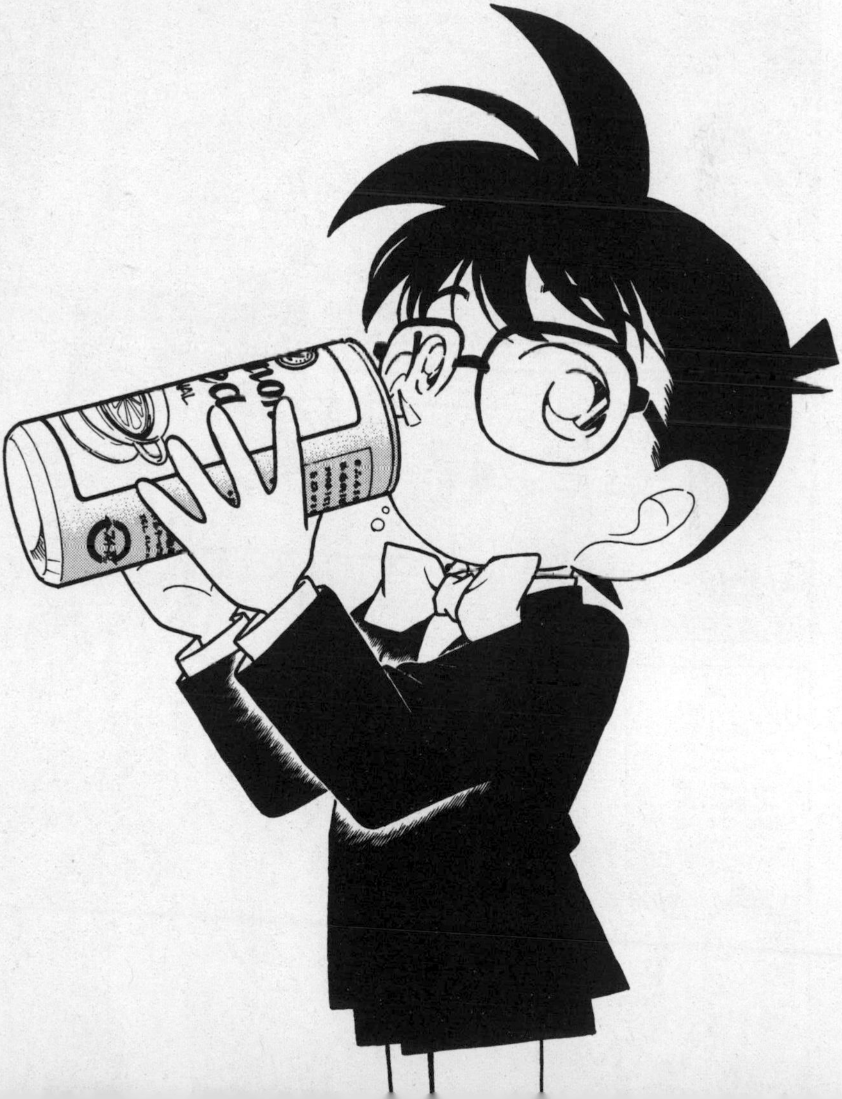

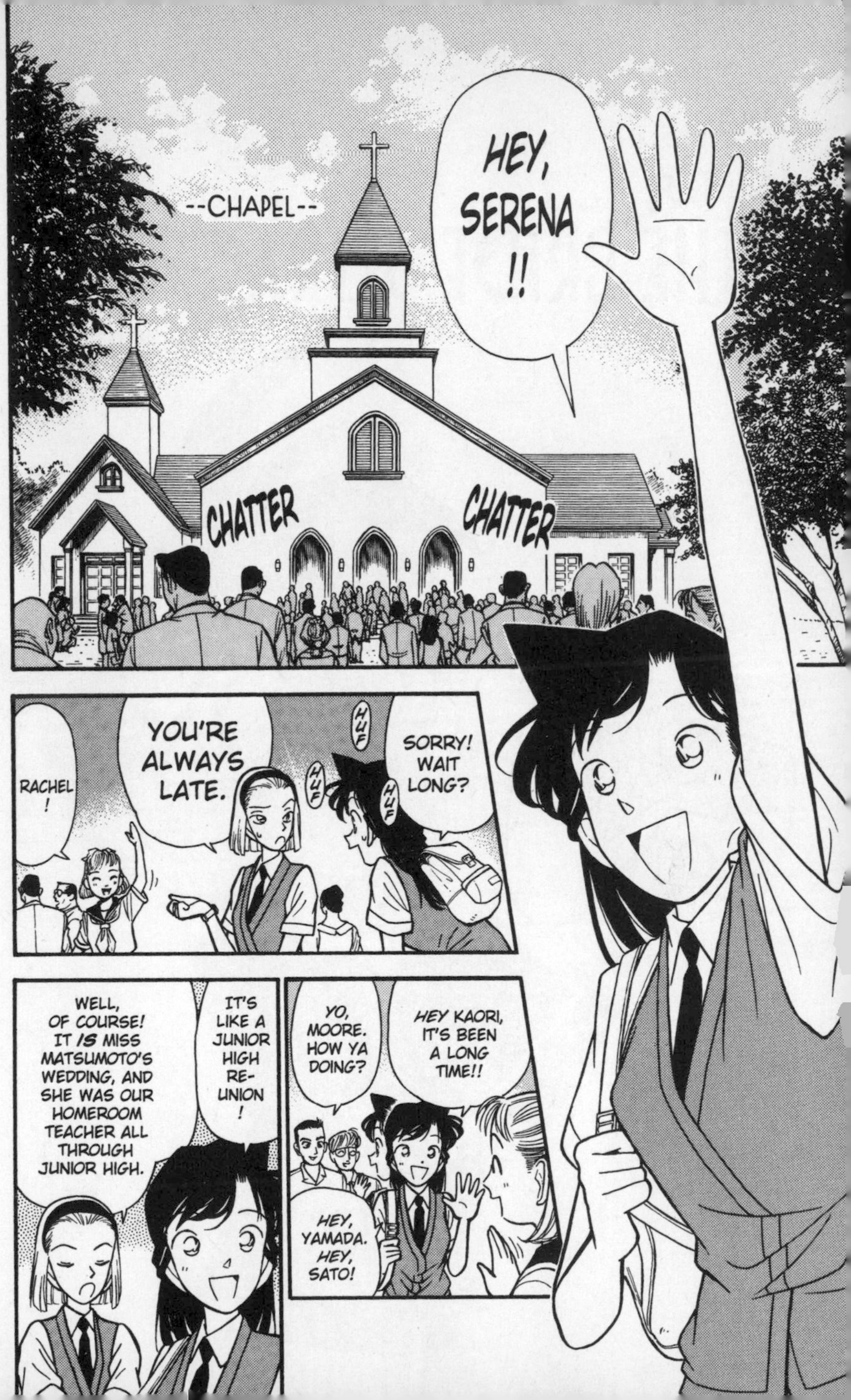
--CHAPEL--
CHATTER
CHATTER
HEY, SERENA!!
SORRY! WAIT LONG?
HUF
HUF
HUF
YOU'RE ALWAYS LATE.
RACHEL!
HEY KAORI, IT'S BEEN A LONG TIME!!
YO, MOORE. HOW YA DOING?
HEY, YAMADA. HEY, SATO!
IT'S LIKE A JUNIOR HIGH RE-UNION!
WELL, OF COURSE! IT *IS* MISS MATSUMOTO'S WEDDING, AND SHE WAS OUR HOMEROOM TEACHER ALL THROUGH JUNIOR HIGH.

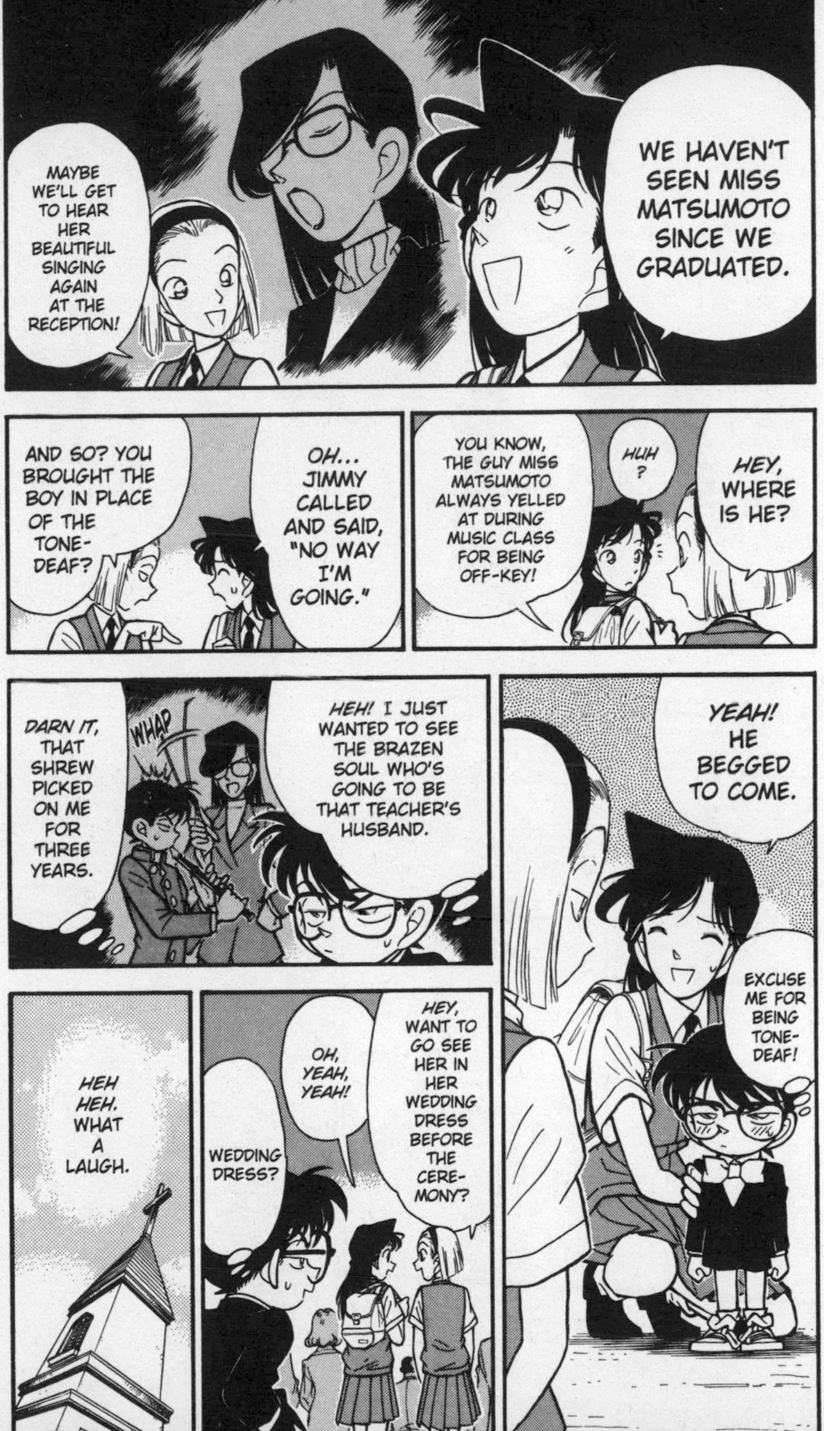
WE HAVEN'T SEEN MISS MATSUMOTO SINCE WE GRADUATED.
MAYBE WE'LL GET TO HEAR HER BEAUTIFUL SINGING AGAIN AT THE RECEPTION!
HEY, WHERE IS HE?
HUH?
YOU KNOW, THE GUY MISS MATSUMOTO ALWAYS YELLED AT DURING MUSIC CLASS FOR BEING OFF-KEY!
OH... JIMMY CALLED AND SAID, "NO WAY I'M GOING."
AND SO? YOU BROUGHT THE BOY IN PLACE OF THE TONE-DEAF?
YEAH! HE BEGGED TO COME.
EXCUSE ME FOR BEING TONE-DEAF!
HEH! I JUST WANTED TO SEE THE BRAZEN SOUL WHO'S GOING TO BE THAT TEACHER'S HUSBAND.
WHAP
DARN IT, THAT SHREW PICKED ON ME FOR THREE YEARS.
HEY, WANT TO GO SEE HER IN HER WEDDING DRESS BEFORE THE CERE-MONY?
OH, YEAH, YEAH!
WEDDING DRESS?
HEH HEH. WHAT A LAUGH.

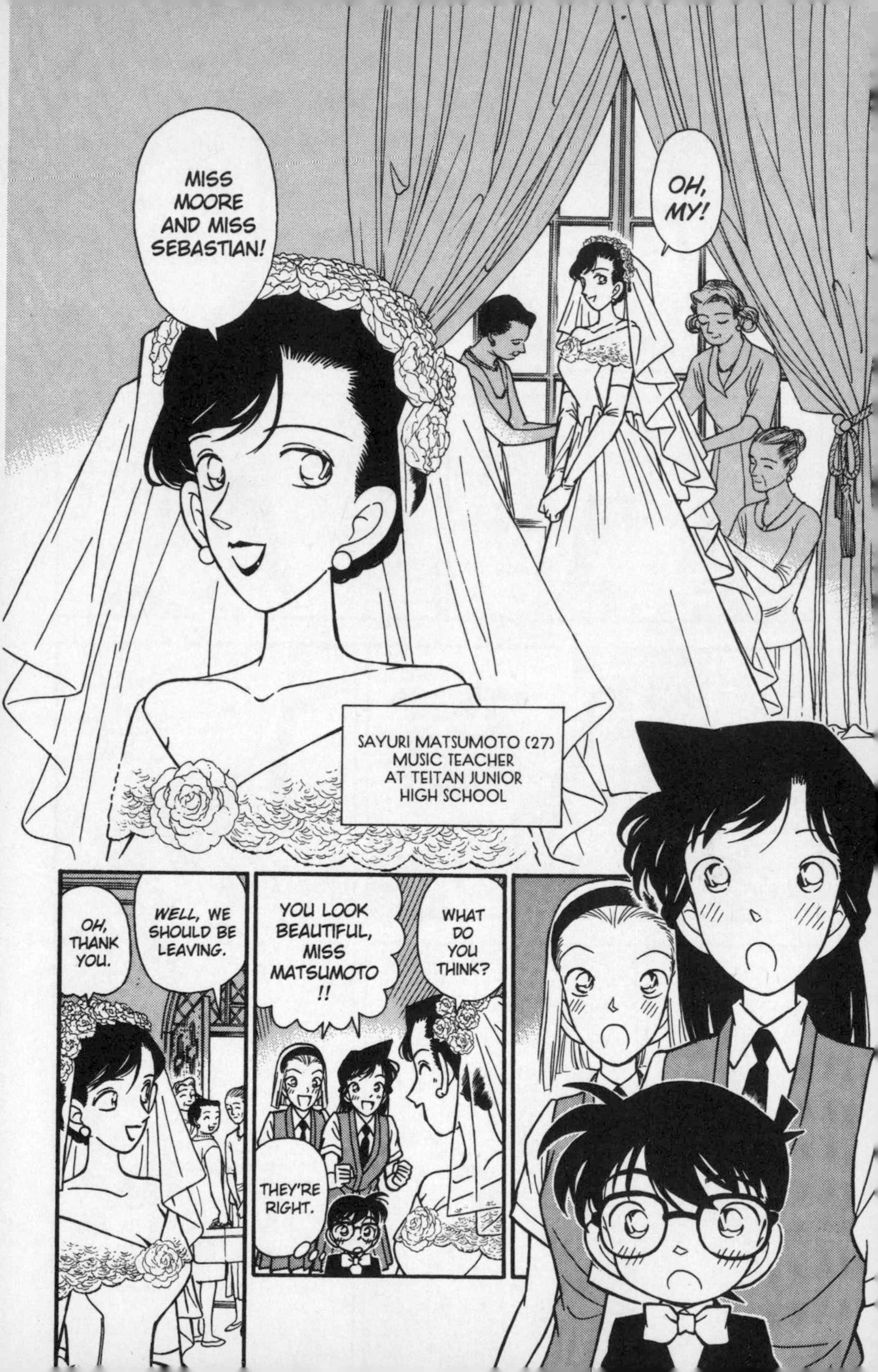
OH, MY!
MISS MOORE AND MISS SEBASTIAN!
SAYURI MATSUMOTO (27) MUSIC TEACHER AT TEITAN JUNIOR HIGH SCHOOL
WHAT DO YOU THINK?
YOU LOOK BEAUTIFUL, MISS MATSUMOTO !!
THEY'RE RIGHT.
WELL, WE SHOULD BE LEAVING.
OH, THANK YOU.

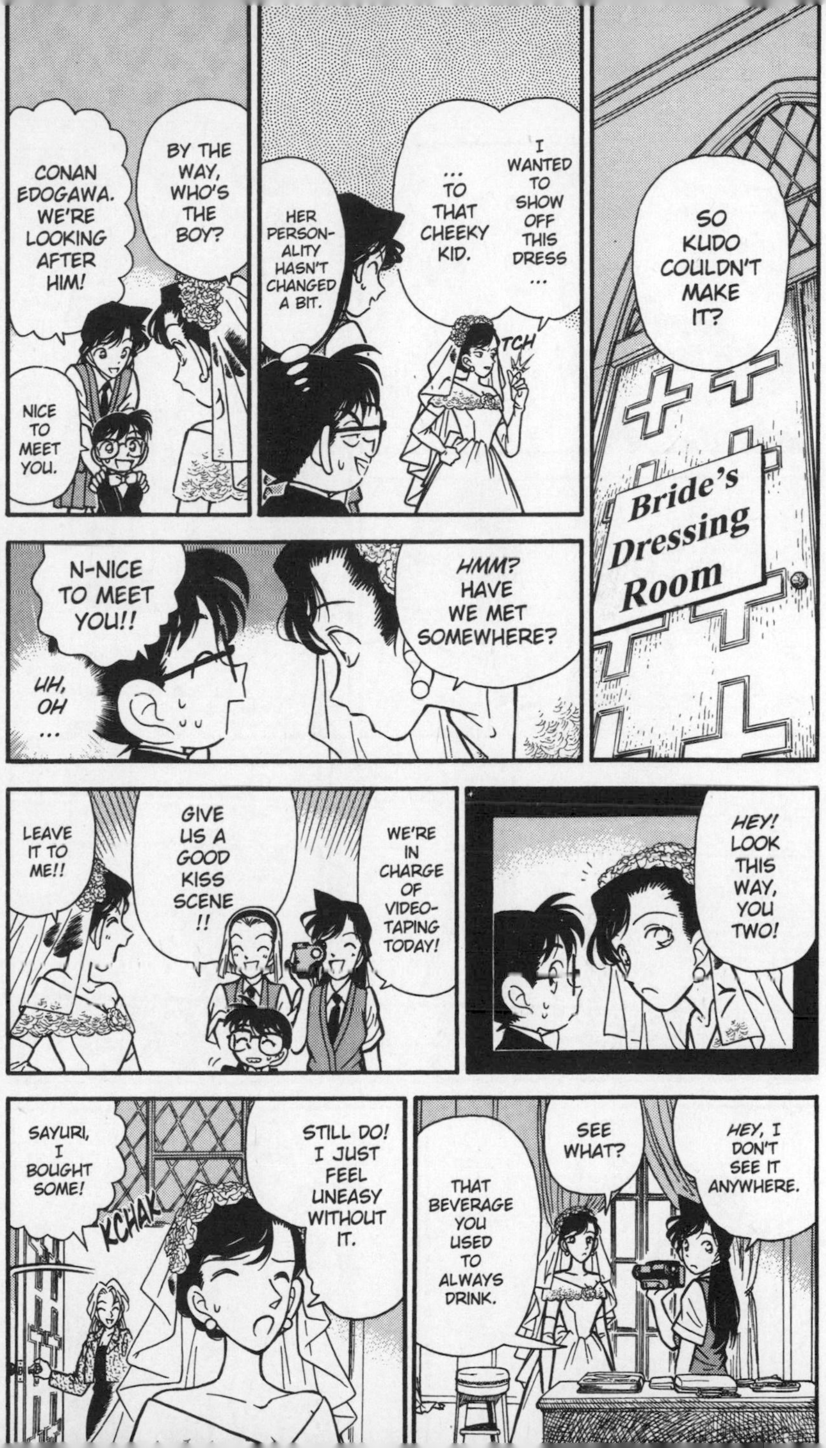
SO KUDO COULDN'T MAKE IT?
Bride's Dressing Room
I WANTED TO SHOW OFF THIS DRESS ...
... TO THAT CHEEKY KID.
TCH
HER PERSONALITY HASN'T CHANGED A BIT.
BY THE WAY, WHO'S THE BOY?
CONAN EDOGAWA. WE'RE LOOKING AFTER HIM!
NICE TO MEET YOU.
HMM? HAVE WE MET SOMEWHERE?
N-NICE TO MEET YOU!!
UH, OH ...
HEY! LOOK THIS WAY, YOU TWO!
WE'RE IN CHARGE OF VIDEOTAPING TODAY!
GIVE US A GOOD KISS SCENE!!
LEAVE IT TO ME!!
HEY, I DON'T SEE IT ANYWHERE.
SEE WHAT?
THAT BEVERAGE YOU USED TO ALWAYS DRINK.
STILL DO! I JUST FEEL UNEASY WITHOUT IT.
KCHAK
SAYURI, I BOUGHT SOME!

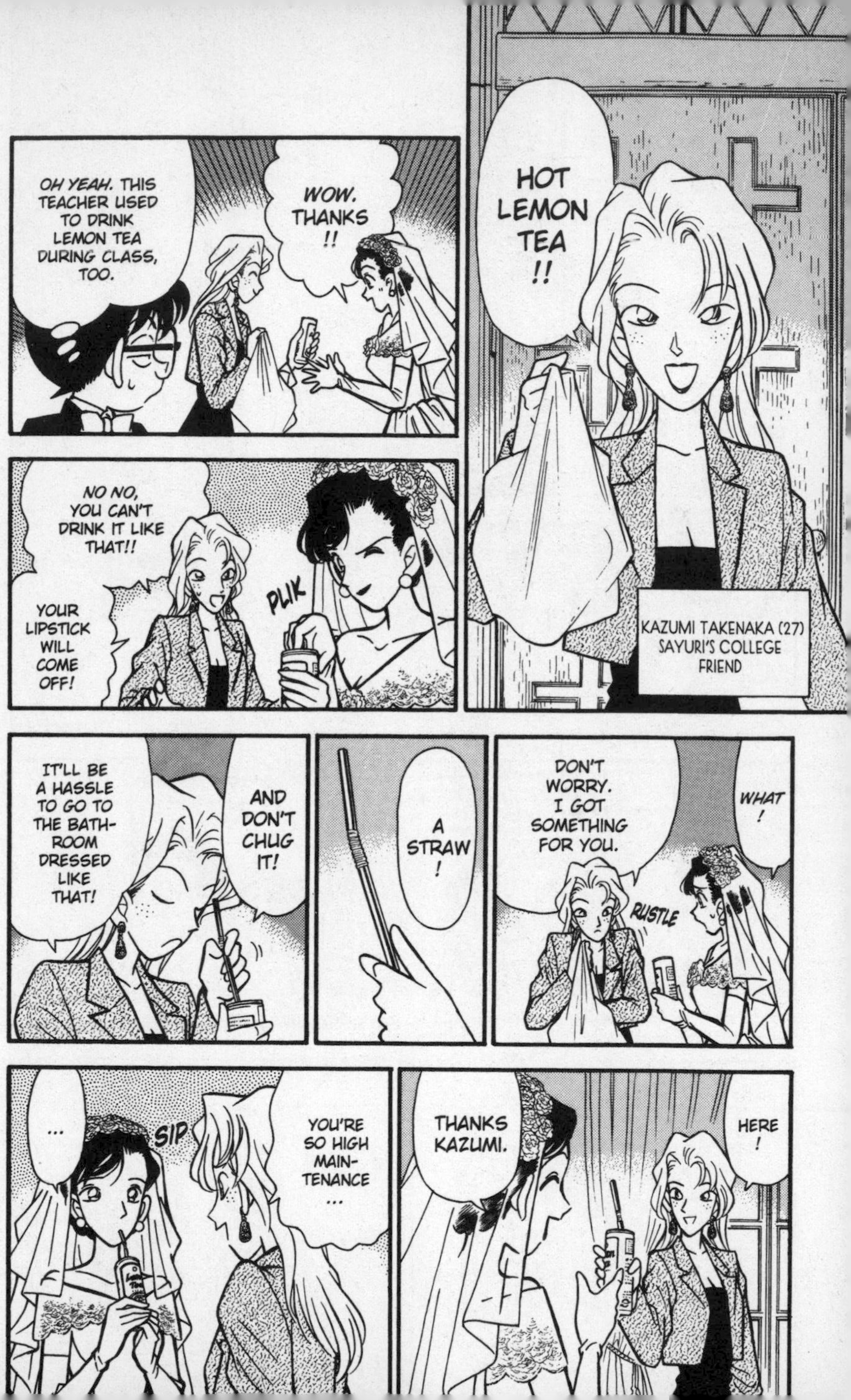
HOT LEMON TEA !!
KAZUMI TAKENAKA (27) SAYURI'S COLLEGE FRIEND
WOW. THANKS !!
OH YEAH. THIS TEACHER USED TO DRINK LEMON TEA DURING CLASS, TOO.
NO NO, YOU CAN'T DRINK IT LIKE THAT!!
PLIK
YOUR LIPSTICK WILL COME OFF!
WHAT !
DON'T WORRY. I GOT SOMETHING FOR YOU.
RUSTLE
A STRAW !
AND DON'T CHUG IT!
IT'LL BE A HASSLE TO GO TO THE BATH-ROOM DRESSED LIKE THAT!
HERE !
THANKS KAZUMI.
YOU'RE SO HIGH MAIN-TENANCE ...
SIP
...

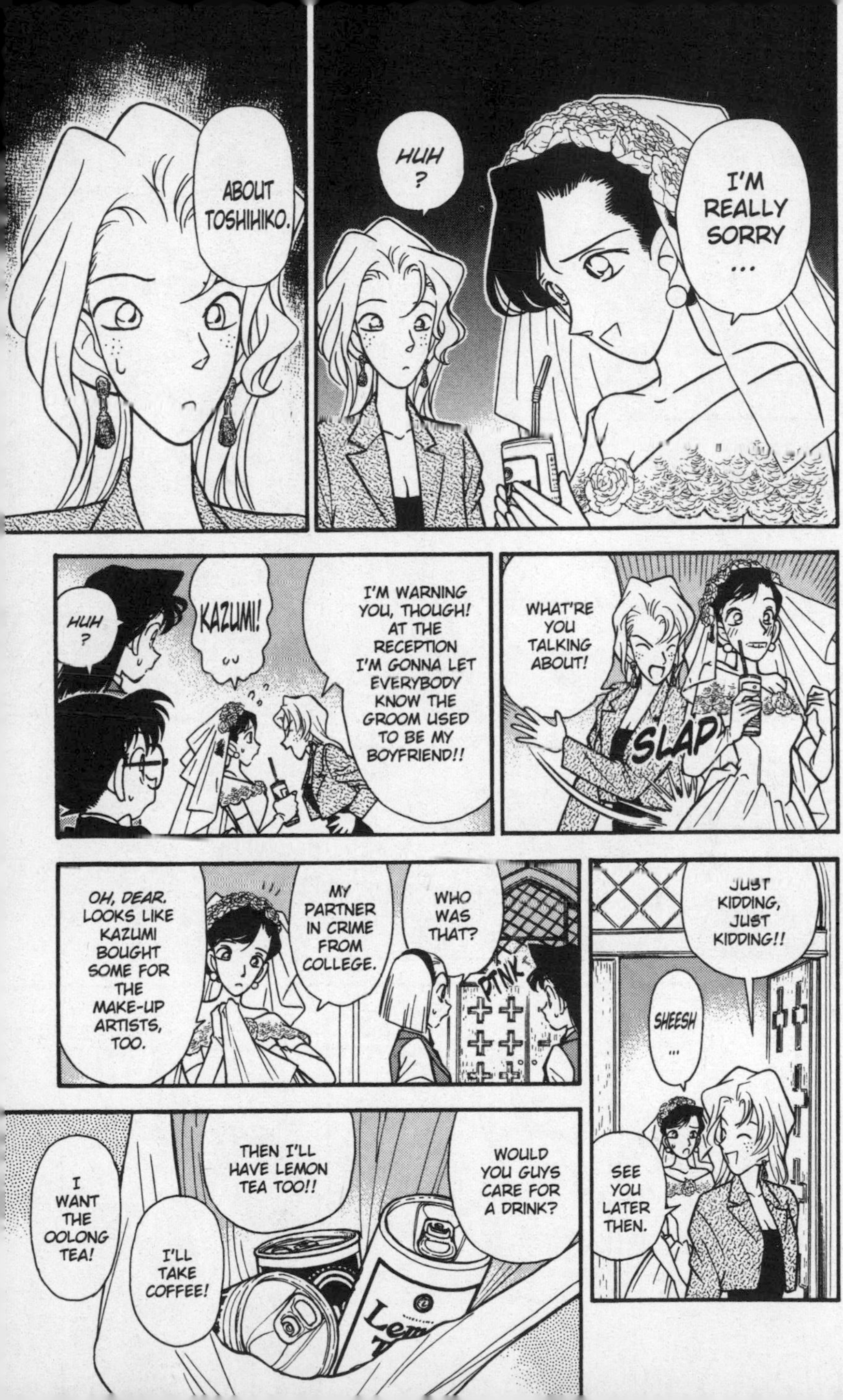
I'M REALLY SORRY ...
HUH ?
ABOUT TOSHIHIKO.
WHAT'RE YOU TALKING ABOUT!
SLAP
I'M WARNING YOU, THOUGH! AT THE RECEPTION I'M GONNA LET EVERYBODY KNOW THE GROOM USED TO BE MY BOYFRIEND!!
KAZUMI!
HUH ?
JUST KIDDING, JUST KIDDING!!
SHEESH ...
SEE YOU LATER THEN.
WHO WAS THAT?
PTNK
MY PARTNER IN CRIME FROM COLLEGE.
OH, DEAR. LOOKS LIKE KAZUMI BOUGHT SOME FOR THE MAKE-UP ARTISTS, TOO.
WOULD YOU GUYS CARE FOR A DRINK?
THEN I'LL HAVE LEMON TEA TOO!!
I'LL TAKE COFFEE!
I WANT THE OOLONG TEA!

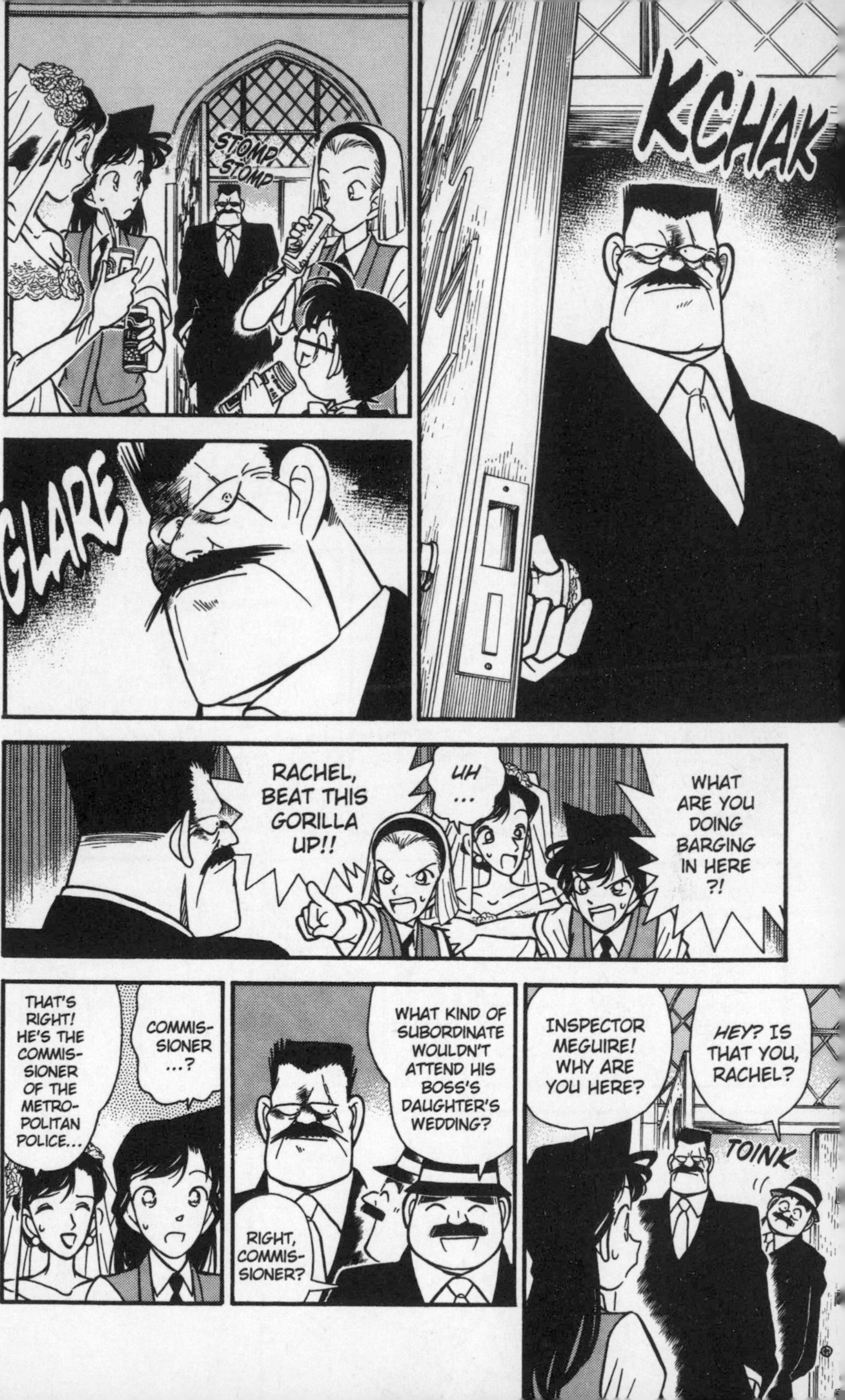
KCHAK
STOMP STOMP
GLARE
WHAT ARE YOU DOING BARGING IN HERE ?!
UH ...
RACHEL, BEAT THIS GORILLA UP!!
HEY? IS THAT YOU, RACHEL?
INSPECTOR MEGUIRE! WHY ARE YOU HERE?
TOINK
WHAT KIND OF SUBORDINATE WOULDN'T ATTEND HIS BOSS'S DAUGHTER'S WEDDING?
RIGHT, COMMISSIONER?
COMMISSIONER ...?
THAT'S RIGHT! HE'S THE COMMISSIONER OF THE METROPOLITAN POLICE...

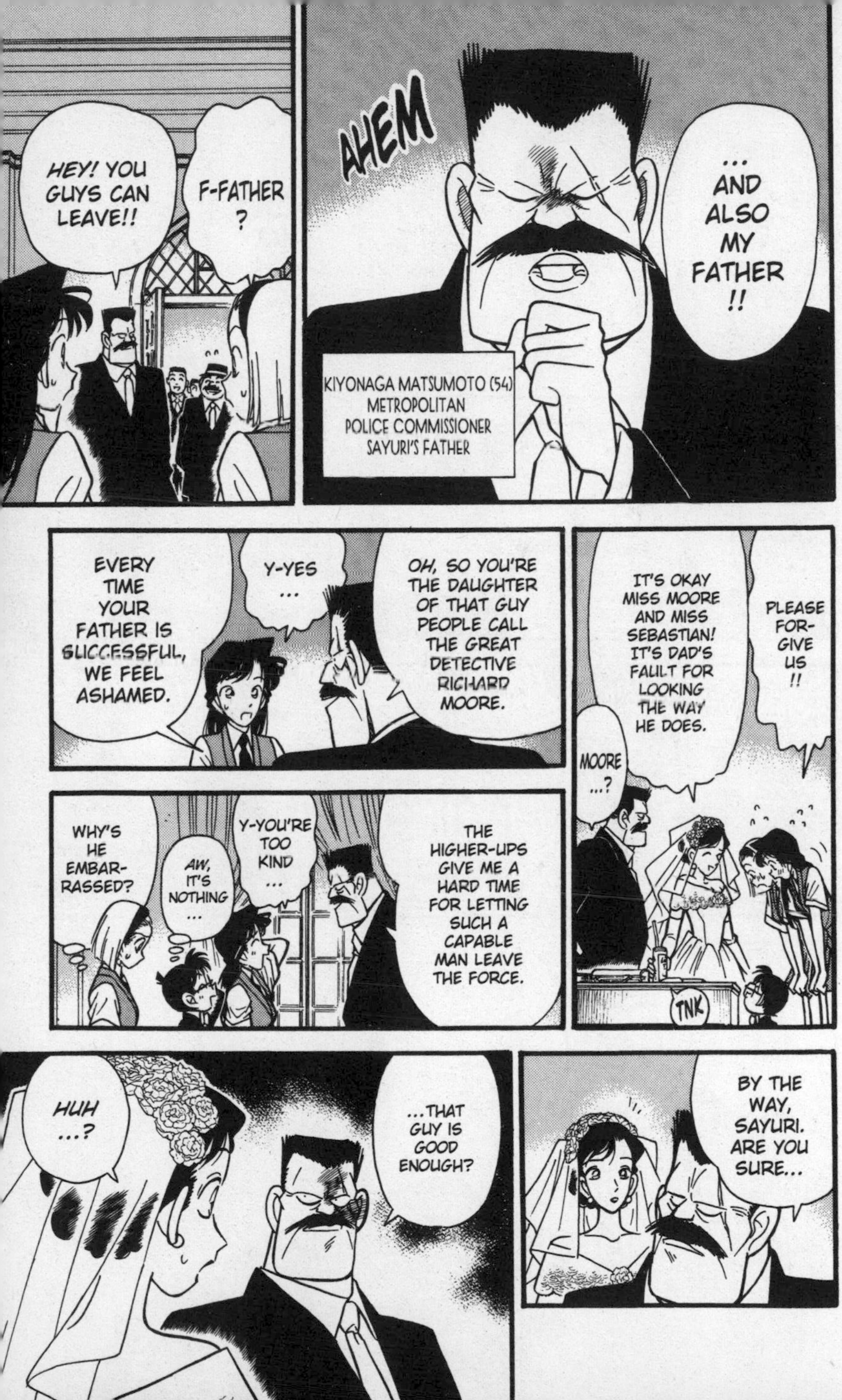
...AND ALSO MY FATHER!!
AHEM
KIYONAGA MATSUMOTO (54) METROPOLITAN POLICE COMMISSIONER SAYURI'S FATHER
F-FATHER?
HEY! YOU GUYS CAN LEAVE!!
PLEASE FOR-GIVE US!!
IT'S OKAY MISS MOORE AND MISS SEBASTIAN! IT'S DAD'S FAULT FOR LOOKING THE WAY HE DOES.
MOORE...?
TNK
OH, SO YOU'RE THE DAUGHTER OF THAT GUY PEOPLE CALL THE GREAT DETECTIVE RICHARD MOORE.
Y-YES...
EVERY TIME YOUR FATHER IS SUCCESSFUL, WE FEEL ASHAMED.
THE HIGHER-UPS GIVE ME A HARD TIME FOR LETTING SUCH A CAPABLE MAN LEAVE THE FORCE.
Y-YOU'RE TOO KIND...
AW, IT'S NOTHING...
WHY'S HE EMBAR-RASSED?
BY THE WAY, SAYURI. ARE YOU SURE...
...THAT GUY IS GOOD ENOUGH?
HUH...?

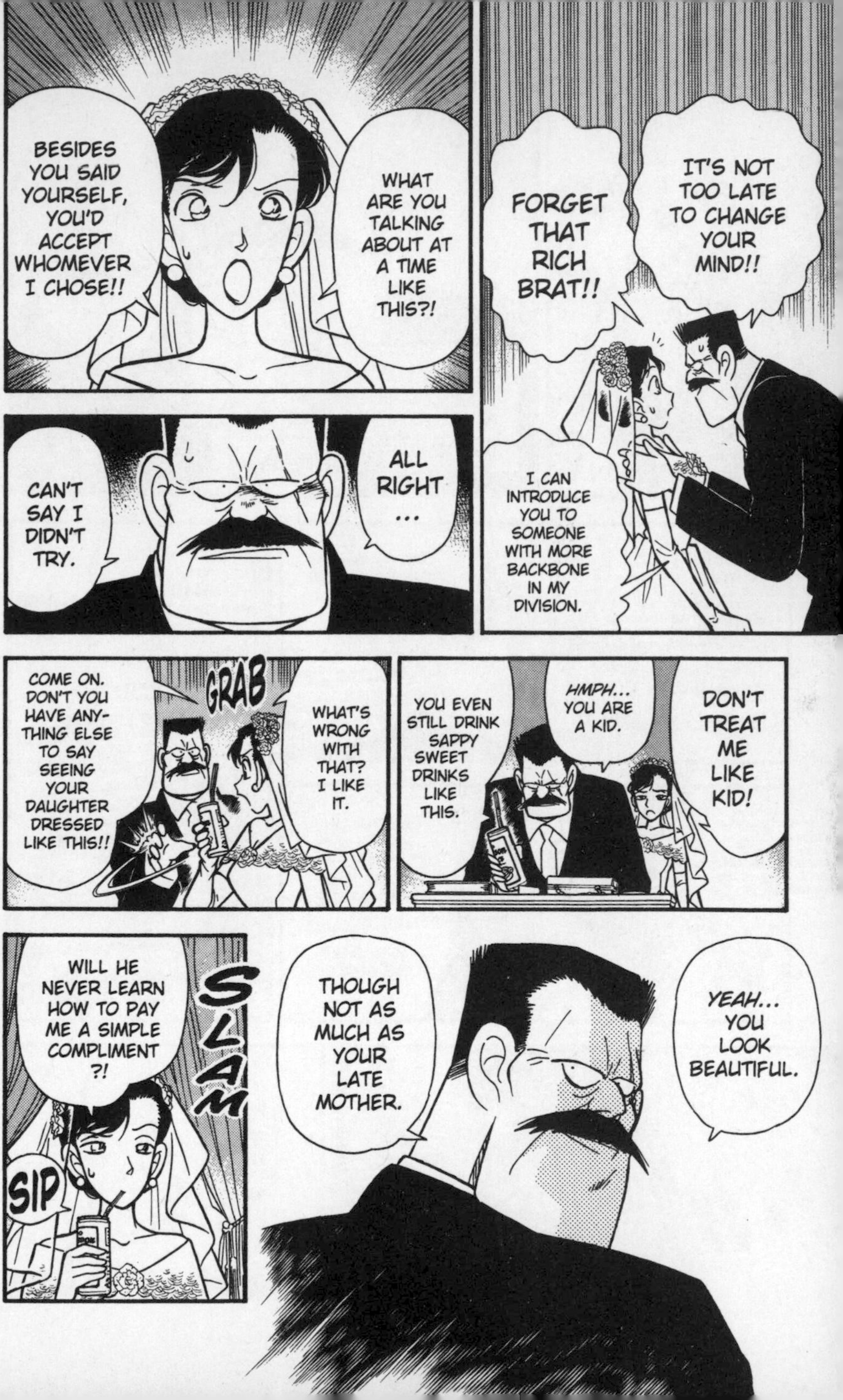
IT'S NOT TOO LATE TO CHANGE YOUR MIND!!
FORGET THAT RICH BRAT!!
I CAN INTRODUCE YOU TO SOMEONE WITH MORE BACKBONE IN MY DIVISION.
WHAT ARE YOU TALKING ABOUT AT A TIME LIKE THIS?!
BESIDES YOU SAID YOURSELF, YOU'D ACCEPT WHOMEVER I CHOSE!!
ALL RIGHT ...
CAN'T SAY I DIDN'T TRY.
DON'T TREAT ME LIKE KID!
HMPH... YOU ARE A KID.
YOU EVEN STILL DRINK SAPPY SWEET DRINKS LIKE THIS.
WHAT'S WRONG WITH THAT? I LIKE IT.
GRAB
COME ON. DON'T YOU HAVE ANYTHING ELSE TO SAY SEEING YOUR DAUGHTER DRESSED LIKE THIS!!
YEAH... YOU LOOK BEAUTIFUL.
THOUGH NOT AS MUCH AS YOUR LATE MOTHER.
SLAM
WILL HE NEVER LEARN HOW TO PAY ME A SIMPLE COMPLIMENT?!
SIP

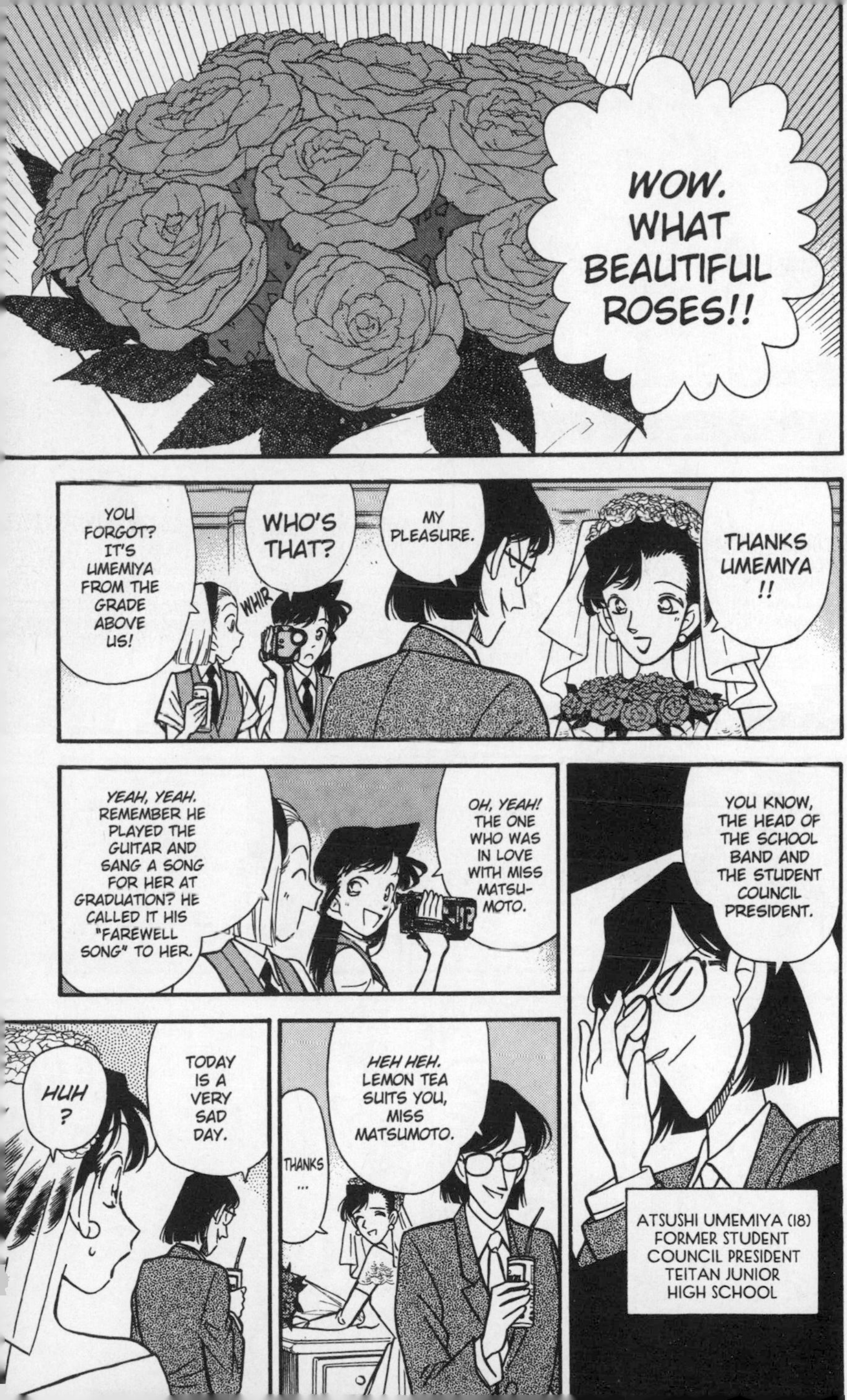
WOW. WHAT BEAUTIFUL ROSES!!
THANKS UMEMIYA!!
MY PLEASURE.
WHO'S THAT?
WHIR
YOU FORGOT? IT'S UMEMIYA FROM THE GRADE ABOVE US!
YOU KNOW, THE HEAD OF THE SCHOOL BAND AND THE STUDENT COUNCIL PRESIDENT.
ATSUSHI UMEMIYA (18) FORMER STUDENT COUNCIL PRESIDENT TEITAN JUNIOR HIGH SCHOOL
OH, YEAH! THE ONE WHO WAS IN LOVE WITH MISS MATSU-MOTO.
YEAH, YEAH. REMEMBER HE PLAYED THE GUITAR AND SANG A SONG FOR HER AT GRADUATION? HE CALLED IT HIS "FAREWELL SONG" TO HER.
HEH HEH. LEMON TEA SUITS YOU, MISS MATSUMOTO.
THANKS ...
TODAY IS A VERY SAD DAY.
HUH ?

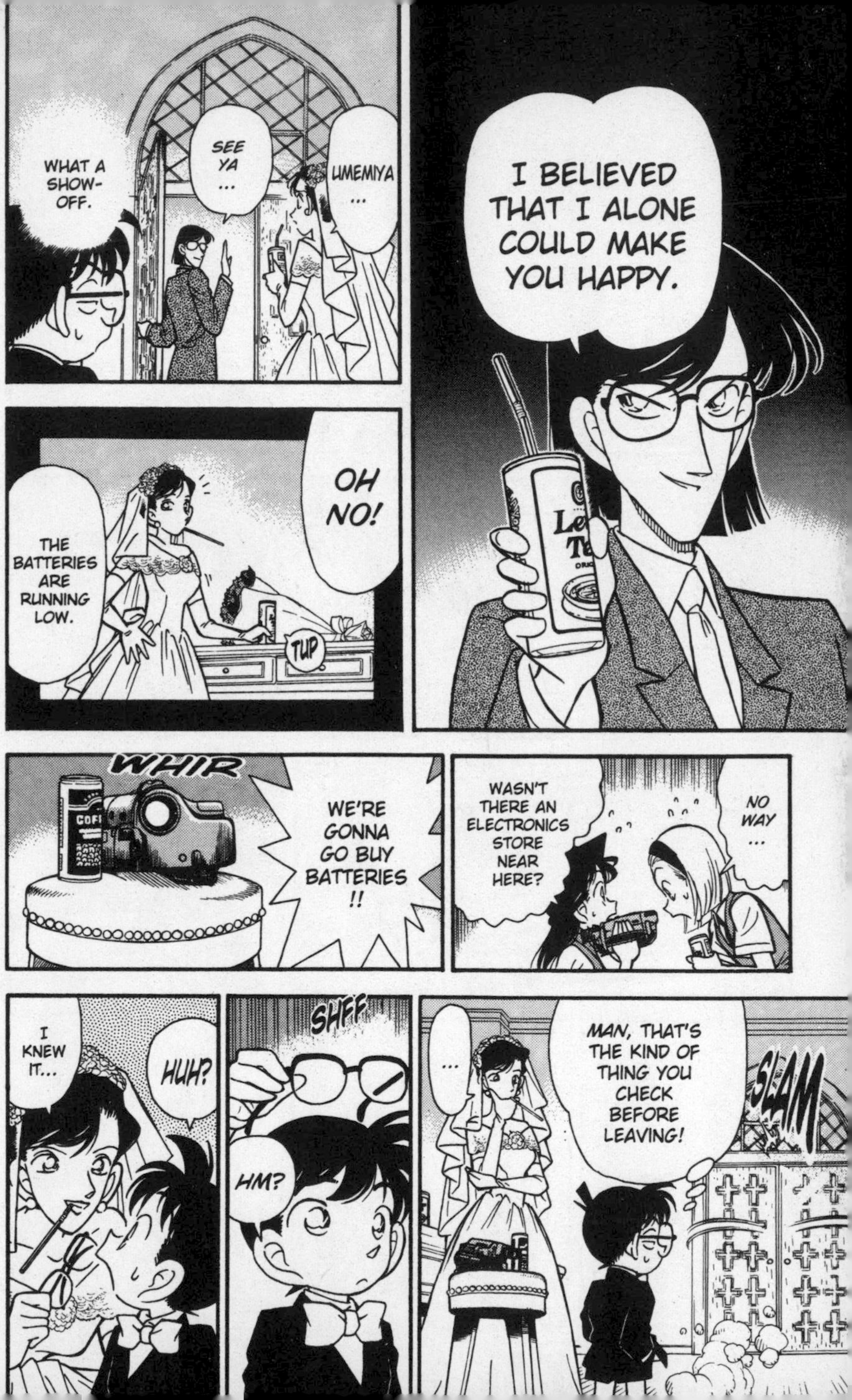

I BELIEVED THAT I ALONE COULD MAKE YOU HAPPY.
UMEMIYA ...
SEE YA ...
WHAT A SHOW-OFF.
OH NO!
THE BATTERIES ARE RUNNING LOW.
TUP
NO WAY ...
WASN'T THERE AN ELECTRONICS STORE NEAR HERE?
WHIR
WE'RE GONNA GO BUY BATTERIES !!
MAN, THAT'S THE KIND OF THING YOU CHECK BEFORE LEAVING!
SLAM
...
SHFF
HM?
HUH?
I KNEW IT...

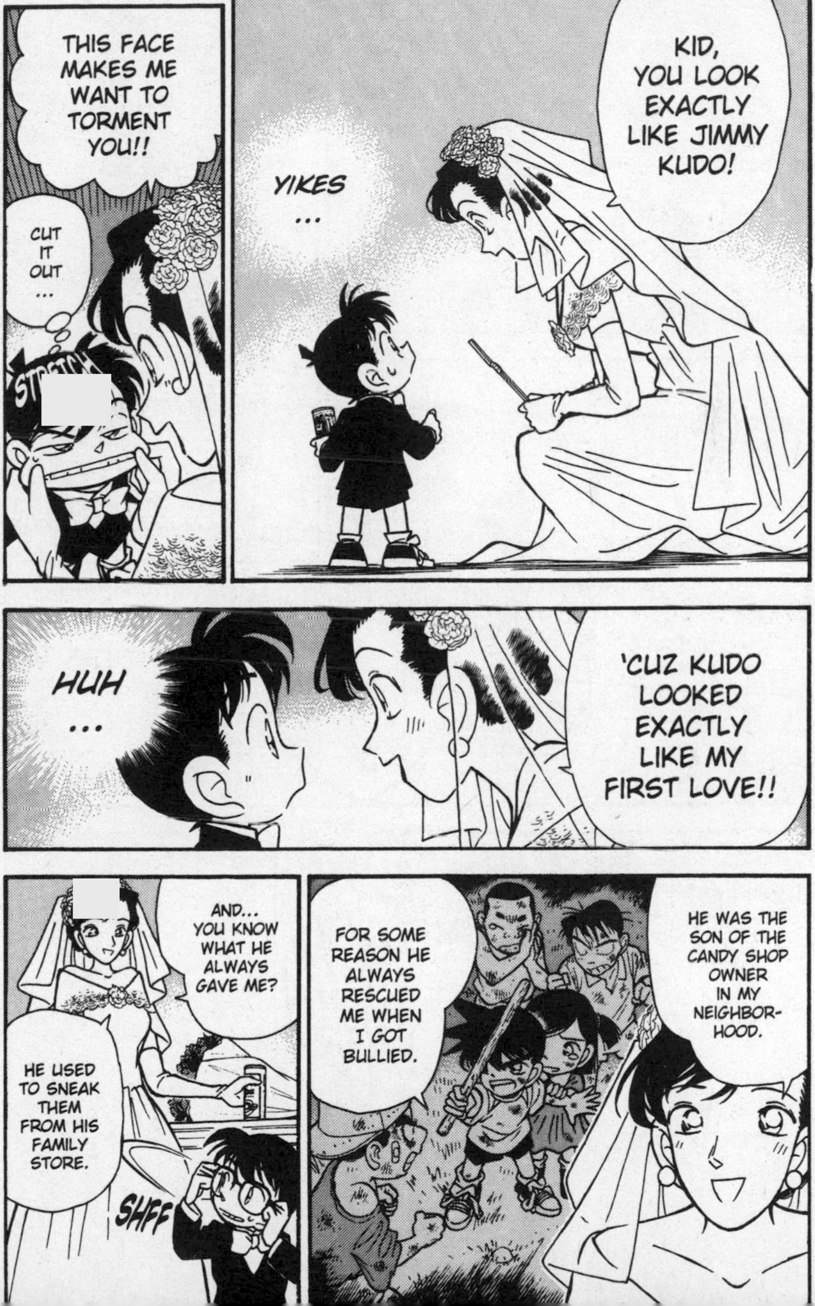
KID, YOU LOOK EXACTLY LIKE JIMMY KUDO!
YIKES ...
THIS FACE MAKES ME WANT TO TORMENT YOU!!
CUT IT OUT ...
'CUZ KUDO LOOKED EXACTLY LIKE MY FIRST LOVE!!
HUH ...
HE WAS THE SON OF THE CANDY SHOP OWNER IN MY NEIGHBOR-HOOD.
FOR SOME REASON HE ALWAYS RESCUED ME WHEN I GOT BULLIED.
AND... YOU KNOW WHAT HE ALWAYS GAVE ME?
HE USED TO SNEAK THEM FROM HIS FAMILY STORE.
SHFF

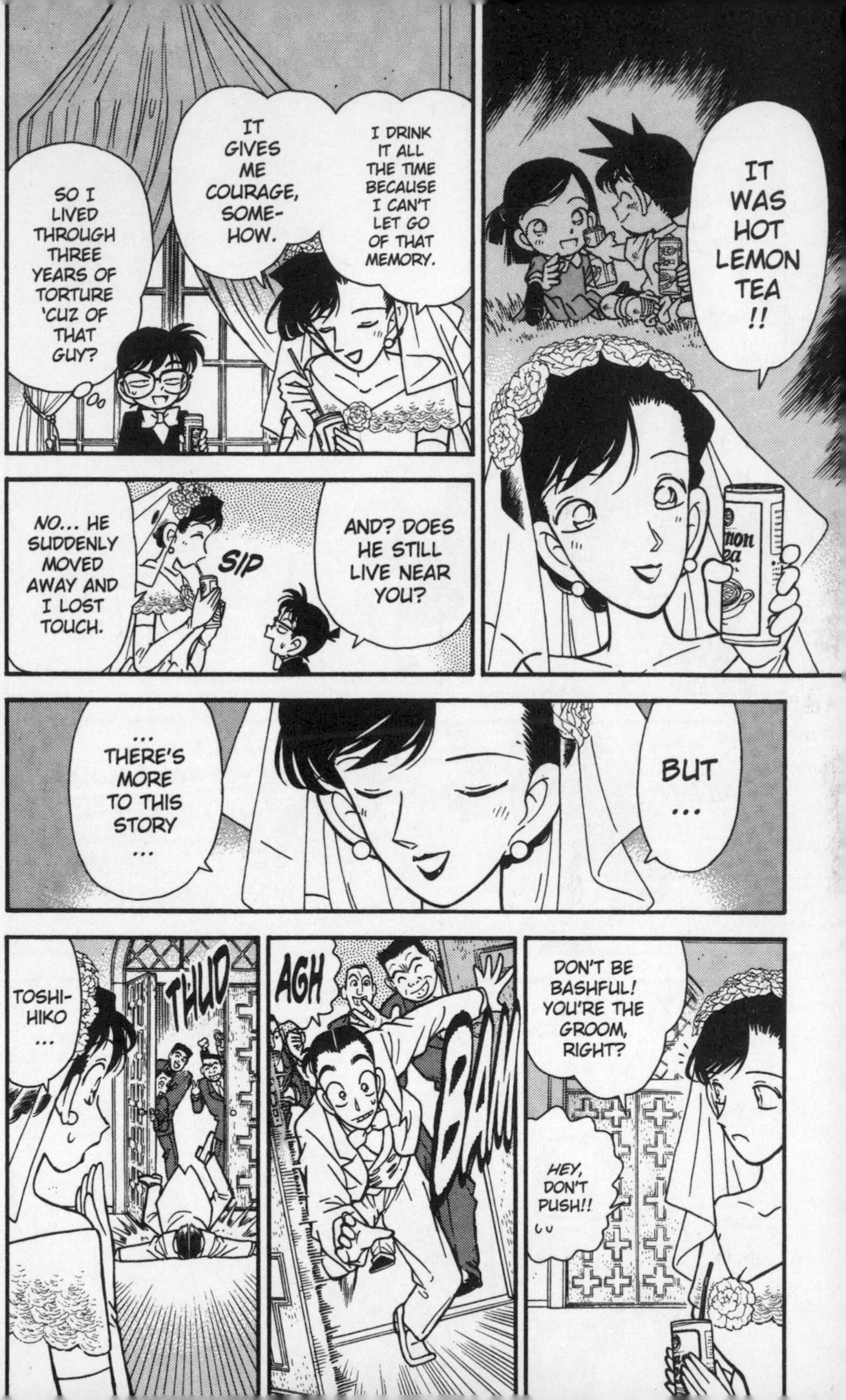
IT WAS HOT LEMON TEA!!
I DRINK IT ALL THE TIME BECAUSE I CAN'T LET GO OF THAT MEMORY.
IT GIVES ME COURAGE, SOME-HOW.
SO I LIVED THROUGH THREE YEARS OF TORTURE 'CUZ OF THAT GUY?
AND? DOES HE STILL LIVE NEAR YOU?
SIP
NO... HE SUDDENLY MOVED AWAY AND I LOST TOUCH.
BUT...
...THERE'S MORE TO THIS STORY...
DON'T BE BASHFUL! YOU'RE THE GROOM, RIGHT?
HEY, DON'T PUSH!!
AGH
BAM
THUD
TOSHI-HIKO...

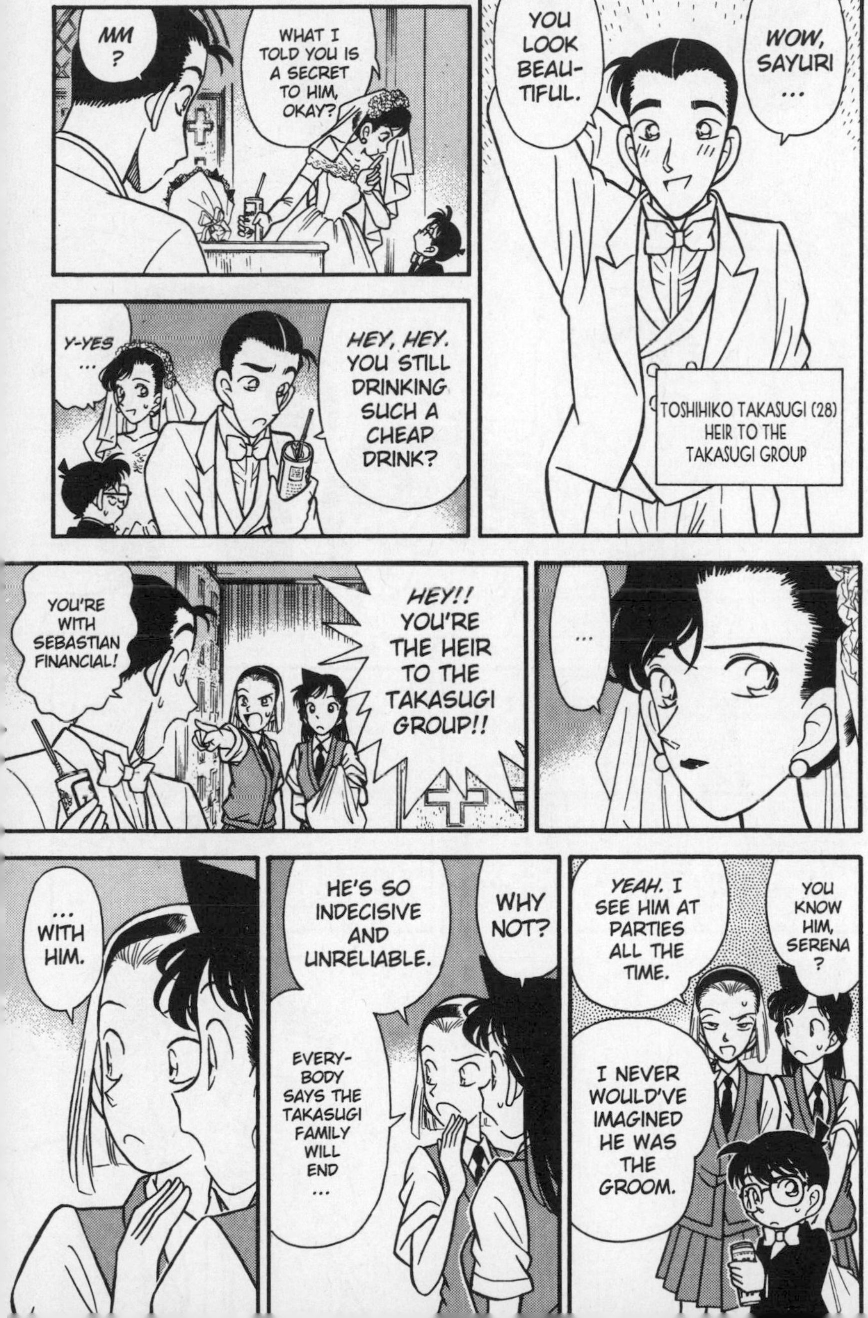
WOW, SAYURI ...
YOU LOOK BEAU-TIFUL.
TOSHIHIKO TAKASUGI (28) HEIR TO THE TAKASUGI GROUP
WHAT I TOLD YOU IS A SECRET TO HIM, OKAY?
MM ?
HEY, HEY. YOU STILL DRINKING SUCH A CHEAP DRINK?
Y-YES ...
...
HEY!! YOU'RE THE HEIR TO THE TAKASUGI GROUP!!
YOU'RE WITH SEBASTIAN FINANCIAL!
YOU KNOW HIM, SERENA ?
YEAH. I SEE HIM AT PARTIES ALL THE TIME.
I NEVER WOULD'VE IMAGINED HE WAS THE GROOM.
WHY NOT?
HE'S SO INDECISIVE AND UNRELIABLE.
EVERY-BODY SAYS THE TAKASUGI FAMILY WILL END ...
... WITH HIM.

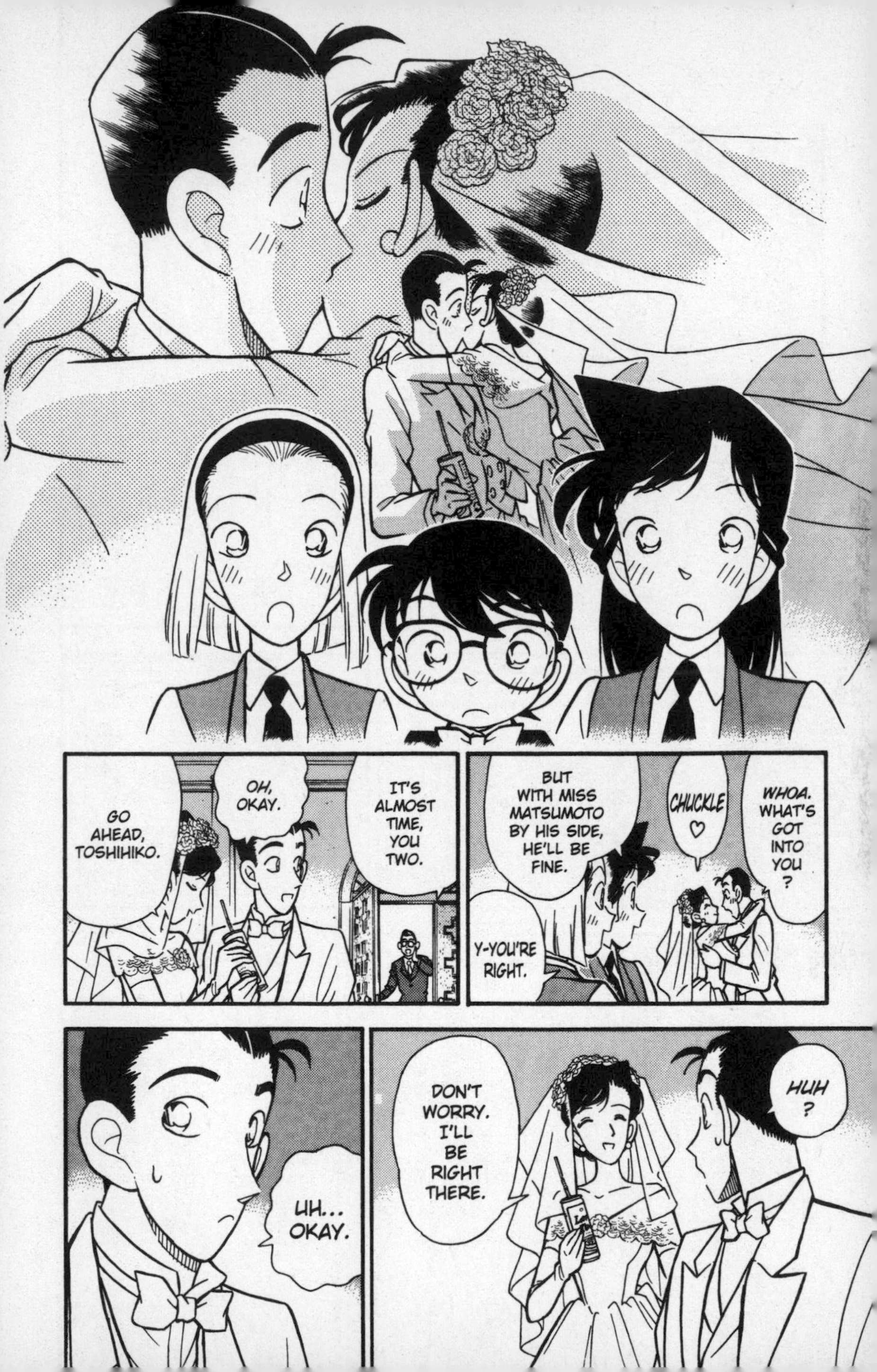
WHOA. WHAT'S GOT INTO YOU ?
CHUCKLE ♡
BUT WITH MISS MATSUMOTO BY HIS SIDE, HE'LL BE FINE.
Y-YOU'RE RIGHT.
IT'S ALMOST TIME, YOU TWO.
OH, OKAY.
GO AHEAD, TOSHIHIKO.
HUH ?
DON'T WORRY. I'LL BE RIGHT THERE.
UH... OKAY.

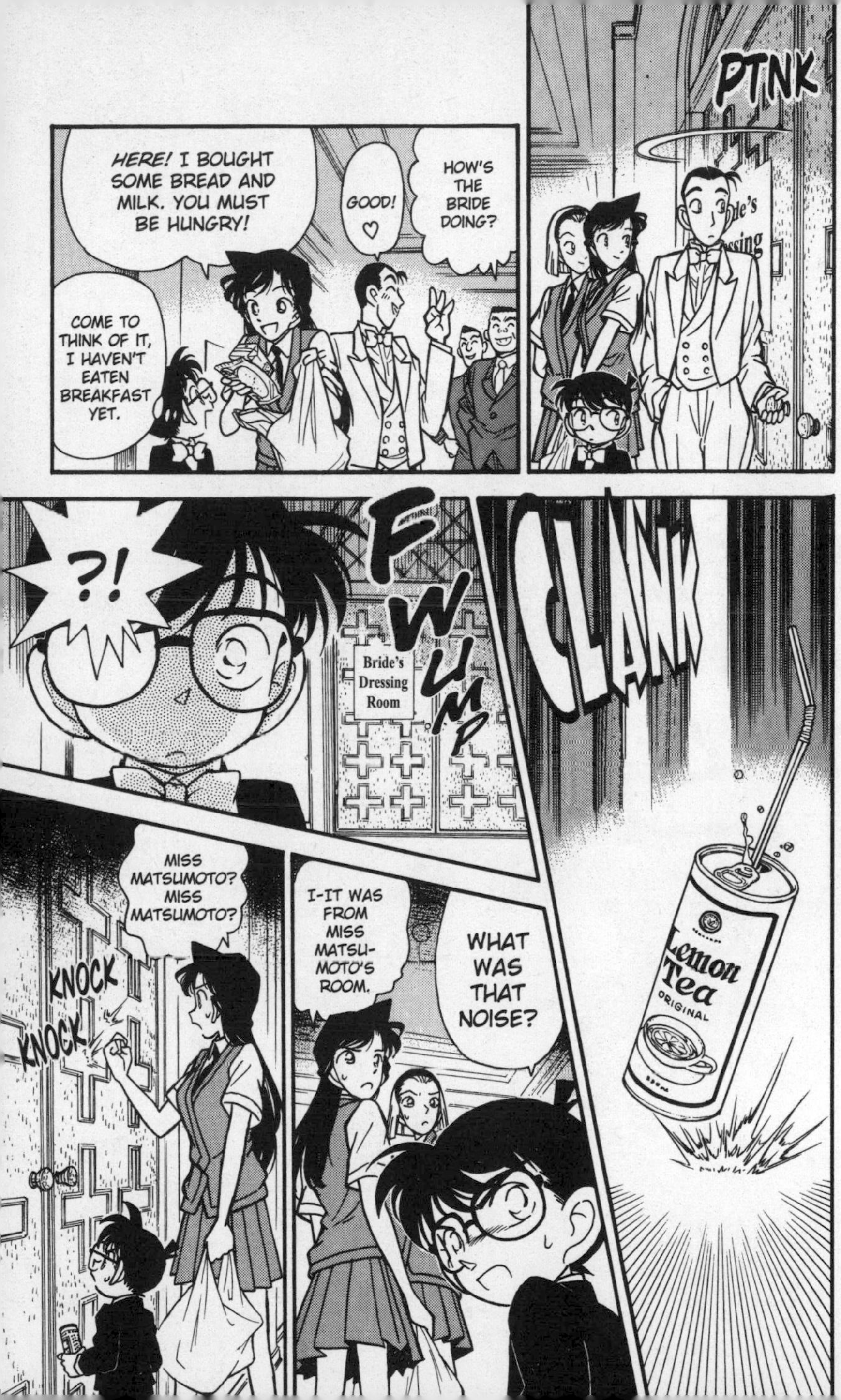
PTNK
Bride's Dressing
HOW'S THE BRIDE DOING?
GOOD! ♡
HERE! I BOUGHT SOME BREAD AND MILK. YOU MUST BE HUNGRY!
COME TO THINK OF IT, I HAVEN'T EATEN BREAKFAST YET.
CLANK
Lemon Tea ORIGINAL
FWUMP
Bride's Dressing Room
?!
WHAT WAS THAT NOISE?
I-IT WAS FROM MISS MATSU-MOTO'S ROOM.
MISS MATSUMOTO? MISS MATSUMOTO?
KNOCK
KNOCK

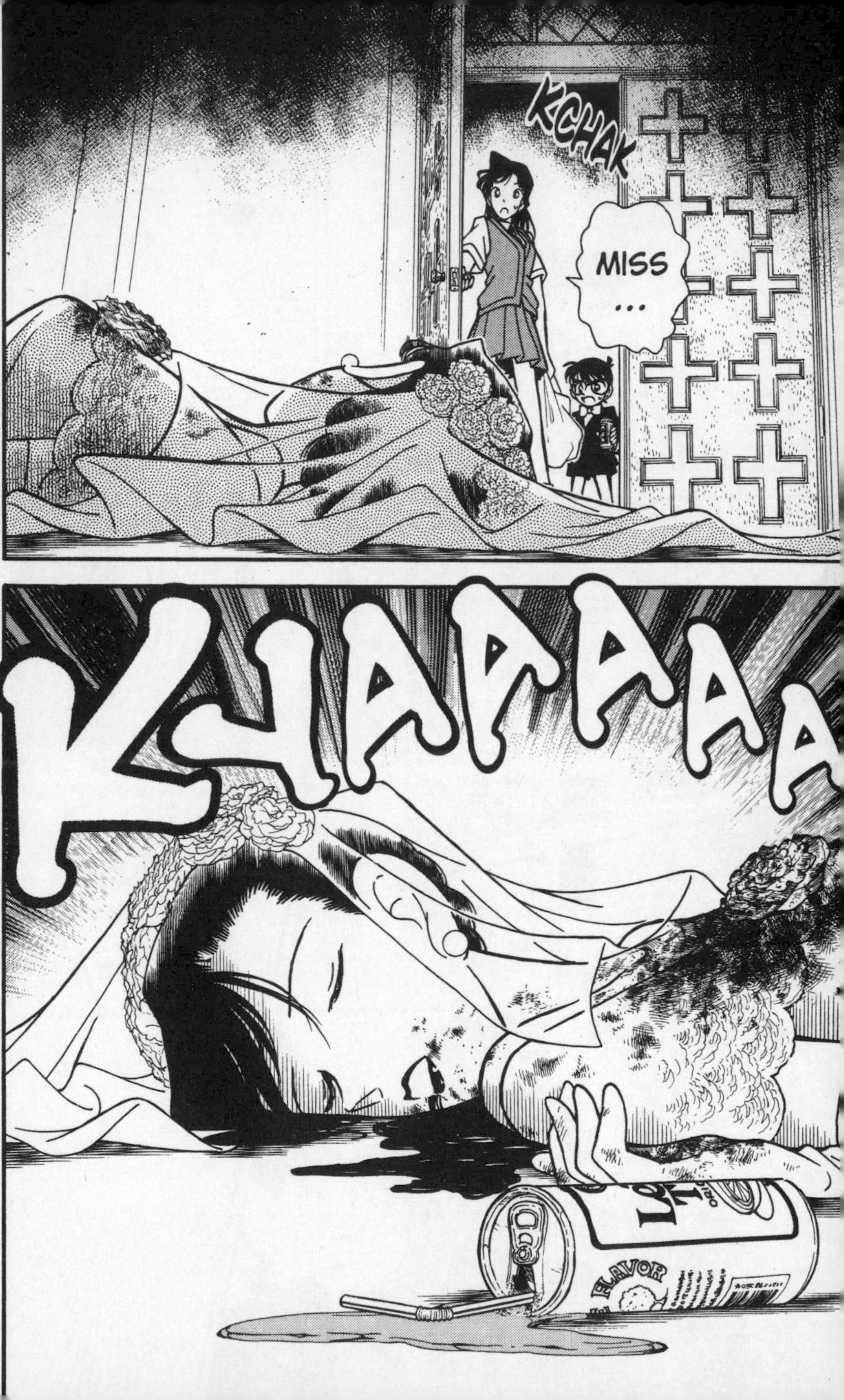
KCHAK
MISS ...
KYAAAA

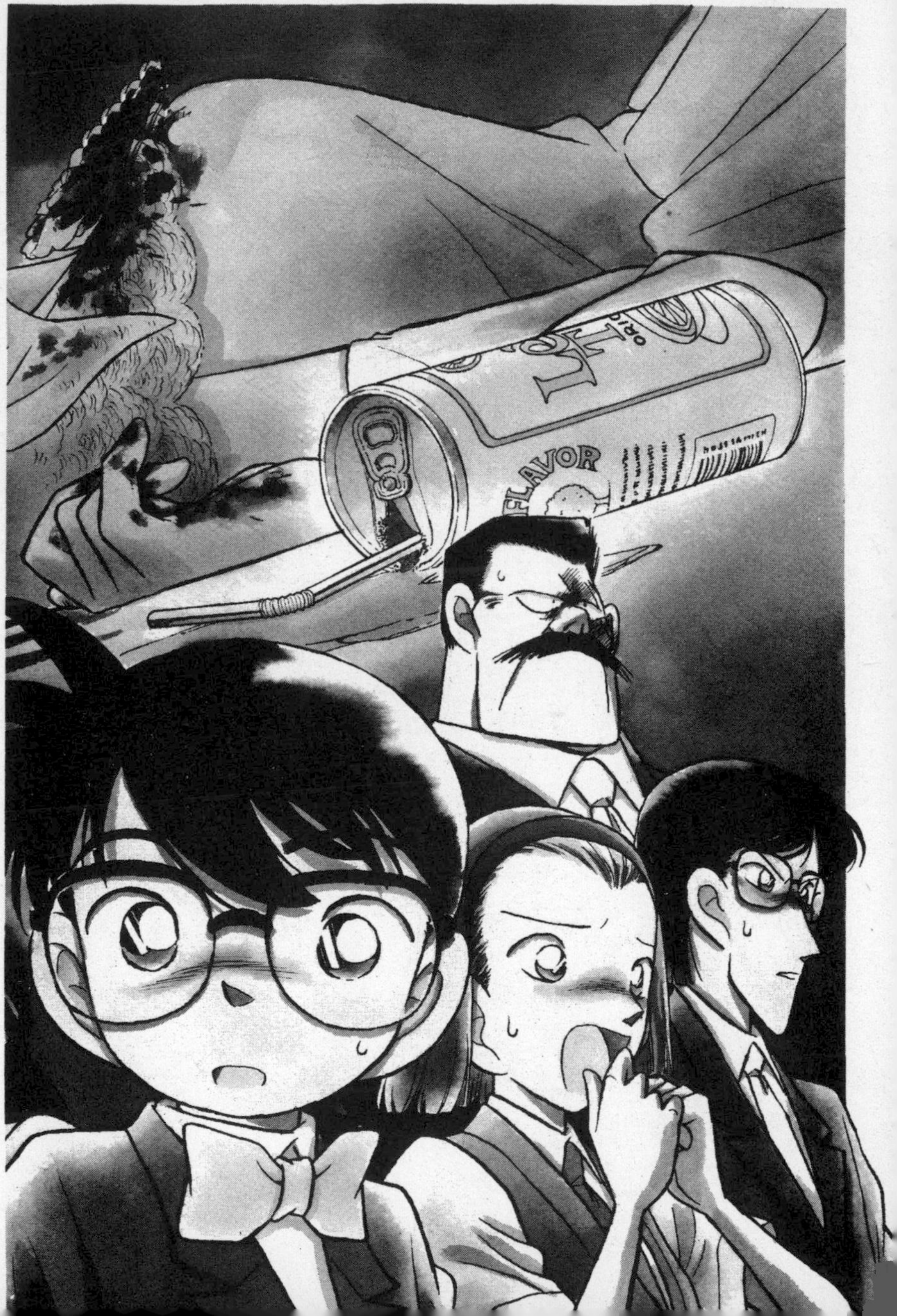
FLAVOR

FILE 9: FORBIDDEN LEMON TEA?!

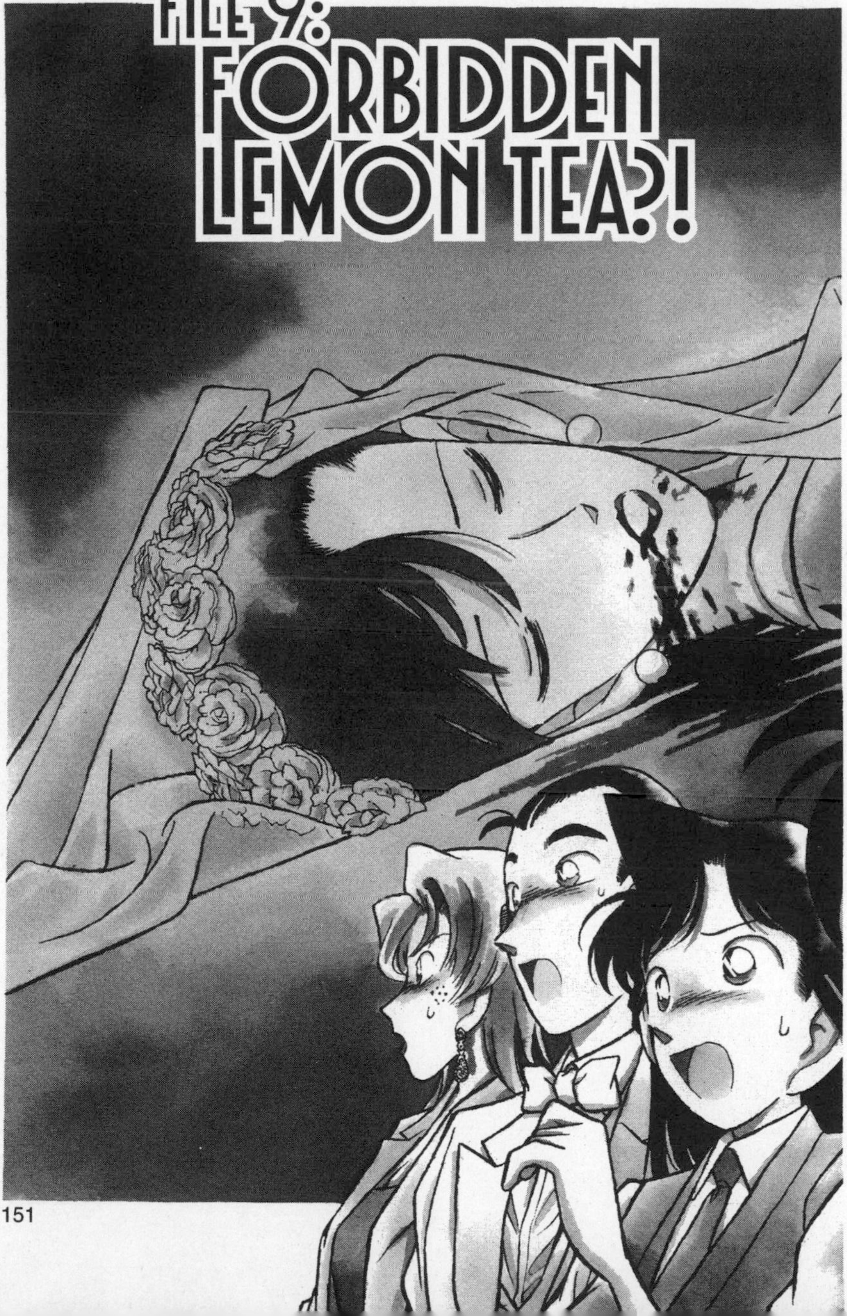

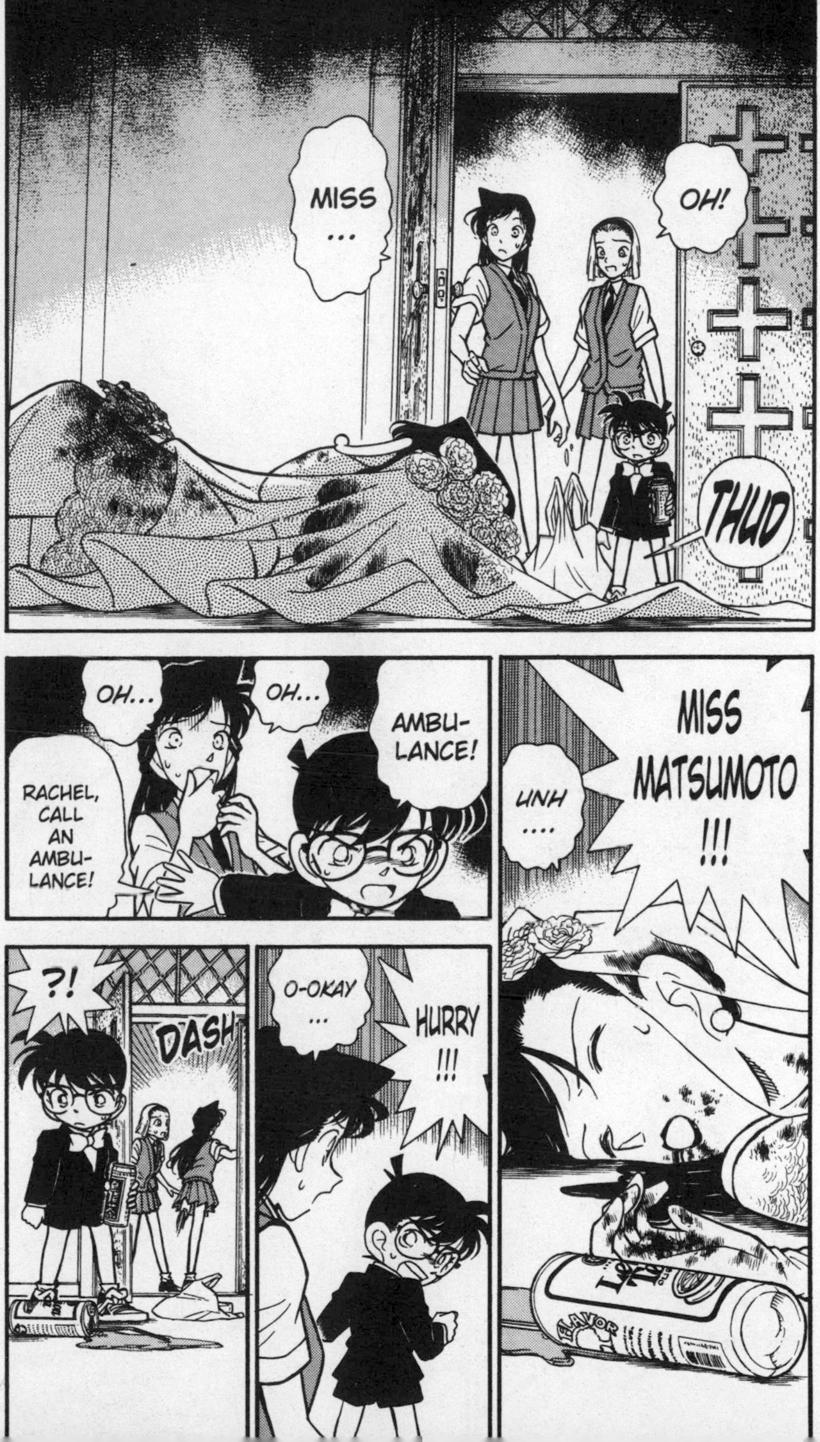
OH!
MISS ...
THUD
MISS MATSUMOTO !!!
UNH ....
OH...
OH...
AMBU-LANCE!
RACHEL, CALL AN AMBU-LANCE!
O-OKAY ...
HURRY !!!
?!
DASH

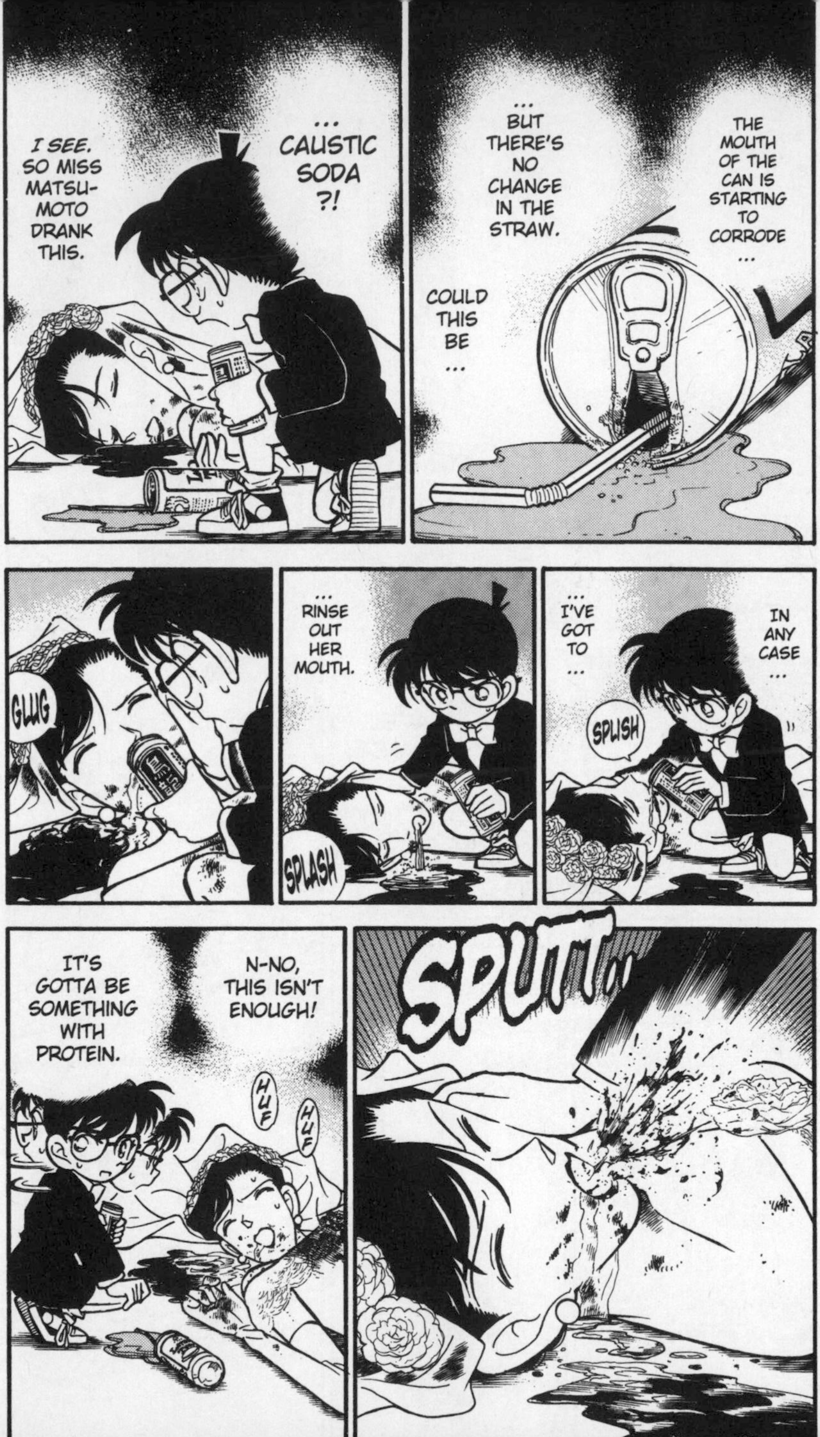
THE MOUTH OF THE CAN IS STARTING TO CORRODE ...
... BUT THERE'S NO CHANGE IN THE STRAW.
COULD THIS BE ...
... CAUSTIC SODA ?!
I SEE. SO MISS MATSU-MOTO DRANK THIS.
IN ANY CASE ...
... I'VE GOT TO ...
SPLISH
... RINSE OUT HER MOUTH.
SPLASH
GLUG
SPUTT..
N-NO, THIS ISN'T ENOUGH!
IT'S GOTTA BE SOMETHING WITH PROTEIN.
HUF
HUF

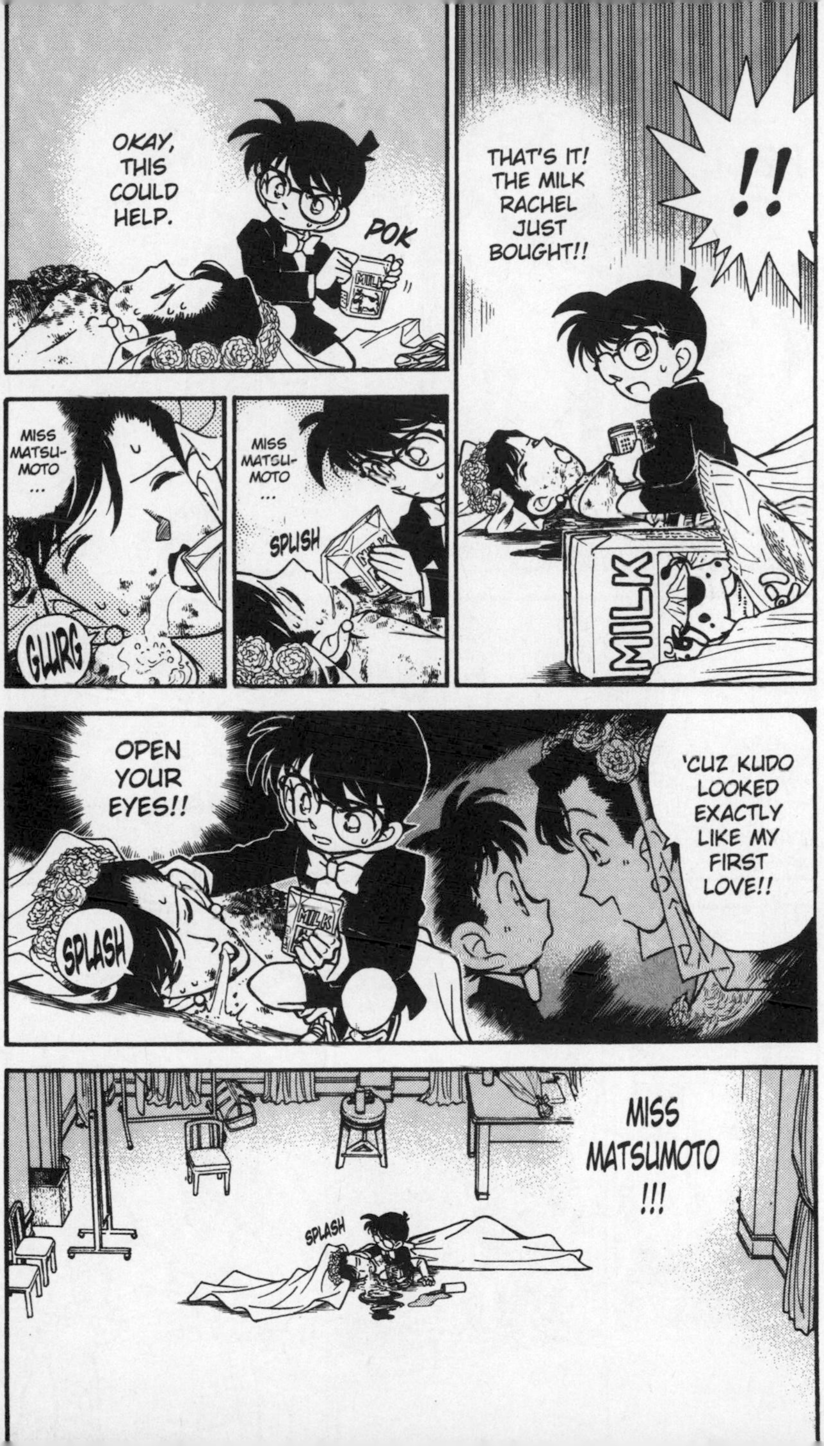
!!
THAT'S IT! THE MILK RACHEL JUST BOUGHT!!
MILK
OKAY, THIS COULD HELP.
POK
MILK
MISS MATSU-MOTO ...
SPLISH
MISS MATSU-MOTO ...
GLURG
'CUZ KUDO LOOKED EXACTLY LIKE MY FIRST LOVE!!
OPEN YOUR EYES!!
SPLASH
MILK
MISS MATSUMOTO !!!
SPLASH

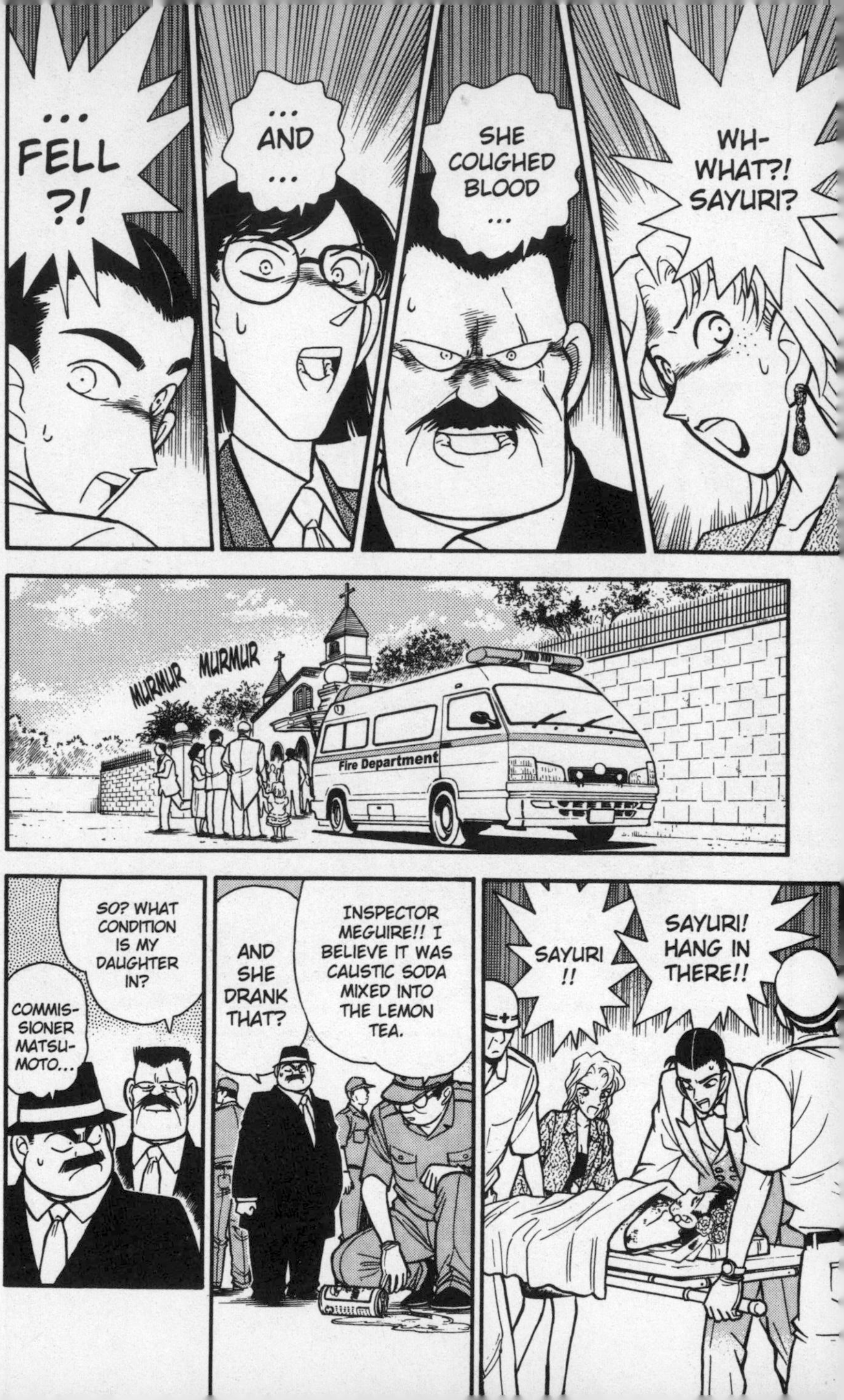
WH- WHAT?! SAYURI?
SHE COUGHED BLOOD ...
... AND ...
... FELL ?!
MURMUR MURMUR
Fire Department
SAYURI! HANG IN THERE!!
SAYURI !!
INSPECTOR MEGUIRE!! I BELIEVE IT WAS CAUSTIC SODA MIXED INTO THE LEMON TEA.
AND SHE DRANK THAT?
SO? WHAT CONDITION IS MY DAUGHTER IN?
COMMIS- SIONER MATSU- MOTO...

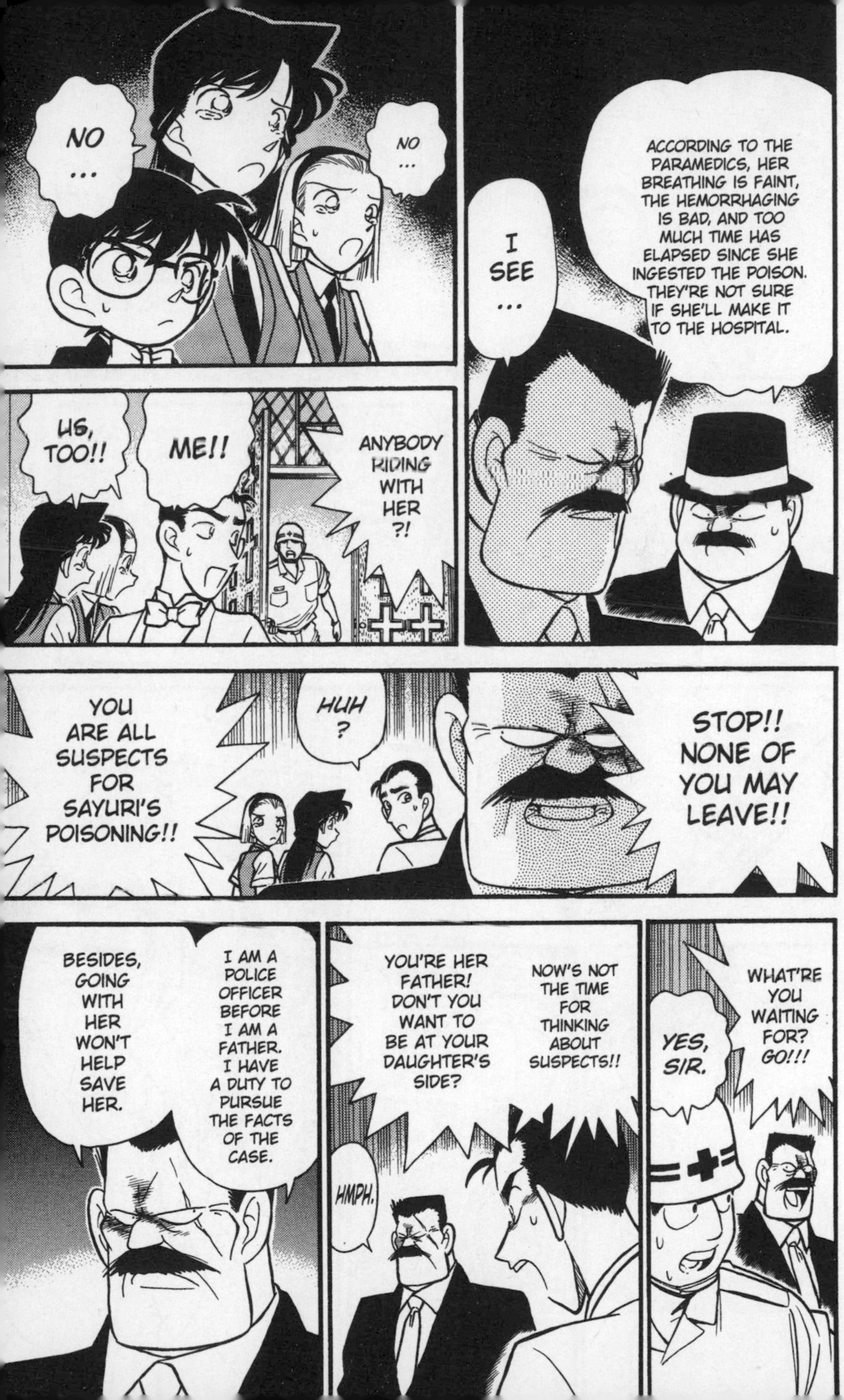
ACCORDING TO THE PARAMEDICS, HER BREATHING IS FAINT, THE HEMORRHAGING IS BAD, AND TOO MUCH TIME HAS ELAPSED SINCE SHE INGESTED THE POISON. THEY'RE NOT SURE IF SHE'LL MAKE IT TO THE HOSPITAL.
I SEE ...
NO ...
NO ...
ANYBODY RIDING WITH HER ?!
ME!!
US, TOO!!
STOP!! NONE OF YOU MAY LEAVE!!
HUH ?
YOU ARE ALL SUSPECTS FOR SAYURI'S POISONING!!
WHAT'RE YOU WAITING FOR? GO!!!
YES, SIR.
NOW'S NOT THE TIME FOR THINKING ABOUT SUSPECTS!!
YOU'RE HER FATHER! DON'T YOU WANT TO BE AT YOUR DAUGHTER'S SIDE?
HMPH.
I AM A POLICE OFFICER BEFORE I AM A FATHER. I HAVE A DUTY TO PURSUE THE FACTS OF THE CASE.
BESIDES, GOING WITH HER WON'T HELP SAVE HER.

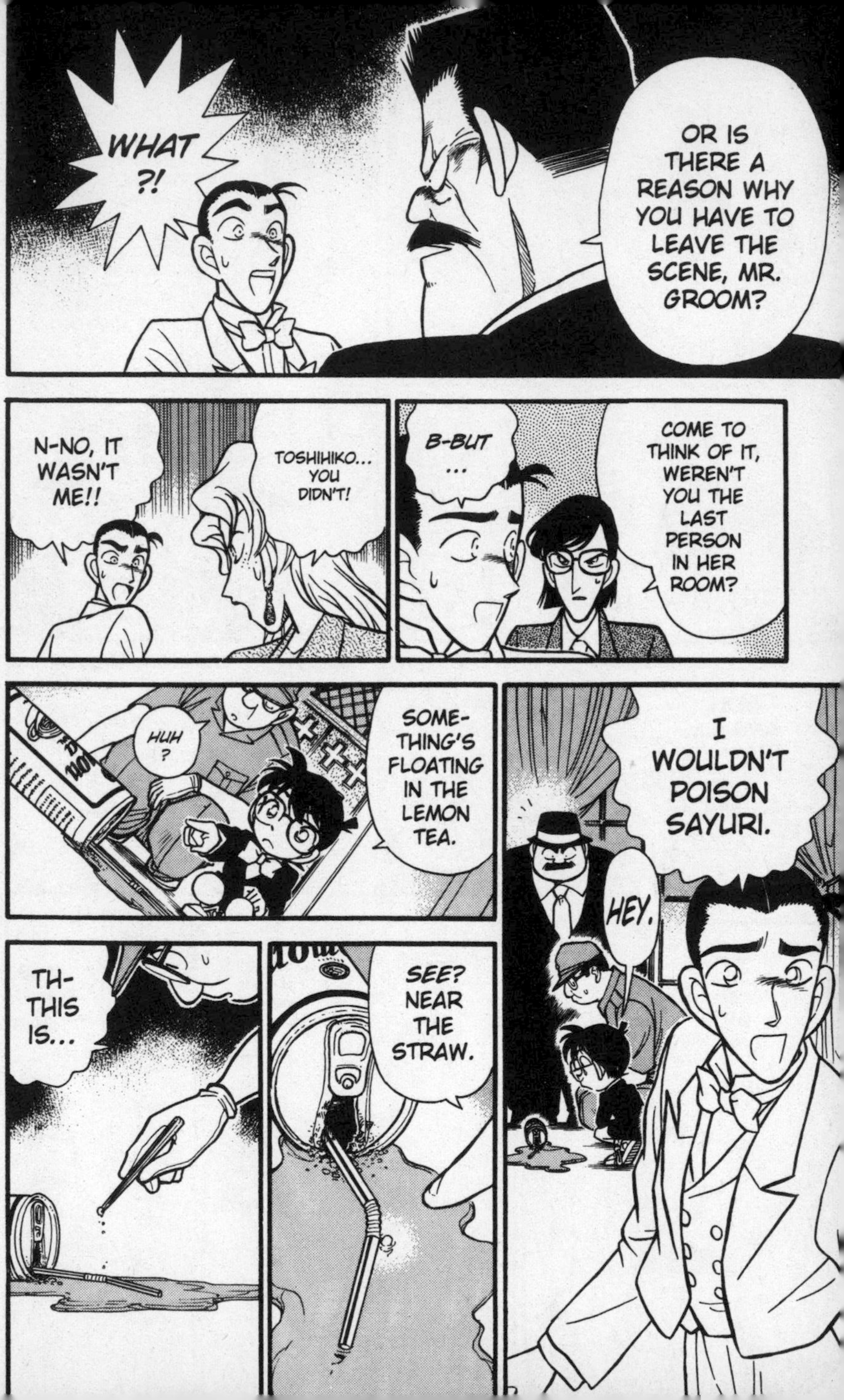
OR IS THERE A REASON WHY YOU HAVE TO LEAVE THE SCENE, MR. GROOM?
WHAT ?!
COME TO THINK OF IT, WEREN'T YOU THE LAST PERSON IN HER ROOM?
B-BUT ...
TOSHIHIKO... YOU DIDN'T!
N-NO, IT WASN'T ME!!
I WOULDN'T POISON SAYURI.
HEY.
SOME-THING'S FLOATING IN THE LEMON TEA.
HUH ?
SEE? NEAR THE STRAW.
TH-THIS IS...

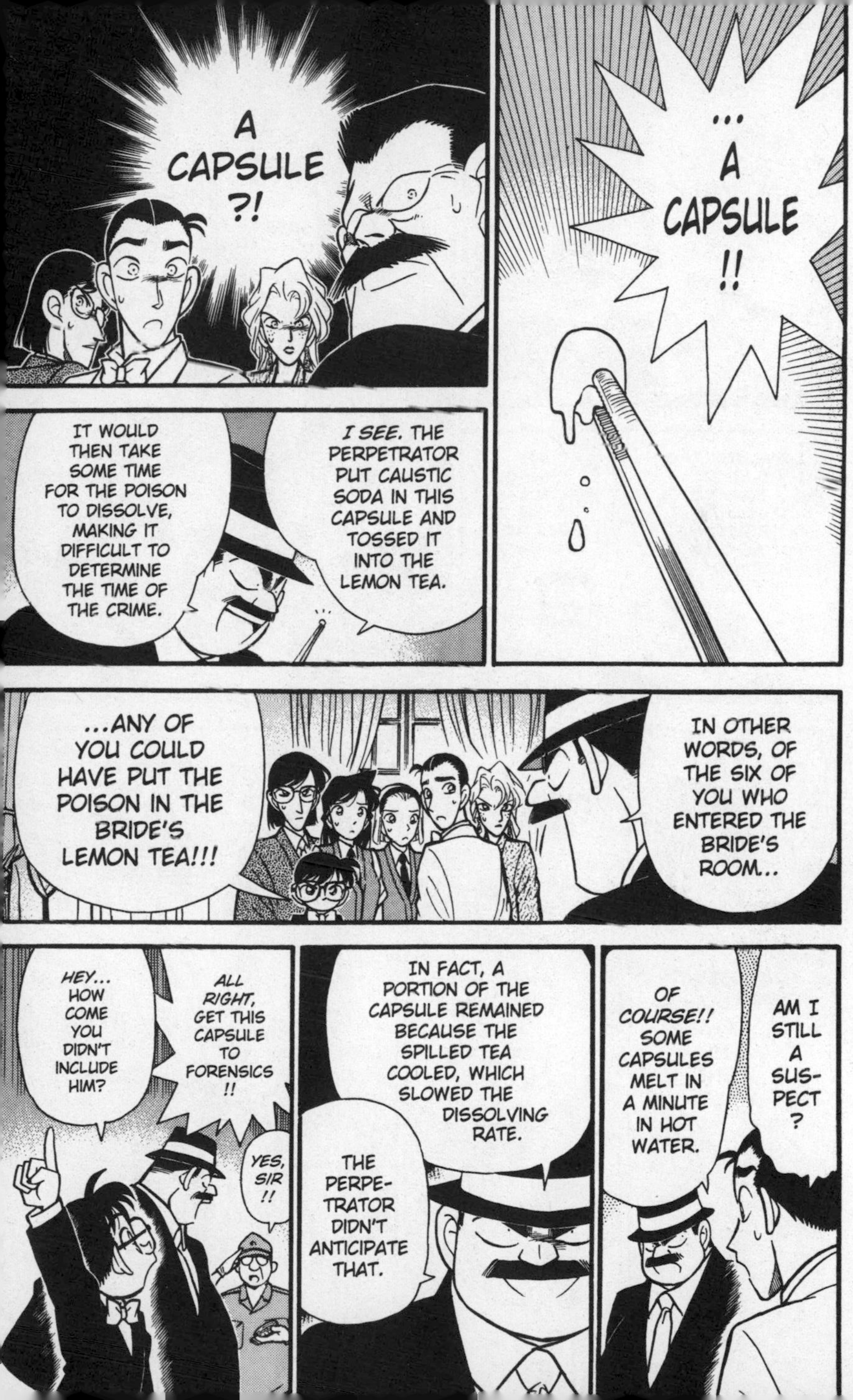
... A CAPSULE !!
A CAPSULE ?!
I SEE. THE PERPETRATOR PUT CAUSTIC SODA IN THIS CAPSULE AND TOSSED IT INTO THE LEMON TEA.
IT WOULD THEN TAKE SOME TIME FOR THE POISON TO DISSOLVE, MAKING IT DIFFICULT TO DETERMINE THE TIME OF THE CRIME.
IN OTHER WORDS, OF THE SIX OF YOU WHO ENTERED THE BRIDE'S ROOM...
...ANY OF YOU COULD HAVE PUT THE POISON IN THE BRIDE'S LEMON TEA!!!
AM I STILL A SUS-PECT?
OF COURSE!! SOME CAPSULES MELT IN A MINUTE IN HOT WATER.
IN FACT, A PORTION OF THE CAPSULE REMAINED BECAUSE THE SPILLED TEA COOLED, WHICH SLOWED THE DISSOLVING RATE.
THE PERPE-TRATOR DIDN'T ANTICIPATE THAT.
ALL RIGHT, GET THIS CAPSULE TO FORENSICS !!
HEY... HOW COME YOU DIDN'T INCLUDE HIM?
YES, SIR !!

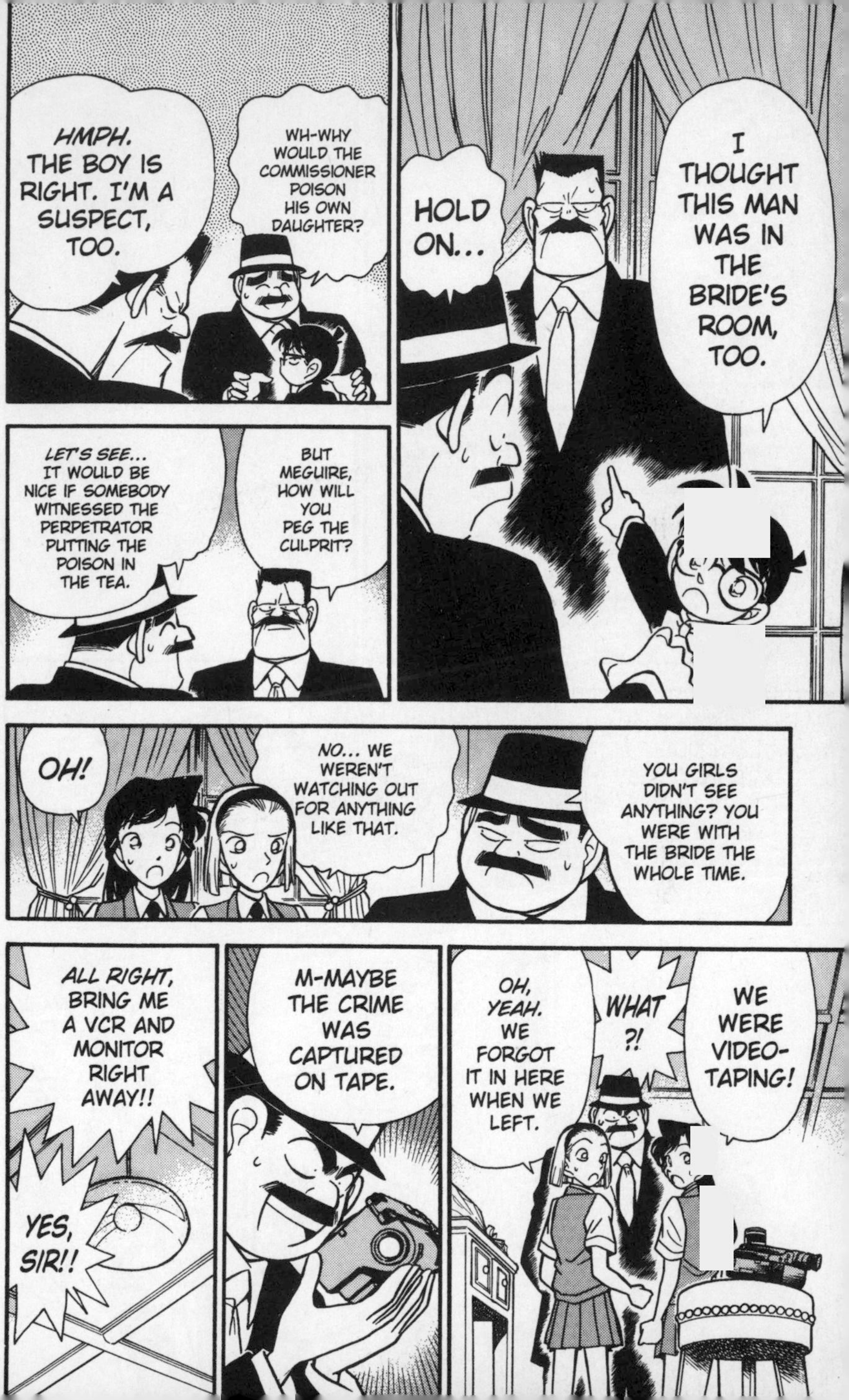

I THOUGHT THIS MAN WAS IN THE BRIDE'S ROOM, TOO.
HOLD ON...
WH-WHY WOULD THE COMMISSIONER POISON HIS OWN DAUGHTER?
HMPH. THE BOY IS RIGHT. I'M A SUSPECT, TOO.
BUT MEGUIRE, HOW WILL YOU PEG THE CULPRIT?
LET'S SEE... IT WOULD BE NICE IF SOMEBODY WITNESSED THE PERPETRATOR PUTTING THE POISON IN THE TEA.
YOU GIRLS DIDN'T SEE ANYTHING? YOU WERE WITH THE BRIDE THE WHOLE TIME.
NO... WE WEREN'T WATCHING OUT FOR ANYTHING LIKE THAT.
OH!
WE WERE VIDEO-TAPING!
WHAT ?!
OH, YEAH. WE FORGOT IT IN HERE WHEN WE LEFT.
M-MAYBE THE CRIME WAS CAPTURED ON TAPE.
ALL RIGHT, BRING ME A VCR AND MONITOR RIGHT AWAY!!
YES, SIR!!

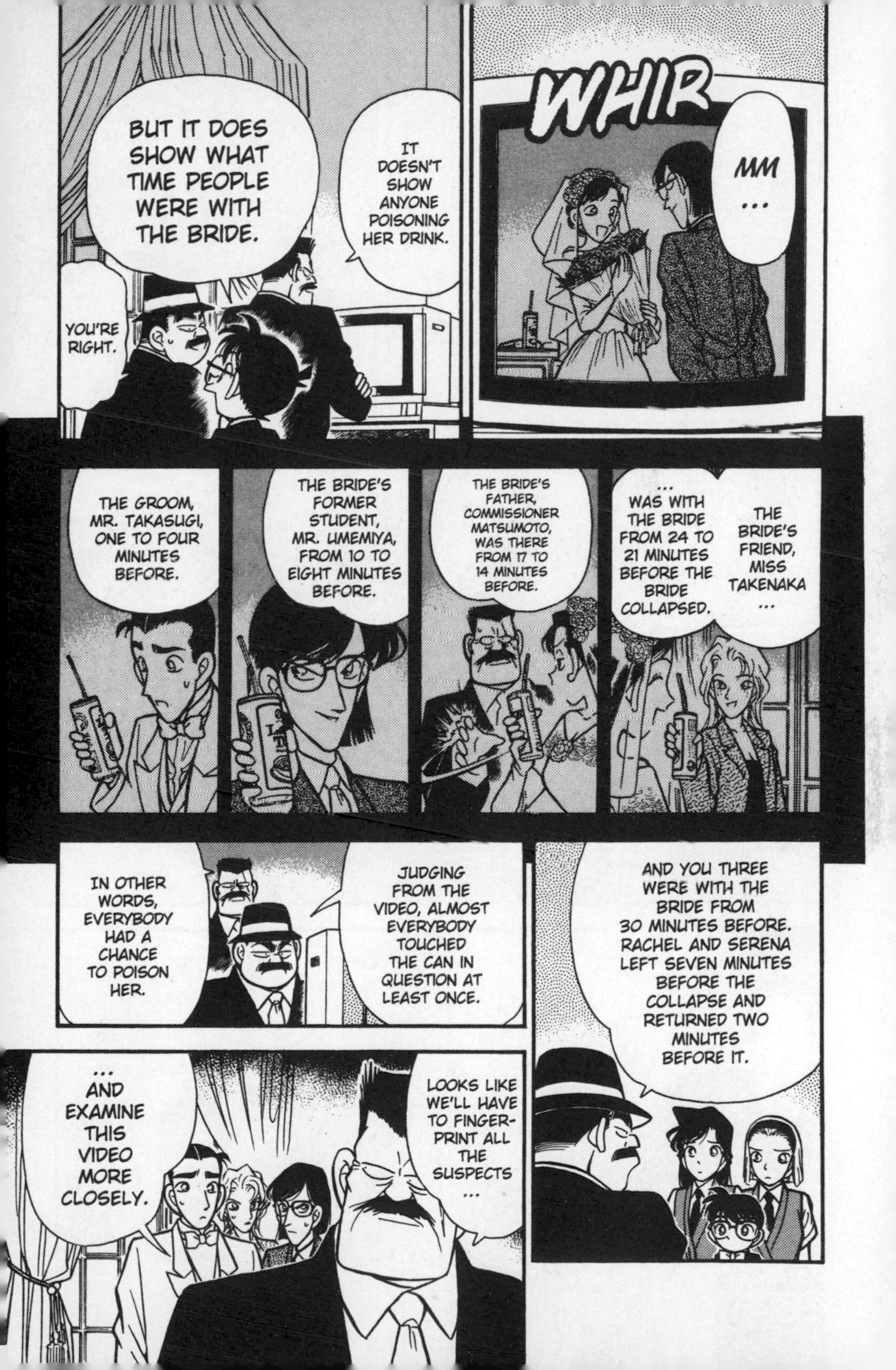
WHIR
MM ...
IT DOESN'T SHOW ANYONE POISONING HER DRINK.
BUT IT DOES SHOW WHAT TIME PEOPLE WERE WITH THE BRIDE.
YOU'RE RIGHT.
THE BRIDE'S FRIEND, MISS TAKENAKA ...
... WAS WITH THE BRIDE FROM 24 TO 21 MINUTES BEFORE THE BRIDE COLLAPSED.
THE BRIDE'S FATHER, COMMISSIONER MATSUMOTO, WAS THERE FROM 17 TO 14 MINUTES BEFORE.
THE BRIDE'S FORMER STUDENT, MR. UMEMIYA, FROM 10 TO EIGHT MINUTES BEFORE.
THE GROOM, MR. TAKASUGI, ONE TO FOUR MINUTES BEFORE.
AND YOU THREE WERE WITH THE BRIDE FROM 30 MINUTES BEFORE. RACHEL AND SERENA LEFT SEVEN MINUTES BEFORE THE COLLAPSE AND RETURNED TWO MINUTES BEFORE IT.
JUDGING FROM THE VIDEO, ALMOST EVERYBODY TOUCHED THE CAN IN QUESTION AT LEAST ONCE.
IN OTHER WORDS, EVERYBODY HAD A CHANCE TO POISON HER.
LOOKS LIKE WE'LL HAVE TO FINGER-PRINT ALL THE SUSPECTS ...
... AND EXAMINE THIS VIDEO MORE CLOSELY.

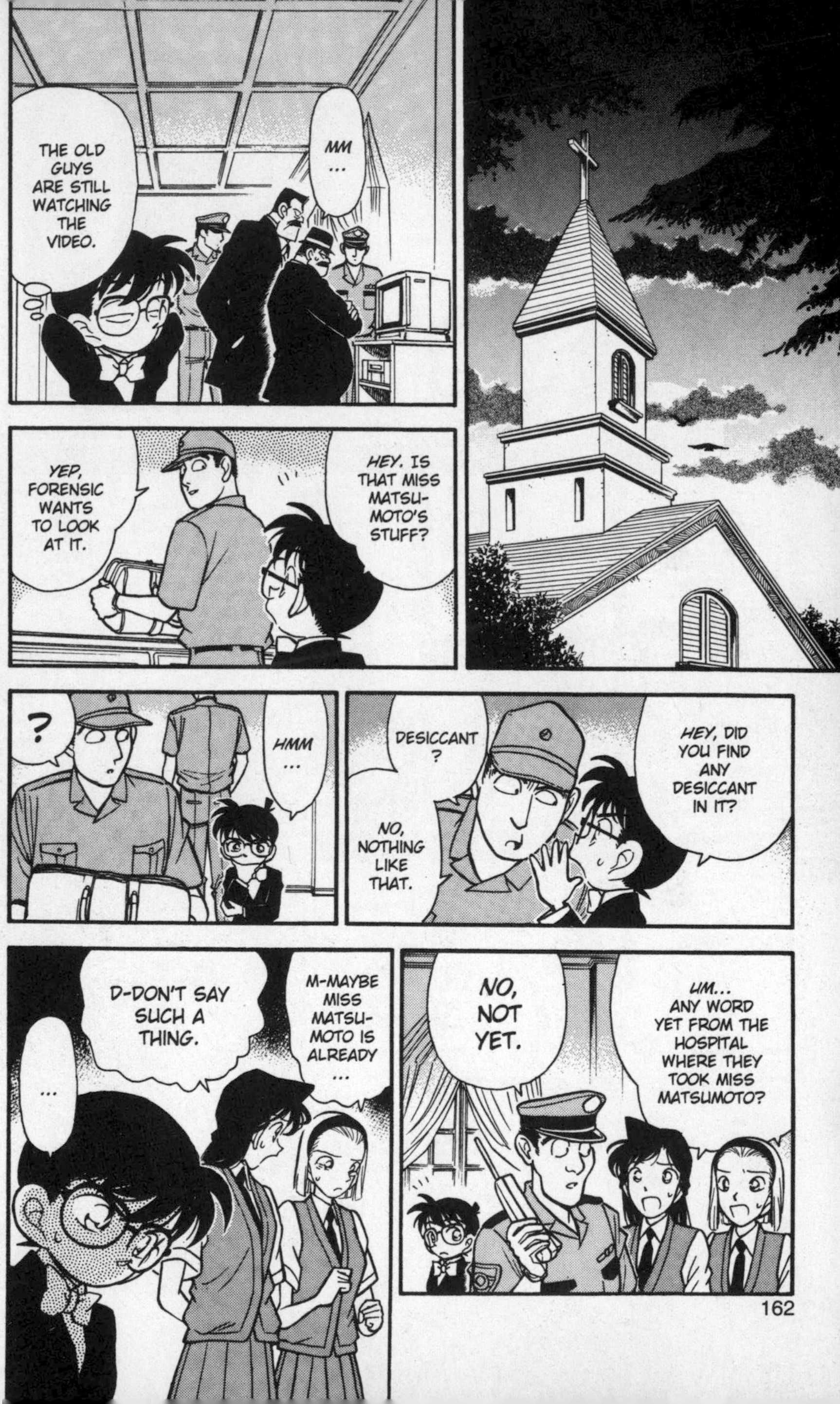
MM ...
THE OLD GUYS ARE STILL WATCHING THE VIDEO.
HEY. IS THAT MISS MATSUMOTO'S STUFF?
YEP, FORENSIC WANTS TO LOOK AT IT.
HEY, DID YOU FIND ANY DESICCANT IN IT?
DESICCANT?
NO, NOTHING LIKE THAT.
HMM ...
?
UM... ANY WORD YET FROM THE HOSPITAL WHERE THEY TOOK MISS MATSUMOTO?
NO, NOT YET.
M-MAYBE MISS MATSUMOTO IS ALREADY ...
D-DON'T SAY SUCH A THING.
...

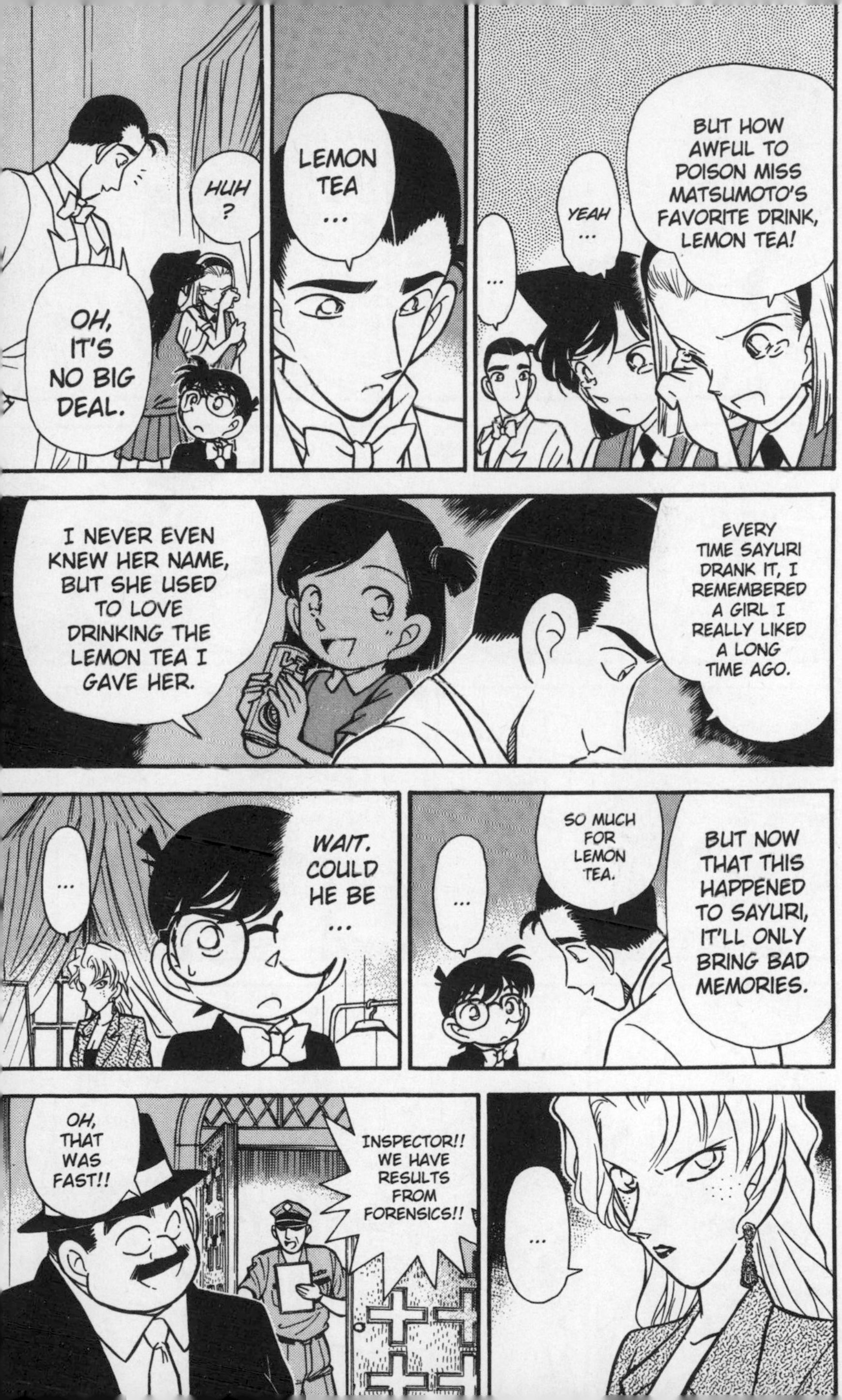
BUT HOW AWFUL TO POISON MISS MATSUMOTO'S FAVORITE DRINK, LEMON TEA!
YEAH ...
...
LEMON TEA ...
HUH ?
OH, IT'S NO BIG DEAL.
EVERY TIME SAYURI DRANK IT, I REMEMBERED A GIRL I REALLY LIKED A LONG TIME AGO.
I NEVER EVEN KNEW HER NAME, BUT SHE USED TO LOVE DRINKING THE LEMON TEA I GAVE HER.
BUT NOW THAT THIS HAPPENED TO SAYURI, IT'LL ONLY BRING BAD MEMORIES.
SO MUCH FOR LEMON TEA.
...
WAIT. COULD HE BE ...
...
...
INSPECTOR!! WE HAVE RESULTS FROM FORENSICS!!
OH, THAT WAS FAST!!

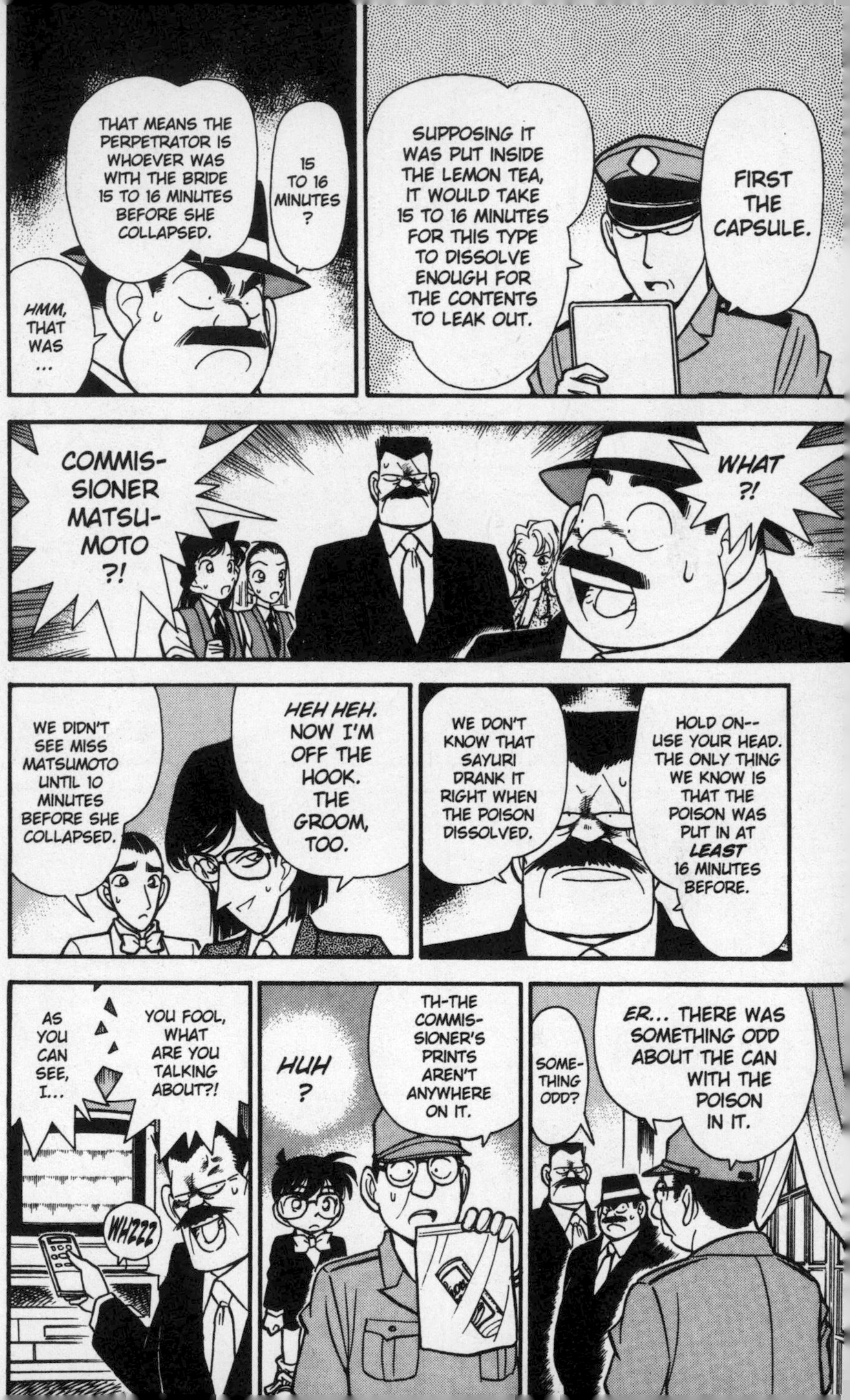
FIRST THE CAPSULE.
SUPPOSING IT WAS PUT INSIDE THE LEMON TEA, IT WOULD TAKE 15 TO 16 MINUTES FOR THIS TYPE TO DISSOLVE ENOUGH FOR THE CONTENTS TO LEAK OUT.
15 TO 16 MINUTES?
THAT MEANS THE PERPETRATOR IS WHOEVER WAS WITH THE BRIDE 15 TO 16 MINUTES BEFORE SHE COLLAPSED.
HMM, THAT WAS...
WHAT?!
COMMISSIONER MATSUMOTO?!
HOLD ON-- USE YOUR HEAD. THE ONLY THING WE KNOW IS THAT THE POISON WAS PUT IN AT LEAST 16 MINUTES BEFORE.
WE DON'T KNOW THAT SAYURI DRANK IT RIGHT WHEN THE POISON DISSOLVED.
HEH HEH. NOW I'M OFF THE HOOK. THE GROOM, TOO.
WE DIDN'T SEE MISS MATSUMOTO UNTIL 10 MINUTES BEFORE SHE COLLAPSED.
ER... THERE WAS SOMETHING ODD ABOUT THE CAN WITH THE POISON IN IT.
SOMETHING ODD?
TH-THE COMMISSIONER'S PRINTS AREN'T ANYWHERE ON IT.
HUH?
YOU FOOL, WHAT ARE YOU TALKING ABOUT?!
AS YOU CAN SEE, I...
WHZZZ

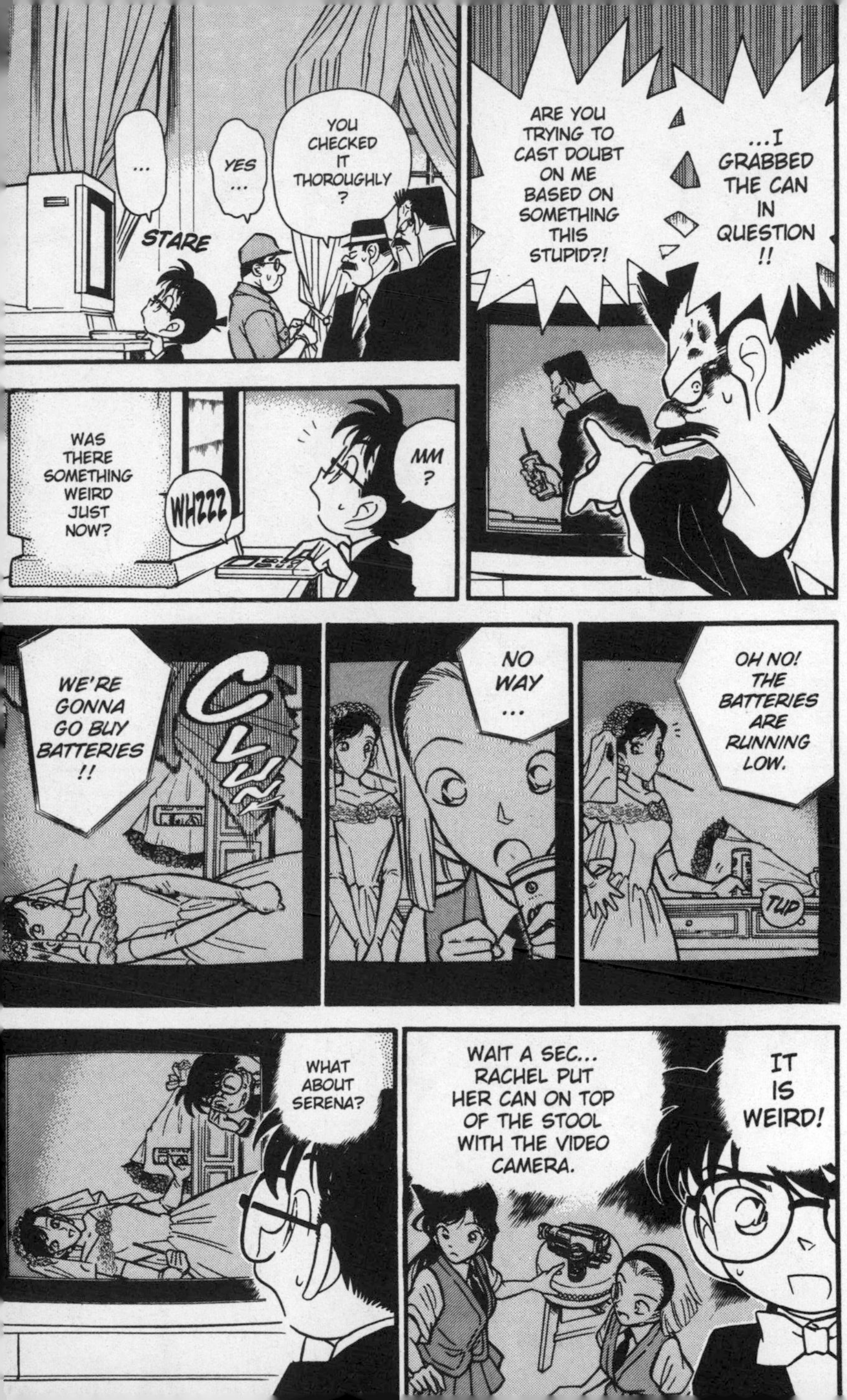
...I GRABBED THE CAN IN QUESTION!!
ARE YOU TRYING TO CAST DOUBT ON ME BASED ON SOMETHING THIS STUPID?!
YOU CHECKED IT THOROUGHLY?
YES...
...
STARE
MM?
WHZZZ
WAS THERE SOMETHING WEIRD JUST NOW?
OH NO! THE BATTERIES ARE RUNNING LOW.
TUP
NO WAY...
WE'RE GONNA GO BUY BATTERIES!!
IT IS WEIRD!
WAIT A SEC... RACHEL PUT HER CAN ON TOP OF THE STOOL WITH THE VIDEO CAMERA.
WHAT ABOUT SERENA?

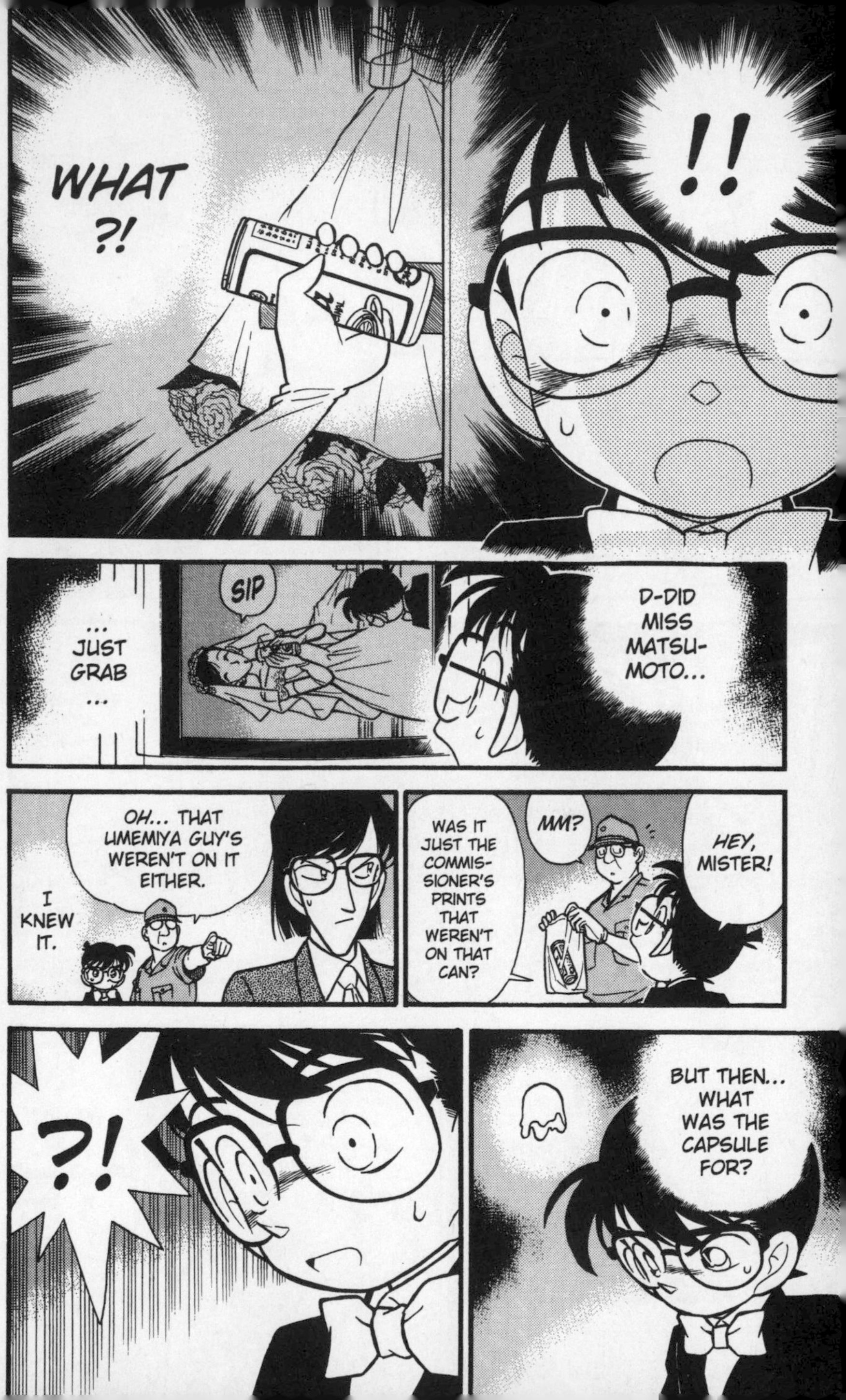
!!
WHAT ?!
D-DID MISS MATSU-MOTO...
SIP
... JUST GRAB ...
HEY, MISTER!
MM?
WAS IT JUST THE COMMIS-SIONER'S PRINTS THAT WEREN'T ON THAT CAN?
OH... THAT UMEMIYA GUY'S WEREN'T ON IT EITHER.
I KNEW IT.
BUT THEN... WHAT WAS THE CAPSULE FOR?
?!

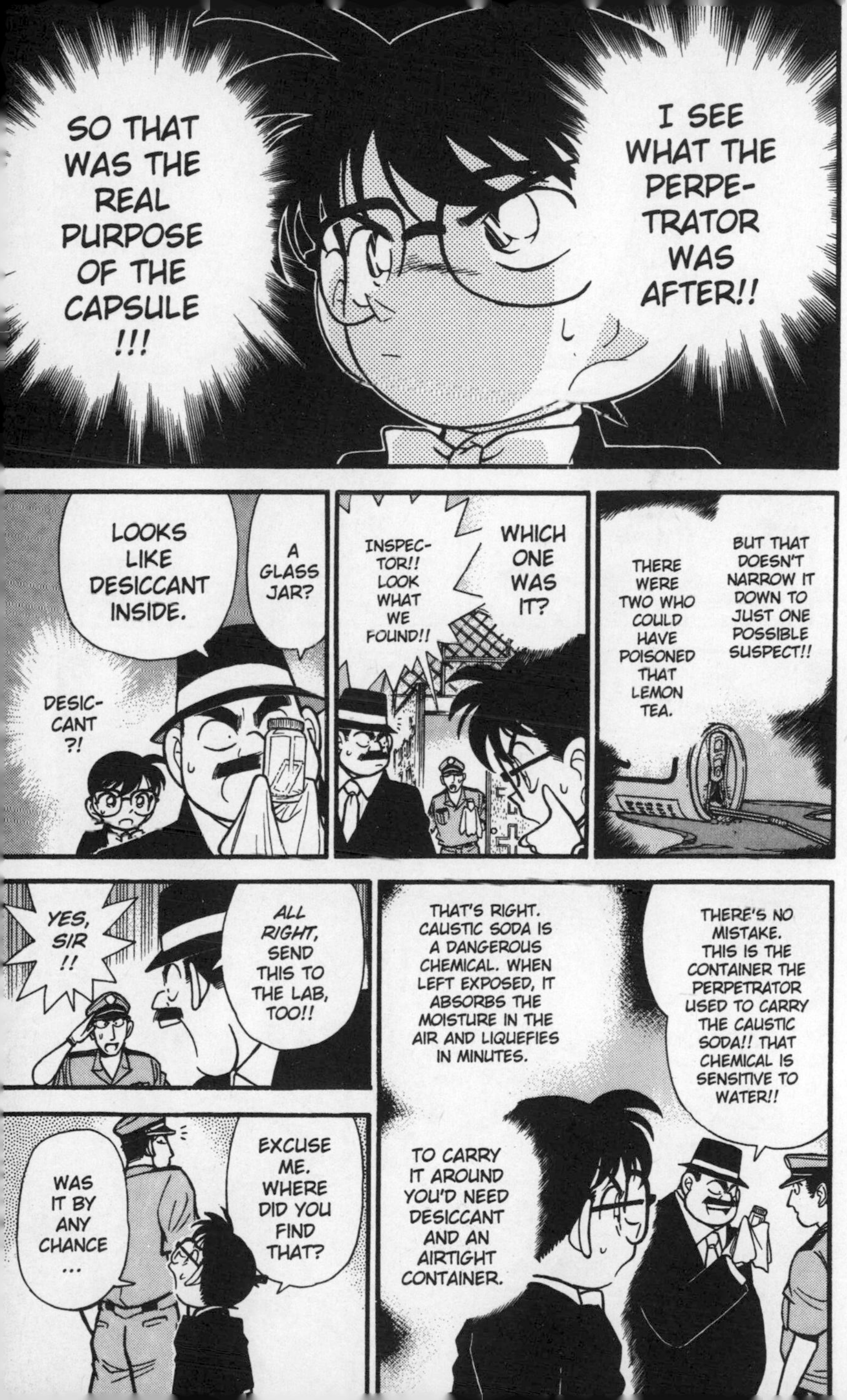
I SEE WHAT THE PERPE-TRATOR WAS AFTER!!
SO THAT WAS THE REAL PURPOSE OF THE CAPSULE!!!
BUT THAT DOESN'T NARROW IT DOWN TO JUST ONE POSSIBLE SUSPECT!!
THERE WERE TWO WHO COULD HAVE POISONED THAT LEMON TEA.
WHICH ONE WAS IT?
INSPEC-TOR!! LOOK WHAT WE FOUND!!
A GLASS JAR?
LOOKS LIKE DESICCANT INSIDE.
DESIC-CANT?!
THERE'S NO MISTAKE. THIS IS THE CONTAINER THE PERPETRATOR USED TO CARRY THE CAUSTIC SODA!! THAT CHEMICAL IS SENSITIVE TO WATER!!
THAT'S RIGHT. CAUSTIC SODA IS A DANGEROUS CHEMICAL. WHEN LEFT EXPOSED, IT ABSORBS THE MOISTURE IN THE AIR AND LIQUEFIES IN MINUTES.
TO CARRY IT AROUND YOU'D NEED DESICCANT AND AN AIRTIGHT CONTAINER.
ALL RIGHT, SEND THIS TO THE LAB, TOO!!
YES, SIR!!
EXCUSE ME. WHERE DID YOU FIND THAT?
WAS IT BY ANY CHANCE...

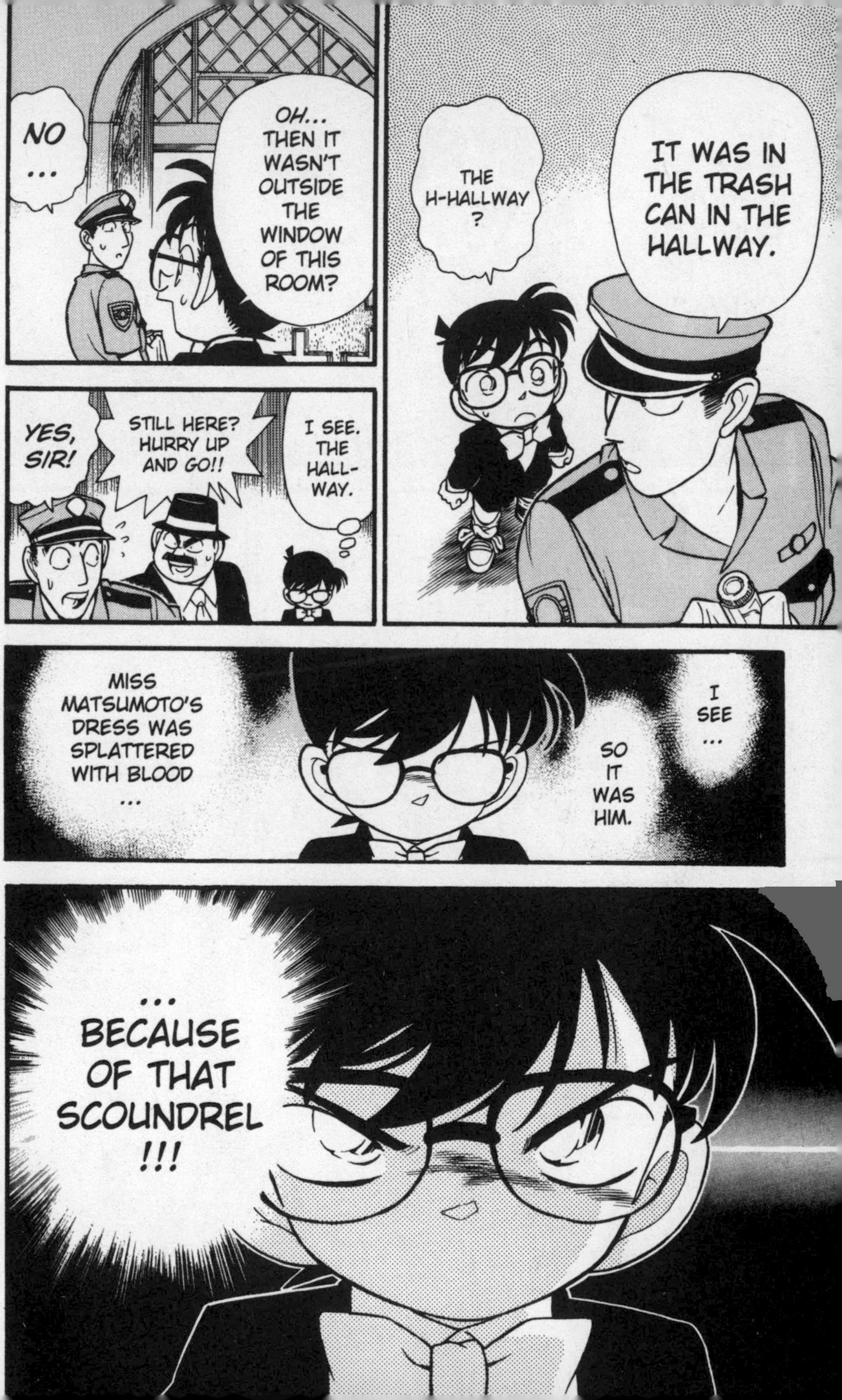
IT WAS IN THE TRASH CAN IN THE HALLWAY.
THE H-HALLWAY ?
OH... THEN IT WASN'T OUTSIDE THE WINDOW OF THIS ROOM?
NO ...
I SEE. THE HALL-WAY.
STILL HERE? HURRY UP AND GO!!
YES, SIR!
I SEE ...
SO IT WAS HIM.
MISS MATSUMOTO'S DRESS WAS SPLATTERED WITH BLOOD ...
... BECAUSE OF THAT SCOUNDREL !!!

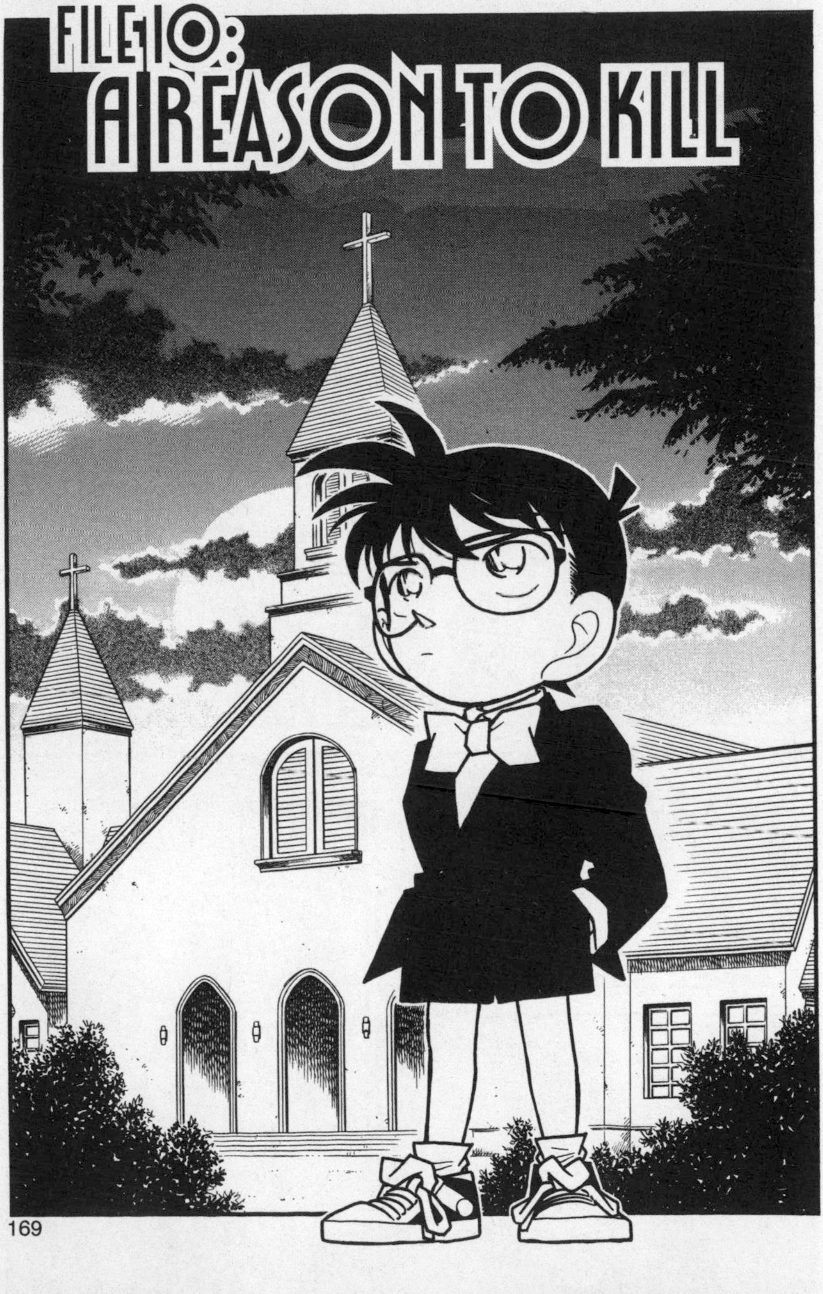
FILE 10:
A REASON TO KILL

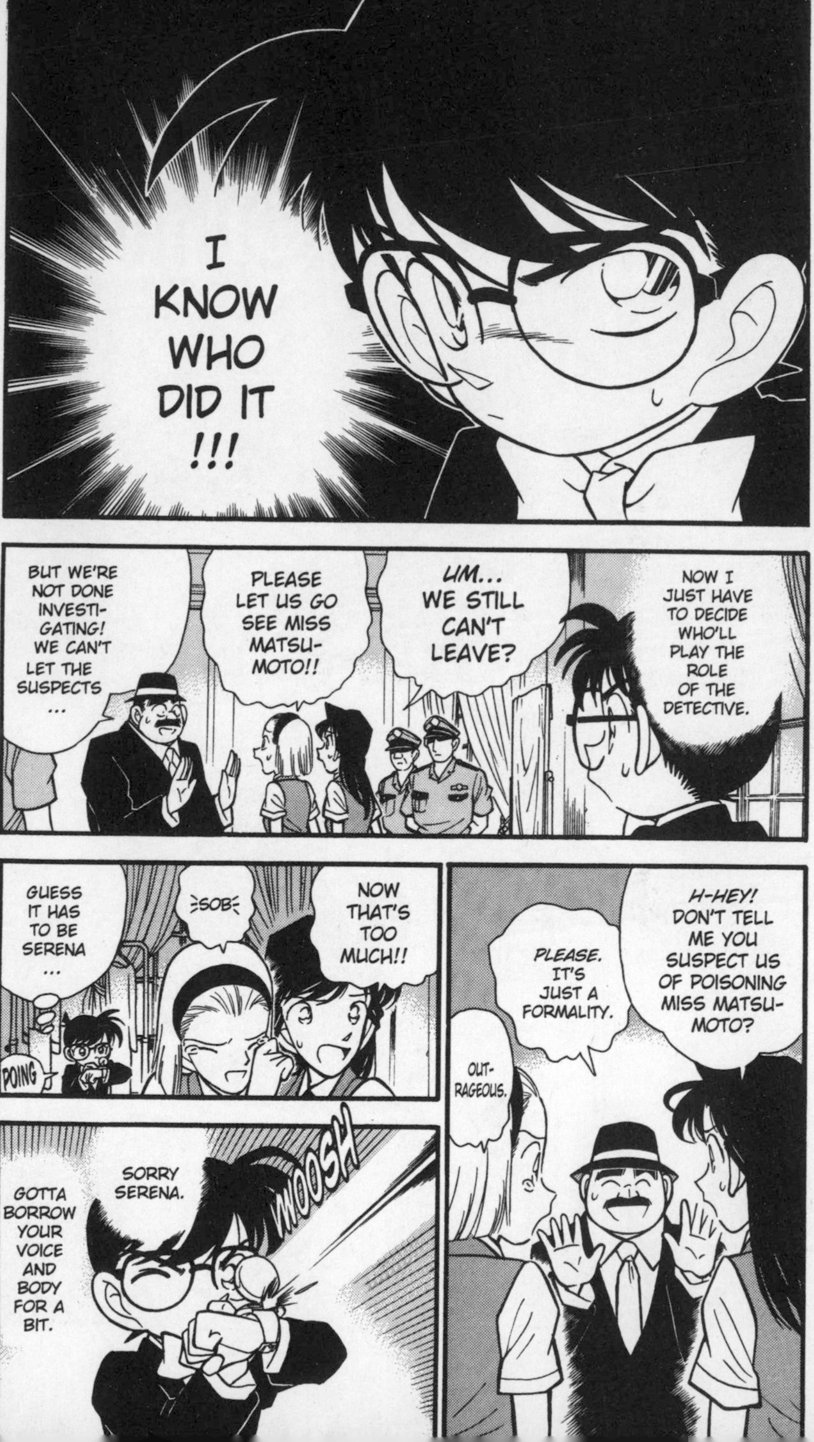
I KNOW WHO DID IT !!!
NOW I JUST HAVE TO DECIDE WHO'LL PLAY THE ROLE OF THE DETECTIVE.
UM... WE STILL CAN'T LEAVE?
PLEASE LET US GO SEE MISS MATSU-MOTO!!
BUT WE'RE NOT DONE INVESTI-GATING! WE CAN'T LET THE SUSPECTS ...
H-HEY! DON'T TELL ME YOU SUSPECT US OF POISONING MISS MATSU-MOTO?
PLEASE. IT'S JUST A FORMALITY.
OUT-RAGEOUS.
NOW THAT'S TOO MUCH!!
SOB
GUESS IT HAS TO BE SERENA ...
POING
WOOSH
SORRY SERENA.
GOTTA BORROW YOUR VOICE AND BODY FOR A BIT.

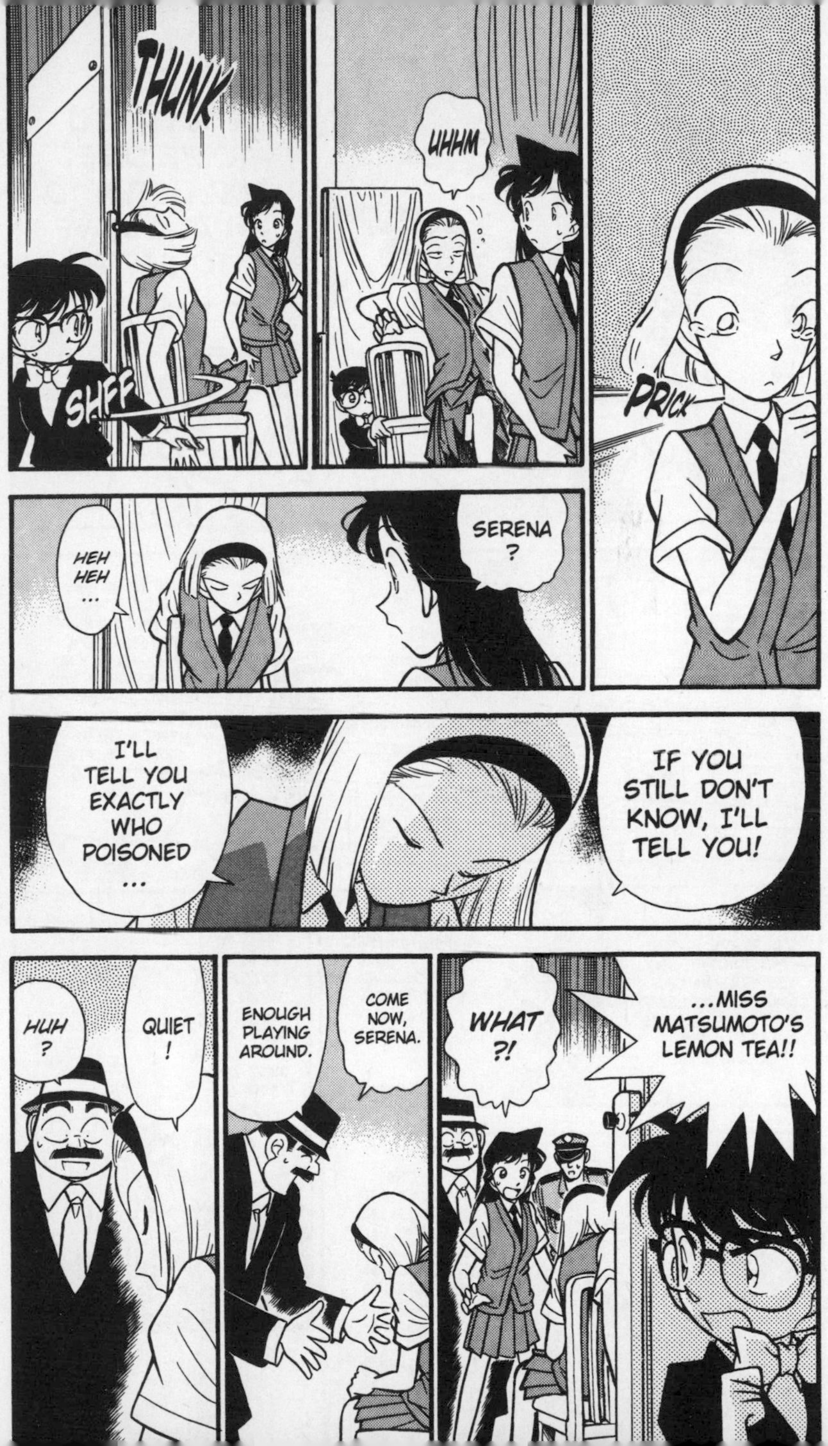
PRICK
UHHM
THUNK
SHFF
SERENA ?
HEH HEH ...
IF YOU STILL DON'T KNOW, I'LL TELL YOU!
I'LL TELL YOU EXACTLY WHO POISONED ...
...MISS MATSUMOTO'S LEMON TEA!!
WHAT ?!
COME NOW, SERENA.
ENOUGH PLAYING AROUND.
QUIET !
HUH ?

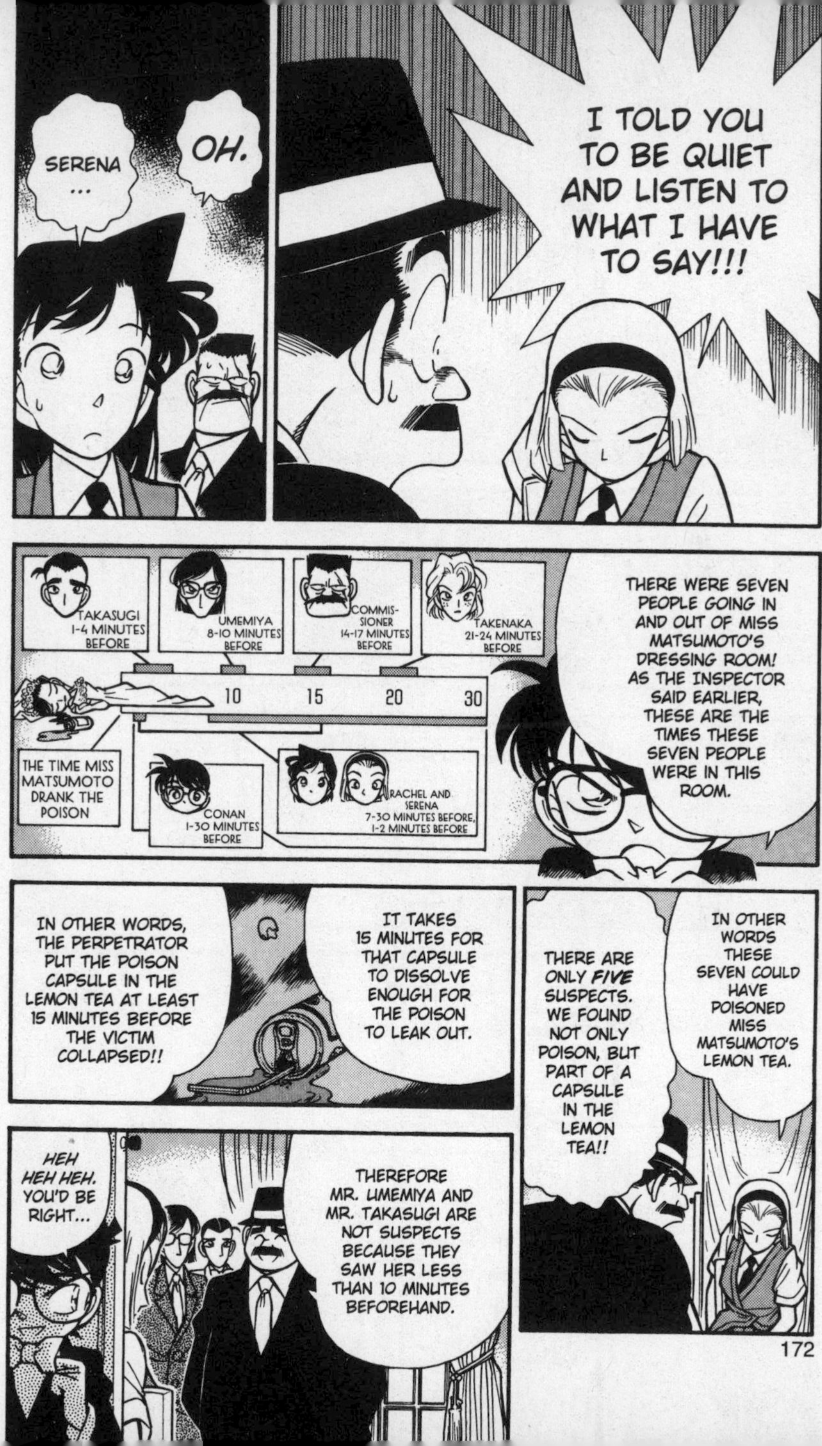
I TOLD YOU TO BE QUIET AND LISTEN TO WHAT I HAVE TO SAY!!!
OH.
SERENA ...
THERE WERE SEVEN PEOPLE GOING IN AND OUT OF MISS MATSUMOTO'S DRESSING ROOM! AS THE INSPECTOR SAID EARLIER, THESE ARE THE TIMES THESE SEVEN PEOPLE WERE IN THIS ROOM.
TAKENAKA 21-24 MINUTES BEFORE
COMMIS-SIONER 14-17 MINUTES BEFORE
UMEMIYA 8-10 MINUTES BEFORE
TAKASUGI 1-4 MINUTES BEFORE
10
15
20
30
RACHEL AND SERENA 7-30 MINUTES BEFORE, 1-2 MINUTES BEFORE
CONAN 1-30 MINUTES BEFORE
THE TIME MISS MATSUMOTO DRANK THE POISON
IN OTHER WORDS THESE SEVEN COULD HAVE POISONED MISS MATSUMOTO'S LEMON TEA.
THERE ARE ONLY *FIVE* SUSPECTS. WE FOUND NOT ONLY POISON, BUT PART OF A CAPSULE IN THE LEMON TEA!!
IT TAKES 15 MINUTES FOR THAT CAPSULE TO DISSOLVE ENOUGH FOR THE POISON TO LEAK OUT.
IN OTHER WORDS, THE PERPETRATOR PUT THE POISON CAPSULE IN THE LEMON TEA AT LEAST 15 MINUTES BEFORE THE VICTIM COLLAPSED!!
THEREFORE MR. UMEMIYA AND MR. TAKASUGI ARE NOT SUSPECTS BECAUSE THEY SAW HER LESS THAN 10 MINUTES BEFOREHAND.
HEH HEH HEH. YOU'D BE RIGHT...

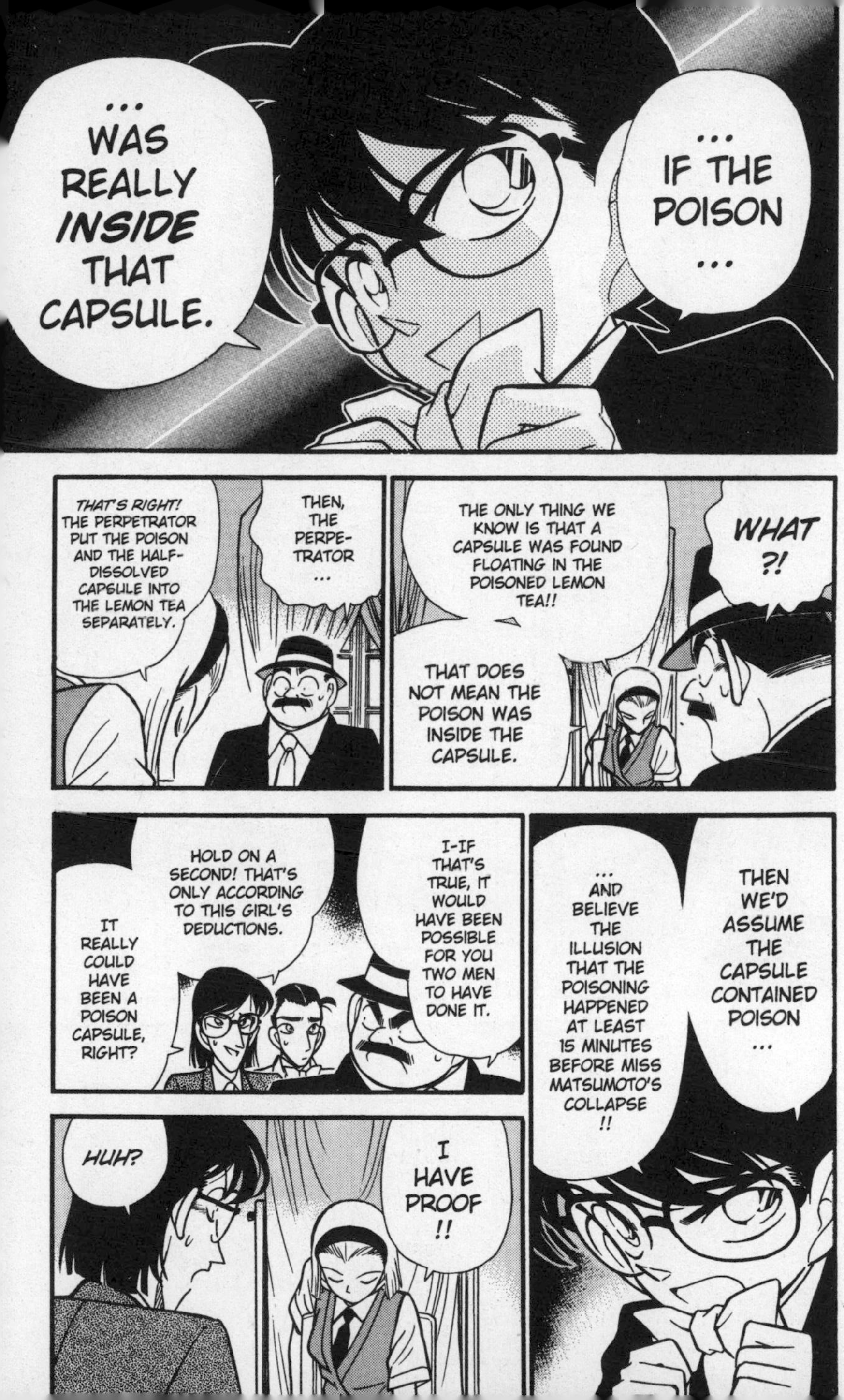
... IF THE POISON ...
... WAS REALLY *INSIDE* THAT CAPSULE.
WHAT ?!
THE ONLY THING WE KNOW IS THAT A CAPSULE WAS FOUND FLOATING IN THE POISONED LEMON TEA!!
THAT DOES NOT MEAN THE POISON WAS INSIDE THE CAPSULE.
THEN, THE PERPE-TRATOR ...
THAT'S RIGHT! THE PERPETRATOR PUT THE POISON AND THE HALF-DISSOLVED CAPSULE INTO THE LEMON TEA SEPARATELY.
THEN WE'D ASSUME THE CAPSULE CONTAINED POISON ...
... AND BELIEVE THE ILLUSION THAT THE POISONING HAPPENED AT LEAST 15 MINUTES BEFORE MISS MATSUMOTO'S COLLAPSE !!
I-IF THAT'S TRUE, IT WOULD HAVE BEEN POSSIBLE FOR YOU TWO MEN TO HAVE DONE IT.
HOLD ON A SECOND! THAT'S ONLY ACCORDING TO THIS GIRL'S DEDUCTIONS.
IT REALLY COULD HAVE BEEN A POISON CAPSULE, RIGHT?
I HAVE PROOF !!
HUH?

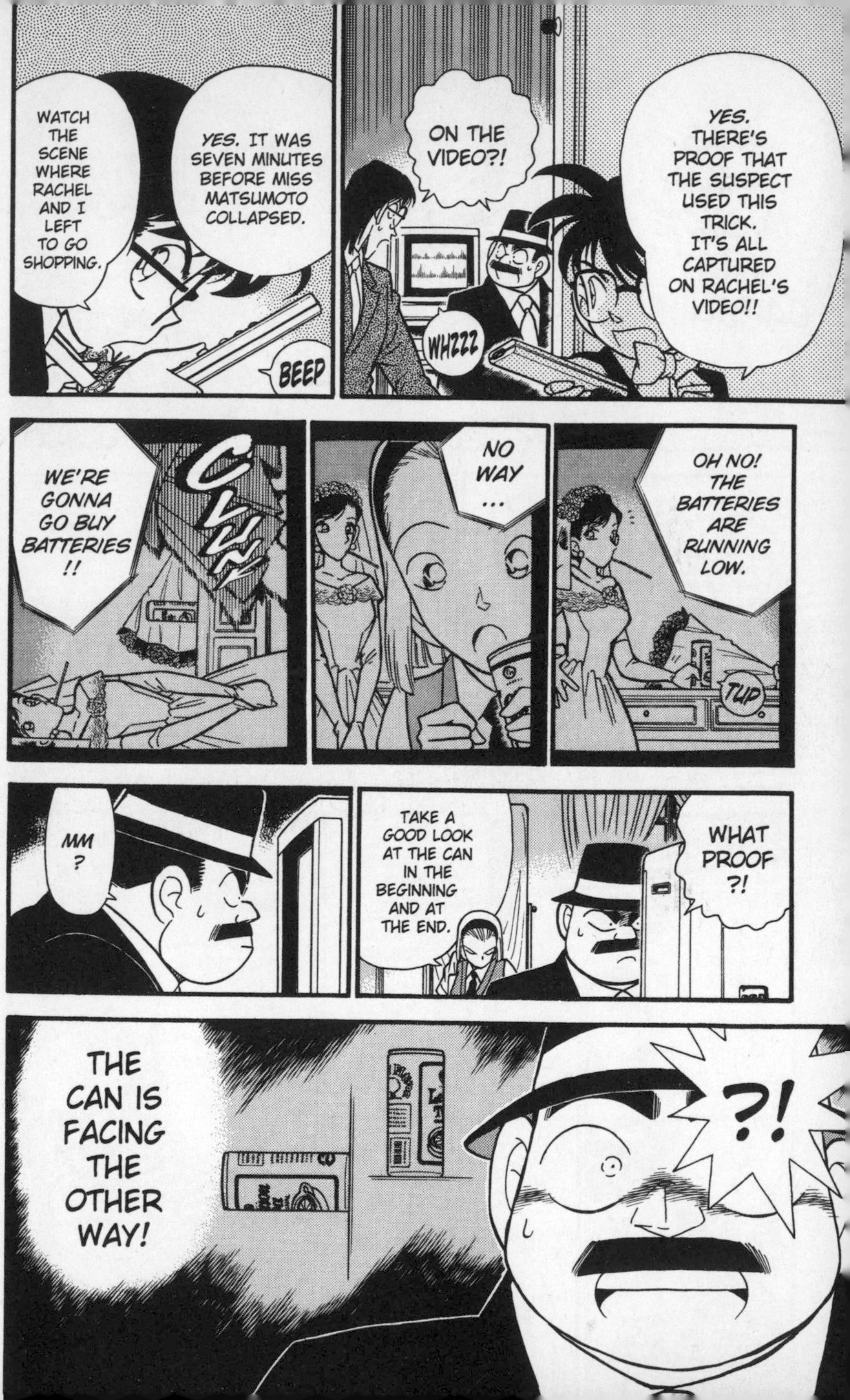
ON THE VIDEO?!
YES. THERE'S PROOF THAT THE SUSPECT USED THIS TRICK. IT'S ALL CAPTURED ON RACHEL'S VIDEO!!
WHZZZ
YES. IT WAS SEVEN MINUTES BEFORE MISS MATSUMOTO COLLAPSED.
WATCH THE SCENE WHERE RACHEL AND I LEFT TO GO SHOPPING.
BEEP
OH NO! THE BATTERIES ARE RUNNING LOW.
TUP
NO WAY ...
WE'RE GONNA GO BUY BATTERIES!!
WHAT PROOF?!
TAKE A GOOD LOOK AT THE CAN IN THE BEGINNING AND AT THE END.
MM?
?!
THE CAN IS FACING THE OTHER WAY!

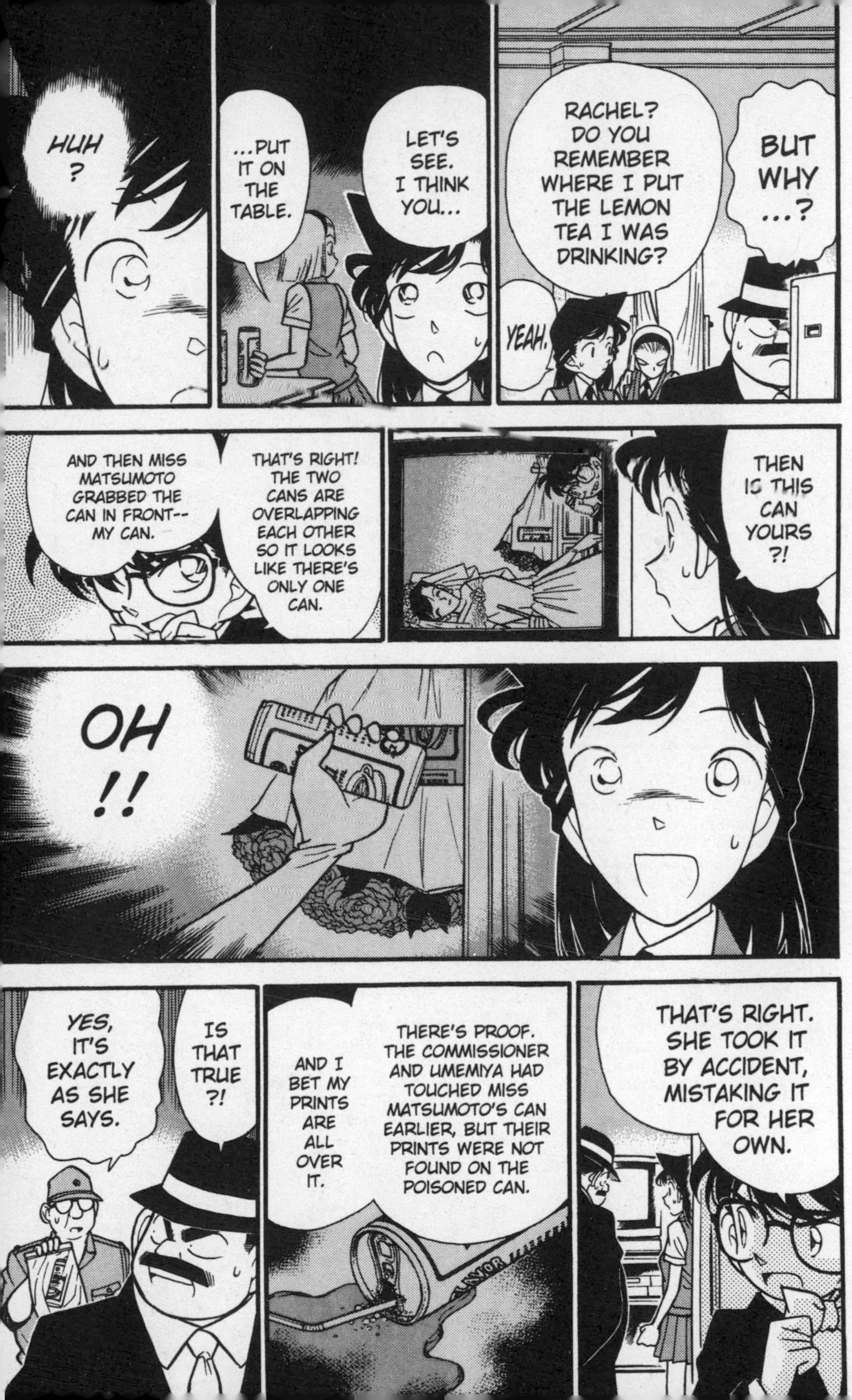
BUT WHY ...?
RACHEL? DO YOU REMEMBER WHERE I PUT THE LEMON TEA I WAS DRINKING?
YEAH.
LET'S SEE. I THINK YOU...
...PUT IT ON THE TABLE.
HUH ?
THEN IS THIS CAN YOURS ?!
THAT'S RIGHT! THE TWO CANS ARE OVERLAPPING EACH OTHER SO IT LOOKS LIKE THERE'S ONLY ONE CAN.
AND THEN MISS MATSUMOTO GRABBED THE CAN IN FRONT-- MY CAN.
OH !!
THAT'S RIGHT. SHE TOOK IT BY ACCIDENT, MISTAKING IT FOR HER OWN.
THERE'S PROOF. THE COMMISSIONER AND UMEMIYA HAD TOUCHED MISS MATSUMOTO'S CAN EARLIER, BUT THEIR PRINTS WERE NOT FOUND ON THE POISONED CAN.
AND I BET MY PRINTS ARE ALL OVER IT.
IS THAT TRUE ?!
YES, IT'S EXACTLY AS SHE SAYS.

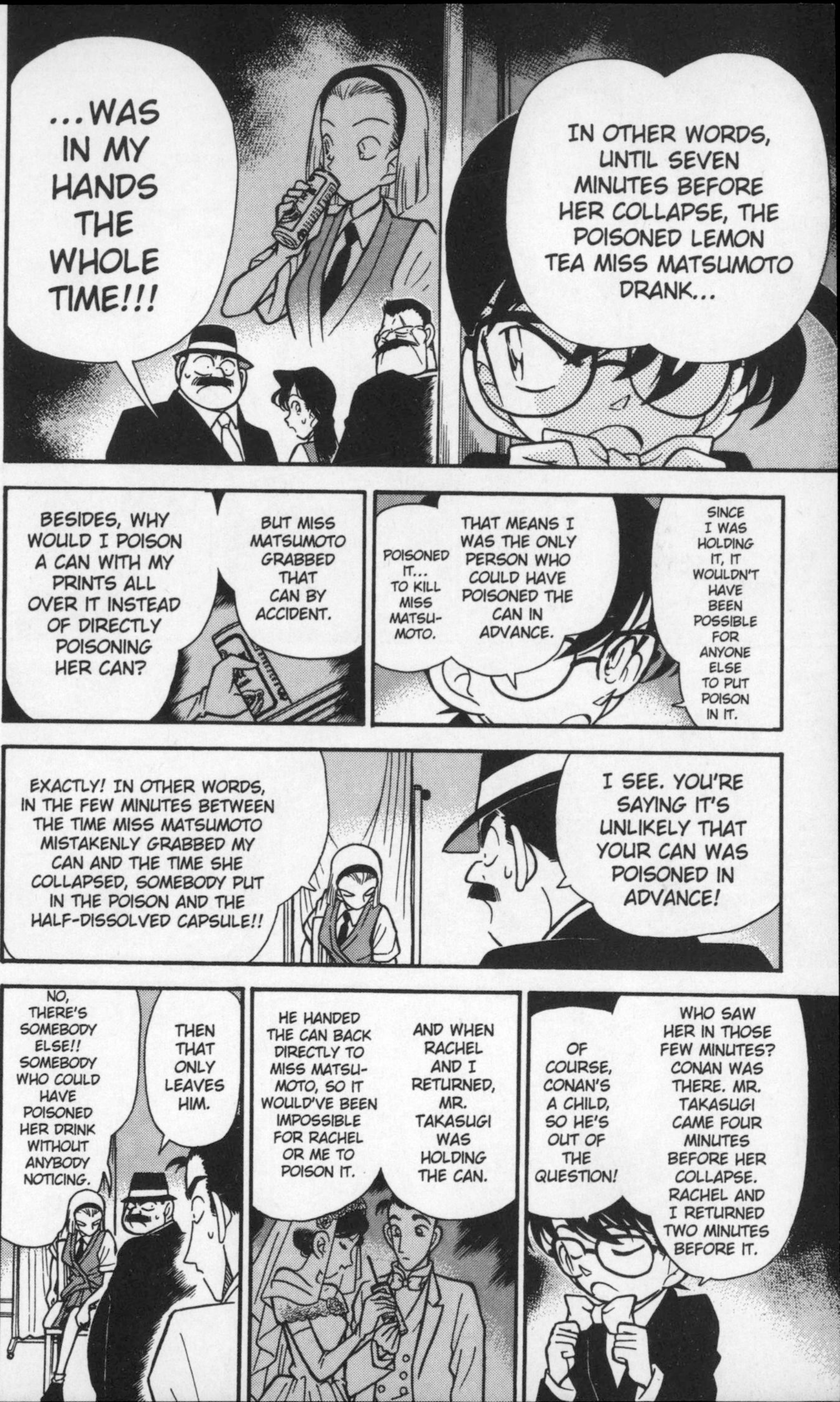
IN OTHER WORDS, UNTIL SEVEN MINUTES BEFORE HER COLLAPSE, THE POISONED LEMON TEA MISS MATSUMOTO DRANK...
...WAS IN MY HANDS THE WHOLE TIME!!!
SINCE I WAS HOLDING IT, IT WOULDN'T HAVE BEEN POSSIBLE FOR ANYONE ELSE TO PUT POISON IN IT.
THAT MEANS I WAS THE ONLY PERSON WHO COULD HAVE POISONED THE CAN IN ADVANCE.
POISONED IT... TO KILL MISS MATSU-MOTO.
BUT MISS MATSUMOTO GRABBED THAT CAN BY ACCIDENT.
BESIDES, WHY WOULD I POISON A CAN WITH MY PRINTS ALL OVER IT INSTEAD OF DIRECTLY POISONING HER CAN?
I SEE. YOU'RE SAYING IT'S UNLIKELY THAT YOUR CAN WAS POISONED IN ADVANCE!
EXACTLY! IN OTHER WORDS, IN THE FEW MINUTES BETWEEN THE TIME MISS MATSUMOTO MISTAKENLY GRABBED MY CAN AND THE TIME SHE COLLAPSED, SOMEBODY PUT IN THE POISON AND THE HALF-DISSOLVED CAPSULE!!
WHO SAW HER IN THOSE FEW MINUTES? CONAN WAS THERE. MR. TAKASUGI CAME FOUR MINUTES BEFORE HER COLLAPSE. RACHEL AND I RETURNED TWO MINUTES BEFORE IT.
OF COURSE, CONAN'S A CHILD, SO HE'S OUT OF THE QUESTION!
AND WHEN RACHEL AND I RETURNED, MR. TAKASUGI WAS HOLDING THE CAN.
HE HANDED THE CAN BACK DIRECTLY TO MISS MATSU-MOTO, SO IT WOULD'VE BEEN IMPOSSIBLE FOR RACHEL OR ME TO POISON IT.
THEN THAT ONLY LEAVES HIM.
NO, THERE'S SOMEBODY ELSE!! SOMEBODY WHO COULD HAVE POISONED HER DRINK WITHOUT ANYBODY NOTICING.

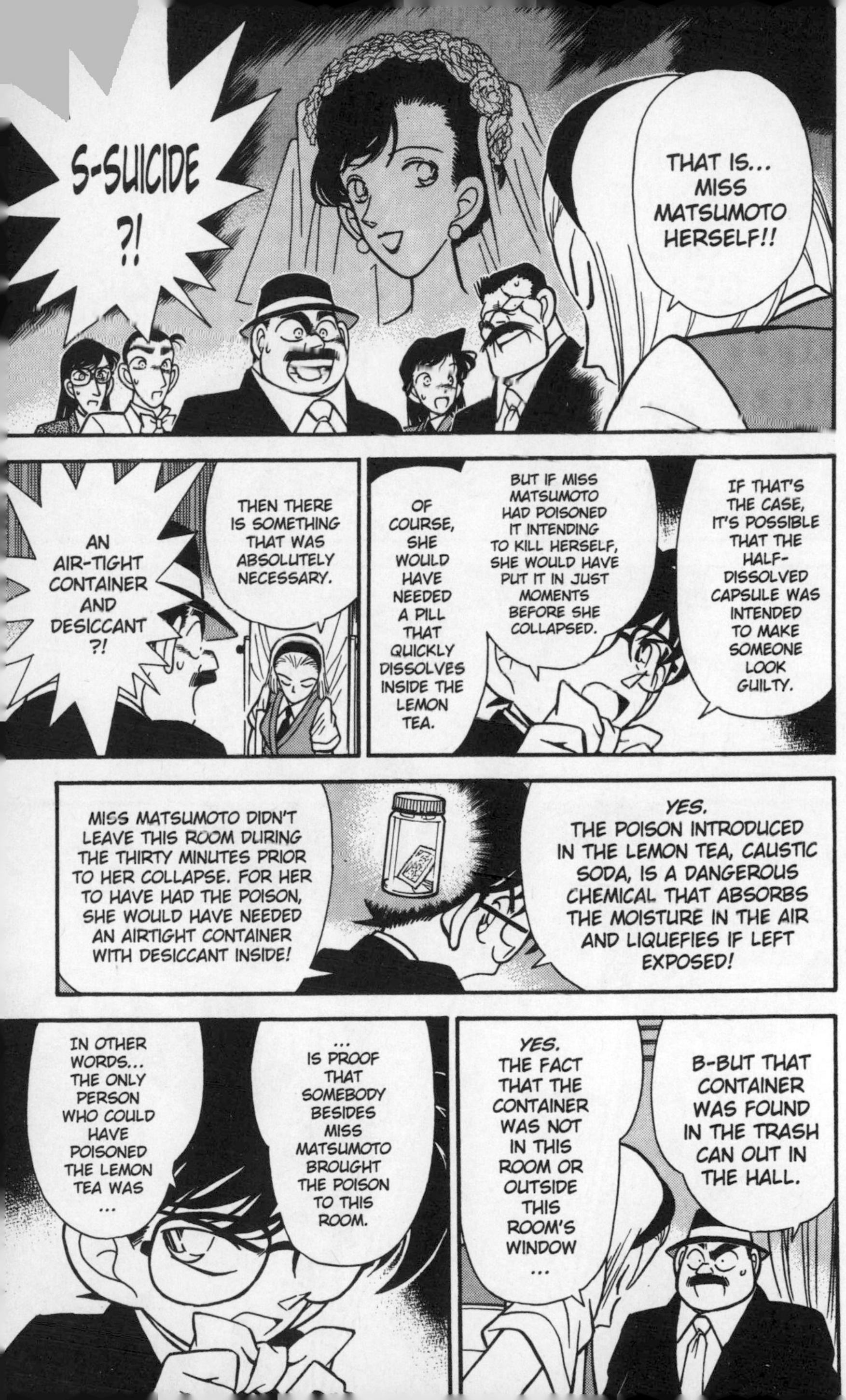
THAT IS... MISS MATSUMOTO HERSELF!!
S-SUICIDE ?!
IF THAT'S THE CASE, IT'S POSSIBLE THAT THE HALF-DISSOLVED CAPSULE WAS INTENDED TO MAKE SOMEONE LOOK GUILTY.
BUT IF MISS MATSUMOTO HAD POISONED IT INTENDING TO KILL HERSELF, SHE WOULD HAVE PUT IT IN JUST MOMENTS BEFORE SHE COLLAPSED.
OF COURSE, SHE WOULD HAVE NEEDED A PILL THAT QUICKLY DISSOLVES INSIDE THE LEMON TEA.
THEN THERE IS SOMETHING THAT WAS ABSOLUTELY NECESSARY.
AN AIR-TIGHT CONTAINER AND DESICCANT ?!
YES. THE POISON INTRODUCED IN THE LEMON TEA, CAUSTIC SODA, IS A DANGEROUS CHEMICAL THAT ABSORBS THE MOISTURE IN THE AIR AND LIQUEFIES IF LEFT EXPOSED!
MISS MATSUMOTO DIDN'T LEAVE THIS ROOM DURING THE THIRTY MINUTES PRIOR TO HER COLLAPSE. FOR HER TO HAVE HAD THE POISON, SHE WOULD HAVE NEEDED AN AIRTIGHT CONTAINER WITH DESICCANT INSIDE!
B-BUT THAT CONTAINER WAS FOUND IN THE TRASH CAN OUT IN THE HALL.
YES. THE FACT THAT THE CONTAINER WAS NOT IN THIS ROOM OR OUTSIDE THIS ROOM'S WINDOW ...
... IS PROOF THAT SOMEBODY BESIDES MISS MATSUMOTO BROUGHT THE POISON TO THIS ROOM.
IN OTHER WORDS... THE ONLY PERSON WHO COULD HAVE POISONED THE LEMON TEA WAS ...

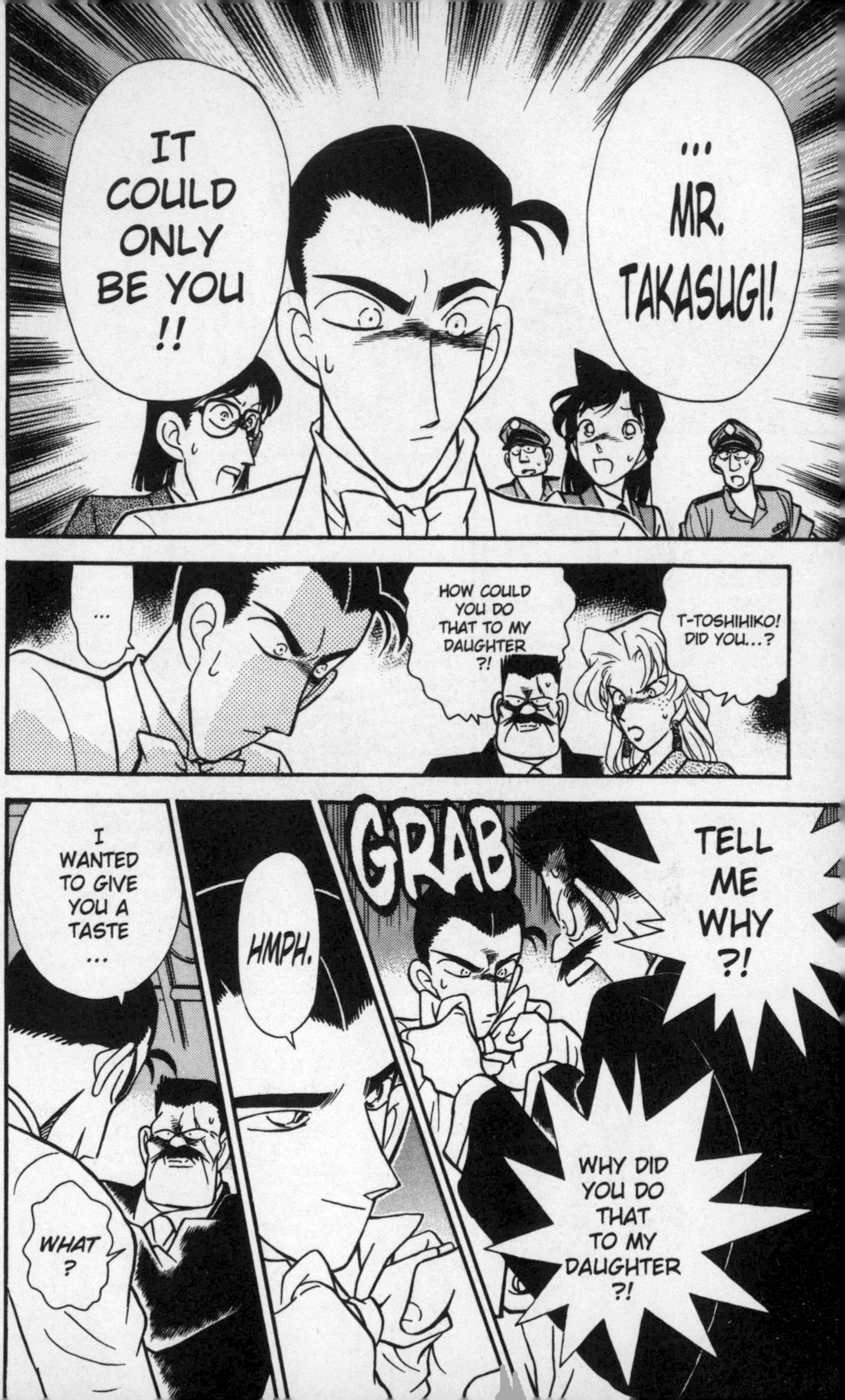
... MR. TAKASUGI!
IT COULD ONLY BE YOU !!
T-TOSHIHIKO! DID YOU...?
HOW COULD YOU DO THAT TO MY DAUGHTER ?!
...
TELL ME WHY ?!
GRAB
WHY DID YOU DO THAT TO MY DAUGHTER ?!
HMPH.
I WANTED TO GIVE YOU A TASTE ...
WHAT ?

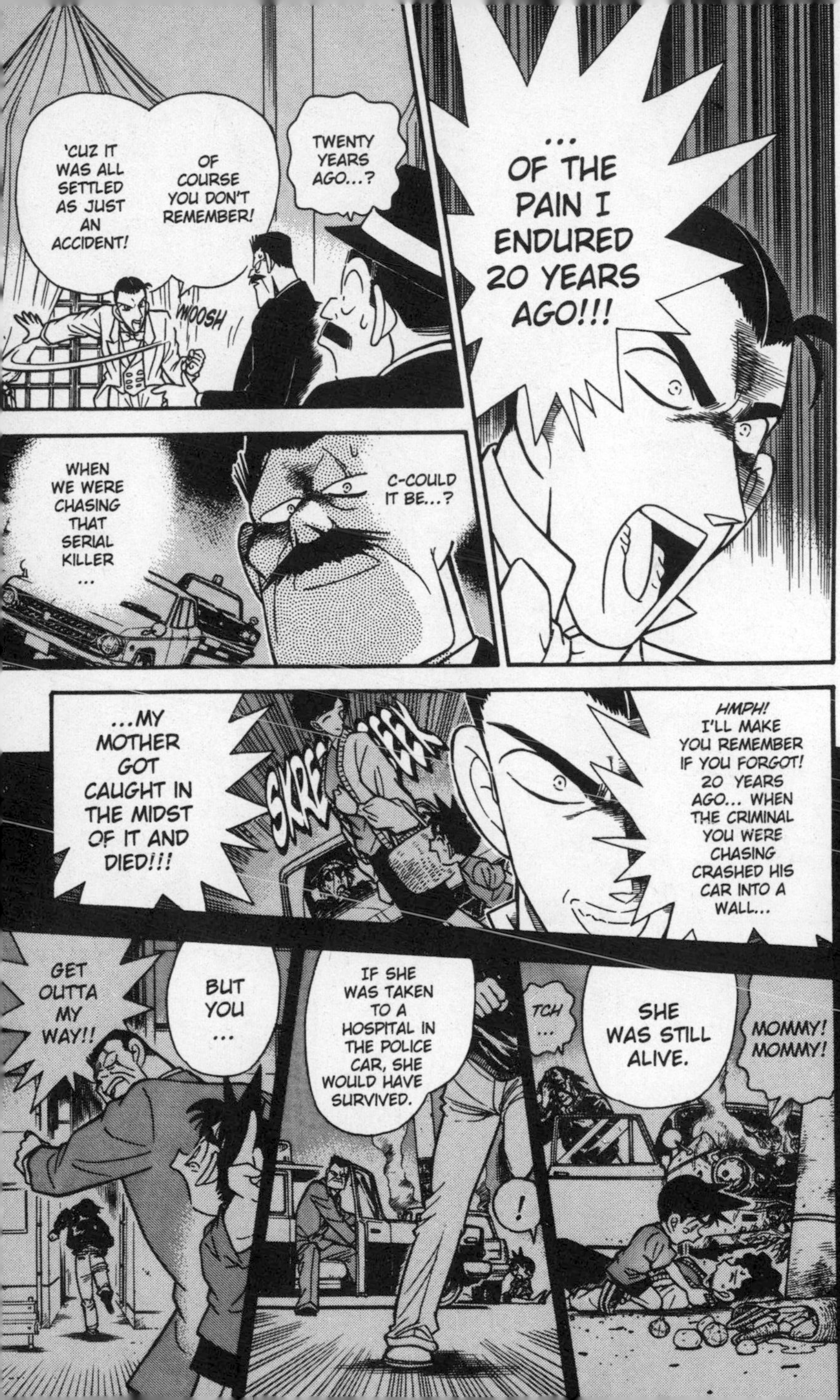
... OF THE PAIN I ENDURED 20 YEARS AGO!!!
TWENTY YEARS AGO...?
OF COURSE YOU DON'T REMEMBER!
'CUZ IT WAS ALL SETTLED AS JUST AN ACCIDENT!
WOOSH
C-COULD IT BE...?
WHEN WE WERE CHASING THAT SERIAL KILLER ...
HMPH! I'LL MAKE YOU REMEMBER IF YOU FORGOT! 20 YEARS AGO... WHEN THE CRIMINAL YOU WERE CHASING CRASHED HIS CAR INTO A WALL...
SKRE
...MY MOTHER GOT CAUGHT IN THE MIDST OF IT AND DIED!!!
MOMMY! MOMMY!
SHE WAS STILL ALIVE.
TCH ...
!
IF SHE WAS TAKEN TO A HOSPITAL IN THE POLICE CAR, SHE WOULD HAVE SURVIVED.
BUT YOU ...
GET OUTTA MY WAY!!

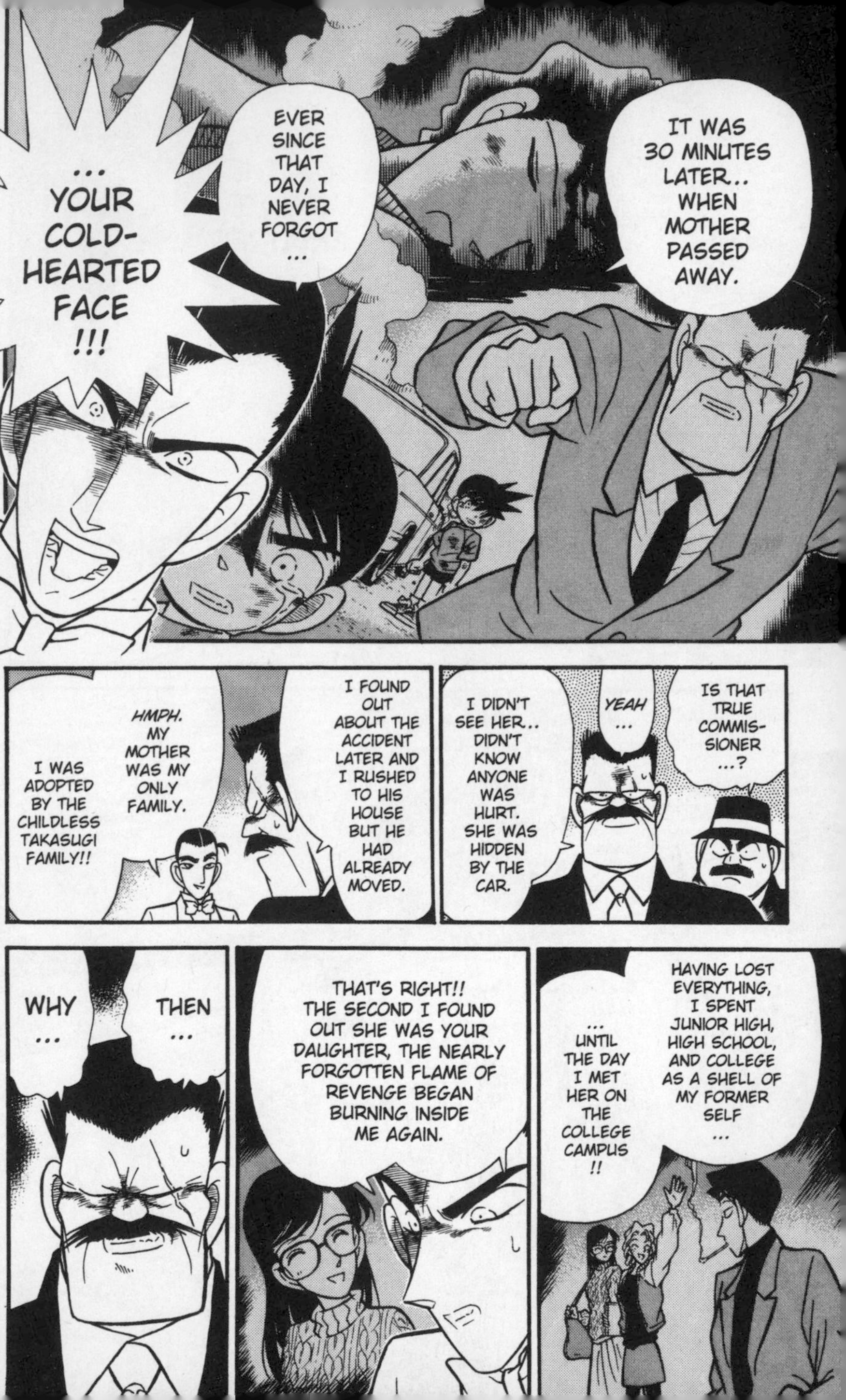
IT WAS 30 MINUTES LATER... WHEN MOTHER PASSED AWAY.
EVER SINCE THAT DAY, I NEVER FORGOT ...
... YOUR COLD-HEARTED FACE !!!
IS THAT TRUE COMMISSIONER ...?
YEAH ...
I DIDN'T SEE HER.. DIDN'T KNOW ANYONE WAS HURT. SHE WAS HIDDEN BY THE CAR.
I FOUND OUT ABOUT THE ACCIDENT LATER AND I RUSHED TO HIS HOUSE BUT HE HAD ALREADY MOVED.
HMPH. MY MOTHER WAS MY ONLY FAMILY.
I WAS ADOPTED BY THE CHILDLESS TAKASUGI FAMILY!!
HAVING LOST EVERYTHING, I SPENT JUNIOR HIGH, HIGH SCHOOL, AND COLLEGE AS A SHELL OF MY FORMER SELF ...
... UNTIL THE DAY I MET HER ON THE COLLEGE CAMPUS !!
THAT'S RIGHT!! THE SECOND I FOUND OUT SHE WAS YOUR DAUGHTER, THE NEARLY FORGOTTEN FLAME OF REVENGE BEGAN BURNING INSIDE ME AGAIN.
THEN ...
WHY ...

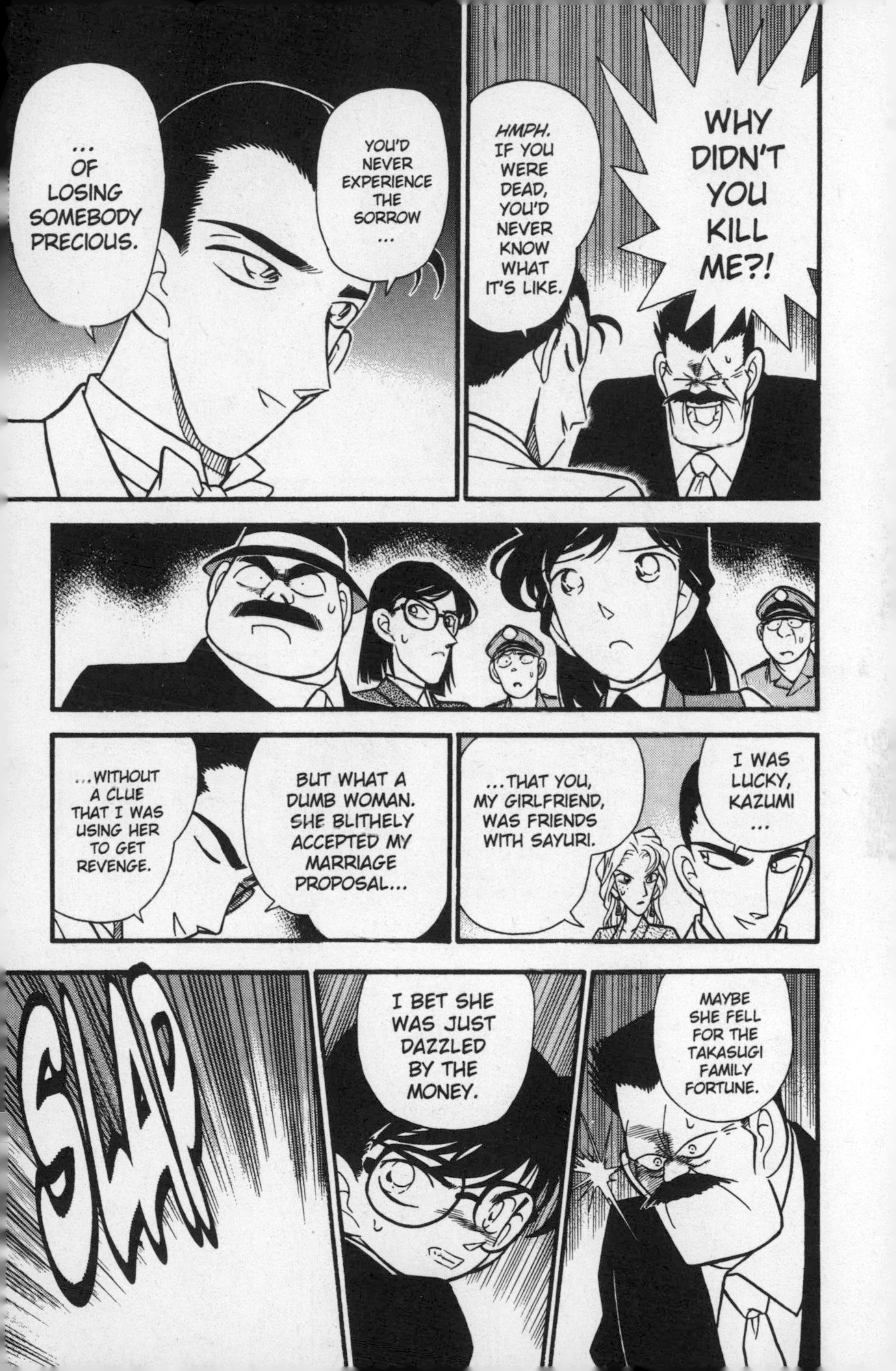
WHY DIDN'T YOU KILL ME?!
HMPH. IF YOU WERE DEAD, YOU'D NEVER KNOW WHAT IT'S LIKE.
YOU'D NEVER EXPERIENCE THE SORROW ...
... OF LOSING SOMEBODY PRECIOUS.
I WAS LUCKY, KAZUMI ...
...THAT YOU, MY GIRLFRIEND, WAS FRIENDS WITH SAYURI.
BUT WHAT A DUMB WOMAN. SHE BLITHELY ACCEPTED MY MARRIAGE PROPOSAL...
...WITHOUT A CLUE THAT I WAS USING HER TO GET REVENGE.
MAYBE SHE FELL FOR THE TAKASUGI FAMILY FORTUNE.
I BET SHE WAS JUST DAZZLED BY THE MONEY.
SLAP

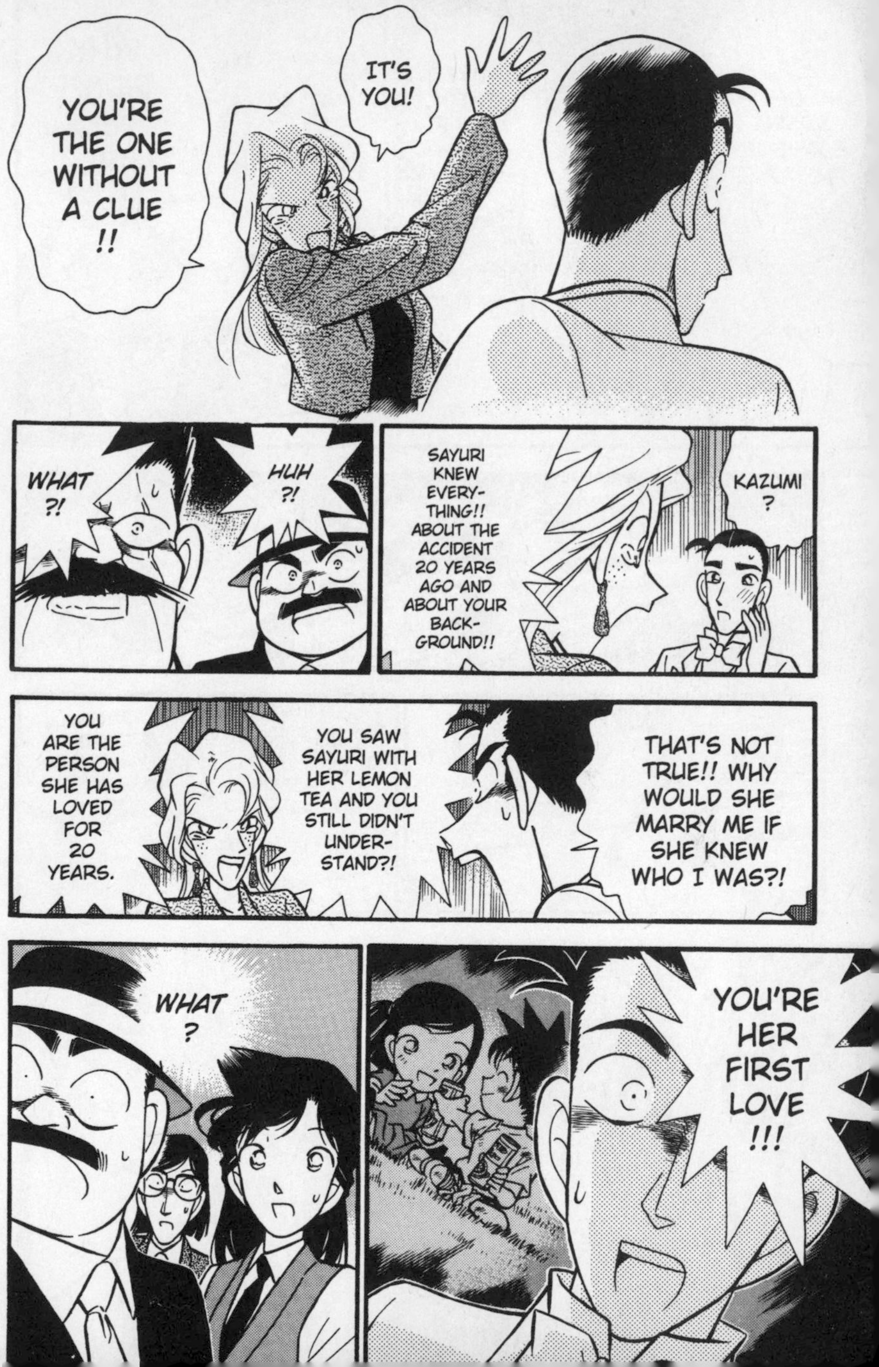

IT'S YOU!
YOU'RE THE ONE WITHOUT A CLUE !!
KAZUMI ?
SAYURI KNEW EVERY-THING!! ABOUT THE ACCIDENT 20 YEARS AGO AND ABOUT YOUR BACK-GROUND!!
HUH ?!
WHAT ?!
THAT'S NOT TRUE!! WHY WOULD SHE MARRY ME IF SHE KNEW WHO I WAS?!
YOU SAW SAYURI WITH HER LEMON TEA AND YOU STILL DIDN'T UNDER-STAND?!
YOU ARE THE PERSON SHE HAS LOVED FOR 20 YEARS.
YOU'RE HER FIRST LOVE !!!
WHAT ?

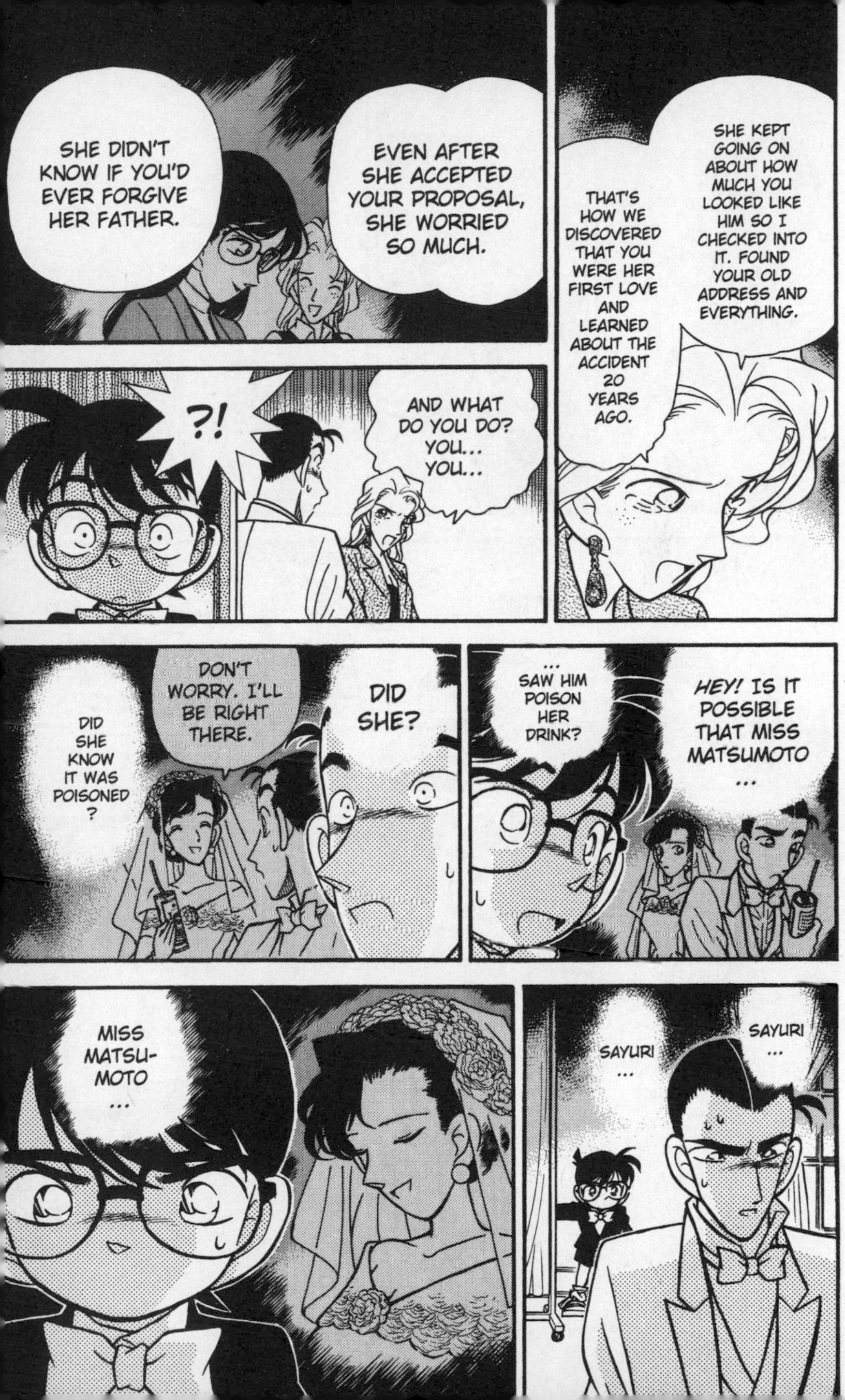

SHE KEPT GOING ON ABOUT HOW MUCH YOU LOOKED LIKE HIM SO I CHECKED INTO IT. FOUND YOUR OLD ADDRESS AND EVERYTHING.
THAT'S HOW WE DISCOVERED THAT YOU WERE HER FIRST LOVE AND LEARNED ABOUT THE ACCIDENT 20 YEARS AGO.
EVEN AFTER SHE ACCEPTED YOUR PROPOSAL, SHE WORRIED SO MUCH.
SHE DIDN'T KNOW IF YOU'D EVER FORGIVE HER FATHER.
AND WHAT DO YOU DO? YOU... YOU...
?!
HEY! IS IT POSSIBLE THAT MISS MATSUMOTO ...
... SAW HIM POISON HER DRINK?
DID SHE?
DON'T WORRY. I'LL BE RIGHT THERE.
DID SHE KNOW IT WAS POISONED ?
SAYURI ...
SAYURI ...
MISS MATSU-MOTO ...

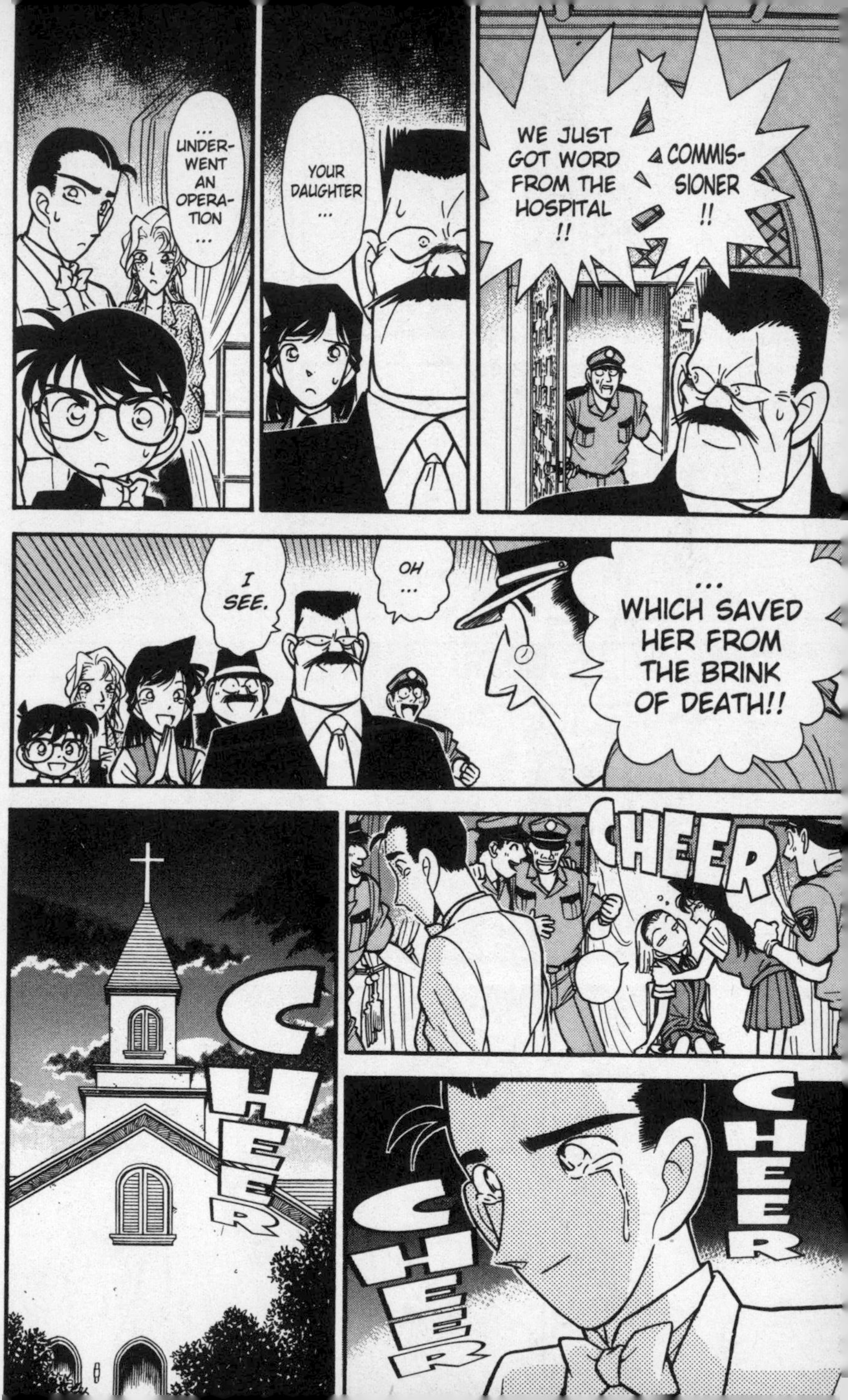
COMMISSIONER !!
WE JUST GOT WORD FROM THE HOSPITAL !!
YOUR DAUGHTER ...
... UNDERWENT AN OPERATION ...
... WHICH SAVED HER FROM THE BRINK OF DEATH!!
OH ...
I SEE.
CHEER
CHEER
CHEER
CHEER

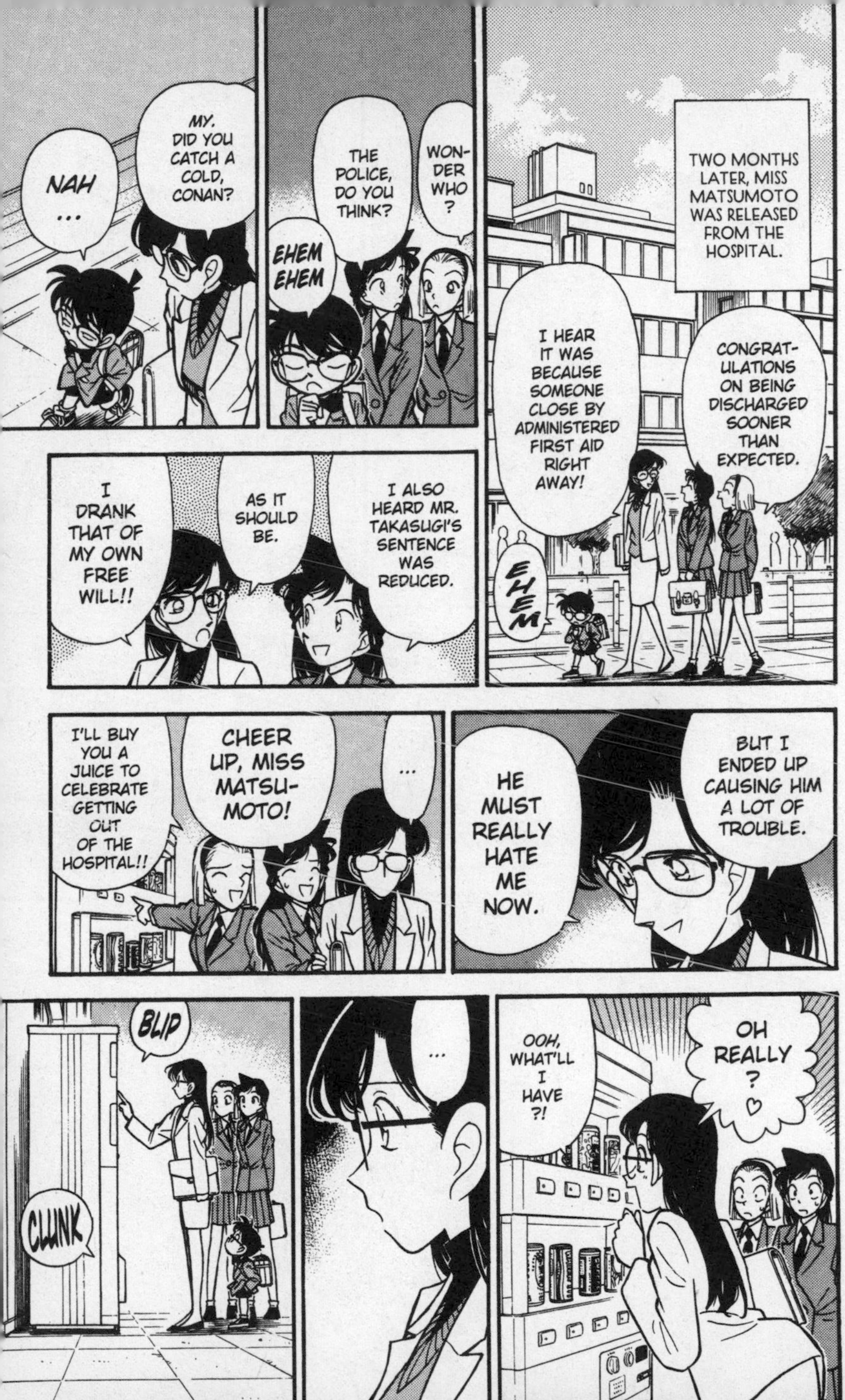

TWO MONTHS LATER, MISS MATSUMOTO WAS RELEASED FROM THE HOSPITAL.
CONGRATULATIONS ON BEING DISCHARGED SOONER THAN EXPECTED.
I HEAR IT WAS BECAUSE SOMEONE CLOSE BY ADMINISTERED FIRST AID RIGHT AWAY!
EHEM
WONDER WHO?
THE POLICE, DO YOU THINK?
EHEM EHEM
MY. DID YOU CATCH A COLD, CONAN?
NAH ...
I ALSO HEARD MR. TAKASUGI'S SENTENCE WAS REDUCED.
AS IT SHOULD BE.
I DRANK THAT OF MY OWN FREE WILL!!
BUT I ENDED UP CAUSING HIM A LOT OF TROUBLE.
HE MUST REALLY HATE ME NOW.
...
CHEER UP, MISS MATSUMOTO!
I'LL BUY YOU A JUICE TO CELEBRATE GETTING OUT OF THE HOSPITAL!!
OH REALLY? ♡
OOH, WHAT'LL I HAVE?!
...
BLIP
CLUNK

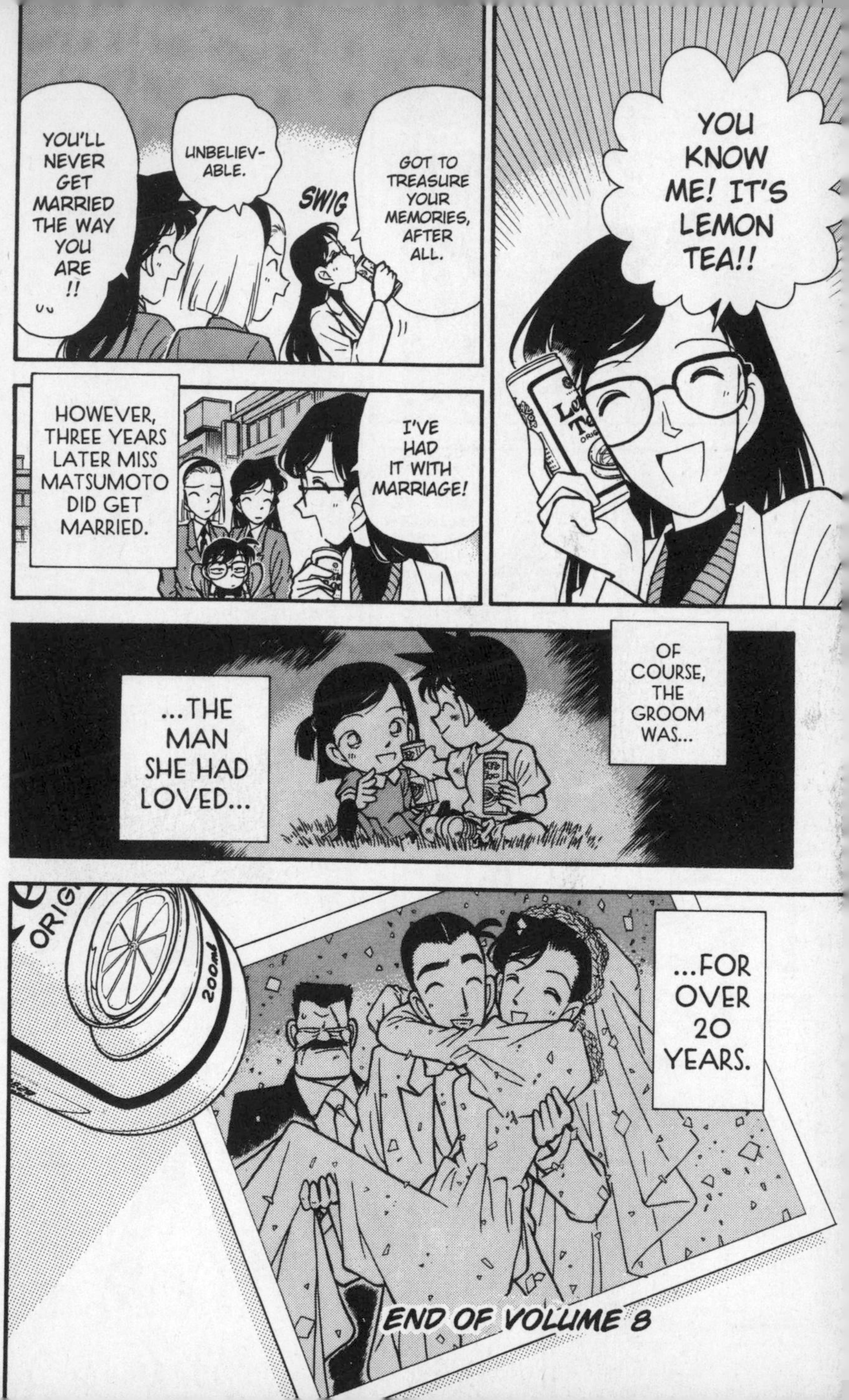
YOU KNOW ME! IT'S LEMON TEA!!
GOT TO TREASURE YOUR MEMORIES, AFTER ALL.
SWIG
UNBELIEVABLE.
YOU'LL NEVER GET MARRIED THE WAY YOU ARE!!
I'VE HAD IT WITH MARRIAGE!
HOWEVER, THREE YEARS LATER MISS MATSUMOTO DID GET MARRIED.
OF COURSE, THE GROOM WAS...
...THE MAN SHE HAD LOVED...
...FOR OVER 20 YEARS.
200ml
END OF VOLUME 8

Hello, Aoyama here.

The streets are filled with Christmas songs and people eagerly look forward to the holy night... While I'm so busy I hardly get a break for the Obon holidays or New Year's!! Please, Santa, give me the gift of another me!

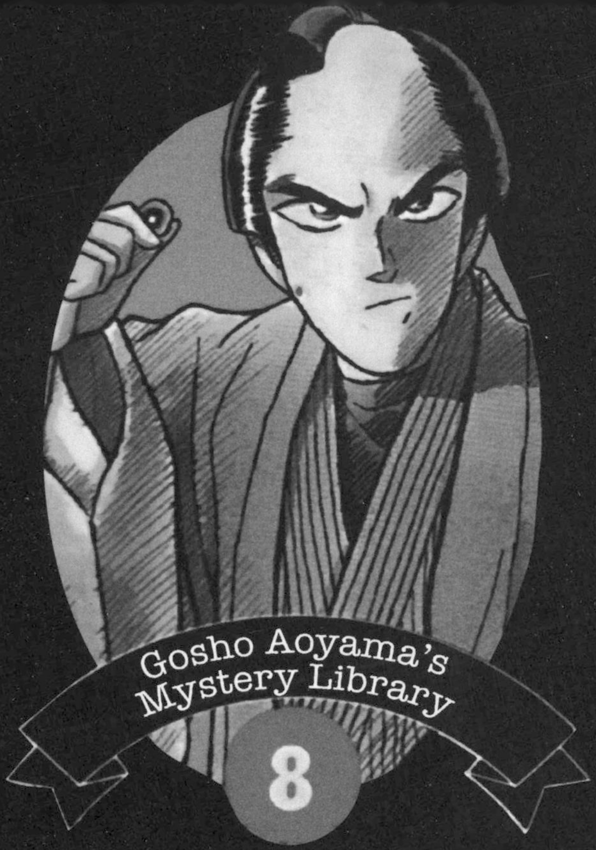
Gosho Aoyama's
Mystery Library
8

ZENIGATA HEIJI

When you think of a great, hip and dashing detective who protects the peace of Edo, you're thinking of the criminal-catcher, Heiji, also known as Zenigata Heiji!! The master of capture created by novelist Kodo Nomura, lives in the poor neighborhood of Kanda Myoujinshita with his wife. He loves smoking and when he's free he can be found playing a game of shogi on the veranda. Heiji's best move is none other than the "Coin Toss"!! He gets 10 out of 10, never missing his target with the four *mon* coins he throws. A friend to the common man and a hater of dishonesty, he never takes bribes so he's deep in debt and two months behind on his rent. It is the raffish Hachigoro (famous for saying, "Boss, we got trouble") who helps Heiji and his wife Oshizu. Oshizu, who always strikes a good luck flint when her husband leaves, is Heiji's biggest supporter. I wish he'd be a bit more frugal with his coin tosses for Oshizu's sake. I recommend ***Zenigata Heiji Torimono Hikae*** (The Casebook of Zenigata Heiji).

Editor's note: Nomura Kodo wrote close to 400 episodes involving detective Zenigata Heiji. A museum dedicated to the author has been open since 1995 in Shiwa, Japan.

CASE CLOSED IS A STEAL
THE PROOF IS IN THE PRICE

CATCH THE CAPERS ON DVD FOR UNDER $30 A SEASON!

You should be watching funimation.com/case-closed

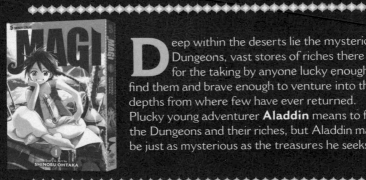

Hey! You're Reading in the Wrong Direction!

This is the **end** of this graphic novel!

To properly enjoy this VIZ graphic novel, please turn it around and begin reading from **right to left.** Unlike English, Japanese is read right to left, so Japanese comics are read in reverse order from the way English comics are typically read.

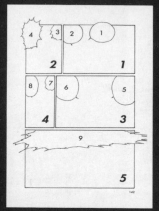

Follow the action this way.

This book has been printed in the original Japanese format in order to preserve the orientation of the original artwork. Have fun with it!